MIND–BODY PROBLEMS

MIND–BODY PROBLEMS

PSYCHOTHERAPY WITH
PSYCHOSOMATIC DISORDERS

Edited by

Janet Schumacher Finell, Ph.D.

JASON ARONSON INC.
Northvale, New Jersey
London

This book was set in 12 pt. Centaur by Alabama Book Composition of Deatsville, Alabama, and printed and bound by Book-mart Press of North Bergen, New Jersey.

Library of Congress Cataloging-in-Publication Data

Mind—body problems : psychotherapy with psychosomatic disorders /
    edited by Janet Schumacher Finell.
        p.   cm.
    Includes bibliographical references and index.
    ISBN 1-56821-654-8 (alk. paper)
    1. Somatoform disorders—Treatment.   2. Medicine, Psychosomatic.
3. Mind and body.   I. Finell, Janet Schumacher.
RC552.S66M56   1997
616.89—dc20   96-38977

Printed in the United States of America on acid-free paper. Jason Aronson Inc. offers books and cassettes. For information and catalog write to Jason Aronson Inc., 230 Livingston Street, Northvale, New Jersey 07647-1731. Or visit our website: http://www.aronson.com

CONTENTS

ACKNOWLEDGMENTS

A word of thanks to the contributors for their hard work. The area of psychosomatics (or somatic illness) is of vital importance in the everyday work of the therapist. Not only do many patients with a variety of symptomatology suffer from accompanying somatic mind–body or psychosomatic ailments, but the importance of the role of these ailments in the transference and in the overall treatment dynamics cannot be overlooked. The writers of these chapters have ventured into this controversial area of psychotherapeutic ideas and practice, and it is hoped that this volume will provide a useful guide for fellow practitioners.

CONTRIBUTORS

Bertrand Agus, M.D.
Associate Professor of Medicine, New York University Medical School, and a practicing rheumatologist; member, Rheumatic Diseases Study Group at New York University School of Medicine; Attending Physician, Lupus Clinic of Bellevue Hospital, for twenty-six years; former chief of rheumatology, St. Clare's Hospital and Beekman Downtown Hospital in New York City. He is widely known as a lecturer on various medical subjects and has directed courses at the New York University Postgraduate Medical School. He is also an author of many scientific papers in the field of rheumatology.

Suzan Anson, Ph.D.
Private practice, New York, NY; member, National Psychological Association for Psychoanalysis, New York, NY; former faculty, Hofstra University Graduate Art Therapy Program, Hempstead, NY, and School of Fine Arts, California State University Long Beach; Co-founder, the George Whitmore Foundation, Inc.

Carolyn Celentano, ACSW
Vice President, Society for Psychoanalytic Training, New York, NY; Director of Faculty and Curriculum, Institute for Psychoanalytic Education and Training, New York, NY; Associate Professor, Suffolk Community College, Selden, NY; member, International Federation for Psychoanalytic Education; New York State Society for Clinical Social Workers, Committee on Psychoanalysis; Council of Psychoanalytic Psychotherapists; private practice, Port Jefferson, NY.

Andrea Corn, Psy.D.
Currently completing residency in psychology with specialty in working with children and adolescents; completed internship at Miami Children's

Hospital, Miami, FL; completed doctorate at Nova Southeastern University, FL; past affiliations include the Mailman Center for Child Development, Davie, FL, and the Family Center at Nova Southeastern University; currently a psychoanalytic candidate at the Southeast Florida Institute for Psychoanalysis and Psychotherapy.

Michael Eigen, Ph.D.

Faculty, Senior Member, and Control/Training Analyst, National Psychological Association for Psychoanalysis, New York, NY; Clinical Associate Professor of Psychology and Supervisor, New York University Postdoctoral Program in Psychotherapy and Psychoanalysis.

B. Sue Epstein, Ph.D.

Training and Supervisory Psychoanalyst, Institute for Psychoanalysis and Psychotherapy of New Jersey; Field Supervisor, Graduate School of Applied Professional Psychology, Rutgers University.

Frederick Feirstein, NCPsyA

Faculty, National Psychological Association for Psychoanalysis, New York, NY.

Janet Schumacher Finell, Ph.D.

Training and Supervisory Psychoanalyst, National Psychological Association for Psychoanalysis, New York, NY, and Institute for Psychoanalysis and Psychotherapy of New Jersey (IPPNJ) and Faculty IPPNJ; private practice, New York, NY, and Millburn, NJ.

Elizabeth Flynn Campbell, NCPsyA

Member, National Psychological Association for Psychoanalysis, New York, NY; editorial board, *Psychoanalytic Review*; private practice, New York, NY.

Leonore M. Foehrenbach, CMHC

Faculty and Training Analyst, New York Center for Psychoanalytic Training; Faculty and Training Analyst, Institute for Psychoanalytic Education and Training, New York, NY; Editorial Review Board, *The New York Counselor*.

Paula Freed, LCSW, BCD
Member, Institute for Psychoanalysis and Psychotherapy of New Jersey.

Laura Arens Fuerstein, MSW, LCSW
Supervisor, Senior Training and Control Analyst, Faculty Member, the New York Center for Psychoanalytic Training and the Institute for Psychoanalysis and Psychotherapy of New Jersey; Fellow, New Jersey Society for Clinical Social Work; author of various published professional papers, including several in *The Psychoanalytic Review*.

Marvin Hurvich, Ph.D.
Professor of Psychology, Long Island University, Brooklyn Center; Faculty Member, Training and Supervisory Psychoanalyst at the Institute for Psychoanalytic Training and Research, the New York University Postdoctoral Program, and the New York Freudian Society; member, International Psychoanalytic Association; private practice, New York, NY. He is co-author (with Leopold Bellak and Helen Gediman) of *Ego Functions in Schizophrenics, Neurotics and Normals*, and has published on borderline and narcissistic pathology, and on annihilation anxieties. He is currently writing a book on theoretical, clinical, and empirical aspects of annihilation anxieties.

Josephine Kirby, M.A.
Psychoanalytic psychotherapist; affiliated with Ecumenical Consultation Center; Bereavement Facilitator, Hospice of Long Island, NY.

Robert C. Lane, Ph.D.
Director, Postdoctoral Institute of Psychoanalysis and Psychotherapy; Program Director, Intensive Psychodynamic Psychotherapy Clinic; Psychoanalytic Scholar in Residence, Nova Southeastern University, Center for Psychological Studies; Director Emeritus, Long Island Division, New York Center for Psychoanalytic Training; Past President and Founding Father of the Division of Psychoanalysis, American Psychological Association.

Harriette Podhoretz, Ph.D.
Member, Faculty, Training Analyst, author, lecturer, National Psychological Association for Psychoanalysis, New York, NY.

Charlotte Schwartz, MSS, CSW

Psychoanalyst, private practice; formerly Assistant Professor of Pediatrics, New York Medical College; Adjunct Clinical Professor, Smith College School for Social Work; Training Analyst, National Psychological Association for Psychoanalysis and the New York Society for Psychoanalytic Training.

Amira Simha-Alpern, Ph.D.

Graduate of Long Island University; candidate in the Postdoctoral Program in Psychoanalysis and Psychotherapy, the G. F. Derner Institute of Advanced Psychological Studies, Adelphi University; Staff Psychologist at Just-Kids Diagnostic and Treatment Center, Middle Island, Long Island. Area of research: bulimia.

Joseph Simo, Ph.D.

Private practice, New York, NY; Past President, Council of Psychoanalytic Psychotherapy; Past President, Society of Psychoanalytic Training; Director, Institute for Psychoanalytic Education and Training, New York City; teacher, lecturer, and supervisor in the United States, Mexico, South America, and Europe; author of numerous psychoanalytic papers.

PART I

The Development of
Psychosomatic Disorders

CHAPTER ONE

Alexithymia and Mind–Body Problems

JANET SCHUMACHER FINELL

The ego "is first and foremost a body-ego."

Freud

This book focuses on mind–body problems in contemporary psychotherapeutic practice. It contains case reports that cover a variety of psychosomatic[1] disorders. Two of the central issues that have appeared in the body of literature on psychosomatic disorders are the meaning of symptoms from a historical and theoretical perspective and the concept of *alexithymia*. This term refers to the psychosomatic patients who display asymbolic and concrete thinking and have difficulty identifying and communicating feelings.

---

1. By the term *psychosomatic* I mean the seven traditional psychosomatic diseases (duodenal ulcer, bronchial asthma, rheumatoid arthritis, ulcerative colitis, essential hypertension, neurodermatitis, and thyrotoxicosis), somatoform disorders as well as other psychophysiological conditions, such as fibromyalgia and panic attacks. This includes illness in which there appears to be a strong emotional component with or without tissue change.

THE ROLE OF MEANING

Early psychosomatic theory reflected Freud's thinking about conversion hysteria. Although Freud did not write about psychosomatic disorders in the general body of his work, his thinking on hysteria became the model for this field. Conversion symptoms were seen by Freud as symbolic of unconscious meaning expressed in bodily rather than psychical ways (see Chapter 2).

Early psychosomatic writers believed that specific diseases were linked to specific conflicts. For example, asthma was believed to involve a stifled cry for the mother's love along with fear of maternal rejection, while dermatitis was believed to represent a conflict between wishes for maternal touch and punishment (Alexander 1950, Alexander et al. 1968). These writers were founders of the specificity theory, which held that all psychosomatic illness involved dependency longings, but specific illnesses were believed to correlate with specific conflicts and wishes. Alexander's determinants included constitutional predisposition, external conditions, and chronic repressed emotions and conflicts, as Taylor (1987) points out. The fact that bodily symptoms were seen as an outcome of particular conflicts and fantasies identified the theory as one of specificity.

Most early writers differentiated the symbolism Freud wrote of in conversion hysteria from the type that occurred in the vegetative or nonvoluntary symptoms in psychosomatic states. For these writers, the symptoms themselves were seen as not having primary symbolic meaning in and of themselves, but were associated with predictable conflicts and emotions.

In time, writers on psychosomatics began to look at the importance of preoedipal factors. Fenichel (1945) wrote of organ neuroses and pregenital conversion symptoms. Sperling (1967) stressed pregenital factors in her work with patients with inflammatory bowel disease. Some writers focused on regression to early fixation points (Deutsch 1953) and the role of the ego in regression (Schur 1955). Giovacchini (1993) wrote of fragmentation, splitting, and projective defenses in borderline psychosomatic patients.

Winnicott (1966) emphasized the dissociation in psychosomatic illness between mind and body and between the functions of different caregivers of the patient. He saw the splitting of the ego organization as the "true illness" rather than the somatic symptoms themselves. Dissociation was described as a defense against somatic dysfunction and psychic conflict. He believed it is important in treating these patients to work with the fantasy of the "inside, and what is there to be found, and how it got there, and what to do with it" (p. 512). In one case the mother was the ill person while it was the child who had the symptom. Underneath the symptom lay the threat of disintegration. Integration of contradictory, split-off feelings was feared as leading to annihilation of the self. Omnipotent self-care behaviors defended against these overwhelming anxieties. Winnicott (1949) saw the symptoms as having positive value in that it forced a return to emphasis on the body rather than the intellectual part of the mind, which became activated in "cataloging" impingements and environmental failures. In developing a mind-psyche rather than a psyche-soma, the false self displayed compliance and false self behavior, either caregiving or complying with the outside world.

In spite of the multidimensional approach advocated by some of the early writers, Taylor (1987) and Hogan (1995) criticize their mind—body causality approach with its "mysterious leap" from mind to body, which involves linearity. According to Taylor, this approach does not take into account the importance of the interaction between self and object that is such an integral part of development. The emerging self has impact on the external objects who respond accordingly. Early psychoanalytic thinking stressed the unilateral impact on the child by the caregivers. Hogan is also critical of the linear model, which erroneously considers temporal contiguity, the simultaneous occurrence of certain emotions with certain bodily symptoms, as proof of cause and effect, when in fact one can only prove parallelism between mind and body.

Taylor (1987) gives a detailed account of the importance of object relations in psychosomatic cases. In this theory he draws on the work of Winnicott, McDougall, Bion, and others. In a later publication (1993) Taylor details his clinical work; he uses an approach that draws more heavily on self psychology, but he also enables the patient to ultimately identify feelings of rage, anger, shame, and sadness. He teaches his patient "to identify and accurately label these feelings for himself [which] gradually provided [increased] use [of] the symbolic system of language to modulate distressing emotions" (p. 588).

In time, the patient becomes more able to deal with all kinds of difficult feelings, including rage. Early in the treatment Taylor does not respond to material involving rageful feelings, and he follows Kohut (1977) in considering aggression a disintegration by-product of an ego unable to process intense feelings. Later in the treatment, through identifying and naming intense feelings, somatic symptomatology is lessened.

An inconsistency between theoretical thinking and practice shows up in Hogan's (1995) argument, in which he claims that it can often be proven that mental and physical reactions occur simultaneously, which "rules out causality." He raises questions about the implication in conversion that mind causes body in a linear model (which would imply some time difference between mental and physical reactions), but then reverts back to the use of conversion, claiming that "the term *conversion* is so established that I cannot foresee any important immediate changes in the use of it, so I shall continue to comply, with the understanding that I am using it only in its historical sense" (p. 96).

He reverts back to the mind—body causality he has been criticizing. As justification for this about-face, he cites the excellent results achieved by Sperling in her work with children with bowel diseases. He too believes that the results he has achieved with patients with inflammatory disease of the colon further supports the continued use of the drive-defense model in work with psychosomatic problems. He believes that the concept of alexithymia reflects defense rather than deficit. When defenses around feelings are analyzed, repressed emotions can be brought to the surface. He gives examples of the capacity of his patients to process feelings of sadism and in doing so achieve relief from their inflammatory colon disease.

Contemporary theory on psychosomatics espouses a multicausal approach exploring constitutional predisposition, reality stressors, and social and neurological factors. The role of the neurotransmitters, particularly serotonin, has received much publicity recently with Prozac, Paxil, and Zoloft frequently prescribed in the hope that they will ease underlying depression and lessen psychosomatic illness. Recent research on psychoneuroimmunology has focused on the link between stress and immunology (Hornig-Rohan 1995) and is still in its preliminary stage. Researchers at New York University (Waldholz 1993) identified a thickening in brain neural pathways as a result of trauma. They believe that a neurological change in structure is at work in posttraumatic stress disorders. Goleman (1995) reports on research that discovered actual shrinkage of the hypothalamus, which affects short-term memory and leaves subjects more prone to flashbacks, nightmares, and trouble with concentration. This research added the role of cortisol to that of adrenalin as a stress-related biological element in promoting impaired immune defenses and such diseases as hypertension and diabetes.

The role that separation and loss play in biological reactions was discussed by Mushatt (1989), Hofer (1984), and Pipp and Harmon (1987). Hofer describes relationships as regulators in humans and in studies of rat pups. The sense of permanent loss of a needed attachment disregulates biological rhythms. In bereavement, biological responses are affected. Pipp and Harmon question how, following Hofer's work, "homeostatic regulation after separation" (p. 649) is regained. We appear to be "biologically connected to those with whom we have close relationships" (p. 651). They suggest that with loss of the attachment, some aspects of the homeostatic regulation become internalized while others are distributed among several close relationships.

In his excellent review on the interaction between developmental and biological interrelationships in disease, Taylor (1992) reviews research that shows that alexithymic individuals are not only more prone to disease as a result of faulty processing and conceptualizing of emotions, thereby being unable to cognitively deal with distressing affects, but also are more prone to display failures in autonomous functioning. "The alexithymic individual's vulnerability to illness is attributed primarily to deficits in the cognitive processing of emotions" (p. 475). He further proposes that "the failure to process emotions cognitively so that they are experienced as conscious feeling states leads to a focusing on and amplification of the somatic component of emotional arousal" (p. 475).

As a result of their tendency to rely on external objects for self-regulation and self-esteem, alexithymic individuals are more vulnerable to separations and loss in their environment. These object impairments become played out in the transference and can be worked on in treatment. Engel and Schmale (1967) believe that feelings of withdrawal and helplessness-hopelessness responses are related to endocrinological and immunological changes and being prone to illness. One cannot help wondering to what extent heightened adrenal/cortisol levels over time interfere not only with health but with cognitive processing and reality testing. Taylor (1992) cites Freud's (1926b) statement cautioning against searching for answers in endocrinology and the autonomic nervous system. Considering the research being reported on endocrinology in this "Decade of the Brain," Freud's statement is certainly ironic.

Bibring's (1968) belief that the "ego's shocking awareness of its own helplessness in regard to its (narcissistic) aspirations" (p. 175) gives rise to depression is worth considering here. The shocklike experiences that occur in the child in the course of misattuned and intrusive experiences with parents in all likelihood trigger heightened cortisol secretion that overtaxes the mind–body connection. Energy could conceivably be drawn away from normal body functioning to energic fight-or-flight responses that cause exhaustion, lowered immunity, and disease. Energy expended in attempting to transform painful misattunement into love and recognition undoubtedly extracts its toll on the body systems. Feelings of anxiety and helplessness are most probably paralleled by a bodily state of excitement, exertion, and exhaustion. Furthermore, chronic stressful mind–body conditions over a long period of time in people who ultimately develop type A, overcontrolled, driven behavior, with its accompanying readiness to anger and the fight response, could understandably promote unhealthy biological reactions.

The role of early trauma appears to be important, and the psychosomatic sufferer is perceived by some contemporary theorists as sharing certain qualities with addicted people—essentially unsatisfactory inner objects and poor inner self-regulation (Connors 1994, McDougall 1974, Taylor 1987). Both addicted and somatic types are seen as turning to external objects to regulate their impulses and emotions. To the extent that the trauma overwhelmed the ego, the person feels helpless and not in control of his or her survival. It may be that those later experiences that resonate with the ego's earlier shocklike experience prepare the way for the regressive reactions that some theorists have stressed.

In all likelihood the failure of the mother to help the child transform its raw sensations and stimuli coming from within and without floods the immature ego with helpless shock, which intertwines with the faulty emotional development that is found in individuals with alexithymia. The parental experience seems to be alternately impinging and distancing; thus, the child never has the emotional attunement with the caregiving individual needed to develop the adequate internalizations and structure to help bind stimuli. The environmental failure contributes to a state of flooding, in which anxiety reaches traumatic proportions, causing excitation of neural impulses that make indelible impressions on the most primitive reactions of the brain. In this state of helpless panic, narcissistic depletion occurs as the emerging self tries to make sense of a disordered and chaotic world. The energy expended in coping with this troubled situation further interferes with appropriate growth. When, as Winnicott (1951, 1960) writes, object attachments interfere with rather than promote resolution of omnipotent longings, creativity and symbolization fail to develop optimally. Following this thinking, the "spontaneous gesture" (1960, p. 145) may show itself as a pathological somatic response rather than a normal developmental gesture meant to obtain the mother's attention.

James (1979), too, believes not only that psychosomatic disorders reflect a failure of internalization, in which the person seeks to relive the early unsatisfying object relationship, but also that with the illness the patient has a purpose in living. Through the "regime that inevitably becomes a way of life" (p. 414), the patient reverses an underlying sense of futility. This suggests the presence of a fundamental depression and narcissistic injury in these cases. In focusing on self issues, Rodin (1984, 1991) cautions that the patient often displays a wish to be literally "held" by the therapist, and one needs to be alert to reactions of disappointment transferentially. Citing Freud's (1923) famous statement that the ego "is first and foremost a body-ego (p. 27)," Rodin, like Taylor, believes that somatization replaces cognitive processing of affects when caregivers were unable to help the child transform raw bodily experiences into cognition. Somatization needs to be understood in the intersubjectivity of the transference. As a message to the therapist, the patient may wish alternately to be held, to be understood, to get relief from the somatic symptoms, and to establish a connection to the therapist through them. The patient's wishes for responsiveness from the therapist around the symptoms are central in the transference. Rodin (1991) states, "In the therapeutic situation, the physical symptoms served not only to insure the continued interest of the therapist but also to ward off fears of abandonment" (p. 377).

Somatic experience replaces self experience and reflects deep anxieties over fragmentation and disintegration. Like other writers on alexithymia, Rodin stresses the need to link physical symptoms to an awareness of accompanying feelings. He writes of the meaning of physical symptoms that arise in the course of psychotherapy and can reflect wishes for physical soothing. The tendency to experience emotions physically rather than psychically in all probability reflects early traumatization "by empathic failures in their primary relationships" (1984, p. 261).

ALEXITHYMIA IN MIND–BODY PROBLEMS

Work with psychosomatic sufferers offers a rich body of clinical evidence in which one can study the important problem of alexithymia. De M'Uzan (1974) describes the process of "pensée opératoire" or operatory-concrete thinking that characterizes this type of individual. The term *alexithymia* is coined from the Greek *a lexis* and *thymos*, meaning not having the words for feelings (Sifneos 1975). This term describes a deficiency in emotional expressiveness.

Recent research discussed by Taylor (1994) found evidence of personality traits identified with alexithymia only in certain conditions, among them posttraumatic stress, somatization, and eating, panic, and substance-abuse disorders. Some healthy individuals also display alexithymia. Taylor and his colleagues constructed a twenty-item scale (Twenty-Item Toronto Alexithymia Scale) with a three-factor structure—"difficulty identifying feelings; . . . difficulty describing feelings to others; and . . . externally oriented thinking" (Taylor 1994, p. 66). Proneness to somatization, the experience of states of unpleasant emotions, narrow range of interest, lack of imaginativeness, and poor resilience in the face of stress suggest that alexithymia "is a deficiency in the area of affects" (p. 69).

Alexithymic individuals tend to respond with descriptions of external events when questioned about feelings and fantasies (Nemiah and Sifneos 1970). Nemiah (1975) believes that these patients could not elaborate their fantasies, unlike hysterics who often have a rich fantasy life. These patients have a difficult time reflecting on inner processes and generally respond poorly to "uncovering analytic" approaches but do better with "supportive measures" (p. 6).

Krystal (1982) further elaborates on this thinking, linking alexithymia to early traumatic states. He found similarities between drug withdrawal and posttraumatic states. Feelings are not processed and used as signals, and emotions are vague and unspecific. These patients are overdependent on reasoning and are often described as "dull, colorless, and boring" (Krystal 1982, p. 359). They externalize their feelings and are monotonous in their fantasy life. Both substance-dependent patients and psychosomatics who are alexithymic tend to have limited capacity for self-soothing and self-gratifying.

As one of the most important and creative contributors to psychoanalytic technique with psychosomatic patients, McDougall (1974, 1989) believes that feelings that are not processed through language can activate somatic problems—a form of archaic hysteria. Certain experiences are foreclosed from the mind, they are not connected with memory, language, and symbols. These patients are "normopaths"—people who seem normal but have grave difficulty in reaching their feelings through the analytic process. They display flattened affect and detachment, and are mechanical and robotic. Alexithymia "as advanced by Nemiah and Sifneos [arises] largely from neuroanatomical defects" (McDougall 1989, p. 25). She agrees with Nemiah that not all psychosomatic sufferers display alexithymia nor do all alexithymics display psychosomatic disorders. While she expresses a preference for the term *disaffected* over *alexithymia*, she draws on both terms to describe her patients' behavior.

McDougall believes that another important characteristic of many somatizing patients is the absence of a good internalized object with whom they can identify in times of need for self-soothing and self-care. Their mothers failed to provide optimum space, being either too intrusive or too distant for them to move from bodily experiences to words and feelings. They were not protected from external or internal stimuli, and did not store memories in language. The fathers were uninvolved, leaving the child at the mercy of the impinging mother. In contrast to psychotics, who project monstrous primitive images to the outside world, these patients experience a failure in the projective process. They develop anxiety about their body rather than project their inner dread to an object perceived as persecutory, as in psychosis. They lack an important step in their development and use their objects addictively to close a psychic space or gap.

One of McDougall's (1974) important contributions is her assisting in the development of a fantasy that is related to the somatic symptom. The fantasy developed is of a sadomasochistic nature and becomes "hystericalized" or "obsessionalized." In other words, the patient becomes overwhelmingly anxious and preoccupied with the fantasy, which becomes the means for working through the somatic problems. Hogan (1995), however, suggests that McDougall and the patient do not actually create a fantasy that is not already there; rather, the fantasy is repressed. He stresses defense over development and believes that analysis of drive and defense brings such fantasies to consciousness.

WORKING THROUGH: PSYCHOSOMATOSIS AND THE MUMMIFIED COUNTERTRANSFERENCE

Countertransference issues loom large in writing on mind–body problems. The countertransference reported most frequently with alexithymic patients is boredom, sleepiness, and difficulty in maintaining a connection to the patient. As a result of the patient's deadening, the therapist too can become alexithymic—deadened and mummified. Avoiding succumbing to these feelings is of central importance in work with these patients. They operationalize and concretize their thought processes and fantasy life so consistently that the therapist feels that he or she has mutated into a mummy and in so doing can avoid psychic life along with the patient. Such a development enables the terrified, hidden, and more alive self of the patient to remain in hiding.

It is at this point that creativity and courage on the part of the therapist are needed. These patients are projecting their psychic deadness onto the therapist. The lack of space to symbolize and play leaves them with a paucity of creativity. They express themselves concretely and operationally since more abstract imagery and emotional expressiveness is either too threatening or simply not available.

ALEXITHYMIA AND THE THERAPIST

Krystal (1982) points out that therapists can be as alexithymic as patients. He feels that alexithymia can occur in well-functioning therapists: "Thus the occurrence of alexithymia among psychoanalysts and other psychotherapists makes these people particularly prone to miss these problems in their patients" (p. 374).

When the therapist has an underlying tendency to display alexithymia, the work with these patients becomes more difficult. It can be particularly hard for therapists who struggle to identify their own inner processes. In referring to the classical psychosomatic disorders, Sperling (1967) believes that "psychosomatic disorders are common and widespread among analysts" (p. 352).

Being a therapist, generally speaking, enlivens one's psychic life. However, if both patient and therapist are numbed, the situation becomes deadlocked. Defenses on the part of the therapist include daydreaming, falling asleep, preoccupation with the patient's physical problems, and frustration over the lack of stimulation coming from the patient. The patient becomes the nonattuned mother, only minimally interested in and involved with the child. The therapists' selves become annihilated and mummified. Rather than feel anxiety, depression, loss, disappointment, and emptiness as countertransference reactions, they join the patient in becoming preoccupied with the physical problem being discussed.

TECHNIQUES WITH ALEXITHYMIC PATIENTS

One way of dealing with these patients is to work backward from symptoms to feelings. The therapist is like a detective trying to deduce what occurred in the patient's mind that triggered the psychosomatic outburst. Asking questions helps the patient discover that some external event aroused strong emotions that were not processed psychically but were strangulated and shifted into somatic expression. An alternate way of looking at the process is that an event failed to occur in the mind and instead was experienced only somatically. If emotions are viewed as biological or somatic events, they can go unprocessed (Taylor 1996, personal communication). Whether an object relations failure or terror over impulses is uppermost, the failure to process emotional reactions is a central feature of mind—body problems.

Psychosomatic patients incorporate suffering into their important object relationships. In many cases, the parent was attentive only when the child was ill. The inability of the parent to cathect the child when it was healthy provides a prototype of later mind—body problems. Sperling (1967) writes of the mother's involvement with the child on issues of its helplessness, submission, and dependency, while rejecting the child for displaying aggression and autonomous strivings. The absence of illness signifies loss, abandonment, and annihilation to these patients, which can give rise to a powerful negative therapeutic reaction. Bodily symptoms are positively rather than negatively cathected. Health symbolizes loss of the love of the object, loss of the object, and ultimately annihilation.

These losses contrast with the series of losses and separations that

Freud (1926a) believed trigger anxiety reactions, essentially anxiety over underlying instinctual wishes. He viewed only the first loss as biological—separation from the mother at birth—since it resulted from the infant's helpless dependence on her for survival. Later losses—loss of the mother as an object, loss of the penis (for boys), loss of the object's love, and loss of the superego's love—Freud saw as essentially psychological. It is interesting that contemporary psychosomatic theory includes biology as well as psychology as a causative factor. Neurotransmitters, certain hormone levels, as well as the sense of loss, separation, and helplessness, can be viewed as interacting in psychosomatic reactions. The child internalizes the illness-centered caregiving that represented the mother's style of mothering. In keeping with Bollas's (1987) thinking that the patients treat themselves the way they were treated by the mothering objects, one sees in psychosomatically ill patients a form of self-care that focuses heavily on bodily illness and bodily dysfunction rather than on feelings. To use Bion's thinking, the alpha process—the change of primitive, raw, nonsymbolized (beta) experience to symbolic thinking and the capacity to express emotions verbally—only partially occurred (Grinberg et al. 1977).

When the mother suffered psychosomatically, the process of identification occurred so that some of the psychosomatic illness reflects the unconscious identificatory tie to the mother. Relinquishing this tie can signify unbearable object loss. Alexithymia, too, represents an identification with a deadened part of the parent, which is incorporated into the patient's psychic structure. The patient may know intellectually that the therapist wants to hear about fantasies, sexual wishes, and so on, but this has an unreal quality to him or her. Only the somatic bodily reactions are cathected libidinally and aggressively. The other psychic experiences are unavailable to some psychosomatic sufferers (not all somatic sufferers are alexithymic and vice versa). Some of these individuals may be patterned through years of faulty mind–body reactions to experience emotions mainly somatically.

SUMMARY

Techniques that are potentially helpful with alexithymic patients are as follows:

1. It is important to encourage the development and elaboration of feelings and wishes. The therapist may need to help the patient create and identify feelings and fantasies where previously there were none.
2. When appropriate, the therapist should interpret and analyze defenses around character traits—deadening and flatness of affect—that relate to the lack of feelings and fantasies. Pointing out the contrast between the content of what the patient is discussing and the inappropriateness or deadness of affect may be helpful. It may be necessary to question the patient about what feelings are being avoided as stressful or anxiety-provoking material is reported in a robotic-like manner. The patient is undoubtedly not aware of this discrepancy between content and affect and the therapist must be careful not to cause narcissistic injury, which would lead the patient to withdraw.
3. The therapist must use the countertransference to ascertain which feelings might be defended against or unavailable. In particular, the therapist must draw on projective identification, identifying feelings the patient is projecting to the therapist through induced feelings and introducing the patient to these feelings in a benign and patient manner.
4. In therapy's supportive relationship, in which the patient is free to expose previously repressed, discounted, or foreclosed wishes and longings, in particular wishes for closeness and dependency longings, the patient may find it possible to feel a degree of trust never before experienced. Constant attention to the transference, in particular disappointment and feelings of misattunement, should be uppermost in the therapist's mind and sensitively brought into the process. The meaning of the symptom to the patient should be explored. The fantasy of the patient's insides and what is happening, following Winnicott (1966), should be explored.
5. Conflicts around dependence, which show up as omnipotent self-care and caregiving or rescuing behavior of others, should be explored. The patient alternately pushes away the therapist, arouses countertransference wishes on the part of the therapist to hold and soothe the patient regarding issues of somatic suffering, and triggers helpless feelings in the face of what may at times seem like unreasonable impasses.

These issues present very difficult challenges to psychotherapy.

ACKNOWLEDGMENT

Many thanks to Graeme J. Taylor for reading and commenting on this chapter.

REFERENCES

Alexander, F. (1950). *Psychosomatic Medicine.* New York: Norton.

Alexander, F., French, T. M., and Pollock, G. H. (1968). *Psychosomatic Specificity, Vol. 1: Experimental Study and Results.* Chicago: University of Chicago Press.

Bibring, E. (1968). The mechanism of depression. In *The Meaning of Despair,* ed. W. Gaylin, pp. 154–181. New York: Science House.

Bollas, C. (1987). *The Shadow of the Object.* New York: Columbia University Press.

Connors, M. E. (1994). Symptom formation: an integrative self-psychological perspective. *Psychoanalytic Psychology* 11 (4):509–523.

de M'Uzan, M. (1974). Psychodynamic mechanisms in psychosomatic symptom formation. *Psychotherapy of Psychosomatics* 23:103–110.

Deutsch, F. (1953). *The Psychosomatic Concept in Psychoanalysis.* New York: International Universities Press.

Engel, G. L., and Schmale, A. H. (1967). Psychoanalytic theory of somatic disorder: conversion, specificity and the disease onset situation. *Journal of the American Psychoanalytic Association* 15:344–365.

Fenichel, O. (1945). *The Psychoanalytic Theory of Neurosis.* New York: Norton.

Freud, S. (1923). The ego and the id. *Standard Edition* 19:12–66.

——— (1926a). Inhibitions, symptoms and anxiety. *Standard Edition* 20:77–174.

——— (1926b). The question of lay analysis. *Standard Edition* 20:183–250.

Giovacchini, P. L. (1993). *Borderline Patients, the Psychosomatic Focus and the Therapeutic Process.* Northvale, NJ: Jason Aronson.

Goleman, D. (1995). Severe trauma may damage the brain as well as the psyche. *The New York Times,* August 1, p. C3.

Grinberg, L., Sor, D., and Tabak de Bianchedi, E. (1977). *Introduction to the Work of Bion.* Northvale, NJ: Jason Aronson.

Hofer, M. A. (1984). Relationships as regulators: a psychobiologic perspective on bereavement. *Psychosomatic Medicine* 46:183–197.

Hogan, C. C. (1995). *Psychosomatics, Psychoanalysis, and Inflammatory Disease of the Colon.* Madison, CT: International Universities Press.

Hornig-Rohan, M. (1995). Stress, immune mediators, and immune-mediated disease. *Advances: The Journal of Mind-Body Health* 2:31.

James, M. (1979). The non-symbolic nature of psychosomatic disorder: a test case of both Klein and classical theory. *International Review of Psycho-Analysis* 6:413–422.

Kohut, H. (1977). *The Analysis of the Self.* New York: International Universities Press.

Krystal, H. (1978). Trauma and affects. *The Psychoanalytic Study of the Child* 33:81-116. New Haven, CT: Yale University Press.

—— (1982). Alexithymia and the effectiveness of psychoanalytic treatment. *International Journal of Psychoanalytic Psychotherapy* 9:353–378.

McDougall, J. (1974). The psychesoma and the psychoanalytic process. *International Review of Psycho-Analysis* 1:437–459.

—— (1989). *Theaters of the Body.* New York: Norton.

Mushatt, C. (1989). Mind-body-environment: toward understanding the impact of loss on psyche and soma. *Psychoanalytic Quarterly* 44:81–106.

Nemiah, J. C. (1975). Alexithymia: theoretical considerations. *Psychotherapy of Psychosomatics* 28:199–206.

Nemiah, J. C., and Sifneos, P. E. (1970). Affect and fantasy in patients with psychosomatic disorders. In *Modern Trends in Psychosomatic Medicine*, vol. 2, ed. O. W. Hill, pp. 26–34. London: Butterworth.

Pipp, S., and Harmon, R. J. (1987). Attachment as regulation: a commentary. *Child Development* 58:648–652.

Rodin, G. (1984). Somatization and the self: psychotherapeutic issues. *American Journal of Psychotherapeutic Issues* 38:7–263.

—— (1991). Somatization: a perspective from self-psychology. *Journal of the American Academy of Psychoanalysis* 19:367–384.

Schur, M. (1955). Comments on the metapsychology of somatization. *Psychoanalytic Study of the Child* 10:110–164. New York: International Universities Press.

Sifneos, P. E. (1975). Problems of psychotherapy of patients with alexithymic characteristics and physical disease. *Psychotherapy of Psychosomatics* 26:65–70.

Sperling, M. (1967). Transference neurosis in patients with psychosomatic disorders. *Psychoanalytic Quarterly* 36:342–355.

Taylor, G. J. (1987). *Psychosomatic Medicine and Contemporary Psychoanalysis.* Madison, CT: International Universities Press.

———— (1992). Psychosomatics and self-regulation. In *Interface of Psychoanalysis and Psychology*, ed. J. W. Barron, M. N. Eagle, and D. S. Wolitzky. Washington, DC: American Psychological Association.

———— (1993). Clinical application of a dysregulation model of illness and disease: a case of spasmodic torticollis. *International Journal of Psycho-Analysis* 74:581–595.

———— (1994). The alexithymia construct: conceptualization, validation, and relationship with basic dimensions of personality. *New Trends in Experimental and Clinical Psychiatry* 10:61–74.

Waldholz, M. (1993). Study of fear shows emotions can alter 'wiring' of the brain. *The Wall Street Journal*, September 29, pp. A1, A12.

Winnicott, D. W. (1949). Mind and its relation to the psyche-soma. In *Collected Papers*, pp. 243–254. London: Tavistock, 1958.

———— (1951). Transitional objects and transitional phenomena. In *Collected Papers*, pp. 229–242. London: Tavistock, 1958.

———— (1960). Ego distortion in terms of true and false self. In *The Maturational Processes and the Facilitating Environment*, pp. 140–152. Madison, CT: International Universities Press, 1965.

———— (1966). Psychosomatic illness in the positive and negative aspects. *International Journal of Psycho-Analysis* 47:510–516.

CHAPTER TWO

Developmental Determinants of Psychosomatic Symptoms

LEONORE FOEHRENBACH, CAROLYN CELENTANO,
JOSEPHINE KIRBY, AND ROBERT C. LANE

The sorrow that has no vent in tears makes other organs weep.

> Henry Maudsley,
> British anatomist

Curiosity has been one of man's greatest assets as a cognitive being. The compelling desire to know resulted in a gradual but amazing mastery of the environment and to an ever-increasing knowledge about the human species. Through the ages, one of the most intriguing of all challenges has been to understand the esoteric nature of man and the behaviors that are a part of this being. It was inevitable that the inquiring search for truth and for cause and effect led inevitably to the enigmatic connection that exists between body and mind. As far back as Greek and Roman civilizations, the relationship between psyche and soma was known to have an influence on one's state of health and the development and progress of illness and disease. However, it was not until sixty years ago that any real interest in psychosomatic medicine as we know it today began to take its place in the investigative research of physicians (Sheehan and Hackett 1978). Subsequently, there was little real development in the field and interest became sidetracked. Presently, however, with renewed interest and improved research methodologies, there has been a resurgence of curiosity about psychosomatic influences, centering on the role that the mind plays in pathology, treatment, and cure of both physical and mental disorders.

This chapter presents a brief overview of the investigation into psychosomatic determinants of illness, with considerable emphasis on the emerging scientific findings of the past ten years.

Over 100 years ago, Freud described a "leap" that moved in the direction of mind to body. In studies on hysteria and in conversion symptoms, Freud (1893/1955) recognized the psyche's power over the soma. He described these manifestations as a body expression of compromise between a forbidden wish or impulse and the defense against that desire. Simply put, the overwhelming urge to kick an offensive sibling can be prevented by the body suddenly taking over with a paralysis of the leg. And so it was in the case of one of Freud's (1905/1953) women patients who sat at her ill father's bedside. When her repressed oedipal sexual desires pressed for consciousness, the result was the conversion of this instinctual wish to the paralysis of the arm that would have reached out to express that desire.

In the 1940s and '50s, Alexander (1950) collected data on his patients who seemed to have psychosomatic elements in their case histories and categorized them into seven psychosomatic disorders: asthma, ulcers, colitis, hypertension, thyroid disorder, dermatitis, and arthritis. The attempt at the time was to connect certain stimuli with specific organ choices. For example, skin with its eruptive and oozing sores represented unrecognized weeping on the inside. The other disorders were also linked to symbolic meaning. But in the following years, the data supplied did not necessarily prove this theory. Moreover, many other manifestations of body illness were added to these seven original psychosomatic maladies: all of the addictions, the eating disorders, migraines, accident proneness, and the lowering of immunity. In fact, whatever involves a body or organ reaction needs to be explored for its psychological component. Body and mind are truly inseparable.

In the 1950s brain researchers speculated that distressing emotions, instead of being relayed to the neocortex (word center) and finding expression in the symbolic use of words, were immediately sent to autonomic pathways for processing and were translated into a kind of "organ language." Max Schur (1955) went further and hypothesized that the causation of psychosomatic diseases came from conflict between wish and conscience, but also was influenced by disturbances in mother–infant interaction and in subsequent object relationships. After a new frontier was opened with these pieces of research, almost 20 years passed before the theories were given much attention by psychosomatricians.

In the 1970s, the French psychosomaticists Marty, de M'Uzan, and David (1963) began to notice that many of their physically ill patients could not describe images or fantasies. They seemed to have no ability to explain feelings and their analytic sessions were flat and operational or mechanical. At the same time in the United States, analysts Nemiah and Sifneos (1970) studied psychosomatic patients and found that these people could not verbally express their feelings or affects and had a striking lack of imagery and other symbolic functions. They coined the term *alexithymia*—(*a-*) without, (*lexi-*) words, (*thymia*) emotions (no words for feelings)—and felt that psychic functioning was of central importance in many diseases.

Joyce McDougall (1980, 1989, 1991), working with the French psychosomaticists, the British object relationists, and the infant researchers here and abroad, took up these theories and has written extensively about this subject, beautifully encapsulating the thoughts of others into a logical and clear hypothesis of the intricacies of both psyche and soma in the life of an individual—perhaps from the person's very conception. This chapter explores the theoretical picture (in relation to the psychodynamics behind it) that these recent advances and hypotheses present.

Picture the baby—newly born, removed from its warm and nurturing intrauterine life, and totally helpless. It is hungry, it has pain, it is cold and wet, it has discomfort—these feelings are physical in nature. It is afraid, anxious, frustrated, and it fears annihilation and extinction—this is psychic pain. Both of these categories, physical and psychic, produce tremendous tensions that press for release. These are stressful energies and are expressed in the only way a neonate knows—it cries, its arms and legs wave about in global spasmodic movements, in short, it tries to release these pressures through body action. There is no differentiation between physical or psychic pain, merely a reaction to pain. The infant possesses no symbolic, imaginative psychic apparatus to mitigate, to neutralize this energy. This very lack is what we often see duplicated in the adult life of our psychosomatic patients. Something is lacking; there seems to be no psychic reality to be called upon for relief of overwhelming tensions. Such people act operationally and mechanically. They are like robots and have no sense of emotion. Not only are they wordless, they are affectless. McDougall (1989) feels that for these persons, the "leap" Freud spoke of goes in the opposite direction—from primitive body expression to mind, to that special structure that can recognize psychic pain and form compromises and judgments that permit the neutralization of tension.

Here are two patients who, in the course of treatment, are examples of the theoretical dimensions we are examining.

Dave is a 28-year-old married social work student. He lives a great distance from the therapy office but commutes to school and treatment. He entered treatment a year and a half ago complaining of panic attacks, which included hyperventilation, chest pains, palpitations, and dizziness. He had been in therapy before with a female therapist who used relaxation exercises to help him calm down. This was successful in reducing his anxiety for a short time, but the underlying feelings generating the anxiety always returned, bringing increased anxiety each time. This resulted in what he described as "states of terror."

Sue came to therapy because her husband had left her, and she was overwhelmed with fear and anxiety. She was small and gaunt. She sat hunched over and looked like a pathetic waif. Her early sessions were disjointed, combined with continuous weeping. She wore gloves (the month was June) and explained that she suffered from Raynaud's disease and there was very little that she could do. There was a lost quality about Sue. The important object in her life had abandoned her and she was left in total despair. As she described her marriage—she presented a picture of a little child, always cold and helpless—the therapist often was puzzled by her inability to call upon her psychic reality to deal with the pain both during the marriage and at present. Although she was not able to verbalize her anguish, she presented it most vividly by her physical appearance: her body was undernurtured, underloved.

Let's explore for a moment how the symptomatology of these two patients developed. What is the something that seems to be missing, that permits them to be so flooded with pain? Where are the structures that are needed to deal with body responses to overwhelming stimuli?

Let's return to the infant. The baby has no symbolic capability and no psychic apparatus as yet. It is a primitive, physically resting entity. How does this part of intellectual function, this mental mechanism, come into being? The scenario is as follows: baby feels stomach pain and is helpless, and, fearing extinction, it cries. Mommy comes, milk and comfort are given, the pain is gone. Safe and secure, the baby can now drift off to sleep. The next step in this primitive maturation might be that the baby hears the sound of Mommy coming, and the image of what she does that brings about a feeling of being safe and pain free is resonated in memory. It is possible now for the baby to wait a bit and the feelings of abandonment and extinction are delayed. Here we see the thought formation in its crudest state—the beginning of the diminishment of symbiosis and the start of a process that is a precursor to a psychic apparatus. Melitta Sperling (1952) says, "We find on closer investigation in every psychosomatic case, that the patient lives in an emotional symbiosis with one object in his environment, who does not have to be the actual mother but who somehow, in the patient's unconscious, serves the dynamic function of a mother figure" (p. 286). McDougall (1989) points out essentially the same thing as Sperling when she says, "Sometimes the dead area of despair that so often inhabits our analysands is masked by an addictive dependence on significant others who are experienced as in infancy as a part of themselves" (p. 38).

> Dave told the therapist recently how upset he gets when his wife won't pay attention to him. If she is reading, for example, and he's in the same room, he'll "do things" (i.e., act "cute" or "funny"), to get her to notice him. He says that although this appears to make them "feel close," in actuality they're not. He will follow her from room to room, like a "puppy dog" trying to get some attention from her. Although he is frequently away from home, he becomes anxious and upset if she is the one who leaves and he finds himself alone.

> In the beginning of therapy, it took a long time for Sue to form an internal picture of the therapist to hold on to the memory traces between sessions, so that when she felt a sense of abandonment she would contact the therapist in order for the pain to go away. During the session, she needed constant empathy and support. As the session would come to an end, she very often would ask the therapist to reiterate what had been said. Then, that same day, there would be a message from Sue asking the therapist to phone her. She would say that

she couldn't remember what the therapist had said to her and would she please tell her again. Other times she would say she couldn't remember what it was about but she was all right now. It was obvious that she was unable to internalize the therapist and had to touch her in reality via her voice.

Let us examine the etiology of this psychic ability not developing. In our practices, we see individuals who cannot permit feelings or process the memories of them for use in an ameliorating way. The baby starts in utero with a one body fantasy—baby and Mommy are one (McDougall 1989). Everything that threatens this illusion after birth causes the infant to try desperately to find again that lost intrauterine paradise. The cries and signs of distress cause Mommy on her part to use her warmth, voice, protectiveness, closeness, to re-create the same illusion. When this is done it enables the neonate to form an internal picture of the maternal image and, with security, fall peacefully to sleep. But sleeping requires separation. The baby has a need for that also. So from this body–mind unity must come differentiation, which means recognizing the differences between the two bodies and the formation of the representation of the "other." In other words, the ability to separate the child from the mother, the soma from the psyche, is beginning.

As long as the mother's unconscious wishes do not interfere with the baby's need to merge and then to differentiate, the process can go on. This universal tendency of infants (to merge and to differentiate) allows each baby to form a mental representation of a mother who soothes, cares for, and contains baby's raw emotions. When she is not actually there, the mental picture of her is available. This lays the groundwork for the integration of the mother object in each person's inner world, a piece of that psychic apparatus that eventually allows one, through mental functioning, to perform these caregiving activities for one's self. McDougall (1980) states:

The mother's failure, through being too close or too far away, to fulfill her function as a shield against the stream of stimuli to which her baby is subjected, includes her failure to make sense out of this nonverbal communication. There is then a grave risk that his own capacity to give the rudiments of meaning to what he experiences and to represent psychically his id impulses and their subsequent objects will be impaired. The differentiation between representation and symbol will also be confused eventually. [p. 361]

Sue was deprived of a mother, who was too far away. She doesn't remember having a bed of her own. There were thirteen children and she was number seven. Each night she slept where she was placed—on chairs, on the floor, or in a bed with other siblings. Somehow there was no bed designated for Sue. She remembers being wakened by the tossing and turning of bodies that pushed up against her, pulled the blanket away, and breathed heavily in her face. When asked if she complained, she said she didn't remember except that she sensed that she'd better be quiet or it could be worse. Sue's mother failed to act as a protective shield against outside stimuli and failed to help decode Sue's communications. Sue is unable to integrate a warm protective feeling as a mother to herself or her children.

Dave's mother needed him to be available for her needs. The feeling he associates most with her is of being "used." In her "using," separateness was denied. She would often confide in him and tell him how unhappy she was in her marriage. She gave him money for being her "helper" (i.e., cleaning up after school) and this would become their "secret." It is the way she continues to "give" to him today. Money becomes highly cathected and represents their secret relationship, which causes Dave shame and anger. Being Mommy's "helper" is to be merged with her, allowing no place for autonomy. Whenever Dave feels "used" in a relationship, he experiences strong physical affects that signal his rage, despair, and confusion. To illustrate what happens when this integration has been lacking, Dave recently reported that he was in supervision discussing how one of his clients was "blocking" feelings, not saying what he felt. Dave described feeling as though he were "in a trance" during the session. He felt, he said, like he was the client. "I got blurred about who was who." His inability to differentiate in situations like this leads to feelings of blurriness, confusion, and, in extreme situations, panic.

One of the first psychosomatic illnesses that is observed is infant insomnia, and here we see the mother's own needs and deficiencies setting the stage for this disease. Normally, after feeling secure, warm, fed, and happy, the infant is able to slide into a contented dreamlike state and to feel soothed by images—the internal pictures of the mother and her presence.

Often the baby is not given the space for such reflection because the mother feels the need to keep the infant dependent on her. Out of her own wants she creates the clingy child who feels it cannot live without contact with the significant other. This child who has not been encouraged to differentiate often cannot sleep without physical connection. The psychic structure isn't allowed to form through elaboration of memory traces, and the implications of this in later life are tremendous. As adults, those who have disturbing representations (as with Dave) or no imagery of the mothering figure at all (as with Sue) also frequently suffer from insomnia. It is as though they have understood that they must be the parents to themselves, and are incapable of reliving through thought the primary fusion with Mommy. They must be their own caregivers and stay awake, ever on guard, so that no harm comes to them.

> Sue is devoid of any psychic apparatus. She spends her life searching for a caregiving object. After she was divorced and lived alone, she complained of lying awake most of the night unable to sleep. She would go about the house locking the doors and windows. When she still couldn't sleep, she would compulsively recheck the doors and windows. She imagined that an intruder would steal into the house and harm her. When she could no longer tolerate the anxiety, she would phone her children one by one until there was a response. Invariably the response would be one of anger for being wakened. She would then lie in bed, paralyzed with overwhelming fear. Because she lacked the internal representation of mother's soothing, Sue would lie in a state of expectancy and dread and finally fall asleep from sheer exhaustion.

When the mother has not furthered healthy development as a result of her anxious need to control her offspring's thoughts, emotions, and fantasies, the young child, lacking the growing space between self and mother, cannot organize its own psychic realities to provide caregiving functions for its adult self. Such mothers, in Winnicott's (1953) view, are excessively maternal, not simply good enough but rather overgood. They overlove, overfeed, overcare for, and overworry about the child. Their children feel this as a "psychic" abandonment—the stress is on body alone, the physiological—and the indifference of the mother to their psychological needs and affective states reinforces the split of body–mind rather than its fusion. This is illustrated in a metaphorical way by Dave's memory of the "Sunday meal."

Dave remembers on Sundays there was always a large meal, the aroma of which permeated the house all day long. He remembers all of this food being prepared and the smell of it cooking, but although he could feel and hear the sounds from his noisy stomach signaling his hunger, he was not permitted to eat until evening. On occasion he recalled being allowed a celery stick, for example, but in addition to the deprivation he felt his frustration at having all of this bounty within his reach but unavailable to him, which kept him in a state of anxiety and rage, with no mechanism for processing it. This was the physiological manifestation of his psychic hunger and represented for him the split between his body and his mind.

If the mother makes the baby her sole source of libidinal gratification, the infant's maturation is disrupted and its ability to use transitional phenomena is undeveloped. Normally, the infant substitutes security "blankets," and in doing so chooses an object that embodies the essence of the mother—her smell, her touch—but is in reality a symbol of her soothing and protective function. Transitional objects allow the baby to sleep and feel safe because they are illusions of the mother's presence. Later these objects are replaced by more sophisticated substitutes—dolls, animals, and eventually by the symbolization of verbalization, the word *Mommy*. Through this word we have the re-creation of the feelings, the warmth, and protection felt and now internalized in psychic memory. In this manner, and through many similar instances, the infant becomes a normal, verbal child. The emphasis is moving from soma to psyche, from feelings to words. Psychosomatic individuals, however, continue to use body and organ expression as the only way to release psychic pain, just as they did in infancy.

So far we have been discussing infant development prior to the formation of verbalization and speech. This complicated task of symbolization is not a spontaneous matter. The eventual capacity of the growing toddler to encode linguistically all bodily and emotional experiences is uniquely dependent on the nature of the tie to the mother, for it is Mommy who, in the first instance, must interpret her baby's cries and gestures. She must be attuned to the child so that she can tell in an accurate fashion what it is really feeling.

> The therapist's vacation time always exacerbated Sue's anxiety about separation. No matter how much planning and preparation for it had been done, the therapist's departure and return were attached with anger and devaluation. It was decided that Sue's fear of abandonment would be alleviated through periodic contact. Certain times were designated when she would be called. Each time she was called her response was indifferent and conversation was short.
>
> When the therapist returned, Sue complained that what she did was not satisfactory, that those times when she called were not the times Sue needed her. How reminiscent of her life with the important object. Mother was not attuned to the infant's needs and Sue was not able to relate her feelings in an accurate manner.

After attunement, the fundamental structuring element in the forma-tion of a psychic organization is the symbolization of affect. The mother is the mirroring object and must provide words for the expression of feelings. She perceives that the child is struggling with emotion that it can only enact, since the capacity to reflect has not yet been developed. The maternal object must be able to hold the infant's rage and modify its pain so that the soma-tic and psychic autonomy can be formed. For this to occur, physical sensation and painful affects must become accessible for the symbolic process. Mother acts as an interpreter for her child's cries and gestures. Words are the containers of affect and must be given directly. Mother is the translator that lets the child know *what* it is feeling and the word that stands for the sensation. The child can then become conscious of its body's many changes and messages. It can learn for itself to elaborate symbolically, through thought and imagery, the physical and emotional events that are occurring so that they can be deciphered, understood, and mitigated. This early psychic foundation will determine to a considerable extent the adult potentiality to capture and to recognize one's personal emotional reality and to be able then to communicate it to others. When there is no capacity for symbolization, when affects cannot be identified and tolerated, then not only alexithymia results but also perhaps an inability to feel at all. Feelings are dangerous and one learns to eject them without perceptual recognition.

Emotions of frustration, distress, despair, guilt, and rage may therefore be expressed only through the soma. Information about how to deal with important life issues are unavailable for use as a means that could permit a person to think clearly, judge and weigh a situation, and then take appropriate action. For these persons, situations capable of invoking psychic pain and conflict have been refused access to the psyche and can then only be taken over by that other information-processing machine, the body, which will reply in place of the mind.

When Sue complains that her sons take advantage of her, she is not clear about her affective reactions. She disperses her feelings and rather than think about them, goes into action, busying herself with other things—she calls it "distraction." Her psychic pain is somatized; then she is able to inform the important objects about her illnesses. They don't respond sympathetically, but begin to recount their own problems. When this happens, Sue says she gets a feeling from childhood. "When they don't understand how I feel, I think of my parents and I want to cry, but I'm not alone, so I can't. I think of my ex-husband and wish I could tell him, but what good would it do? He left me and was not concerned." Since she can't deal with the psychic reality, she continues to send primitive messages that express themselves through somatic discharge.

When Dave is angry, hurt, or disappointed, he has a physical reaction before he has any awareness of what he is feeling. He experiences dizziness, ringing in his ears, a warm sensation throughout his body, and sometimes a general numbness follows. At these times, he has to physically separate himself from the person or situation triggering the reaction. For example, if this happens with his wife, he will leave the room, go somewhere in the house to lie down, and only then is he able to understand what has really taken place.

When the body takes over, we are watching a story in mime. If this tale could be spoken, it would appear that the soma is responding intelligently, given its own interpretation, when it replies to psychological threats as though they were biological ones. Such anger, for instance, knows no psychic outlet that will provide relief, no alternative action to mitigate that fury that threatens to explode and fragment the person into bits. The body, in the service of survival, takes over to maintain life. Often the body's response can be an organ action, such as a stomach secretion or an intestinal contraction. When organs are involved over and over, eventually organic damage develops.

Psychosomatic illness can be life threatening and runs the risk of precipitating a premature death.

When Dave entered treatment, he had symptoms that simulated those present before a heart attack. He suffered from chest pains, flushing, palpitations, clamminess, and dizziness on occasion. Indeed, these symptoms, not treated and unrelenting for long periods of time, can bring about cardiac distress.

After working psychoanalytically for a while, Dave began to experience changes. He described himself as "living in my head," very cerebral. We could speculate about the displacement upward (particularly in light of his sexual symptomatology, to be discussed below). What is significant is his understanding of the need to "think" before he "feels," a change from his prior experience of being overwhelmed by symptoms, with no sense of what he was truly feeling. It's as though living in his head provides him with a boundary, a way of regulating himself, something that had not been provided for him as a child.

Last year, prior to the therapist's vacation, Sue began to develop new illnesses. As the time for the therapist to leave drew closer, Sue seemed to be getting sicker, until one day she reported a litany of her maladies and how busy she was tending to them. They were as follows:

1. a skin cancer that had to be removed, followed by plastic surgery;
2. a cap that had disintegrated in her mouth, and made her feel as though she were swallowing poisonous matter, needed to be replaced;
3. internal bleeding that necessitated a barium enema;
4. high blood pressure that refused to respond to medication.

All in all, she would have the need of a dermatologist, plastic surgeon, dentist, gastroenterologist, and internist.

Since her therapeutic relationship felt threatened because the therapist was going away, Sue communicated a state of despair through organic illness, thus giving her access to caregiving people. (Sue needed five doctors to replace one therapist!)

When the process of symbolization is inadequate, pathological transitional objects are created, which may take the form of addictive substances, addictive relationships, and perverse or addictive sexual behavior. These addictive products are used to disperse mental pain and psychic conflict as a mother might, and they are also magical attempts to fill a void in the inner world—that of the soothing maternal figure. But, as we only too sadly know, magic doesn't work and what we see once again is the person's attempt to achieve pain alleviation and self-cure—an attempt that fails. McDougall (1980) writes:

There is in such cases in later life a breakdown in object relations due to the attempt to make an external object behave like an internalized good mother should and thus repair a psychic gap. The object or situation will then be sought addictively. Basically all addictions are attempts to make an external agent do duty for a missing symbolic dimension. . . . There is an attempt to make substitute objects in the external world do duty for symbolic ones which are absent or damaged in the inner psychic world. The victim of this kind of lack is doomed to endless repetition and addictive attachment to the outer world and external objects. [p. 370]

Dave has been using masturbation compulsively for several purposes. One is to self-soothe and bring himself a degree of comfort when he is anxious or upset. Where Mother was not able to provide this function for him in reality, he has had to resort to using it in fantasy. Masturbation serves the function of restoring physical and psychic equilibrium for him when he is most at odds with himself and feeling overwhelmed. Dave also masturbates when he is enraged and feeling powerless. By using his penis as a weapon, he manages to punish both himself and the fantasied object who has hurt or frustrated him.

Shortly after Sue's husband left her, she met Will and immediately clung to him, literally for her life. He would be the replacement for the missing object she so desperately needed. She expected that he would be there for her as a caregiving mother and that he would repair her inner psychic world.

She reported all the things he did for her—run errands, chauffeur her, help clean her house, garden. Somehow, whatever he did never sufficed, so she would send him away, saying she was better off alone. But the withdrawal was intolerable and she would call him back and repeat the addiction, never to develop the ability to care for herself.

Let us consider what clues we can discover that help us to be cognizant of psychosomatic tendencies in our patients. We may observe a dearth of feelings in their narratives. We may see little or no symbolization in words for affects when emotions do seem to surface. We may even observe that feelings are ejected from perception, unrecognized, forbidden, destroyed, or expressed in body language. There is little capacity for dreaming or imagery. The sessions with such patients have a flat quality.

McDougall finds these patients to be "dis-affected." For them, an emotion—good or bad—may come to consciousness but cannot be worked over. Instead of being contained by words, these feelings are dispersed through an action, as if possessing them was a forbidden thing.

While it is not uncommon to discharge tension in action through eating, engaging in work, or some type of physical activity, disaffected people habitually use action as a defense against mental pain. Acting-out behavior is what we see in their external world, and this can also happen in their inner lives. There may be an internal use of ejection of feelings or "foreclosure" as McDougall (1989) calls it. The hidden story, perhaps the need to rid oneself of a toxic internalization, for example, is demonstrated by vomiting, by gagging, or by diarrhea. Persons who somatize are unaware that they are not dealing with their affects. Rather, they are running away from them. Often the action used is destructive and can include violence, frantic sexual exploits, or perverse behavior.

Early in the treatment, Dave spoke of his perverse fantasies. In large part, he was frightened by what he called his "predator" feelings. He was afraid he would act on these. He spoke of forceful sex, "penetration," and "stalking," and worried about what kind of pervert he was. He sometimes worried about having children for fear of being a child molester. In addition to his anxiety, he was also conveying a message to the therapist about what he experienced in fantasy as his enormous rage and power.

Addiction to sex often emerges and is demonstrated in many ways. Sexuality takes on the many qualities and effects of drug use. The partner as a *person* plays little role in the patient's inner world. Lovers (as with Sue) are used like tranquilizers. Patients who use objects as drugs often complain of feeling misunderstood, lonely, empty. Their objects are used like transitional inanimate things, for self-soothing or as persons to be attacked or controlled. The comfort this brings is short-lived, for the object is not inside, hence the emptiness prevails. A pathological wish for merger, followed by fear at the same time of losing identity and autonomy, is repeated over and over. This pattern is often typified in the course of therapy through the transference. Threats of closeness in the formation of a positive attachment are often dealt with by a negative reaction to the therapist.

Negative transferences must be analyzed quickly, and the therapist must be alert for the early signs of such reactions. Sperling (1952) points out the difficulty in working with a psychosomatic patient in a negative transference. Such patients do not verbalize negative feelings, might not be aware of them, or repress them so completely that the only way they can find an outlet is via their bodies. When it is possible to reconvert a somatic symptom into the feeling or fantasy that caused it, it helps to tolerate this feeling without acting it out in uncontrolled behavior and is decidedly a step forward. It is in the building of one's own psychic understanding and symbolic apparatus that the patient can move from the use of the therapist as the container of his affect storms to the development of his own powers that will serve the same purpose for himself.

Although treatment with psychosomatic patients can be a long and perilous task, with gentle understanding the deficits of early life can be made up. Even severe damage can be repaired by the use of the empathy the therapist extends during the course of the treatment.

In an effort to defend against the all-powerful mother, Sue continuously struggles to maintain control. In therapy, she does this by testing the ground rules. During the past month, due to icy weather conditions, she called to say she could not keep her appointment as she could not drive on ice. When offered another therapy time, her response was, "I don't know how I will be then. Will I be responsible for the make-up time if I can't come?" At the next session, she explained that she felt a great deal of pressure to comply with therapy rules and wanted to alleviate the pressure by coming only once a week. The therapist responded that by doing that the rules would be broken. Sue said it felt like a gun was being held to her head. Her wish to separate and her anger at her inability to do it keep her feeling helpless. Because she is unable to internalize the soothing therapist, she wishes to keep her as a transitional object, a security blanket that she can wrap around her when needed or tear apart and punish.

One day, Dave, who had been rather elated in the earlier part of the session, suddenly got up from his chair, crossed the room, and stood looking at the therapist's framed certificates and pictures. For a few moments he stood this way, then, almost abruptly, returned to his seat and sat huddled and ashamed. After a lengthy silence, he said that he felt like a child who had done something "bad" and needed to be punished. He felt the therapist must surely be angry at his boldness and curiosity. The interpretation about his need to act, as opposed to verbalizing, and a recognition of his desire to "play" in spontaneous fashion (à la Winnicott, affording him this potential space) enabled him to speak about how he had always had to be the "good boy," "the saint," "the parent," to his younger siblings, while there was a whole other side to him that was never acknowledged.

In dealing with mental pain expressed through body language, we are observing primitive pathology that erupts when preneurotic conflicts arise that have not yet achieved mental representation. McDougall finds that at the moment of somatization psychotic anxiety and/or neurotic anxiety is being kept at bay. Neurotic anxiety is concerned with the normal adult rights to a love life, to narcissistic satisfaction, to pleasure, and to friends. Psychotic anxiety is generated over the right to exist, to be alive, and to be wanted. This sense of worthlessness leads to the psychotic fear of the body falling apart, of the mind falling apart and of being pulled into a magnetic, luring black vortex. Patients find this to be the most terrifying thing they know. She further believes that psychosomatic patients are even more damaged than psychotics, for the latter can at least create delusions to fill that void. This in itself is a struggle for self-cure, a symbolic power that the somatist does not possess when confronted by the void that threatens basic identity. This is experienced as a great, blank, black cessation of life itself.

SUMMARY

How can we as therapists use the information presented here to the greatest advantage in our practices? Here are some points to consider:

1. When a patient comes to treatment, we begin to form a picture of his or her tone and the emotional level of the communicative style. If the tenor of the sessions appears to be affectless or mechanical and flat, with little or no imagery in the material and few words used to describe feelings, the therapist should be vigilant for more overt signs of somatization.

2. Acting-out behavior, in the external world, is another verification that the capacity to use words and other symbolic methods of expression is absent. Addictive usages of substances or objects may also be necessary to mitigate pain. The therapist should also ascertain if body or organ expression is used as a means of handling overwhelming stimuli.

3. When the therapist repeatedly hears the complaint, "You don't understand," he or she should be on the alert. Understanding and attunement are very important to persons who do not have the good object integrated within. This phrase should be perceived as a strong plea for empathy, a longing for the therapist to be the symbiotic other who knows what the patient is feeling without the need to have it verbalized directly.

4. Through the use of the transference, compensation for the deficits of infancy is possible. The therapist acts in this relationship as a better mother than the patient has ever known. This includes accurate identification of the affect the patient is feeling, a deciphering of the

emotion and causation underlying it, and an understanding of what this sensation means in the patient's experience.

5. Through the use of memory, containment of affect, and decoding of feelings, the creations of the symbolic use of words as containers of emotion become a reality. It is through this procedure that the ability to think through, to mitigate anxiety, and to form judgment comes into being.

6. Patients often must use us through our own countertransferences to be the receivers of what they cannot express in words. This is especially so with those who are used to the soma speaking for them. So often the reactions we have and the feelings that are created within us by the patient are purposeful and are messages for us to identify and use, for this is the only way the patient can communicate. The therapist should look for his or her own feelings and decipher them.

7. Through the use of empathy and gentle understanding, it becomes possible to develop an understanding of the body's messages. Psyche and soma can unite. Individuation becomes possible. Thus, movement from dependency on another to true maturity can proceed.

8. Emotion itself can be owned, experienced, and utilized in a positive fashion. Internal and external conflicts can be contained and mitigated, and the fullness and richness of life can be enjoyed.

Those who can think can laugh,
Those who can only feel, must cry.

Leonore Foehrenbach

Addendum

Here is a follow-up at the present time in the cases of Sue and Dave.

Sue has begun to internalize the therapist; she doesn't call between sessions. The therapist can go on vacation without contacting her and vice versa. She uses catch phrases: "I'm better off alone." "I need to mother myself." "I can't expect others to guess what I want."

Breaking her addiction to Will, Sue is able to say, "He causes other problems when he's around. I can't do what I want when he's around. I need him for many things but now I'm asking myself, Do I really need him?" She recognizes that the relationship is toxic.

Trying to individuate from important objects, Sue says, "They don't hear me when I tell them what I want. I guess I don't tell them. I have no words." Sue has just started to learn that there is a psychic reality and how to listen to it and find words for it, rather than continually hurt her body. "I have to learn the words," she said. "I never know what to say. My body parts are worn out."

Presently, Dave is just several months shy of receiving his master's degree. This week signals an end to his treatment. He has many conflicting feelings concerning this. On the one hand it is another loss for him, one of many he has experienced in his life. He is aware of feelings of great sadness along with some confusion about who he is and what he wants to do with his life. On the other hand, he has gained much from his therapy, however brief. He is able to process more of what he is feeling when he is feeling it. He can put into words what his body once spoke for him almost exclusively. He is much less isolated and speaks of choices. He feels, for example, that he is more differentiated from his wife. At the same time he feels closer to her. This issue came up in a discussion of therapists in his community. He indicated that where in the past he'd had a supervisor give him a referral to therapy, he might now consider his own options and choices. This has the sound of differentiation.

REFERENCES

Alexander, F. (1950). Emotional factors in different diseases: psychosomatic disorders. In *Psychosomatic Medicine*, pp. 83–200. New York: Norton.

Freud, S. (1893/1955). Studies on hysteria. *Standard Edition* 2:25–307.

——— (1905/1953). Fragment of an analysis of a case of hysteria. *Standard Edition* 7:7–122.

Marty, P., de M'Uzan, M., and David, C. (1963). *L'investigation Psychosomatique*. Paris: Presses Universitaires de France.

McDougall, J. (1980). *Plea for a Measure of Abnormality*. New York: International Universities Press.

————— (1989). *Theaters of the Body*. New York: Norton.

————— (1991). *Theaters of the Mind: Illusion and Truth on the Psychoanalytic Stage*. New York: Brunner/Mazel.

Nemiah, J., and Sifneos, P. (1970). Affect and fantasy in patients with psychosomatic disorders. In *Modern Trends in Psychosomatic Medicine*, vol. 2, ed. O. W. Hill, pp. 26–34. London: Butterworth.

Schur, M. (1955). Comments on the metapsychology of somatization. *Psychoanalytic Study of the Child* 10:119–164. New York: International Universities Press.

Sheehan, D., and Hackett, T. (1978). Psychosomatic disorders. In *The Harvard Guide to Modern Psychiatry*, ed. A. M. Nicholi, Jr. Cambridge: Harvard University Press.

Sperling, M. (1952). Psychotherapeutic techniques in psychosomatic medicine. In *Specialized Techniques in Psychotherapy*, ed. G. Bychowski and J. L. Despert. New York: Basic Books.

Winnicott, D. W. (1953). Transitional objects and transitional phenomena. *International Journal of Psycho-Analysis* 34:89–97.

CHAPTER THREE

Freud's View of the Mind–Body Connection

SUZAN ANSON

> I suspect that we are here concerned with unconscious processes of thought which are twined around a wire; so that on another occasion one might find other lines of thought inserted between the same points of departure and termination. Yet a knowledge of the thought-connections which have been effective in the individual case is of a value which cannot be exaggerated for clearing up the symptoms.
>
> Freud 1905a, p. 102

It has been nearly 100 years since the patient Freud called Dora appeared in his consulting room. In a brief treatment lasting only eleven weeks, Freud was confronted with a dizzying array of physical symptoms to sort through and treat using the psychoanalytic method. Dora fled treatment prematurely—a result of negative transference—leaving the disappointed Freud to try to make sense of what had happened. Initially he was enthusiastic. He confided to Fliess that this was "'a case that has smoothly opened to the existing collection of picklocks'" (Masson 1985, p. 427). Freud was hopeful that this case would fully support his sexual theories and psychoanalytic technique, which was based on the analysis of material from two dreams. Nonetheless, the case miscarried, with a premature termination that was painful for Freud.

He had been casting about for a case that would pull him out of his ennui and financial worries, one that would spark him and enable him to explicate his sexual theory. Dora would become that patient. Commenting on the initial draft of the case, Freud expressed his mixed feelings about Dora: "'It contains resolutions of hysterical symptoms and glimpses of the sexual-organic foundation of the whole. It is the subtlest thing I have written so far and will put people off even more than usual. Still, one does one's duty and does not write for the day alone'" (Masson 1985, p. 433).

In another letter, he elaborated on the origin of Dora's symptoms:

"The main thing in it is again psychology, the utilization of dreams, and a few peculiarities of unconscious thought processes. There are only glimpses of the organic [elements], that is, the erotogenic zones and bisexuality. . . . It is a hysteria with tussis nervosa [nervous cough] and aphonia [loss of voice], which can be traced back to the character of the child's sucking, and the principal issue in the conflicting thought processes is the contrast between an inclination toward men and an inclination toward women." [Masson 1985, p. 434]

Oscar Rie, Freud's sister-in-law Minna's physician, had initially pressed Freud to allow him to read the case, but he apparently conveyed some negativity or lack of interest afterward. Freud then turned to Fliess for acknowledgment, but the friendship was waning and he did not find encouragement there either. Consequently, Freud did not publish the case until 1905.

Freud's correspondence with Fliess gives us a glimpse into Freud's physicianly preoccupation with physical symptoms; his letters are peppered with reports of his own illnesses and those of his family and colleagues.

Before Dora entered Freud's consultation room, Freud had spent a decade studying and writing about the distinctions between the actual (also referred to as true) neuroses and the psychoneuroses. Briefly, the actual neuroses, including neurasthenia, anxiety neurosis, and hypochondria, correspond to modern psychosomatic conditions; there is no underlying fantasy or conflict to be found in the symptoms. Freud felt that the case of the true neuroses was somatic dysfunctions arising from disrupted sexual functioning. The defining aspect of the psychoneuroses (a wide category that includes hysteria and some psychoses, such as paranoia) was the presence of psychic conflict.

In 1890 Freud published a paper exploring his theories on the mind–body connection that Nadelman (1990) notes presages contemporary issues in psychosomatic medicine. In this paper, Freud addressed the impact of psychological factors on physical health and the creation of disease states, touching upon the role the mind plays in the creation of physical pathology, predisposition to disease, impairment of immunological factors, and pain. Importantly, Freud addressed the role volition plays in positively affecting the outcome of illness—from the point of view of both the patient and the physician. Faith in the treatment, faith in the doctor's competence, and the "healing" personality of the physician were recognized by Freud to be important factors in treating disease.

Based on his research into the psychoneuroses and actual neuroses, Freud concluded that in patients who suffered from a "nervous" condition, such as neurasthenia or hysteria, symptoms originated from "a change in the action of their minds on their bodies" (1905b, p. 286). Looking beyond specific physical symptoms, Freud felt that the problem involved the entire nervous system. He speculated that affects—and how they were experienced—had a physical impact on the body. Depressed immunity, manifest anatomical changes (including organ disease), failure or success in overcoming illness, and even death could be attributed to strong affects. Certain patients, Freud noted, were predisposed to develop illness if stress exceeded a particular threshold level.

In his view of a unified psyche-soma, he connected the effect of thought on physiological processes. Freud speculated that all thoughts had a physical impact on the body, as excitations or stimuli were discharged into smooth or striated muscles. Freud held the view that the capacity to tolerate and to process affects had a role in the development of illness, anticipating the work of Taylor (1992) and others who attribute psychosomatic illness to disorders of self-regulation. Nadelman points out that although the ideas in this paper are 100 years old, Freud's thinking touches on contemporary issues in the relationship between psychoanalysis and psychosomatics.

During the years of his correspondence with Fliess, Freud not only took note of the various afflictions that beset his household but also freely discussed his own maladies, which ranged from writer's cramp to migraines and depression, many of which seem to reflect his general unhappiness with his life circumstances. During his self-analysis, Freud noted the shifting nature of his psychosomatic symptoms—inexplicably, his cardiac symptoms gave way to gastrointestinal problems (Masson 1985). He continued to use his correspondence with Fliess as a means of sharing, in detail, his own symptoms. As an example, in a letter dated September 27, 1899, Freud reveals his nearly hypochondriacal preoccupation with his changing symptoms:

"Dear Wilhelm,

For the record:

Sept. 11—inexplicable ill humor

Sept. 12—cardiac weakness with mild headache

Sept. 14–18—bad days, moody; cardiac fatigue

Tuesday, Sept. 19—headache without cardiac pain (traveling)

Since then, rather good days

Today, Sept. 27, initially a trace of headache without other manifestations." [Masson 1985, p. 375]

Ever alert to interpret the meaning of his symptoms or those of his family, Freud attributed his son's maladies to hysteria: " 'Ernest is laid up with a bad insect bite. . . . Ever since the boy lost a front tooth, he has been continually hurting himself; he is full of wounds, like Lazarus, yet at the same time totally reckless and as though anesthetic. I ascribe it to a slight hysteria. He is the only one whom the former nurse treated badly' " (Masson 1985, p. 367).

Shortly after beginning treatment with Dora, Freud's sister-in-law Minna began to suffer from a baffling constellation of painful gastrointestinal symptoms, puzzling both to Freud and her physician, Oscar Rie. Minna remained ill throughout Dora's treatment, showing improvement five days after Freud finished writing up Dora's case. In the wake of his abbreviated treatment of Dora, Freud continued his attempt to understand the underlying causes of Minna's illness, confiding to Fliess, " 'A functional or neurotic illness surely cannot be diagnosed. The whole business is uncanny' " (Masson 1985, p. 434).

DISTINGUISHING THE PSYCHONEUROSES
FROM THE TRUE NEUROSES

Freud's thinking was forever in flux, subject to refinement and redefinition, so it is useful to distinguish early definitions of neurosis and psychoneurosis from later formulations that evolved to coincide with the development of the structural theory.

In early formulations, actual neurosis as defined by Freud (1894) was divided into three "pure forms": neurasthenia, anxiety neurosis, and hypochondria. These conditions were thought to be the result of either excessive or impoverished libidinal states.

Freud defined neurasthenia as a malady resulting from impoverished libido, which was characterized by physical tiredness, intracranial pressure, dyspepsia (indigestion), constipation, organ irritability, weakening or inhibition of function, spinal paresthesia, and impoverishment of sexual activity.

Excessive accumulation of libido was thought to produce anxiety neurosis, a condition where physical tension remained located in the soma, which could be experienced in a number of ways: generalized irritability; hypersensitivity to noise; free-floating anxiety; anxiety attacks, or any number of somatic equivalents including sweating, congestion, dyspnea (shortness of breath or labored breathing), and palpitations—all symptoms, Freud noted, that corresponded to physiological responses to normal sexual intercourse); awakening in fright—*pavor nocturnus*; vertigo; phobias; digestive disorders, and paresthesia.

In Freud's view, anxiety neurosis was the somatic equivalent of hysteria. Anxiety neurosis (an actual neurosis) occurs as a result of the deviation of excess excitation into the soma. Hysteria (a psychoneurosis) arises from psychic conflict. Three factors linked them: accumulation of excitation, psychical inadequacy that resulted in abnormal somatic processes, and a "deflection of excitation" (1894, p. 105) into the somatic field. Both neuroses share similar physical symptoms that may be either chronic or episodic.

Freud attempted to clarify the confusions and contradictions arising between the etiology of the actual neuroses and the psychoneuroses. He was clear that both arose from the libido. He was careful to state that sexual function influenced both the psychic life and somatic functioning. However, he was emphatic in separating out what he felt to be analyzable. Limiting the role of psychoanalysis to its ability to reveal the unconscious, Freud (1920) observed that

> the problems of the true neuroses, whose symptoms probably originate in direct toxic damage, yield no point of attack to psychoanalysis. Psychoanalysis can do little for their elucidation, and must leave the task to biological-medical research. . . . The symptoms of the true neurosis—such as pressure in the head, sensations of pain, irritability

of an organ, weakening or inhibition of a function—these have no meaning, no psychic significance. [p. 336]

Maintaining the view that libidinal imbalances were the root of the neuroses, Freud speculated, "We shall not be surprised to discover that the true neuroses are the direct somatic consequences of sexual disturbances" (p. 336).

Freud believed the source of pain in the psychoneuroses was real. "Once upon a time this pain was real, a direct sexual toxic symptom, the physical expression of libidinous excitation" (1920, p. 339). He added that libidinal excitement—either normal or pathological—contributed to symptom development in hysteria. Through the analysis of hysterical symptoms, pain could be seen to be a displacement and elaboration that provided a substitute gratification for libidinous fantasies or memories.

Freud observed that it was possible for the symptom in an actual neurosis to be the kernel from which a psychoneurotic symptom developed. He believed the (actual) neurotic symptom was often created as a result of a physical condition such as an injury or an inflammation. But once the symptom was manifest, unconscious fantasies could find expression through it. The symptom could then evolve into the conflict or pain of either a psychoneurosis or a "mixed neurosis." He maintained that through psychoanalysis it would be possible to relate each hysterical symptom to its etiology, as the examination of each symptom would yield a specific meaning.

In 1920 Freud commented on the blurrings of definitions among the neuroses, which included actual neuroses and psychoneuroses. "The terms are all widely used but their connotation is vague and uncertain" (p. 338), he wrote, noting that often they were blended together or combined with a psychoneurotic condition, which he called a mixed neurosis. He concluded that it was not useful to discuss the actual neuroses in a discussion of psychoanalysis because to do so would "prove sterile for the purpose of psychoanalysis" (p. 338).

At the time Dora's case was written, the psychoneuroses were composed of the transference neuroses or narcissistic neuroses, subsuming conversion hysteria and anxiety hysteria (phobia). Laplanche and Pontalis (1973) distinguish between two types of conversion hysteria: paroxystic hysteria (emotional crises accompanied by theatricality) and long-lasting hysteria (including anesthesia, hysterical paralyses, and lumps in the throat).

Anxiety hysteria occurs as a phobic response to specific external objects. Laplanche and Pontalis note that the hysterical response has a specificity to "certain kinds of identification, certain mechanisms (repression), in an emergence of the oedipal conflict occurring mainly in the phallic-oral libidinal spheres" (p. 195). Freud defined conversion as a "malady through representation" (cited in Laplanche and Pontalis, p. 195), encompassing unconscious fantasy, a defensive conflict, repression, identification, and transference.

In 1920, discouraged by those who wished to blend the psychoneuroses with the actual neuroses, Freud observed: "I think they have gone too far and have not chosen the road which leads to progress" (p. 338). Later on, as Waelder (cited in Taylor 1992) noted, Freud's followers disregarded Freud's 1920 view, making the assumption that the actual neuroses would eventually yield evidence of intrapsychic conflict. As a result, psychoanalysis of psychosomatic conditions was initiated.

Fenichel (1945) cautioned that the term *psychosomatic* implied a dualism that he felt was not true. For Fenichel, every disease could be considered to be psychosomatic: "No 'somatic' disease is entirely free from psychic influence—an accident may have occurred for psychogenic reasons, and not only resistance against infections but all vital functions are continually influenced by the emotional state of the organism—even the most 'psychic' conversion may be based on a purely 'somatic' compliance" (p. 237).

Fenichel felt Freud's use of the term *neurotic* for different disturbances was imprecise. He proposed new terms to distinguish between somatic changes based on either conversion or "organ neuroses." Conversion symptoms are based on fantasies translated into a "body language," which are accessible to therapy in the same way that a dream provides the key to the unconscious fantasy. "Organ neurotic" symptoms refer to physical symptoms resulting from nonspecific emotional stress. Fenichel maintained that symptom relief was obtained if the attitude that prevented reduction of stress could be analyzed. "The change of function cannot be 'analyzed' because it has no unconscious meaning; however, the attitude that produced it can be analyzed, and if the attitude is given up, or the state of being dammed up is overcome, the involuntary consequences likewise disappear" (p. 264).

Brenner (1974) observed that although Fenichel classified neurasthenia and anxiety neurosis as clinical entities, there is little mention of actual neuroses in case material since Freud. In contemporary usage psychosomatic conditions have replaced the actual neuroses.

THE CASE OF DORA

It is useful to review the main elements of Dora's history, which reads like a modern soap opera (for an excellent summary of the case, see Gay 1988, pp. 246–255). Dora, an intensely neurotic, hysterical young woman, was brought by her father to Freud for treatment at the age of 18. Her neurotic symptom—a chronic dyspnea—began at age 8, and was continuing, much elaborated, at the time she began her analysis with Freud. Her parents had become alarmed after discovering a suicide note she had written.

Dora's behavior had become increasingly difficult. She was unhappy with herself and her parents, and with good reason. The environment Dora had lived in throughout her adolescence was highly eroticized and full of pretense. Her tubercular and syphilitic father had been having an affair with Frau K., a family friend and his former nurse. Dora's mother, whom Dora had little use for, was an obsessive-compulsive housekeeper who apparently had no sexual interest in her husband. Dora's father had moved the family to Vienna to facilitate contact with Frau K. Dora had discovered the affair and even colluded with her father to maintain it. Meanwhile, Frau K. had befriended Dora, often sharing her bedroom with her. Frau K.'s husband was enamored of Dora; his attempt to eroticize their relationship had begun when Dora was 14. Dora's father, intent on preserving his liaison with Frau K., had not objected to Herr K.'s long-standing erotic interest in Dora. When an attempted seduction by Herr K. failed and Dora accused him, he denied it. Worse, her father concluded that what had happened was only a fantasy, and refused to break off the relationship with the K.'s. Dora's response to this lack of protection and betrayal was depression, irritability, and suicidal ideation.

Dora's Symptoms

One might imagine how confounding it would be today to have a patient presenting with the sheer number of symptoms that Dora presented to Freud. It is remarkable that Freud was able to be so open-minded in his efforts to untangle the numerous symptoms Dora experienced, and to find unconscious meaning in most of them after carefully ruling out organic disease.

Early in treatment the following nineteen symptoms were enumerated: chronic dyspnea, hemicranial headaches, migraine, nervous coughing—*tussis nervosa*—catarrh, hoarseness, aphonia (loss of voice), fever, fatigue—*taedium vitae*—lack of concentration, fainting with loss of consciousness, convulsions, delirium, amnesia, "petite hysterie" including hysterical unsociability, depression, irritability, suicidal ideation, and a history of childhood bedwetting and thumb-sucking. During the course of treatment Freud would uncover ten more symptoms: abdominal pains mimicking appendicitis— "ovarian neuralgia"—leukorrhea (abnormal, whitish vaginal discharge), palpitations, nervous asthma, obsessional preoccupations, tactile hallucinations, eating disorder, locomotor disturbances (dragging her right foot), irregular menstruation, and constipation.

These symptoms provided Freud with the basis to apply his metapsychological principles, lending weight to his theory that sexual disturbances were the root cause of both the psychoneuroses and the actual neuroses. He eventually concluded that "sexuality . . . provides the motive power for every single symptom, and for every single manifestation of a symptom. The symptoms of this disease are nothing else than *the patient's sexual activity*. . . . Sexuality is the key to the problem of the psychoneuroses and of the neuroses in general" (1905a, p. 137).

The Dora case enabled Freud to explore different aspects of hysteria: the motivation for illness, the role of somatic compliance, and the multidetermined nature of symptoms in relation to the unconscious and oedipal sexual fantasy.

Freud originally thought that the motive for illness in hysteria was not apparent until the particular form of an illness had manifested. He distinguished this from the liability to being ill. He observed that "the neurotic escapes the conflict *by taking refuge in illness*" (1920, p. 332). In a footnote (added 1923) to the case of Dora, Freud refined these notions, distinguishing the primary gains from the secondary gains that resulted from becoming ill. Primary gains could be either internally or psychologically motivated (*paranosic gain*), or externally (*epinosic gain*) motivated, for example, by difficult relationships or circumstances. He pointed out that a flight into illness represents a convenient solution that reduces the need for psychic effort. This enables the individual to retreat from underlying psychic conflicts.

Guilt, remorse, and desire for punishment are among the internally motivated factors contributing to illness. In Dora's case, her self-reproaches were displaced onto the father. Freud felt these internal factors were more easily accessible therapeutically than externally motivated factors. External factors—situational or relationship factors—also play an important role in motivating illness. These external factors were felt by Freud to be more problematic.

Dora's case led Freud to refine his ideas concerning the origin and gratification of secondary gain. Observing that children quickly learn that illness is one path to obtaining special attention from the parents, Freud ventured that this behavior is likely to be repeated in adulthood.

Citing the conflict that secondary gain presented, he wrote, "The ego wants to rid itself of the pain of the symptoms without relinquishing the gain of illness, and that is impossible" (1920, p. 333). Freud noticed that Dora knew Frau K.'s retreat into illness was a convenient way to avoid sexual activity with her husband. As he noted, "She had also learned from Frau K. what useful things illnesses could become" (1905a, p. 48).

At the same time, he was convinced that constitutional factors contributed to hysteria. Dora's father had syphilis at the time of her conception, leading Freud to believe (based on the analysis of other patients) that there was a "neuropathic" constitution in the offspring of syphilitic parents.

Analyzing the patient's intention to become ill and convincing the patient of that fact became a prime task in the analysis of hysteria. Freud initially felt the motive for Dora's illness was to induce her father to love her and to break up the relationship with Frau K. Only after Dora fled treatment did Freud realize he had erred in failing to see the importance of Dora's homosexual transference to Frau K.

Recognizing the mutual influence on the psyche and the soma, Freud emphasized that every symptom required participation from both sides. A hysterical symptom could not be generated without somatic compliance, in which a physical symptom could not be repeated unless there was an unconscious meaning attached to it. Without somatic compliance, symptoms would be limited to purely mental expression, resulting in phobias or obsessions.

As an example of somatic compliance, Freud discovered that Dora's episodic attacks of aphonia (loss of voice) symbolized her love for Herr K. Freud made this connection after discovering that the duration of Dora's attacks corresponded to the same length of time as Herr K.'s business trips, usually three to six weeks. Typically, Herr K. kept up a correspondence with Dora when he traveled, sending her long letters and postcards. During his absence Dora would lose her voice; yet she found that writing came quite easily to her during these intervals. She maintained her connection to Herr K. through writing. Freud noted that "speech had lost its value because she could not speak to *him*. . . . Writing gained in importance, as being the only means of communication with the absent person" (1905a, p. 50).

Freud established linkages between the "necessary somatic prerequisite" and later symptoms. In hysteria, he felt the motive force was intensified by repressed sexuality and unconscious perverse activities. Freud linked Dora's early childhood memory of thumb-sucking while fondling her brother's ear lobe to her erotization of sucking. This eroticized somatic compliance of the oral zone predisposed her to fantasies of sucking on Herr K.'s penis. Interestingly, Freud noted that this sucking fantasy was based on a preoedipal fantasy of sucking at the breast, but he did not elaborate on what disturbances in the mother—child dyad led Dora to attempt self-soothing through these behaviors.

Freud elaborated on the multidetermined nature of symptoms; linking the symptom to several unconscious mental processes, he stressed that "a symptom signifies the representation—the realization—of a phantasy with a sexual content, that is to say, it signifies a sexual situation" (1905a, p. 58). He noted that the symptom could represent several meanings simultaneously or several meanings in succession, sometimes over the course of years. Dora's dyspnea and hoarseness are representative of the migration of meaning of her symptoms over time. These shifting meanings could represent fantasies or be based on identifications.

Symptoms Based on Identifications

Dora's identification with both parents' various illnesses contributed to the nature of her symptoms; Dora's family members and her circle of acquaintances provided a fertile ground for the development of symptoms through identification.

Dora's parents had tuberculosis; her father had a continual cough and dyspnea; her mother eventually died of tuberculosis. The impact of the father's syphilis on Dora can be seen in her identification with her father and with her mother, which became clear during the treatment, and possibly through congenital effects Freud felt might have contributed to her hysteria. Her beloved friend Frau K. had spent months in a sanitorium for "nervous disorders" and had been unable to walk.

Dora's identification with her father provided the basis for her most severe and chronic symptoms, since these symptoms were fused with unconscious sexual fantasy. Freud felt that Dora's coughing had begun as catarrh, resulting from an irritation. Sperling (1973) points out that Dora's selection of a cough was reasonable, since both parents were afflicted with tuberculosis. The hoarseness and dyspnea of the father were imitated by Dora and evolved into a nervous cough, *tussis nervosa*. Freud felt that this cough was multidetermined; it signified her love and concern for her father, but it also served as a reproach, categorized by Freud as "I am my father's daughter. I have a catarrh, just as he has. He has made me ill, just as he has made Mother ill. It is from him that I have got my evil passions, which are punished by illness" (1905a, p. 99).

Freud deduced that the throat irritation was eroticized, and that it became a fixation as a result of her imitation of her father. Her father had used his cough as evidence that he needed to live in a milder climate, but in fact he was traveling to maintain his affair with Frau K.; the transparency of his motive was quickly discovered by the suspicious Dora.

The father's fabrications provided Dora with other opportunities for identification. Dora's suicide note was, according to Freud, apparently based on an identification with a story told by her father. In an effort to disguise a meeting where he had been discovered with his lover, Frau K., he constructed a story in which he reported that he had felt suicidal urges. In this story, he cast Frau K. in the role of the rescuer who had chased him into the woods to dissuade him. Freud believed that Dora's suicidal note, created with knowledge of her father's fabrication, represented longing for a similar relationship.

Following a disagreement with her father, Dora had lapsed into unconsciousness, which she did not recall afterward. Freud connected this behavior to her identification with her father's syphilitic symptoms, which had flared up several years before her suicide note. As a result of syphilis, the father had suffered a "confusional attack, followed by symptoms of paralysis, and slight mental disturbances" (1905a, pp. 26–27).

Dora had reported dragging her right foot shortly after her attack of appendicitis, unlike, but related to, the *tabes dorsalis* (locomotor ataxia) suffered by her father. This inability to walk properly following appendicitis had surprised the doctors, but Freud expected to find that it held unconscious meaning for Dora.

Freud gives scant attention to the role Dora's mother played in her illness. However, several symptoms can be traced to her identification with her mother—an obsessive-compulsive housekeeper—especially Dora's obsessive rumination about her father and Frau K. During a particularly difficult few days during her treatment, Dora berated her father while displaying symptoms similar to her mother's, which had required treatment in a sanitorium. Dora made the assumption that her mother's illness (abdominal pain and discharge) had been sexually transmitted by the father. As it turned out, Dora actually did have leukorrhea, which Freud attributed to masturbation, although in a footnote (1905a; footnote added in 1923) he retracted this statement, holding it out as an "extreme view." In the analysis of Dora's dream, Freud linked her association to the word *wet* to indicate Dora's disgust over her vaginal discharge.

Dora was aware of her mother's reaction of disgust in response to her own discharge, explained by the mother's obsessive cleanliness. Dora blamed her father for infecting her mother, but Freud speculated that she believed he had infected her as well.

When Dora presented with "piercing gastric pains," Freud asked, " 'Whom are you copying now?' " (1905a, p. 48). Dora revealed that she had developed pains similar to those of a cousin, whom she labeled a malingerer. Later in the treatment, Freud would uncover the sexual fantasies underlying this symptom, but initially he focused on Dora's identification with the cousin (whose own gastric pains appeared to be motivated out of sexual conflict).

Symptoms Based on Unconscious Sexual Fantasy

Freud was convinced that sexuality provided the motive force for every hysterical symptom. "The symptoms of this disease are nothing else than the patient's sexual activity" (1905a, p. 137). His interpretation of Dora's erotic fantasies about Herr K., Frau K., her father, and herself provided further explanation for the hysterical source of her symptoms.

Freud attributed Dora's dyspnea, palpitations, and nervous asthma to an identification with her father's labored breathing that she had overheard when her parents were having sex, in Freud's view "detached fragments of the act of copulation" (1905a, p. 97).

It was Dora's assumption that her father was impotent. She suggested to Freud that there were other ways to achieve sexual gratification, revealing her fantasy of Frau K. and her father engaged in oral sex. Freud interpreted Dora's throat irritation, tickling in the throat, and coughing as occurring as a result of her fantasizing about Frau K. and her father engaging in oral sex. Freud noticed that shortly after Dora accepted his interpretation, the cough disappeared, although he was reluctant to attribute this solely to the effectiveness of his interpretation.

In tracing the determinants for Dora's coughing and dyspnea, he evolved the following sequence: there was initially a real irritation of the throat that was eroticized and became fixated. He speculated that the fixation occurred as a result of her ambivalent feelings about her father. The same symptoms shifted to represent her relationship with Herr K., which finally represented, through her identification with Frau K., her wish to have sex with her father.

Freud found Dora's appendicitis symptoms (coinciding with fever, constipation, and irregular menses) to represent a fantasy of childbirth. Initially, he thought Dora had suffered an attack of appendicitis, although he felt the dragging foot that accompanied it carried a meaning to be discovered. Dora revealed her fantasy in an association to her dream: the pains had appeared nine months after Herr K.'s attempted seduction. To Freud, the dragging foot symbolized a "false step," which he interpreted to be Dora's fantasy of having sex with Herr K. and her continuing unconscious fantasies of love for him. (This interpretation was followed with a negative therapeutic reaction as Dora announced that she was leaving treatment.)

Preoedipal Pathology and Developmental Failures

In a footnote to the case of Dora, Freud noted that he had failed to recognize Dora's homosexual longings for Frau K., observing that it was the "strongest unconscious current in her life" (1905a, p. 143). Sperling (1973), following her treatment of a patient with conversion symptoms, concluded that Freud had overlooked the preoedipal origin of conversion symptoms. Sperling had a patient whose conversion symptoms were remarkably similar to Dora's: rapid heartbeat, dizziness, fainting spells, stomachaches, coughing spells, laryngitis resulting in aphonia, migraine headaches, and food allergies.

In Sperling's patient, as with Dora, the onset of the symptoms corresponded to a sexual conflict that reactivated oedipal conflict, guilt, and fear of punishment. Sperling employed classical analytic technique, analyzing the patient's defenses, resistances, and transference. She noticed the patient's regression to preoedipal object relations, and emphasized the importance of the symbiotic relationship with the mother as it was activated in the transference. This represented, in Sperling's view, the root of the conflict. "Internalization of her objects and dealing with them in her body in various organs and functions manifested in somatic symptoms meant to undo real, imagined or anticipated separation (loss)" (1973, p. 753).

In her analysis of this patient, Sperling helped her patient to understand the somatic nature of her resistance, assisting her to move from preverbal (somatic) to verbal communication. As the patient gained cognitive facility in understanding how her conversion symptoms represented her resistance to analysis, Sperling was able to interrupt the manifestation of the somatic behavior. Sperling cautioned that a positive transference allows the patient to stop conversion symptoms before the unconscious fantasies are analyzed.

She posited that sexual temptation results in a defensive regression to a preoedipal fixation. This becomes associated with loss of the mother and generates intense separation anxiety, which becomes activated defensively in the development of a neurotic symptom that she considered to be a proto-symbol or symbolic equivalent. Sperling concluded that a form of symbiotic relating between mother and child forms the basis for conversion symptoms.

Sperling attributed the problem to disturbances in the mother—child dyad in which the mother thwarts the child's assertive strivings and prevents the child from behaving aggressively toward her. Instead, the child is rewarded for submissiveness and dependence, for example, in the special care lavished on the child during illness. The ego of the child is compromised by the mother's inability to allow the child to tolerate anxiety without her intervention. Furthermore, she speculated that a parent's perverse preoccupation with particular organs or zones would have an impact on the site of the symptom.

CONCLUSION

Disturbances between mother and child, as cited by Sperling, predispose the patient to conversion symptoms. In Dora's case, as Sperling makes clear, Dora regressed to preoedipal functioning as the result of a sexual conflict. Freud's primary interest was not the preoedipal relationship; he leaves very little evidence to reconstruct what happened early in Dora's life. It can be speculated that Dora's mother's illnesses (tuberculosis, hospitalization for gynecological disease, obsessive-compulsive disorder) and strained marriage had an impact on Dora's early development.

From a Winnicottian perspective, it is likely that disturbances in the transitional space disturbed her capacities for differentiation, symbolization, and stabilization of inner self and object representations. Taylor (1992) observes that developmental "misattunements" lead to abnormalities in affective development and regulation, which lead to the development of symbiotic relationships that are necessary to maintain homeostasis. Dora's adoration and protection of Frau K. can be seen as an example of this form of relationship.

Taylor has reviewed the developmental, object relations, and self psychology literature to demonstrate that such failures ultimately lead to deficits affecting self-regulation. He observed that patients who are overly dependent on symbiotic relationships are vulnerable to illness when those relationships are disrupted, corresponding to Kohut's concept of the selfobject function. In this formulation, loss of the external object leads to a loss of self-regulatory function, or a disruption of narcissistic equilibrium.

The case of Dora enabled Freud to illustrate the relationship between sexual conflict, unconscious fantasy, and the development of hysterical symptoms. Freud systematically sought out the source of Dora's varied symptoms, attributing them to either organic disease or neurosis. His focus in writing up the case was to demonstrate the impact of the unconscious upon the body, not the effect of the body on the mind.

Current research highlights the relationship between early developmental failures and the deficits that predispose a patient to illness. In

"Psychical (or Mental) Treatment" Freud (1905b) anticipated the importance of positive relationships in stimulating immunological factors and healing, but he did not anticipate the impact of early developmental failures.

Freud's view that difficulties in affective regulation predispose patients to becoming ill is compatible with contemporary views on the importance of self-regulatory function in maintaining health or creating disease. Contemporary theorists have drawn upon developmental and object relations theory to suggest that attachment disturbances, symbiotic attachments, and developmental failures—aspects that Freud did not address in Dora—have an impact on self-regulatory function.

Freud's understanding of the importance of the psyche's effect on the body, including the role of conflict and unconscious fantasy when combined with current developmental and object relations theory, contributes to our evolving, contemporary understanding of psychosomatic disease and immunology.

REFERENCES

Brenner, C. (1974). *An Elementary Textbook of Psychoanalysis.* New York: Doubleday.

Fenichel, O. (1945). *The Psychoanalytic Theory of Neurosis.* New York: Norton.

Freud, S. (1894). The justification for detaching from neurasthenia a particular syndrome: the anxiety-neurosis. In *Collected Papers*, vol. 1, ed. E. Jones, trans. A. and J. Strachey, pp. 76–106. New York: Basic Books.

———— (1905a). Fragment of an analysis of a case of hysteria. In *Collected Papers*, vol. 3, ed. E. Jones, trans. A. and J. Strachey, pp. 13–146. New York: Basic Books.

———— (1905b). Psychical (or mental) treatment. *Standard Edition* 7:283–302.

———— (1920). *A General Introduction to Psychoanalysis.* New York: Boni and Liveright.

Gay, P. (1988). *Freud: A Life for Our Time.* New York: Norton.

Laplanche, J., and Pontalis, J.-B. (1973). *The Language of Psychoanalysis*, trans. D. Nicholson-Smith. New York: Norton.

Masson, J. (1985). *The Complete Letters of Sigmund Freud to Wilhelm Fliess.* Cambridge, MA: Harvard University Press.

Nadelman, M. (1990). Centennial of an overlooked Freud paper on psychosomatics. *Psychoanalytic Quarterly* 59:444–450.

Sperling, M. (1973). Conversion hysteria and conversion symptoms: a revision of classifications and concepts. *Journal of the American Psychoanalytic Association*, 21:745–771.

Taylor, G. (1992). Psychosomatics and self-regulation. In *Interface of Psychoanalysis and Psychology*, ed. J. W. Barron, M. N. Eagle, and J. S. Wolitzky, pp. 464–488. Washington, DC: American Psychological Association.

CHAPTER FOUR

Annihilation Anxiety in Psychosomatic Disorders

MARVIN HURVICH AND AMIRA SIMHA-ALPERN

This chapter focuses on some relationships between psychosomatic symptoms and annihilation anxieties. These are explored in relation to symbolization, alexithymia, deficit, and intrapsychic conflict. Also considered is anxiety associated with secondary psychological reactions to the somatic symptoms once they have become active. We begin with some background.

It has been recognized since antiquity that illness cannot be reduced to merely physical causes (Engel 1977). Gastrointestinal, respiratory, and dermatologic disorders, as well as eating disorders and chronic headaches, have long and regularly been found to have both organic and functional components. They are seen to result from the interaction of several causative factors within the psyche-soma (Drossman 1993, French and Alexander 1941, McDougall 1980). In addition, psychosocial factors such as early life experience, psychological stress, mood, and cultural and familial environments also have been found to influence the individual's susceptibility to illness. The links between psychological and physiological systems are manifold and complex. Proximity of brain centers (Strober et al. 1982), neurological connections between sensory organs and functional systems throughout the central nervous system (CNS), and classical conditioning have all been put forth as possible explanations for the mutual influences between psyche and soma (Drossman 1993).

In psychoanalytic theories the close relationships between the body and psychological functioning are reflected in Freud's writings. In 1905, he pointed out that medical science had long realized that there was a relation between mind and body, but that doctors had emphasized the effects of the body on the mind. Freud concluded that "in . . . some of these patients, the signs of their illness originate from nothing other than *a change in the action of their minds on their bodies* and that the immediate cause of their disorder is to be looked for in their minds" (1905 p. 286). He later offered the view that the ego is initially and preeminently a body ego, meaning that "the ego is ultimately derived from bodily sensations" (1923, p. 26).

Psychoanalytic theory proposes that the ego gradually emerges via the first interaction between a caregiver and an infant around bodily experiences, specifically feeding and elimination. The importance of the mother–infant connection goes beyond the management of the infant's feeding and elimination. It is the prototype of the affective bond that is necessary for internalization, the principal process by which mental structures develop and the ego grows (Blatt and Behrends 1987, Loewald 1970, Schafer 1976). The organization of bodily experiences within the context of mother–child relations constitutes the cornerstone of further psychological organization (Blanck and Blanck 1974).

Although some cognitive capacities exist at birth (Stern 1985), the major experiences of the infant and of the outside world are through his/her body (Krueger 1989, McDougall 1980). Tactile sensations of the mouth through sucking; olfactory, auditory, and visual sensations; kinesthetic sensations of body posture; the agreeable feeling of satiation and disturbance of stomach distention are all internalized (Benedek 1959, McDougall 1980). It is in differentiating sources of body sensations that the infant learns to distinguish between the inside and outside (Fenichel 1945). The tactile sensations of the mother's hand over the infant's body first define the infant's original boundary of the body's surface (Krueger 1989).

Winnicott's (1958) holding environment concept centers on the availability of needed support for the infant. It includes timely and reliable availability, attunement to factors associated with disequilibrium in the subject, and protection of the infant from overstimulation and impingement. He wrote that either *being* or *annihilation* are the only options for an infant during the holding phase. The "good-enough" mother (Winnicott 1960) permits the youngster to bear increasingly intense affective tension but steps in and comforts the baby before his emotions overwhelm him. For Winnicott, the essence of bad mothering is impingement on the infant through failures of attunement and of active adaptation to the infant's needs. Excessive impingement leads to an increased likelihood of premature but overly brittle ego development (Khan 1963) and of an overdeveloped false self (Greenberg and Mitchell 1983, Winnicott 1960).

PSYCHOSOMATIC SYNDROMES

In his early work Cannon (1953) pointed out that psychosomatic conditions are negotiated through the autonomic and neuroendocrine systems. Readying the body to respond to danger defensively, while also playing a key role in maintaining homeostasis through control over digestion, excretion, respiration, and vasomotor operation, are the two main functions of the autonomic nervous system, and they can be antagonistic.

Work done in the 1940s and 1950s was based on what has been characterized as the *specificity* theory. Dunbar (1947) stressed that distinctive personality profiles are related to various psychosomatic symptoms. That is, individuals who have particular personality traits in common are subject to the same psychosomatic illness.

Alexander and his group (1950), on the other hand, underscored comparable specific dynamic conflicts, which, on a background of organic vulnerability, and following a triggering event, tend to result in a particular psychosomatic condition. Alexander and his colleagues specified seven psychosomatic syndromes: bronchial asthma, essential hypertension, neurodermatitis, peptic ulcer, rheumatoid arthritis, thyrotoxicosis, and ulcerative colitis. Recent research has implicated a host of emotional factors in the onset, maintenance, and resolution of these and other conditions. We will give examples from the literature.

Alexander held that the adaptive reactions of the vegetative organs relate to the total situation in which the organism finds itself. While recognizing the importance of organ vulnerability, Alexander (1950) also postulated a specific correlation between the emotional state and its physiological concomitants or sequelae.

Max Schur (1953, 1955) provided an alternative to the specificity hypothesis. He found no one phase of sexuality or of aggression, no one defensive constellation, conflict, or personality style that characterized the patient with a "psychosomatic symptom." He illustrated his views with somatized skin reactions.

In delineating his own formulation of a psychoanalytic view of somatization, Schur placed the reaction of the ego at the center, especially the ego response to the danger inherent in an insoluble conflict. The key issues for him are anxiety and ego regression. Somatization tends to be minimal when the response to anticipated danger is thought-like. This occurs when there is a preponderance of secondary process functioning, and when anxiety and other affects are of low amplitude, which Schur (1955) formulated in terms of the presumed use of neutralized energy. Issues of ego strength and weakness, arrest and deficit are implied here, although Schur focuses on ego regression.

Regression of thinking, from secondary to primary process modes, tends to lead to the failure to neutralize aggressive energy. This may trigger uncontrolled (traumatic, annihilation) anxiety, as well as aggression, depression, and guilt. Schur pointed out that many somatic symptoms reflect pathology of both physical structure and function, which have a psychological component and are complex reactions to experienced insoluble psychic conflicts. Once the physical pathological response to a certain conflict has been instituted, these reactions to the conflict result in regression of various ego functions. Impaired libidinal and ego development, immature object relations, and excessive amounts of early traumatization were found by Schur (1955) to characterize somatizers and resomatizers. This is how many psychoanalysts formulate these issues today.

Sarnoff (1989) agrees with Schur's hypothesis that regression to a psychosomatic phase is sometimes a reaction to the awareness of danger. He also concurs that the patient's own skin may serve as an expression of the conflict as one mechanism associated with the genesis of psychosomatic symptomatology. Sarnoff's more delineated formulation based on Schur's earlier work is that the specific symptom is related to the level of symbolization at the time and stage of functioning to which the patient has regressed in relation to the recently experienced trauma. He assesses the stage of regression reached along two developmental lines: the evolution of the state of consciousness, and from body ego to reality objects. Regarding the latter, fear of physical penetration can lead to or be associated with fear of mental penetration. As a result, fear of curiosity may reflect the above concerns in relation to backward and forward movements along the developmental line that proceeds from psyche to soma (Sarnoff 1989).

Deprived of parental soothing (Humphrey 1986, Ordman and Kirschenbaum 1986) and optimal separateness (Bird 1957, Minuchin et al. 1978, Sperling 1949), psychosomatic patients lack the nurturing and self-regulating aspects in their object representations. In the absence of internal mechanisms to promote calming, soothing, and anxiety regulating, bulimics develop symptoms in which food is used as a transitional object to relieve tension and anxiety (Adelman 1985, Arkema 1981, Giovacchini 1984, 1985, Kafka 1969, Lobel 1981, Morris et al. 1986, Woodall 1987). Like the transitional object, the food enables the bulimic patient to begin to achieve a certain degree of independence from the mother by virtue of the patient's own mental activity. Like the infant who seeks the transitional object when she is most in need of soothing (Tolpin 1971, Winnicott 1953), the bulimic usually turns to food when she experiences or anticipates overwhelming anxiety and depression. Binges are often responses to stress, rejection, and disappointment (Aronson 1986). Similarly, McDougall (1980) reported on a patient who developed eczema attacks and back pains whenever she felt abandoned.

ANNIHILATION ANXIETIES

We begin with the postulate that anxiety represents the first mental awareness of biological imbalance, and is reflected in painful sensations. It is seen as the lifelong initial response to the realization of psychic tension in any circumstance (Schmale 1964).

The annihilation anxiety concept is widely found, under various names, throughout the psychoanalytic literature. It is closely related to Jones's (1927) Ur-Angst and aphanisis, Anna Freud's (1936) instinctual anxiety, Melanie Klein's (1946) psychotic anxiety, Fenichel's (1945) primary anxiety, Schur's (1953) uncontrolled anxiety, Winnicott's (1962) unthinkable anxiety, Bion's (1965) nameless dread, Mahler's (1968) organismic panic, Kohut's (1971) disintegration anxiety, Little's (1981) annihilation anxiety, Tustin's (1972) black hole, Frosch's (1983) basic anxiety, and Grotstein's (1985) prey–predator anxiety.

Psychoanalysts from classical, object relational, and self psychological orientations have all written about annihilation anxieties. The basic issue is helplessness and mortal terror, the fear of imminent destruction. We contend that it is initially preideational, based on somatic memories without an awareness of any specific danger (Jones 1927), and from a developmental time when dangers tend to be experienced as traumatic (Schur 1953). Here, the model for survival-threatening experiences involves the preideational perception of the experiential correlates of disintegration, which reflect apprehended threats to survival. These survival-threatening fears will later attain mental representation (Frosch 1967).

Key to the experience is a feeling of helplessness and powerlessness when the person is faced with inner and/or other dangers against which he presumes he can take no protective or constructive action. It is here seen as a universal potential anxiety: it is a frequent correlate and consequence of *psychic trauma, ego weakness, object loss, and pathology of the self* (Hurvich 1989).

Nine related ideational content areas can be associated with annihilation anxieties:

> fear of being overwhelmed,
> fear of merger,
> fear of disintegration,
> fear of impingement,
> fear of loss of needed support, of abandonment,
> fear of inability to cope,
> fear of loss of self-cohesion,
> concern over survival, and
> responding with a catastrophic mentality.

It should be stressed that the above fears tend to be associated with annihilation anxieties when there is some combination of ego weakness, history of psychic trauma, and disturbances in the sense of self. We will illustrate some relationships between annihilation anxieties and somatic disorders as reported in the literature.

SOMATIZATION AND ANNIHILATION ANXIETIES

In delineating the hypothesis that annihilation anxieties often are consequential for psychosomatic conditions, we find numerous statements in the literature that psychosomatic syndromes tend to be associated with primitive layers of personality and personality functioning (Ruesch 1948). Psychosomatic patients as a group have been found to show residues of early levels of functioning of the personality organization. It has been postulated that the damage caused by physiological reactivity as well as the choice of the organ system involves both psychic and physiologic regression. The latter was seen by Schur (1953) as reflecting a failure of desomatization. Consistent with Freud's (1923) position that the ego is first and foremost a body ego is the view that before the development of language, the body is the only vehicle for representing the manifestations of psychopathology. This channel provides the sole means of defense to avoid a *threat of annihilation* as a result of self-loss anxiety associated with separation and detachment from the primary object. Such reactions may occur as early as eight weeks (Gaddini 1992). Mushatt (1989) concluded that the difficulty in tolerating separation and loss is central for psychosomatic patients. We assume that separation and loss are sometimes so anxiety provoking because their meaning to the subject is that his very existence is threatened, namely, that it triggers annihilation anxieties.

Gaddini (1992) finds bronchial asthma to be manifest as early as the end of the first year of life, and holds that the key troublesome issues are separation and detachment. The beginning of upright locomotion results in the child distancing from the mother. The concurrent learning of language can reactivate the functional connection between speaking and breathing, and the related earlier link between sucking and swallowing, with simultaneous breathing. Later in the second year, and based on the same functional connections between sucking, breathing, and speaking, stuttering may arise.

The danger of losing one's breath is a significant and familiar one to every human being from his earliest years. But it is rendered unconscious over time. Harnik (1930) believed that asthma was first formulated within the libido theory in terms of breathing becoming libidinized; he offered the hypothesis that asthma results from early traumatic incidence of impending suffocation. Related fears are of drowning, choking, vomiting, and the inability to breathe.

Primitive fears of evaporation, which we can see as a variety of annihilation anxiety, may underlie respiratory symptoms generally and asthmatic symptoms more specifically. They derive from the diffuse and amorphous feeling states that arise prior to the establishment of a solid sense of self, which has not been effectively converted into organized and integrated symbolic mental representations due to necessary but insufficient holding and containing by a maternal presence. The evaporation threat persists in an untransformed concrete sensory experience state that is both expressed and contained as a respiratory symptom (Mitrani 1993, 1995). Mitrani (1993, 1996) sees psychosomatic symptoms as a response to prey—predator anxiety (Grotstein 1985), which involves a somatosensory-level protofantasy that serves as an early defensive effort.

The skin is the first contact surface between the mother and the infant, and tends to stand for a figurative representation of the ego boundaries and the self container (Bick 1968). Skin disease can be understood as an attempt to reconstitute self boundaries and sense of self. Body mutilation in borderline patients has been conceptualized as their way of feeling alive. It is also a more concrete way to reexperience body boundaries. These patients' boundaries are blurred and they are easily overwhelmed by the experience that their body is being invaded by external forces.

Theorists have stated that the failure of psychosomatic patients to control their experience of anxiety is due to the ineffectiveness (deficits) of their signaling system. Annihilation anxiety has been specifically related to a defective signaling capacity (Fenichel 1945).

Deficits in the area of self-regulation are found in psychosomatic patients and in others prone to annihilation anxieties. Deprived of parental soothing and separateness, psychosomatic patients lack adequate nurturing and self-regulation aspects in their object representations.

Studies on specific ego deficits in bulimic women have consistently noted that bulimics form insecure attachments (Becker et al. 1987). Their interpersonal relationships are marked by lack of autonomy (Becker et al. 1987), social isolation (Johnson and Larson 1982), fear of abandonment (Becker et al. 1987, Patton 1992), anxiety about being criticized or rejected by others (Bulik et al. 1991, Johnson and Larson 1982), and an excessive need for approval. Bulimics react and respond, but rarely initiate, while relying heavily on external support, guidance, and structure, without which they feel fragmented and incomplete (Goodsitt 1985, Swift and Letven 1984).

Another series of studies (Aronson 1986, Piran 1988, Piran and Lerner 1988, Smith, Hillard, and Roll 1991, Smith, Hillard, Walsh et al. 1991) indicated that bulimic patients have relatively undifferentiated object representations. An assessment of object representation on the Rorschach test (Parmer 1991, Piran and Lerner 1988, Simha-Alpern and Solanto, in press a) revealed more references to primitive interpersonal modes of experience by bulimics. Symbiotic merging, fusion, narcissistic mirroring, and separation themes were all included in the bulimic responses. The frequency of vomiting, in particular, was associated with themes of insufficient boundaries, more preoccupation with fears of engulfment and merger, and more primitive anxieties. These data suggest that bulimics' sense of identity is probably easily overwhelmed or fragmented when negative introjects are evoked. Relationships are perceived as threatening merger and engulfment, where the participants do not experience themselves as separate entities (Simha-Alpern and Solanto, in press a).

Along with preoccupations with issues of control and autonomy, both patients with eating disorders (Jackson, Beaumont et al. 1993, Jackson, Tabin et al. 1993, Simha-Alpern and Solanto, in press a, b, Von Weizsäcker 1964) and asthma patients (Straker 1979) are preoccupied with issues of death and dying. Fear of death is equated with fear of loss of the object or fear of catastrophic disintegration that separateness may entail (Jackson, Tabin et al. 1993). More generally, Lifton (1979/1983) holds that psychosomatic conditions have their origins in the death equivalents of early childhood, as does the emotion of despair, and are associated with a lasting sense of meaninglessness in an unfulfilled life.

Psychosomatic conditions have been understood as a response to a perceived existence-threatening life situation from which the subject can find no satisfactory way to escape (Luby 1963). McDougall (1989) sees psychosomatic symptoms, whatever the degree of physiological damage they bring about, to be attempts at psychic survival. She holds that psychic trauma experienced especially during the separation-individuation period substantially increases the person's susceptibility to psychosomatic conditions. Some psychosomatic symptoms constitute an attempt at protection against danger to life. She describes archaic anxieties behind psychosomatic symptoms, related to underlying fantasies of both bodily and mental fragmentation.

The affective aspect of annihilation anxiety can be found to reflect a range of intensities, from extreme to mild, from full blown to tamed, from uncontrolled to controlled (Schur 1953). The more uncontrolled the anxiety, the more likely it is to be associated with mental disorganization.

Anxiety and depression are the affects most commonly associated with psychosomatic disorders. Anxiety/panic attacks include physiological symptoms such as shortness of breath, dizziness, palpitation, trembling, sweating, choking, nausea, paresthesia, flushes, chills, and chest pains (Drossman 1993). These panic attacks are often experienced as fear of losing control of bodily processes and of motility, and of dying (*DSM-IV* 1994, Hurvich 1989). Panic disorders may be seen as psychosomatic conditions.

Similar complaints have been reported by patients who suffer from eating disorders (Bulik et al. 1991, Buree et al. 1990, Parmer 1991, Patton 1992, Schwalberg et al. 1992, Simha-Alpern and Hurvich, in preparation, Steer and Cooper 1988, Striegel-Moore et al. 1993, Strober 1981), asthma (Straker 1979), and ulcerative colitis (Engel 1955). Wilson (1989) likewise holds that the fundamental fear of all psychosomatic patients is the fear of loss of control of bodily functions. Three major factors have been suggested as causative in the development of a psychosomatic disorder in the individual case: (1) an organic predisposition; (2) a psychological predisposition, that is, ego weaknesses; and (3) less than optimal, even traumatic, environmental circumstances (Levitan 1989a).

In a study now in preparation, relationships between annihilation anxieties and postoperative surgical recovery are being explored (Hurvich and Kerasiotis in progress). We are focusing on the ways in which the activation of underlying annihilation anxieties in medical patients facing imminent surgery are associated with postoperative recovery time and complications. The threat of surgery typically increases psychic regression, experienced threats to the body image, danger to a sense of ego intactness, and feelings of helplessness. Preliminary observations, which must be supported by more extensive data, indicate that when preoperative levels of annihilation anxieties are high, recovery time from the particular surgical procedure is delayed and postoperative difficulties are increased. This appears to be due to excessive anxiety, increased tendencies toward hypochondriacal concerns, depressive affect, decrease in sexual interest, and increased anger. These can lead to interference with immune function, development of infection, blaming of medical personnel, noncompliance with medical recommendations, and expensive additional medical workups. Secondary annihilation anxiety plays an important role here.

From a psychoanalytic point of view, psychosomatic symptoms have three major functions in the management of anxiety. First, they provide an avenue for the expression of affect that is otherwise repressed or dissociated. Bodily symptoms are representations of sensations and feelings that are experienced in a presymbolic manner. Second, psychosomatic symptoms can serve to protect the person from experiencing anxiety and painful affect. Third, psychosomatic symptoms are concrete mechanisms that facilitate maintaining interpersonal connectedness, preserving an intact personality structure and reconstituting boundaries when the person is facing disintegrating anxiety. We now consider the issue of the relationship between psychosomatic conditions and disturbances in symbolization.

SYMBOLIZATION

Symbolization involves displacement, the substitution of one idea or mental representation for another. Since the symbolizing function can be seen to form the bridge between the psyche and the soma (McDougall 1989), disturbances in symbolic functioning would be expected in psychosomatic conditions. More specifically, when a conflict is symbolized, this permits dealing with the cognitive aspect of the associated affects, such as anxiety. When adequate symbolization does not occur, the person can only deal with the physiological aspects of his/her affective responses, and this renders them more prone to psychosomatic disturbances.

McDougall (1980) suggests that psychosomatic symptoms reflect an archaic experience devoid of emotions and conflicts. The core of these disorders is impoverished symbolic representations, in which the body takes over and follows its own laws of functioning. It is not a translation of a psychic wish such as in neurotic illness but rather it is an organic disorder with physiological dysfunctioning, which results from a lack of psychic representations.

Psychosomatic patients are fixated on their concrete body as a self-soothing device due to an impairment in their capacity for symbolization (Krueger 1989, Sugarman and Kurash 1982). The insufficient development of this cognitive capacity to symbolize the maternal object interferes with relinquishing the use of the mother's body as a transitional object, and hinders differention from her. The bulimic's body is experienced *as* her mother, not *like* her mother. This is due to the concrete and preoperational level of her thought functioning. Bingeing becomes an experience of symbolic reunion. And purging is processed as a separation from the mother, which often has the psychic meaning of annihilating her (Sugarman and Kurash 1982).

Of the various views on the failure of symbolization, Freud's (1895) first anxiety theory involved the idea that there is an absence or interference with psychical working over of the stimulation. So there is a failure of mental representation, and the stimulus is shunted into a bodily channel. Winnicott (1949/1958) formulated that a split between mind and body results from inconsistent early mothering, and this interferes with the psychic (symbolic) representation of the body. He also held that psychosomatic symptoms reflect primitive defensive activity against psychotic anxieties.

A selectively empathic mother who responds only or mainly to limited aspects of the child's experience (Kohut 1971) or a mother who is unable to provide the child with appropriate space to facilitate symbolization as a substitute for actual body sensations (McDougall 1980) excludes part of the child's unshared experience, leaving it fixated at a presymbolized level. The instinctual body is therefore disconnected or split off from the mind. This part is denied existence through psychic impoverishment, where feelings are not registered because they are not represented symbolically (McDougall 1980).

But while there is interference with symbol formation, primitive or proto symbols do characterize psychosomatic symptoms and may be reflected in body language. In this case, the psychosomatic symptom has an excess meaning beyond the physical phenomenon itself. Thus, the respiratory spasm of asthma can symbolize an unconscious effort to retain attachment to key objects as well as to destroy the symbolized incorporated figures. This is a deeper level of interpretation with greater implications than Alexander's view of asthma as a "cry for the mother," although the latter also reflects surplus meaning (Wilson 1989). Similarly, torticollis may be a bodily manifestation of a feeling that the mate is a "pain in the neck."

Lifton (1979/1983) maintains that in psychosomatic conditions the mind has regressed to a primitive, virtually desymbolized, and distorted body language. Eventually the afflicted organ or organ system comes to symbolize the principal affective content of the person's life. Image-feelings of separation, disintegration, and inertia-stagnation are in the background of psychosomatic ailments, which Lifton sees as death equivalents.

ANNIHILATION ANXIETY, PSYCHIC DEFICIT, AND PSYCHOSOMATIC SYMPTOMS

It was mentioned earlier that annihilation anxiety is associated with ego weakness, traumatic events, and problems with self-cohesion. These will now be discussed in relation to psychosomatic conditions.

Following the view that the ego is defined by its functions, we specify which functions are especially implicated in connection with annihilation anxieties. First, as Schur (1953) emphasized, traumatic or uncontrolled anxiety is associated with a regression in the function of reality testing. Here, the loss of the distinction between past and present results in potential danger being experienced as present danger. A case can be made that regressive loss of this distinction is more likely when there are preexisting weaknesses and developmental arrests in the components of reality testing (Hurvich 1970).

Another relevant ego function deficit is the failure to achieve reliable affect signal functions. Levitan (1989b) suggests that what mobilizes psychosomatic patients to focus inappropriately or excessively on the outside reality, at the expense of fantasy and symbolic thinking, is the feebleness of the guidance systems that are based on affect. Adhering to external cues is probably a way to compensate for this internal deficit.

This issue also relates to alexithymia, since the affective deficit in that condition is reflected in emotions not being available as signals for the self. In this condition there is both a cognitive and an affect deficit. The cognitive deficit is seen in the area of symbol formation, manifested by difficulties in creating fantasies. This issue is also found in many psychosomatic patients. While often well adjusted to external reality, with good vocational functioning, these persons show an insufficient connection with their own psychic reality, and a paucity of ideas and of imagination.

The affective deficit in alexithymia is also found typically in psychosomatic patients. There is a poverty of emotional experience, and emotions are not available as signals for the self. This is because of the overemphasis on sensory perception at the expense of reflective awareness. As a result, the person reports physical sensations when he is asked to describe his feelings.

Research studies indicate that somatization may or may not be associated with alexithymia in a given case, but somatizers do demonstrate a tendency toward alexithymia. And the clinical observations that evolved into the concept of alexithymia (namely, no words for emotions) were first made on patients with psychosomatic disorders (Sifneos 1973). Patients described as alexithymic are prone to developing psychosomatic symptoms because they experience vague, relatively undifferentiated affect precursors, which are more somatic than fully delineated affects (Krystal 1988). McDougall holds that the deficit is based on the absence of an identification with a caregiving mother. Lifton (1979/1983) maintains that physiological malfunctioning in psychosomatic conditions serves as a replacement for other kinds of obstructed emotions. Others (Wilson 1989) have emphasized the intrapsychic conflict reflected in alexithymic patients' symptoms.

Alexithymia is frequently found in persons who have suffered traumatic experience, where there is a fear of affects and an attempt to block them (Krystal 1979). Krystal also pointed out that alexithymia is often found together with anhedonia, which is a traumatically related residual. Physiological regression reflects a failure of desomatization, and can be understood as a revival of the infantile traumatic state (Schur 1953). Psychic trauma, the actual neuroses, failure of symbolization, alexithymia, and a tendency toward somatization are all related.

SECONDARY ANXIETY

Schur (1953) discussed secondary anxiety as a response to regressive reactions, including resomatization, that perpetuate anxiety response chains. Here, anxiety and feelings of helplessness may become dangers themselves, sometimes resulting in an even more severe disequilibrium than the original danger. When there is a regression to a preverbal, pre-ego stage, anxiety may develop in reaction to a somatization that itself did not generate conscious anxiety. Schur gave as an example a patient who, upon realizing that he had perspired during his sleep, then became anxious. The perspiration awareness activated a tuberculosis phobia that included death fears, as well as both masturbation and enuretic connections, which constituted psychic dangers to the regressed ego. Schur formulated that secondary anxiety may be activated as a result of regressive anxiety reactions such as somatization and resomatization, thereby perpetuating anxiety cycles. We add that this anxiety is often related to annihilation concerns, especially that the somatic manifestation is the sign of a fatal illness.

PSYCHOSOMATIC CONDITIONS AND INTRAPSYCHIC CONFLICT

The conflict view sees the symptom as a compromise among a symbolic representation of the repressed sexual or aggressive drive/fantasy, a defense against the conflictual tendency, and a punishment for having it. Freud's hypothesis that behind the fear lies the wish includes the desire to gratify many kinds of forbidden longings. There is a terror of retaliatory punishment from a primitive archaic superego. We contend this terror of the primitive superego is a version of annihilation anxiety. A number of workers hold that all psychosomatic patients have an archaic, impulsive, primitive superego (Wilson 1989).

The symptoms of bulimia represent an amalgamation of oral, anal, and phallic-oedipal conflicts. The traditional approach notes the equation of the mouth and vagina. Binge eating is, therefore, viewed as symbolic genital activity, an enactment of a conflictual sexual wish. At the same time, the symptoms in bulimia represent a defensive displacement to the mouth of the phallic masturbatory stimulation. It is a defensive regression to oral hunger as a substitute for the guilt- and anxiety-producing wish for incestuous impregnation. The common abuse of laxatives and the central role of the toilet in the regurgitation rituals highlight the importance of the anal conflicts and the regressive displacement of genital wishes by anal ones. Vomiting is an expression of a physical revulsion punishment for the forbidden wishes (Schwartz 1988).

Similarly, peptic ulcer has been perceived as a vengeful bite, that is, a punishment for infantile wishes to bite the mother's breast (Garma 1950). It is also likely that this fantasy is a response to the symptom, rather than its predecessor.

As already mentioned, McDougall (1989) understands psychosomatic symptoms as attempts to protect the organism from primitive yearnings that are experienced as life threatening. These symptoms include defensive endeavors against fears of merging, engulfment, and abandonment. In these cases, anticipation of annihilation danger consists of a regressive warning signal to the body that, as in the preverbal infant, is not in verbal-symbolic form. Rather, it is carried from the mental sphere to the body as a primitive nonverbal impulse, expressed in the psychosomatic symptom as organ speech (Sharpe 1940/1950) by body language.

We end this discussion with some illustrations of Rorschach responses of some bulimic patients that reflect annihilation anxiety concerns. Before presenting these, however, here is the comment of a patient high in annihilation anxiety as measured by the Hurvich Experience Inventory (HEI) (Hurvich et al. 1993, Levin and Hurvich 1995).

As this bulimic patient told me:

> This body thing, fat/thin, food/diet has been an obsession all my life and has tortured me every day of my life. Once in a while I get a handle on it. But it doesn't last. The moment I start to lose weight and feel good and look good is when it falls apart. I think it has to do with sexual feelings and self-confidence. I do not feel those things, and when my body starts to look normal my mind says, "This does not fit." I get terrified and I start eating in a rebellious manner and gaining weight. It's like I'm telling the world I don't care, I can eat whatever I want. And I do it like I am beating myself, stuffing myself till I want to explode. At first the food tastes good, but after awhile I can't even taste it anymore. It becomes a mania, some kind of mad dash to eat as much as I can before I explode. It's like a beating. But I don't throw up much anymore. I guess I feel that won't work anymore. It's hopeless, I will never be thin.

CASE ILLUSTRATION

To clarify our theoretical viewpoint we present two women who suffer from an eating disorder and who report both somatic complaints and severe anxiety. These two subjects were interviewed as part of our study on annihilation anxiety in bulimic women (Simha-Alpern and Hurvich, in preparation). The following discussion is based on their responses to the

Hurvich Experience Inventory (HEI-30) (Levin and Hurvich 1995, Table 4–1), their Rorschach protocols analyzed according to the Rorschach Scoring for Annihilation Anxiety (Benveniste et al. 1996, Hurvich et al. 1993), and their responses to the Intimacy Status Interview (ISI) (Orlofsky 1989).

A number of formal factors, such as fabulized combinations, deviant verbalizations, and absurd logic, are found in the following responses. Our focus here is on annihilation content.

The formal factors are consequential in terms of the extent of adaptive disruption associated with the annihilation content. A scale of assessing the formal level of responses has just been developed (Hurvich et al. 1996), and is being used in current studies along with the annihilation anxiety content scale.

Case 1

Linda is a 21-year-old single Caucasian undergraduate student. She reported suffering from both an eating disorder and asthma since age 13, precipitated by leaving her homeland and migrating to the United States. During the worst month of her eating problems, Linda was binge eating and purging between two and five times a day. She purged with self-induced vomiting (four times per day), laxatives, diet pills, and water pills. She exercised about 2½ hours a day, chewed food and spat it out two to three times a day, and fasted for 24 hours about once a week. During the time of our study Linda was presenting with less frequent bulimic symptoms. She stated that just before her bingeing episodes she experiences intense feelings of emptiness, excitation, disgust, loneliness, boredom, guilt, and depression. She reported being extremely fearful of becoming fat, which does not lessen as she loses weight, and that she is preoccupied with thoughts of food, weight, or eating all the time.

An analysis of Linda's responses on the HEI, as well as her Rorschach protocol, reflects an unclear sense of self and tenuous boundaries. She maintained an intense cathexis of her body as a concrete container for her amorphously experienced self. On the HEI, she endorsed frequent insecurities about her identity, often being uncertain who she really is, keeps searching for an identity she is not sure she quite has, and often feels she has more than one self. Consistently, many of her Rorschach responses reflect

Table 4–1. Cases 1 and 2: Responses on the Hurvich Experience Inventory–Revised

	Case 1	Case 2
1. I feel I could shatter into bits.	1	3
2. I am very afraid of fear.	3	2
3. I am not sure who I really am.	4	3
4. I worry about my survival.	3	4
5. I feel like I am destroyed as a person.	3	3
6. Experiencing strong emotions frightens me.	3	1
7. I am afraid of getting emotionally close to others.	1	4
8. I feel terror and panic.	2	3
9. My body feels like it doesn't belong to me.	4	2
10. I think about my world coming to an end.	3	2
11. I had frightening nightmares as a child.	4	4
12. I feel the dread of dying at any moment.	3	2
13. I feel I have more than one self.	3	2
14. I feel intruded on, mentally or physically.	2	3
15. I keep searching for an identity I don't quite have.	3	4
16. I have a fear of catastrophe.	2	2
17. I need someone to reassure me when I become afraid.	1	3
18. I worry about my physical health.	3	2
19. I feel I can't pull myself together.	2	2
20. I have frightening dreams (nightmares).	2	2
21. As a child I was afraid of dying.	2	4
22. I have a fear of falling in space.	1	2
23. I feel anxious when I am left alone.	2	2
24. It's hard to get over something that makes me nervous.	2	2
25. I feel like I'm being overwhelmed.	3	3
26. I fear getting swept up and lost in another person.	2	4
27. I fear loss of control of myself.	2	4
28. I fear being unable to think or act.	2	4
29. I feel I can't cope with things.	2	2
30. I fear being abandoned.	1	4
Total	71	84

Note. The numbers 1–4 reflect how accurately the statements describe the subject's experience. 1=Never; 2=Not very often; 3=Often; 4=Very often.

her fear of loss of self-cohesion. Her response to card VIII suggests a sense of an uncohesive self:

Response: I see a strange animal. The face of a parrot, the body of a rhinoceros, the legs of a leopard or tiger with a tail of a lizard.
Inquiry: On the left a parrot head, on the right a human head, on the left this one has a prominent sharp nose and his mouth is open, and this one looks more furry, well-combed like a bear. Both look like scavengers looking for prey.

The strange, disintegrated figure is both needy (open mouth) and devouring ("looking for prey"). In the next illustration, Linda perceives mythical figures who symbolize life-threatening creatures (poisonous snakes). The humans are so absorbed with each other (excessive need for support) that they are oblivious to the dangers facing them. There is some confusion between the people and the mythical figures.

Response: Two people with wings like goddesses. I also see two poisonous snakes (points to D1); one is a male and one is a female, both are showing a powerful strength and they belong to the goddesses, like they are their symbols. The goddesses are holding them in their hands showing them. The people are kissing.
Inquiry: The wings are attached to its body, the faces right here, the kind of hats they wear, like the Greek goddess; they are not humans. This is a male and this is a female. The one on my left is a male and the one on my right is a female and it coincides with the snakes, the left snake being a male and the right snake being a female. It's coming together now to me: the two gods are flying these two humans, the gods have the power and these two humans are not even realizing that the gods are lifting them up in the air, because this male and female are so in love with each other, so into their own world that they are not realizing what's going on outside of their own little world. You can tell who is who by the shape of their heads.

In spite of Linda's yearning for omnipotent figures, her ambivalence toward them is illustrated shortly after her first response, where they are experienced as intrusive and aggressive. Many responses reflect her fear of being impinged upon and damaged by dangerous and omnipotent creatures. Her responses contain scary percepts (masks, skulls, frightening persons, dragons, poisonous snakes), themes of people being attacked, and percepts of damaged and mutilated figures. These creatures with combined features (the head of Godzilla and the body of a snail) underscore the absence of self-integration (suggesting identity diffusion). We additionally note the grandiose (Godzilla) and weak, devalued (snail) images in this amalgamated but unintegrated implied self-image, and the wolves (oral aggressive creatures) that are threatened with annihilation and must fight for their lives.

(Card VIII):

Response: I see two dinosaurs, two Godzillas and their bodies, just the head is of Godzilla and the body is of a snail, they look like friendly Godzillas, but the other one is looking for a fight. They found their victim and it's a wolf, each one of them is holding a wolf (D1). And each wolf that each one of them is holding seems like it is fighting for its life.
Inquiry: It's the long neck and small arms and the legs, mouth with tiny eyes and small hands. Its body looks like it was converted into this big snail shell.

The menacing quality of the figures is reflected in another response to card IX, where she sees wrinkled babies who encounter a scary, evil man who gives her the creeps and a very uncomfortable feeling, but she denies she's afraid of him.

Linda's self-perception as a powerless being who is in danger of becoming overwhelmed by dominant figures is woven in with her fear of being unable to cope, execute control, and effectively negotiate her life circumstances. In one of her responses to card III she saw two elves with their heads stuffed into something, suggesting a view of herself as a small elf unable to use its head to make decisions, and thus her sense of being unable to cope.

In a semistructured interview (Orlofsky 1989), Linda stated that when she is by herself all she can think about is food. Meeting people makes her forget about food and is her only way of controlling her eating. She constantly needs to have a boyfriend and does not break up a dissatisfying relationship without making sure that she has another man in place. Nevertheless, her intimate relationships tend to be superficial and lack open communication and deep emotional involvement. She tends to idealize her partners, becomes very sensitive to their criticism, and devalues herself. It appears that Linda's dependency on other people stems from the fact that they serve her with self-definition and regulatory functions to compensate for her lack of an integrated sense of self. The mirroring of other people regulates her self-esteem, which she needs in order not to feel depleted and empty. Many of her Rorschach responses reflect her insecure balance and a fear of loss of needed support, such as people whose tenuous balance is in check, and figures falling.

Consistent with her fears of losing her sense of self and of being overwhelmed and impinged upon, Linda is also experiencing fear of disintegration. However, she cannot articulate this fear. Rather, it is described on a somatic level. As she reports on the HEI, she often feels that her body doesn't belong to her. There are a number of responses on both the HEI and the Rorschach that reflect concerns about her physical health and about the intactness of her body. The protocol contains many vital internal organ responses, percepts of disembodied or dissolving objects, and themes of death and dying. These suggest anxiety about body intactness and about survival. These fears are reflected in her response to the first card, often referred to as the self-presentation card.

Response: A skeleton. If you just . . . it's gray, holes inside the structure at the top that you find on the floor, if you walk in the woods. It's a decayed skeleton. [What makes it look like that?] Here, it's a gloomy color, it's gray not white bones and it has dirt, dirt from the ground, it's a lot, its color, it's a dead object. It's small, not as big as it looks on the paper.

Another example is her response to card II:

Response: Lungs.
Inquiry: The whole thing. [What makes it look like that?] The shape looks like a tissue of lungs.

As Linda's self is not sufficiently integrated to carry out self-soothing functions reliably, it renders her more prone to resort to body sensations to regulate overwhelming, intense feelings. The several lung responses on the Rorschach are likely related to her tendency to experience psychological stress in terms of breathing difficulties generally, and asthmatic symptoms more specifically.

Case 2

Melissa is a 21-year-old single Caucasian woman who was living with her recovering alcoholic parents and attending a local school for undergraduate studies. She attempted to leave home for college, but returned after one semester. She presented with a history of eating problems, anxiety, and hypoglycemia. Melissa reported being preoccupied with her eating habits, which worsened at age 18, since she was 11 years old. During the time of our study Melissa was binge eating about three times a month, and vomiting twice a month. She exercised 1½ hours a day, and stated that she has an intense fear of becoming fat, which does not lessen when she loses weight.

As Melissa described herself: "I have many sides to my personality, and sometimes I don't know if I am trying to change to please who I am with. I am still trying to establish a solid sense of identity that will be a foundation no matter who I am with and when I am alone." She added that she is always afraid she has nothing inside her, "no core to pull myself together." She stated that she has difficulties letting people, especially men, get close to her. Being involved in a relationship with a man triggers the fear of losing control and of losing her mind. Nevertheless, she needs approval, security, and love, which she tries unsuccessfully to gain through sexual relationships. Her love objects are usually uncommitted men, and her romantic relationships tend to be superficial.

Melissa began feeling an overwhelming anxiety at age 13 and was treated with tranquilizers for a short period of time. On the HEI she endorsed the statement that she often feels terror and panic and that she had very frequent nightmares as a child. Her Rorschach protocol was consistent with this report. Nineteen out of her twenty-four responses reflected themes of annihilation anxiety, according to our scoring manual.

Many of her responses reflect her fear of being overpowered by either a dangerous and omnipotent figure or by her own internal urges, and contain scary percepts (masks, skulls, frightening persons, dragons, snakes). Furthermore, she specifically mentioned a sense of fear and fright. In her response to card I she reexperiences a terrifying situation and expresses her fear of being overwhelmed:

Response: Reminds me, in a scary way, with a scary face, of a pagan goat god. This could look like a scary mask. When I was a child I was preoccupied with everything that looked like an evil spirit, I was full of guilt.

Inquiry: Mask is more an impression of feelings. Ominous feelings represented by the skull, the mask. An association from when I was a biologist. I am still interested in painting skulls, but I would not do it because it is still an association with evil things. Just the shape, it's out of proportion but it's my mental association. It's my mental impression with no feeling or emotional connection.

Her archaic sense of danger is so pervasive that these themes appear already in her response to the first card. Many comments she made referring to her own personal experience and early childhood only reinforce the impression of the acuteness of these preoccupations in her own life. It was, therefore, difficult for her to distance herself from the cards. Her protocol continues with similar responses that mention scary objects and personal discomfort. For example, a response 746 to card IX:

Response: This one looks scary. Definitely reminds me of fear things. It looks like two griffins or dragons facing each other. This is fantastic.

Inquiry: This is the snout, the ears, horns. Like I see them more as horns. These are the eyes, bent, sitting like that. They are in profile. Claws. I'd like to paint that too. Or someone being sat upon. Two of these creatures sitting on his shoulders. Like the expression you have a monkey on your shoulders.

In her following response to card IX her fear of being overwhelmed is reinforced as she said:

Response: It also looks like a person, a human, with a large mask on like a Viking with horns on it. The big scary mask they wear. Or a mask of an animal. Would wear a big scary mask.
Inquiry: Like a man wearing an animal skull as a mask. To me it's a scary thing.

Associated with her fear of being overwhelmed Melissa also experiences fear of being impinged upon by another person. Her response to card IV:

Response: This is a guy riding a motorcycle, a big Biker Dude coming at you at the front. An imposing figure. If you stand in front of him he would just knock you right down.
Inquiry: This looks like a head and this looks like handlebars. These are the big feet, and this is the white silhouette. [?] The shape. It's a man, a scary person with big hands, big claws.

Other facets of her fear of being impinged upon are reflected in themes of animated objects being damaged or mutilated. An example of her fear of being damaged is her response to card VI:

Response: A snake, one that was hit by a car, was flattened out. The snake had a bad day. [?] The shape.

Given Melissa's tenuous boundaries and uncertain identity it is not surprising that she is very often concerned with being overwhelmed and impinged upon by another person. Intimate relationships bear the danger of merger and engulfment, and thereby threaten her sense of self. Indeed, Melissa acknowledged on the HEI that she is very often afraid of being swept up and lost in another person, that she is afraid of getting emotionally close to others, and that she often feels intruded on. An amalgamation of her fear of being overwhelmed by others, her fear of being impinged upon and damaged or depleted, as well as her fear of disintegration when facing interpersonal interaction, is illustrated in her response to card X:

Response: If I look at it in a scary way, a person being attacked. Looks like small creatures flying at a person, someone being overwhelmed. Like in the movie *The Fantastic Voyage*. These people are introjected into some-one's body, a silly science fiction movie. Like Raquel Welch gets into the brain and an antibody doesn't recognize her and flies at her, attacking her, trying to kill her. They thought she was a germ in a person's body. Scary, it looks like they already got the heart, you see it's gone.

Inquiry: These things are attacking someone. It's a central part, a bronchi bent off, or an aorta where the heart should be connected and it's empty. This is like creatures. They are on the neck, like two little Gambians or something. She is being overwhelmed with these things flying at her.

Melissa's lack of a solid sense of identity can be understood against the background of her complicated relationships with her parents. As a paren-tified child of alcoholics, Melissa developed strong ties to them. When she was asked about her closest relationship she stated: "My mother, that's my closest relationship, but also the most complicated one, and the root of my difficulties." This is probably why she was unable to separate appropriately from her mother and came back home after only a short stay at an out-of-town college. Her response to card III (sometimes assumed to be the interpersonal card) demonstrates the dependency of a parental figure on its child for stability and the fear of loss of needed support (represented by tenuous balance) with a possible separation:

Response: I am sorry, it's again two people with children. Two women holding babies.

Inquiry: (demonstrates) They were swinging their babies and their babies' feet touch. It's so obvious to me, not that everyone could see it. But it is so primitive. This could be a gorilla. Most people don't stand like this, which is interesting. The children are balancing them because otherwise they have high heels and they are in a posture that is not natural to hold without support or a counterbalance. It's symbolic of babies balancing their mothers' lives, of women as nature.

As the symbiotic relationship with her "vital part," that is, mother, breaks down, Melissa is concerned that she will not be able to cope on her own. In an interview she stated: "My biggest fear is to be alive and be unable to think."

Her response to card I reflects her fear of being unable to cope:

Response: It looks like a woman, the hips, her breast, her hands reaching out like this [demonstrates], but she has no hands. If this is a woman she should have a head. This would be a skirt, transparent. These are her legs. That's a scary thing with no hands. She is helpless, she has no brain, she can't go anywhere, and she has a hole in the middle.

It was an artist who painted women with no feet because they were helpless and they could not escape. They could not do anything with their lives.

The percept of a woman who is "helpless," "has no brain," "can't go anywhere," and can't do anything with her life likely reflects her own lack of a sense of agency and the ability to affect her life.

Melissa has difficulty regulating her affect. She responded on the HEI that she often feels overwhelmed and needs someone to reassure her when she becomes afraid. Melissa's affect was characterized by intense and fluctuating moods. She described herself in this way: "I'm very emotional: if I am up I am very happy, but if I'm down it's usually equally as intense." She often experiences extreme sadness, anxiety, and irritability. She fluctuates between feeling very independent and wanting love and approval. When she feels this way she attempts to behave perfectly. When she feels rebellious, she wants to break loose and "blow up a building."

Like Linda's, Melissa's internal conflicts and feelings often are experienced on a somatic level. Her fear that either she or her mother will not survive the separation and will suffer a psychological collapse or a psychological disintegration is experienced as fear about the intactness of her body. When her blood sugar drops she panics and fears she is going to die. She produced many internal organ responses such as those to card III:

Response: This looks like a pair of lungs
Inquiry: The red body parts is the same way echoing life in a biological way. This could be big lungs.

Response: This looks like an esophagus with a stomach. I take biology illustration class in the cadaver next semester, and I hope I am strong enough for it.

Inquiry: This could be the stomach. It's beautiful; I'd like to paint it because I see so much in it. I hope this would not trigger me back to childhood. But it's like scuba diving. It's scary at first; you have to do it and then it's not scary. The shape and the color, the fact that they are red, inside parts rather than outside parts, vital parts.

Another example is her last response to card X:

Response: This could be ovaries, in which case the womb is gone.
Inquiry: Ovaries and birth canal, like when you look at the negative image, the white part is the torso and with the legs being this [demonstrates].

She specifically noted the disintegration of vital body parts that are essential for her survival. We know that Melissa developed an eating disorder. Her self-esteem became connected with what she eats, and the reactivation of her body sensations functions as self-soothing experiences that help her negotiate overwhelming affect and stress. This is consistent with her report that various intense feelings precipitate her binge eating and that she cannot feel soothed until she purges. Her vomiting, in particular, is usually precipitated by "a very intense emotionally upsetting event with my parents or boyfriends."

REFERENCES

Adelman, S. A. (1985). Pills as transitional objects: a dynamic understanding of the use of medication in psychotherapy. *Psychiatry* 48(3):246–253.

Alexander, F. (1950). *Psychosomatic Medicine: Its Principles and Applications.* New York: Norton.

We would like to thank Muriel Morris, M.D., for her valuable comments on an earlier draft of this chapter.

Arkema, P. H. (1981). The borderline personality and transitional related-ness. *American Journal of Psychiatry* 138(2):172–177.

Aronson, J. K. (1986). The level of object relations and severity of symptoms in the normal weight bulimic patient. *International Journal of Eating Disorders* 5(4):669–681.

Becker, B., Bell, M., and Billington, R. (1987). Object relations, ego deficits in bulimic college women. *Journal of Clinical Psychology* 43(1):92–95.

Benedek, T. (1959). Parenthood as a developmental phase: a contribution to the libido theory. *Journal of the American Psychoanalytic Association* 7:389–417.

Benveniste, P. S., Papouchis, N., Allen, R., and Hurvich, M. (1996). Rorschach assessment of annihilation anxiety and ego functioning. *Psychoanalytic Psychology*, in press.

Bick, E. (1968). The experience of the skin in early object relations. *International Journal of Psycho-Analysis* 49:484–486.

Bion, W. (1965). *Transformations*. London: Heinemann.

Bird, B. (1957). A specific peculiarity of acting out. *Journal of the American Psychoanalytic Association* 5:630–647.

Blanck G., and Blanck R. (1974). *Ego Psychology, Theory and Practice*. New York: Columbia University Press.

Blatt, S. J., and Behrends, R. S. (1987). Internalization, separation-individuation and the nature of therapeutic action. *International Journal of Psycho-Analysis* 68:279–297.

Bulik, C. M., Beidel, D. C., Duchmann, E., et al. (1991). An analysis of social anxiety in anorexic, bulimic, social phobic, and control women. *Journal of Psychopathology and Behavioral Assessment* 13(3):199–211.

Buree, B. U., Papageorgis, D., and Hare, R. D. (1990). Eating in anorexia and bulimia nervosa: an application of the tripartite model of anxiety. *Canadian Journal of Behavioural Science* 22(2):207–218.

Cannon, W. B. (1953). *Bodily Changes in Pain, Hunger, Fear and Rage*, 2nd ed. Boston: Charles T. Branford.

Diagnostic and Statistical Manual of Mental Disorders IV. (1994). Washington: American Psychiatric Association.

Drossman, D. A. (1993). Psychological considerations in gastroenterology. In *Gastrointestinal Disease, Pathophysiology/Diagnosis/Management*, vol. 1, ed. M. H. Sleisenger and J. S. Fordtran, 5th ed., pp. 3–17. Philadelphia: W.B. Saunders.

Dunbar, F. (1947). *Mind and Body: Psychosomatic Medicine.* New York: Random House.

Engel, G. L. (1955). Studies of ulcerative colitis. III. The nature of the psychologic process. *American Journal of Medicine* 19:231.

——— (1977). Studies for a new medical model: a challenge for biomedicine. *Science* 196:129.

Fenichel, O. (1945). *The Psychoanalytic Theory of Neurosis.* New York: Norton.

French, T., and Alexander, F. (1941). Psychogenic factors in bronchial asthma. *Psychosomatic Medicine Monograph 4.* Washington, DC: National Research Council.

Freud, A. (1936/1946). *The Ego and the Mechanisms of Defense.* New York: International Universities Press.

——— (1963). The concept of developmental lines. *Psychoanalytic Study of the Child* 18:245–265. New York: International Universities Press.

——— (1965). *Normality and Pathology of Childhood.* New York: International Universities Press.

Freud, S. (1895). On the grounds for detaching a particular syndrome from neurasthenia under the description "anxiety neurosis." *Standard Edition* 3:90–139.

——— (1905). Psychical (or mental) treatment. *Standard Edition* 7:283–302.

——— (1923). The ego and the id. *Standard Edition* 19:13–66.

——— (1926). Inhibitions, symptoms and anxiety. *Standard Edition* 20:77–124.

Frosch, J. (1967). Delusional fixity, sense of conviction, and the psychotic conflict. *International Journal of Psycho-Analysis* 48:475–495.

——— (1983). *The Psychotic Process.* New York: International Universities Press.

Gaddini, E. (1992). *A Psychoanalytic Theory of Infantile Experience,* ed. A. Limantini. London: Routledge.

Garma, A. (1950). *Peptic Ulcer and Psychoanalysis.* Baltimore: Williams & Wilkins.

Giovacchini, P. L. (1984). The psychoanalytic paradox: the self as a transitional object. *Psychoanalytic Review* 71:81–104.

——— (1985). The borderline adolescent as a transitional object: common variation. *Adolescent Psychiatry* 12:233–50.

Goodsitt, A. (1985). Self psychology and treatment of anorexia nervosa. In

Handbook of Psychotherapy for Anorexia Nervosa and Bulimia, ed. D. M. Garner and P. E. Garfinkel, pp. 55–82). New York: Guilford.

Greenberg, J. R., and Mitchell, S. A. (1983). *Object Relations in Psychoanalytic Theory*. Cambridge: Harvard University Press.

Grotstein, J. (1985). A proposed revision of the psychoanalytic concept of the death instinct. In *The Yearbook of Psychoanalysis and Psychotherapy*, ed. R. Langs, pp. 299–326. Emerson, NJ: Newconcept Press.

Harnik, J. (1930). One component of the fear of death in early infancy. *International Journal of Psycho-Analysis* 11:283.

Humphrey, L. L. (1986). Structural analysis of parent–child relationships in eating disorders. *Journal of Abnormal Psychology* 95(4):395–402.

Hurvich, M. (1970). On the concept of reality testing. *International Journal of Psycho-Analysis* 51:299–312.

———— (1989). Traumatic moment, basic danger and annihilation anxiety. *Psychoanalytic Psychology* 6(3):309–323.

Hurvich, M., Benveniste, P., Howard, J., and Coonerty, S. (1993). The assessment of annihilation anxiety from projective tests. *Perceptual and Motor Skills* 77:387–401.

Hurvich, M., Borg, D., Brody, S., and Baldwin, D. (1996). A scale for assessing the formal level of individual Rorschach responses. Unpublished Manual.

Hurvich, M., and Kerasiotis, B. (In progress). Annihilation anxiety and postoperative surgical recovery.

Jackson, C., Beaumont, P. J. V., Thornton, C., and Lennerts, W. (1993). Dreams of death: Von Weizsäcker's dreams in so-called endogenic anorexia: a research note. *International Journal of Eating Disorders* 13(3):329–332.

Jackson, C., Tabin, J. K., Russel, J., and Touyz, S. (1993). Themes of death: Helmuth Thomä's "anorexia nervosa" (1967)—a research note. *International Journal of Eating Disorders* 14(4):433–437.

Johnson, C. L., and Larson, R. (1982). Bulimia: an analysis of mood and behavior. *Psychosomatic Medicine* 44:341–351.

Johnson, C. L., Stuckey, M. K., Lewis, L. D., and Schwartz, D. M. (1982). Bulimia: a descriptive survey of 316 cases. *International Journal of Eating Disorders* 2:3–16.

Jones, E. (1927/1948). The early development of female sexuality. In *Papers on Psychoanalysis*. London: Bailliere, Tindall and Cox.

Kafka, J. S. (1969). The body as a transitional object: a psychoanalytic study of a self-mutilating patient. *British Journal of Medical Psychology* 42:207–212.

Khan, M. (1963). The concept of cumulative trauma. *Psychoanalytic Study of the Child* 18:286–306. New York: International Universities Press.

Klein, M. (1946). Notes on some schizoid mechanisms. In *Envy and Gratitude and Other Works, 1946–1963*, pp. 1–24. New York: Delacorte, 1975.

Kohut, H. (1971). *The Analysis of the Self: A Systematic Approach to the Psychoanalytic Treatment of Narcissistic Personality Disorder*. New York: International Universities Press.

Krueger, D. W. (1989). *Body Self and Psychological Self*. New York: Brunner/Mazel.

Krystal, H. (1979). Alexithymia and psychotherapy. *American Journal of Psychotherapy* 33:17–31.

———— (1988). *Integration and Self Healing: Affect-Trauma-Alexithymia*. Hillsdale, NJ: Analytic Press.

Levin, R., and Hurvich, M. (1995). Nightmares and annihilation anxiety. *Psychoanalytic Psychology* 12:247–258.

Levitan, H. (1989a). Onset situation in three psychosomatic illnesses. In *Psychosomatic Medicine: Theory, Physiology and Practice*, vol. 1, ed. S. Cheren, pp. 119–134. Madison, CT: International Universities Press.

———— (1989b). Failure of the defensive functions of the ego in psychosomatic disorders. In *Psychosomatic Medicine: Theory, Physiology, and Practice*, vol. 1, ed. S. Cheren, pp. 135–157. Madison, CT: International Universities Press.

Lifton, R. J. (1979/1983). *The Broken Connection: On Death and the Continuity of Life*. New York: Basic Books.

Little, M. (1981). *Transference Neurosis and Transference Psychosis*. New York: Jason Aronson.

Lobel, L. (1981). A study of transitional objects in the early histories of borderline adolescents. *Adolescent Psychiatry* 9:199–213.

Loewald, H. W. (1970). Psychoanalytic theory and the psychoanalytic process. *Psychoanalytic Study of the Child* 25:45–67. New York: International Universities Press.

Luby, E. (1963). An overview of psychosomatic disease. *Psychosomatics* 4:1–8.

Mahler, M. (1968). *On Human Symbiosis and the Vicissitudes of Individuation*. New York: International Universities Press.

McDougall, J. (1980). *Plea for a Measure of Abnormality.* New York: International Universities Press.

———— (1989). *Theaters of the Body.* New York: Norton.

Minuchin, S., Rosman, N. L., and Baker, L. (1978). *Psychosomatic Families: Anorexia Nervosa.* Cambridge, MA: Harvard University Press.

Mitrani, J. L. (1993). "Unmentalized" experience in etiology and treatment of psychosomatic asthma. *Contemporary Psychoanalysis* 29:314–342.

———— (1995). Toward an understanding of unmentalized experiences. *Psychoanalytic Quarterly* 64:68–112.

———— (1996). *A Framework for the Imaginary: Clinical Explorations in Primitive States of Being.* Northvale, NJ: Jason Aronson.

Morris, H., Gunderson, J. G., and Zanarini, M. C. (1986). Transitional object use and borderline psychopathology. *American Journal of Psychiatry* 143(12):1534–1538.

Mushatt, C. (1989). Loss, separation and psychosomatic illness. In *Psychosomatic Symptoms: Psychodynamic Treatment of the Underlying Personality Disorder,* ed. C. P. Wilson and I. L. Mintz, pp. 33–61. Northvale, NJ: Jason Aronson.

Ordman, A. M., and Kirschenbaum, D. S. (1986). Bulimia: assessment of eating, psychological adjustment and familial characteristics. *International Journal of Eating Disorders* 5:865–878.

Orlofsky, J. L. (1989). *Intimacy Status Rating Manual.* Unpublished manuscript. St. Louis: University of Missouri.

Parmer, J. C. (1991). Bulimia and object relations: MMPI and Rorschach variables. *Journal of Personality Assessment* 56(2): 266–276.

Patton, C. J. (1992). Fear of abandonment and binge eating: a subliminal psychodynamic activation investigation. *Journal of Nervous and Mental Diseases* 180(80):484–490.

Piran, N. (1988). Borderline phenomena in anorexia and bulimia. In *Primitive Mental States and the Rorschach,* ed. H. D. Lerner and P. M. Lerner, pp. 363–376. Madison, CT: International Universities Press.

Piran, N., and Lerner, P. M. (1988). Rorschach assessment of anorexia nervosa and bulimia. In *Advances in Personality Assessment,* ed. C. D. Spielberger and J. N. Butcher, pp. 77–101. Hillsdale, NJ: Lawrence Erlbaum.

Ruesch, J. (1948). The infantile personality: the core problem in psychosomatic medicine. *Psychosomatic Medicine* 10:134.

Sarnoff, C. (1989). Early psychic stress and psychosomatic disease. In *Psychosomatic Symptoms: Psychodynamic Treatment of the Underlying Personality Disorder*, ed. C. P. Wilson and I. L. Mintz, pp. 83–103. Northvale, NJ: Jason Aronson.

Schafer, R. (1976). *Aspects of Internalization*. New York: International Universities Press.

Schmale, A. H. (1964). A genetic view of affects with special reference to the genesis of helplessness and hopelessness. *Psychoanalytic Study of the Child* 19:287–310. New York: International Universities Press.

Schur, M. (1953). The ego in anxiety. In *Drives, Affects and Behavior*, ed. R. Loewenstein, pp. 67–103. New York: International Universities Press.

——— (1955). Comments on the metapsychology of somatization. *Psychoanalytic Study of the Child* 10:119–164. New York: International Universities Press.

Schwalberg, M. D., Barlow, D. H., Alger, S. A., and Howard, L. J. (1992). Comparison of bulimic, obese, binge eaters, social phobics and individuals with panic disorders on comorbidity across *DSM-III-R* anxiety disorders. *Journal of Abnormal Psychology* 101(4):675–681.

Schwartz, H. J. (1988). Bulimia: psychoanalytic perspective. In *Bulimia: Psychoanalytic Treatment and Theory*, ed. H. J. Schwartz, pp. 31–54. Madison, CT: International Universities Press.

Sharpe, E. F. (1940/1950). Psycho-physical problems revealed in language: an examination of metaphor. In *Collected Papers on Psychoanalysis*, ed. M. Brierly. London: Hogarth.

Sifneos, P. (1973). The prevalence of alexithymic characteristics in psychosomatic patients. In *Psychotherapy and Psychosomatics*, ed. J. Ruesch, A. Schmale, and T. Spoerri, pp. 255–262. White Plains, NY: S. Karger.

Simha-Alpern, A., and Hurvich, M. (in preparation). Rorschach annihilation responses in bulimic patients.

Simha-Alpern, A., and Solanto, M. (in press a). The relationships between severity of bulimic symptomatology and developmental levels of object representations.

——— (in press b). The relationships between severity of bulimic symptomatology and interpersonal perception.

Smith, J. E., Hillard, M. C., and Roll, S. (1991). Rorschach evaluation of adolescent bulimics. *Adolescence* 26(103):687–696.

Smith, J. E., Hillard, M. C., Walsh, R. A., et al. (1991). Rorschach assessment of purging and nonpurging bulimics. *Journal of Personality Assessment* 56(2):277–288.

Sperling, M. (1949). The role of the mother in psychosomatic disorders in children. *Psychosomatic Medicine* 11:377–385.

Steer, J., and Cooper, P. J. (1988). The anxiety reduction model of bulimia nervosa: contrary case report. *International Journal of Eating Disorders* 7(3): 385–391.

Stern, D. N. (1985). *The Interpersonal World of the Infant.* New York: Basic Books.

Straker, N. (1979). Bronchial asthma: an example of psychosomatic disorder. In *Clinician's Handbook of Childhood Psychopathology,* ed. M. M. Josephson and R. T. Porter, pp. 195–208. Northvale, NJ: Jason Aronson.

Striegel-Moore, R. H., Silberstein, L. R., and Robin, J. (1993). The social self in bulimia nervosa: public self-consciousness, social anxiety, and perceived fraudulence. *Journal of Abnormal Psychology* 102(2):297–303.

Strober, M. (1981). The significance of bulimia in juvenile anorexia nervosa: an exploration of possible etiology factors. *International Journal of Eating Disorders* 1:28–43.

Strober, M., Salkin, B., Burroughs, J., and Morrell, W. (1982). Validity of the bulimia-restricter distinction in anorexia nervosa. Parental personality characteristics and family psychiatric morbidity. *Journal of Nervous and Mental Disease* 170(6):345–351.

Sugarman, A., and Kurash, C. (1982). The body as a transitional object in bulimia. *International Journal of Eating Disorders* 1(4):57–67.

Swift, A., and Letven, R. (1984). Clinical experience, bulimia and the basic fault: a psychoanalytic interpretation of the bingeing-vomiting syndrome. *Journal of the American Academy of Child Psychiatry* 23(4):489–497.

Tolpin, M. (1971). On the beginnings of a cohesive self, an application of the concept of transmuting internalization to the study of the transitional object and signal anxiety. *Psychoanalytic Study of the Child* 26:316–352. New Haven, CT: Yale University Press.

Tustin, F. (1972). *Autism and Childhood Psychosis.* London: Hogarth.

Von Weizäcker, V. (1964). Dreams in so-called endogenic magersucht (anorexia). In *Evolution of Psychodynamic Concepts: Anorexia Nervosa: A Paradigm,* ed. and trans. M. Kaufman and M. Heiman, pp. 181–197.

New York: International Universities Press. (Reprinted from *Deutsche Medizinische Wochenschrift* 1937, 63:253–257, 294–297.

Wilson, C. P. (1989). Ego functioning in psychosomatic disorders. In *Psychosomatic Symptoms: Psychodynamic Treatment of the Underlying Personality Disorder,* ed. C. P. Wilson and I. L. Mintz. Northvale, NJ: Jason Aronson.

Winnicott, D. W. (1949/1958). Mind and its relation to the psyche-soma. In *Collected Papers,* pp. 243–254. New York: Basic Books.

———— (1953). Transitional object and transitional phenomena. In *Collected Papers,* pp. 229–242. New York: Basic Books, 1958.

———— (1958). The capacity to be alone. In *The Maturational Processes and the Facilitating Environment,* pp. 29–36. New York: International Universities Press.

———— (1960/1965). The theory of the parent–infant relationship. In *The Maturational Processes and the Facilitating Environment,* pp. 37–55. New York: International Universities Press.

———— (1962). Ego integration in child development. In *The Maturational Processes and the Facilitating Environment,* pp. 56–63. New York: International Universities Press.

Woodall, C. (1987). The body as a transitional object in bulimia: a critique of the concept. *Adolescent Psychiatry* 14:179–184.

Zetzel, E. R. (1970). *The Capacity for Emotional Growth.* New York: International Universities Press.

PART II

Trauma and Psychosomatics

CHAPTER FIVE

Posttraumatic Stress Disorder, Somatization, Trauma, and Multiple Losses

Suzan Anson

CASE PRESENTATION

Shortly before beginning this chapter I received two letters from a patient, Elizabeth, who had terminated treatment suddenly several months before.

"I'm happy to say my life has been positive. . . . There's really not much I can complain about (although sometimes I still do!). I'm very grateful for all the help you've given me in the last three years. I could have never reached the point where I am now without you. Thank you so much."

Two months later:

"I miss speaking with you—I guess I should say speaking to you. Everything in my life is content for now. We'll see. . . . I'm keeping a very positive outlook."

My reaction to these letters was mixed; while I was relieved to hear she was content, I regretted that she had fled treatment with so many conflicts and transferential issues remaining. I reflected upon the journey we had taken, which filled me with empathy for her plight, leading me to painfully reconstruct the trauma that brought her such misery and pain in the ensuing years.

Elizabeth's mother and two siblings had been murdered in their home when she was 5 years old. She had been attacked and left to die, bludgeoned in the head with a hammer. She had returned to live with her father and his new wife after a two-year separation, during which she lived with relatives. The trauma was repressed throughout her childhood and adolescence. As an adult, she initiated research into what had happened to her and her family, triggering intense posttraumatic stress disorder (PTSD) symptoms.

The sequelae to the trauma made for a tumultuous treatment and transference; she struggled with her trauma, her intense wishes for attachment, and her fear of helpless loss. At times during this period I felt as bruised as she, as she protected herself against what she craved so intensely— to recapture the experience of the early dyad, uninterrupted by trauma. After receiving these letters, I felt that despite Elizabeth's abrupt termination, she was maintaining her connection to her treatment, leading me to feel hopeful that in the future she might return to treatment to work through more material.

Krystal (1978) defines the phenomenological state of trauma as

> . . . a paralyzed, overwhelmed state, with immobilization, withdrawal, possible depersonalization, evidence of disorganization. There may be a regression in any and all spheres and aspects of mental function and affect expression. This regression is followed by characteristic recuperative attempts through repetition, typical dreams, and eventually by long-term neurotic, characterological, psychosomatic, or other syndromes. [p. 90]

The conclusion Krystal reached, after thirty years' work with Holocaust survivors, was that the sum effect of trauma was the development of overwhelming affects.

Elizabeth displayed the helplessness, the overwhelming affects, and defensive dissociation and numbing that are characteristic of trauma patients. Krystal has noted that a consequence of disturbed affectivity is a "vagueness and loss of specificity of emotional responses" (p. 95), which is characterized by a mixed pattern of physiological responses and is frequently expressed on a physiological basis, with physiological symptoms and psychosomatic illness. Krystal attributes this response to a regression in affective expression characterized by affect dedifferentiation, loss of verbalization, and resomatization.

Krystal differentiates between infantile psychic trauma and adult psychic trauma: the difference lies in the relationship to the affects. In adults, affects by themselves are not a source of trauma, but intense affects can easily overwhelm the child's developing ego. Krystal observes, "It is the overwhelming of the ego, the surrender in total helplessness and hopelessness, and the progression to the catatonoid state that makes a situation traumatic" (p. 101). In this case, Elizabeth's trauma occurred during childhood, but remained protectively repressed until she was an adult. She experienced the traumatic affects as all-encompassing and horrific. What Elizabeth had experienced as a child would be terrible and overwhelming for any adult, but it was in the reliving of the trauma that she was swept away by the intensity of the affects, much as a child would be.

The focus in Elizabeth's treatment was on strengthening her ego functioning and her symbolization processes. It was my hope that, in alignment with Krystal's theory of affect development, this would enable her to differentiate affects, decrease somatization, and increase verbalization. I felt that with those elements in place, she would abandon the repetition compulsion, and, with it, her regressive pull to reunite with the dead.

This case presented a continuing challenge to the frame; Elizabeth resisted as though her life depended on it. She maintained an ego-syntonic relationship to her maladaptive defenses: she liked the adrenalin rush of terror, she liked to move into action to prevent depression, she did not want to give up marijuana or alcohol, and she did not want to risk attachment or dependency.

During the time Elizabeth and I worked together, other elements contributed to my understanding of her symptoms and losses. While the mother could not be faulted for her accidental death, it represented a failure to protect Elizabeth from the horrible trauma and its sequelae: catastrophic loss, life-threatening injury, and physical pain. She endured the pain of separation from her father, plus the strain of hospitalization and multiple surgeries. A second trauma occurred with the denial of the trauma and losses through the creation of a replacement family. This interrupted Elizabeth's mourning, disrupting her ability to maintain an object tie to her mother and dead siblings, and preventing the creation of internal representations of those relationships. The developmental necessity for the child to construct these representations following a death has been emphasized recently through the work of Silverman and colleagues (1992). In the absence of psychotherapy for Elizabeth or her father, the trauma and her losses were repressed. Finally, during childhood and adolescence Elizabeth's aunt and uncle—in effect her surrogate parents after the trauma—died. Finally, she experienced the loss, through an emotional cutoff by her relatives, of relationship to her mother's entire family.

Elizabeth began treatment while she was completing her studies as a graduate student in the social sciences. She remained with me, on and off, for three years before she terminated the treatment after obtaining full-time employment and moving to another state. During the time she worked with me she struggled with intense transference, somatization, survivor guilt, and symptoms of PTSD.

Elizabeth was a very pretty, although initially somewhat unkempt, thin young woman, wearing her thick, long, dark hair loose, often tucked under a collection of unusual hats that she would wear during her sessions. She exhibited an insistent, urgent quality in her communication with me, quickly impressing me with her intelligence and wit. A self-described hysteric who immediately set about to gain my approval, Elizabeth was an extremely likable young woman whose vulnerability and guardedness were visible beneath her affable presentation.

Presenting Problems

Elizabeth came into treatment after experiencing extreme anxiety symptoms and sleep difficulties, reporting that she felt "freaked out" by sudden loud noises. She was always on edge, finding herself constantly crying or on the brink of tears. Hyperalert, easily startled, she feared she was living her life unprotected. In her fantasies she envisioned herself to be in a dangerous environment where she imagined being prey to an unknown assailant. Unable to control escalating feelings of panic, she was terrified of losing control and having the terrifying and debilitating experience of panic. In addition, she was seriously depressed, often prone to suicidal ideation. Elizabeth found the mounting tension and depression she experienced to be unbearable, and was unable to self-soothe without the use of alcohol or drugs. Disturbed sleep patterns and poor self-care exacerbated her symptoms. In sessions she chewed on her torn cuticles and bitten-down nails, clicking her heels together in a rapid rhythm as her anxiety increased during her sessions. I was reminded of the character of Dorothy in *The Wizard of Oz*, who could magically escape her situation with a similar click of the heels. Elizabeth, in contrast, was stuck in her painful reality, unable to escape the trauma she had recently unearthed.

History of the Trauma

Elizabeth's mother and two siblings, a brother and a sister, were murdered in front of her in her home when she was 5 years old. She was the sole survivor of a vicious, unprovoked attack by a psychotic young homeless man who had become obsessed with the family. To her recollection, before this traumatic ending, she had been a member of an idyllic family that was intact and loving. She recalled her parents' marriage with nostalgia; to her recollection, theirs had been a perfect union. The father was successful in his profession, enabling his wife to remain home caring for her three children. Elizabeth thought this was a golden time.

Following the murders, she was sent to live with an aunt and uncle, who she recalled were loving and attentive. Within a few years, she was sent to live with her father in a distant city at the time of his marriage to a second wife. She had difficulty adjusting to her new stepmother, who she felt was cold to her. Eventually two replacement siblings were born.

She became extremely rebellious in her adolescence. At age 18 she came into a substantial inheritance. With the means to escape her unhappy family life, she bought a sleek sports car, went away to college, had a wild time, and traveled extensively. After a trip to Asia, she landed in New York for graduate school. Seeking to find out more about what had happened in her childhood, Elizabeth was encouraged by a friend to research the murders. After retrieving microfilm of newspaper articles, she began to have extreme PTSD symptoms.

The Trauma

On an ordinary morning twenty years before, shortly after breakfast, Elizabeth's father had gone to work and her mother began to attend to her housework. The three children played quietly. Although the sequence of events is unclear, the murderer entered the house, bludgeoned the children with a hammer, and at some point murdered the mother, who was working on another floor in the house. He then tried to disguise the crimes by setting off a homemade bomb, which detonated prematurely, severely maiming him. The father returned later in the day to find his wife and the two younger children dead and Elizabeth barely alive.

Elizabeth was taken to the hospital with a fractured skull, severe concussion, and hemiparalysis. She was unable to speak. Recuperation was slow, as several surgeries were necessary to repair her skull fractures. Large plates were created to replace areas of skull that had been fractured. Miraculously, she regained language and movement with no apparent cognitive defects. She had no memory of what happened to her or her family. Following her release from the hospital, she was sent to live with her aunt and uncle, who provided her with a warm, nurturing environment.

Following her move to live with her father and his new life and wife, she was not encouraged to talk about her losses. The past was never discussed; she sensed that there was a taboo against bringing up her lost siblings and mother. Sensitive to her father's pain, she protected him by keeping silent about her losses. To her recollection, her father never encouraged her to refer to her mother or her lost siblings. He focused, instead, on building a new life. Elizabeth began to protect her father from their grief, deciding to sidestep the issue of the mother and siblings to protect him, fearing that reliving the traumatic feelings of loss would intensify his heart condition and kill him. She had a problematic relationship with her stepmother, whom she cast in the typical role of the cold, wicked, and punitive replacement for her idealized mother. This severe polarization between the good and bad mothers created a stormy, split transference.

Elizabeth thought she remembered asking her father what had happened to her mother and siblings as a child. She thought his response was to put her off, saying, "I'll tell you when you're a little older." She recalled his vagueness describing the deaths: "They died, there was a little explosion." These responses puzzled her; she felt that nothing added up, and she wondered what relationship this had to the scars on her head. With such repression within the family, it was no surprise that PTSD symptoms began as the trauma was reactivated after she retrieved the news clippings. After reading the articles, Elizabeth remembered, "My knees buckled, the words, 'explosion,' 'bloody,' 'bludgeoned' so clear in my mind—I never had any inklings about mass murder."

Initial PTSD Symptoms

Following this triggering event, Elizabeth began to experience a full range of physical sensations that had not been present before. She suffered a sensation of escalating panic that she felt was the effect of her mood upon her body: "I feel it—it's a physical reaction." She continued:

> I feel like an old woman, my bones and muscles are weak, I'm feeling drained and old, tired, no time to go to the gym. I feel overwhelmed with emotions, I can't screen out feelings of rage and hate. . . . I feel I'm going too fast, always nervous, twitching, I get a subtle form of panic, increased heartbeat, out of breath—this comes from nervousness.

Her whole body would start to tremble, she would feel nauseated and dazed, hyperventilating, and begin to feel wobbly, as if electric sensations pulsed through her body. She would develop throbbing headaches, often in response to sessions, frequently reporting that her head was tingling.

She struggled to understand her symptoms, frequently confusing her affect with her somatic complaints. For example, one day she observed, "I don't like anger—my eyes are puffy, my throat feels like I'm getting sick—hysterical, huh?"

To defend against these intolerable feelings, she employed a number of defenses. Up until this time, she had used a manic defense to prevent the breakthrough of affect, either through traveling or physical activity. She worked out in gym "like a madwoman." Now she was aware of the dissociation and depersonalization that left her numb and insulated her from the pain. She denied the impact of the trauma, minimizing it. "What happened to me wasn't so bad," she asserted. Elizabeth alternated between needing physical comfort and a tactile defensiveness that left her unable to tolerate contact.

Initial Phase of Treatment

Elizabeth began treatment at once a week, moved to twice weekly, and began to use the couch. Once on the couch she often needed to retain eye contact, twisting her body around on the couch to keep me in her vision. She struggled not to be flooded with the traumatic material, but she was frequently overcome by the physical symptoms that substituted for the verbalization of affects. Initially, the transference was positive; Elizabeth stated that she felt understood, that the room was soothing, generally experiencing me as a good object whom she felt to be the only one who acknowledged her losses.

In addition to the physical symptoms were defenses and enactments that interfered with establishment of a positive treatment alliance and a holding environment. Protectively she used dissociation, splitting, projection, and isolation of affect. Outside the sessions, her impulsivity led her into dangerous situations.

With increasingly hypervigilance, Elizabeth began to confuse the imagined, unremembered trauma with real-life situations. One day while housesitting, she became terrified when a repairman announced himself at the intercom. Convinced that he was coming to kill her, she barricaded the door, holding a kitchen knife for protection in her panic and confusion.

Elizabeth had initially considered but then ruled out clinical hypnosis, fearing flashbacks that she worried might arise intrusively with a cinematic clarity. She made an effort to cope with her escalating symptoms through self-medication, primarily alcohol and marijuana use. Elizabeth couldn't tolerate the intensity of her affects, frequently gaining relief through projecting and displacing her anger or bouts of intense crying. Her self-care was strained. She often spent the weekend in her bedroom, crying, going without food, rocking herself into a numb state where she could keep the sadness at bay.

In this crisis state, the treatment was preanalytic as I made an effort to create a holding environment for her. During this time I encouraged her to initiate behavioral interventions to help her to self-soothe and to contain breakthroughs of affect that occurred outside treatment. She refused to consider medication.

Six months into treatment, Elizabeth reported her first dream. In the dream she struggled with a red snake that was going to kill her siblings. In the dream the siblings had killed a woman. "It was frightening, I had to kill the snake or it would kill me, though it did, halfway did, I escaped with my brother and sister in the car." Her first association was to the obvious phallic reference, but then she decided that the red snake could be related to a stream of blood, and wondered whether it might represent her blood or that of her siblings. She remembered, "They were dead, then they came back to life" (recalling her replacement siblings). In this dream only the mother is dead. Elizabeth was concerned that the red snake symbolized the memory of lying in a pool of blood for six hours before she was discovered. This increased her fears that a flashback would ensue (which did not occur then or ever during her treatment).

Second Phase of Treatment

As Elizabeth's treatment continued, the transference began to shift to a split transference as she struggled with feelings of love and hate. She became afraid to become dependent on me, fearing attachment. Protectively, she displayed a rebelliousness, voicing her wishes to separate from me, usually by announcing her wish to reduce the number of sessions. At other times she reinstated me as the good mother, showing herself as clingy, needy, and vulnerable. Occasionally she would become regressed on the couch, curling up in a fetal position, comfortably stating, "I feel 8 or 9 or 10." Other times she would notice her regressive behavior, saying, "Listen to me, I'm babbling, just like a baby."

I interpreted these wishes for stability from a genetic standpoint, that she had wished for her relationships to be permanent. She frequently struggled with her loving, dependent feelings, which she had kept protectively isolated behind her spiky, tough-girl facade. Following these struggles, in which she resembled a fitful baby, spent after a tantrum, she would calm down, often reporting that she could easily go to sleep.

These splits were also enacted extratransferentially, as she maintained a similar clingy/dependent vs. hostile, rebellious, rejecting stance with her boyfriend. During the course of treatment, she was able to progress from a destructive relationship to a relationship with a caring and loving man who was able to tolerate her symptoms, affective storms, and conflicts.

Elizabeth began to feel freer not only to talk about her mother and siblings, but also to share mementos of her past—photo albums of her early life before the trauma. She sought reassurance that her reading of the photos confirmed that she had lived an idyllic early life. She overcame her feelings that she couldn't talk about or display photos of her family, and installed an area in her apartment made up of photographs and mementos.

During this time, her self-care improved; she no longer spent entire weekends in bed, crying and hungry. However, she engaged in a form of retraumatization that may also be seen as an effort to remain connected to the dead. Elizabeth revealed that part of the reason she had such difficulty sleeping was because she repeatedly watched horror movies with bloody suicides and murders. Her favorite film, *The Wall*, particularly increased her depression and led her to feel suicidal. She loved to watch Stephen King movies, which, as Lenore Terr (1987) has pointed out, can induce traumatic affects in the viewer. Additionally, she frequently initiated midnight phone conversations with a friend to process details about her research into the murders, which induced feelings of excitement mixed with horror.

She conceded that she liked the adrenalin rush the horror movies and other frightening situations gave her: "Oh, yes," she reported, "I'm addicted to adrenalin. I can feel it through the day periodically, like a shock wave. . . . It's like being a little scared, like I have to keep moving. . . . I get very nervous and anxious." She revealed that she liked the "rush" of the adrenalin, which she sought through her participation in numerous daredevil sports activities. As she related these activities, she induced feelings of heart-stopping terror and dread in me.

We examined the negative effect her lack of self-care had on her physiology, particularly her use of cigarettes, marijuana, alcohol, caffeine, and junk food. These substances soothed her momentarily, but left her feeling even more depressed after their effects subsided. Over the course of treatment her self-care oscillated. At times she was able to maintain a moderate level of reasonable nutrition, rest, and exercise; however, she was unable to maintain these positive behaviors consistently.

Treatment Themes: Survivor Guilt and Suicidal Wishes for Reunion

As Elizabeth's treatment intensified and deepened, she was able to engage in an exploration of the relationship between her survivor guilt, the repetition compulsion as it was displayed through her death wishes, and her periodic risky, suicidal behaviors. Raised in a devoutly Roman Catholic household,

Elizabeth felt responsible to make something of her life, having determined that since she was the sole survivor, God must have some special task in mind for her. This thought only served to put pressure on her and to increase her guilty feelings, since she felt she had been singled out for survival. During this phase of the treatment, my countertransference was frequently intense; I often felt that I just wanted to walk out of the office midsession and go home, feeling that I'd had enough for one day. I felt worn out and wrung out. I wondered if these feelings mirrored Elizabeth's overtaxed coping abilities.

The most tumultuous and perilous period during treatment coincided with the anniversary of the murders. During the first year of treatment Elizabeth sadly observed for the first time that the murders had occurred just before her mother's birthday. Three weeks before the anniversary Elizabeth's anxiety escalated. She became frightened that she'd go crazy and speculated that she'd leave treatment to escape from the feelings pressing in on her. "Maybe I'll have a psychotic break," she worried, then added, "Maybe I'll leave you first, maybe you'll still be here [later on]." Despite my efforts to keep her from acting this out, she fled treatment within a week of the anniversary. She entered the office confidently, adamantly announcing that she was leaving treatment. She induced in me feelings of powerlessness— there was nothing I was able to say to keep her in treatment. I tried interpreting her defensive flight, her anger, her need to see me as an authoritarian disapproving parent, all to no avail. Unable to dissuade her from leaving, I was receptive to the projective identification; after investing so much effort in her treatment, I had strong wishes to retaliate, which surfaced in a fantasy of turning her away when, at a later date, she attempted to return to treatment. I became aware of how abandoned and discarded she must have felt many times after the murders—alone in the hospital, unable to move or to speak, slowly absorbing the impact of the loss of her mother and siblings, longing for her absent father while she remained for several years in the care of her aunt and uncle, attempting to adjust to the newly formed family, feeling she had lost her father to his new wife, and, finally, feeling as though she was perpetually on the periphery of her new family with a cold stepmother whose favoritism for Elizabeth's replacement siblings was not disguised.

Within four months she returned. In the intervening period she had worked through the negative transference and told me that she was feeling less rebellious. She reluctantly admitted that she had made a mistake in leaving treatment so precipitously. In the interim, she had extricated herself from the destructive relationship she had been involved in during the past few years. Elizabeth now recognized that this relationship was retraumatizing; her boyfriend had been consistently withholding and unavailable to her. At times he had been rejecting and cold. She realized that he was making an effort to control her, expecting her to share his depression and isolation. Elizabeth's breakup with the boyfriend had spurred a dramatic scene: he became threatening, endangering his life and hers in a melodramatic suicidal drama. He pleaded with her to resume the relationship, but she was firm in breaking it off.

Elizabeth had met a new man, announcing dreamily that she was "head over heels" in love. For several months the ex-boyfriend's behavior escalated, as he became disconsolate and clingy. He threatened suicide, harassed her, and came close to stalking her in an eerie recapitulation of the obsessional attachment that had preceded the murders of her mother and siblings—a parallel that Elizabeth quickly recognized. Fortunately, her new boyfriend stepped in to protect her, in a way she wished her father might have protected her family, fulfilling a wish for rescue and assuaging her fears.

As Elizabeth settled into this new relationship she began to struggle with oedipal and preoedipal wishes that had been eclipsed in the previous relationship. The sexual part of the relationship became problematic; Elizabeth felt "suffocated" when her boyfriend wanted to have sex, preferring cuddling to what she perceived as the intrusiveness of intercourse. She felt that the suffocating feelings somehow connected to her intense frustration following the trauma. She recalled her aphasia in the hospital following the trauma; her screen memory was that she was being wheeled to another floor in a hospital crib, desperately wanting to speak but unable to get the words out.

As her life stabilized, Elizabeth experienced more successes, which led her to feel filled with pressure. In the classic PTSD sense, she felt she had a foreshortened future. I continued to focus on interpreting her guilt, which she accepted, stating that she didn't feel she deserved a good life. Defensively, she engaged in compulsive behaviors to keep these feelings at bay.

Third Phase of Treatment and Termination

Despite these defenses, Elizabeth continued to experience stability and made progress in her life. She graduated from a master's program in social science, and had settled into her new relationship, which appeared to be nurturing and positive, with prospects for marriage. She continued to have difficulty believing that she deserved any of this. I continued to help her articulate her survivor guilt, depression, and suicidal ideation, which she understood to be an effort to achieve reunion with her lost mother.

Anticipating the loaded intensity of the close juxtaposition of the mother's birthday and the anniversary of the murders during the second year of treatment, I began to focus on her acting out, specifically her manic and compulsive defenses against depression. I attempted to increase her ability for symbolization, encouraging her to stay with treatment, to convert feelings into words rather than taking action. Elizabeth described the struggle both physiologically and emotionally:

> When I'm like that I can't talk—I see that I'm very scared, frightened—it's so hard [to put feelings into words]. My eyes dart and blink, adrenalin starts running, I get tense, I clench my fists, I'm ready to fight. I cover my head and then realize what I'm doing. [She rubs the bridge of her nose to control tears.] A panic attack, I get like a feeling—not an aura—like a brief instance—I can't breathe—my heart beats really fast. I take deep breaths, focus, try to concentrate on my breathing to prevent hyperventilation. [Her feet are fidgeting.] It happens out of nowhere. It happens when I'm late, trying to get organized, when I'm anxious. I feel scared, and need to cry, and need to cry in a big way. Like I need to go back or something. "Okay [she says to herself], here we go again," for 15 to 20 minutes. Like a fix. I say to myself, "Nothing happened," but emotionally I feel someone is trying to kill me. With [her boyfriend] I feel safe enough, I hold myself, rock, say nothing's going to happen. It boggles my mind how traumatized I was.

She began to see the connection between these symptoms and her affects. In one instance, she reported that her eyes had been uncontrollably twitching for over three days. She now noticed that she felt she became a little "crazy" when she tried to suppress a feeling, stating, "I'm holding back feelings, I'm depressed. The feelings are very intense. I'm dazed. If I let go, I don't like the way I feel [depressed]." At other times she was unable to tolerate the affective intensity, reporting, "I'm out of my head with hysteria. I feel I'm overflowing with emotions."

As much as she needed to overcome her defenses, particularly the manic flight, Elizabeth recognized the life-sustaining protective aspects of her defenses, stating, "I can't give up my defenses or I'll die."

When the affect broke through, she experienced the somatic and affective experience as intolerable. She cried,

> I feel like shit. I feel someone's killing my insides. I feel like my soul is being murdered. I feel like I'm being killed sometimes when I cry. I feel someone's killing me, I want it to stop. When I come down, my body twitches. My nerves are shot—I'm terrified.

At other times, she would experience a more stuporous state, which she observed felt "chemically different," where her thinking was dazed, unclear, and slow.

During these periods she was inconsolable. She alternately was clingy then rejecting. Despite her boyfriend's reassurances, she remembered telling him, "Don't hurt me, just leave me here to die—go away. I just want to fall asleep for a long time and not wake up." At times she would cling to him, but other times her tactile defensiveness prevented her from allowing him to touch or hug her. She felt this was overdetermined, that her sensation of being smothered was trauma-derived. She worried that if she allowed him to hug or touch her, her rigidity would dissolve, and she would become helplessly clingy and dependent.

Her sleep rituals were arranged to preserve her sense of security. She couldn't allow her body to be touched. Situating herself touching the wall, Elizabeth would put in her earplugs, nudge her body into the wall behind her, and sleep with the light on. When she slept with her boyfriend, she would awaken him repeatedly in the night. Understandably fatigued by these interruptions, he attempted to put an end to the behavior by telling her that, in his view, this compulsive behavior was actually an effort to see whether he was still alive. This he linked to the trauma, speculating that she had attempted, unsuccessfully, to awaken her dead siblings. She accepted his interpretation and made an effort to stop her behavior.

Elizabeth's fears of attachment were visible in the transference. As her treatment deepened, the number of sessions increased from two to three a week. With the increase in frequency, she began to struggle with her fear of being abandoned, fear of growing too attached to me, and fear that she would become dependent upon me. Unable to tolerate the emergence of loving feelings in the present, she preferred to reserve them exclusively for her mother, remembering, "She loved me, she fulfilled all my needs, she accepted me." To dilute the intense transference, she joined a weekly therapy group. One positive aspect was that it gave her a forum to talk about the murders openly for the first time outside of treatment without shame. The negative aspect was that it enabled her to avoid the intense transferential material. Additionally, she engaged the group in an acting out by enticing them to go out after the session to get drunk with her.

While she struggled in the transference, Elizabeth made strides with her family through openly restoring the memory of her mother and siblings. She found she was no longer interested in protecting her father. She recognized that her need to bring the trauma and its effects into the open became more urgent than her fantasy that discussing this with her father would cause his death. She worked herself up to confronting him. His response demonstrated his inability to accept the impact of the trauma. He found it hard to believe she carried emotional scars from the incident and its aftermath. Elizabeth decided to put her feelings into a letter, which gave her relief, but she was hurt when he told her he did not believe there was such a syndrome as PTSD. She angrily confronted his lack of empathy, suggesting that he, too, could benefit from treatment. After her anger subsided, their relationship became closer.

For the first time, Elizabeth asked for, and received, photographs and possessions that had belonged to her mother. She openly displayed photos on the walls of her apartment, unconcerned with her stepmother's response. No longer feeling shame about what had happened, Elizabeth began to talk freely with her father and siblings about the effects of the trauma on the family. She elicited considerable empathy from her siblings, although not much was forthcoming from her stepmother.

As the anniversary of the murders drew closer during the second year of treatment, Elizabeth's anxiety escalated. After revisiting the murder scene at her boyfriend's prompting, Elizabeth began to attempt to reconstruct what had happened to her and her family, using an intellectual, analytical defense. While this resulted in a renewed empathy for what she had endured as a child, it also triggered PTSD symptoms. She became startled by noises as she reconstructed what it must have been like to be nearly murdered, left for dead, and then to hear and feel the vibrations of the explosion of the bomb, which rocked the house. She recalled recent incidents that led her to feel panic. In one instance she remembered her sensation of helplessness as a homeless man became hostile to her after she refused to give him money as she was stopped in traffic during rush hour. This incident triggered a panic attack experienced by Elizabeth as intense feelings of pressure and rapid heartbeat.

Her somatization continued, particularly sadness, which she frequently attributed to premenstrual syndrome (PMS). The premenstrual hormone shifts exacerbated her symptoms. During this time Elizabeth made efforts to increase her self-care through the implementation of soothing bedtime rituals, but these positive behaviors were at odds with the unconsciously suicidal behaviors that persisted, for example, dissociatively walking into traffic or driving while smoking marijuana late at night in her car, which she likened to a "cocoon."

With the approach of the anniversary of the murders, I made an effort, based on the previous year's failure, to increase the holding environment, hoping that she would refrain from any dangerous behavior and remain in treatment. That was when I suggested to Elizabeth that we increase the number of sessions to three a week.

Her response was ambivalent; she resisted, voicing her wish to quit whenever she felt temporary relief. She rationalized, intellectualized, and said she didn't want to be stigmatized by three-times-a-week treatment. We explored her fears of dependence. I focused on making her more conscious of the manic defenses she had used in the past. I interpreted to her the projective identification, that just as she had become comfortable with three-times-a-week frequency, she was threatening me with abandonment.

She expressed her resistance in physiological terms: "I'm so exhausted, I haven't had time, I have cramps, had a busy day, I'm tired, really tired, I've been going too fast, I am feeling the need to slow down." When she stopped resisting the positive transference and was feeling secure within the frame, she would again put her feelings into bodily equivalents. For example, she described how when beginning her menstrual period she bought a pint of ice cream, which she ate "slowly, wonderfully." In this instance, she reported that she felt fine, commingling feelings and body sensations, reporting that her experience of her stomach as fat and bloated led her to feel satisfied. Eventually she noticed how she was "babbling." Curling up on the couch, heels no longer clicking tensely, she settled in quietly. "I feel so restful, I feel I could fall asleep here. I'm content."

Shortly after this "contented" period, Elizabeth made a pilgrimage to the gravesite where her mother and siblings were buried. She reported that for the first time she spoke to her mother aloud as she stood over the grave. Making an effort to contact her mother, Elizabeth told her she missed her. In her words, she "caught her up with my life," telling her mother tearfully, "I miss you, but I have substitutes." She was exhausted afterward, as she became more fully aware of the hatred she felt for the murderer, whom she could not forgive.

One month before the anniversary she was able to verify her reconstruction of the murders with her father. She was surprised to discover she had repressed an earlier discussion about the murders when she was an adolescent, explaining that her father told her the details when she was 16, but "it didn't sink in."

Her father filled in her gaps in memory, which she found equally difficult to take in the second time. He told her his version of what he saw and what he did; that he found her sitting up, bloody, crying, and conscious. He had discovered the siblings dead on the floor. As she disclosed this information, Elizabeth was unable to remain lying down on the couch, telling me she needed to sit up, maintain eye contact with me, in order to tell the rest of the story. Elizabeth said she felt she was gaining in her ability to contain the trauma in the treatment room and not "spill it" elsewhere.

As the date of the anniversary approached, her anxiety escalated. She alternated between using the couch and sitting up, telling me she wanted to see me. Elizabeth had forgotten that she had fled treatment after the previous anniversary. Her response was one of surprise, "Did I?" After discussing this, she reassured me, "I won't do that again" (she was not able to sustain this resolve). Elizabeth became increasingly depressed, struggling with feelings of low self-esteem.

She became more aware of the relationship between her survivor guilt, the repetition compulsion dangerously enacted, and wishes for reunion. Now aware of her conviction that she, too, should have died, Elizabeth recalled instances where, in the past, she had placed herself in grave danger.

She remembered that several years before, one week prior to the anniversary, with no conscious awareness of the date, she found herself on a skydiving flight, about to leap from the plane. She remembered being terrified, needing reassurance that she wouldn't die, pleading for the attendants to tell her she would survive, then leaping into the void, fearful she would die. For Elizabeth, this was a "total terror experience." Significantly, she had held her head on the way down, as if to protect the plates in her skull. In a later session, she said she felt that this realization represented a breakthrough that helped her to understand the phenomenon of the repetition compulsion clearly. "I can't believe I did that," she reflected, "it [the repetition] was as plain as day."

Her anxiety, paranoia, and fears of annihilation increased. Becoming increasingly afraid, she clung to her boyfriend. She imagined telling him, "I feel everyone is trying to hurt me, and you will leave me, I'll drive you crazy with my madness."

Her behavior in sessions was fitful and agitated. "I feel my world is collapsing, I'm dying," she reported. Elizabeth worried that she would not be able to stop herself from some form of enactment. Terrified by her anger, aggression, and abandonment fears, she lamented, "Every time I feel secure, something happens, and I repeat." She extended this concern into the future, envisioning that she would become phobic as a mother, when her children or she reached the age of her mother at the time of the deaths. She became increasingly fearful of her dependent feelings that she experienced in the transference, voicing her fears that she would never be able to leave treatment. She tried to convince herself that she would stay in treatment despite her fears, telling me, "I'm committed to staying in treatment, I won't leave this year."

Elizabeth observed her self-medication as an effort to mitigate her depression. She refused to consider an antianxiety or antidepressant medication. Her capacity for tolerating and articulating her affects increased. She became more able to express many emotions and sensations: misery, clinginess, irritability, guilt, wishes to regress, in contrast to reporting bodily sensations.

I noticed that Elizabeth had begun to wear hats in every session. "I'm protecting my head," she explained. "I'm afraid it's all going to blow up," fearing flashbacks of the explosion. With constant fears of abandonment or worse, death, she had become hypervigilant, startling easily with noises. "I feel something's going to happen, I'm going to do something, I want to leave and run, get out of town before the sirens." I encouraged her to convert these feelings into words rather than action, which I felt was imminent. I felt as though I was helplessly standing by, about to witness a disaster. Elizabeth struggled against her tendency to take action and flee. During sessions she did not want to hear from me, pushing away me and my words. I suggested to her that she was resisting my interventions, pushing me away, that she needed to slow down and digest what I was saying to her. This she acknowledged, saying, "I've been spitting everything out."

Nonetheless, Elizabeth realized that she needed a holding environment. The notion of becoming dependent undermined her narcissistic self-sufficient coping style, which terrified her. Elizabeth wanted extra sessions or more sessions or double sessions, all the time verbalizing that she probably wouldn't be able to continue treatment once she obtained a full-time job. She was afraid of becoming dependent, afraid of attaching then having to separate. She cried deeply, citing "all this transference crap" as the source of her misery. I addressed her ambivalence: her surface fears of attachment of dependency. I felt she was not yet able to accept her intense fury at her mother for leaving her through death. Instead, I encouraged her to see that she would be helped by learning to tolerate negative transference feelings by staying in treatment, putting her negative feelings into words rather than actions. "You're my symbolic mother, I accept it, I don't like it," she stated in exasperation.

Conflicted over the rekindling of her need for her mother, she became rebellious as she attempted to maintain her autonomy, stating, "I'll come in when I want." Elizabeth noted the adolescent quality of her responses: "I want to be grown up, after all, I have a job, [but] I'm [acting] totally regressed."

On the day before the anniversary date of the murders, on her way to the session, Elizabeth was delayed by a traffic jam that had occurred after a small plane had crashed and exploded near the roadway, tying up traffic for hours. Unable to leave the road, she was eventually directed by police past the accident scene, where she viewed pieces of the victims' clothing and personal belongings strewn near the chalk markings where the bodies had been found. She found herself becoming extremely anxious, fearing that the victims had suffered painful deaths. Commenting on her own feelings of depression at this anniversary time, she took this as a sign, noting, "God must want me to be grateful that I'm alive."

This momentary insight did not allay her suicidal impulses following the anniversary, however. Elizabeth began to drink heavily, relating several instances where she had been out of control. In one instance, she had blacked out after drinking too much at a wedding. According to her boyfriend, she suddenly panicked while they were on the expressway. She began to punch at him, then she tried to exit his car while the car was in motion. Terrified, he pulled to the side of the road, where she curled up in a fetal position against the car door, screaming blood-curdling screams by his recall, acting as though she were being tortured. She had no memory of this event.

Unconscious death wishes became prominent. Within the month, she booked a birthday flight for her boyfriend in a small plane similar to the one that had crashed at the time of the anniversary, medicating herself with marijuana and alcohol before the flight. On a day-to-day basis, she felt she was "zoning out" protectively, by becoming numb while preserving her ability to function.

I confronted her suicidal behavior, which she reacted to with shock and surprise. She resisted my interpretation.

Postanniversary Flight from Treatment

Within a month Elizabeth fled treatment, replicating the pattern of the previous year. In the last session before leaving, she angrily confronted me, as she struggled with her feelings of dependence: "I don't know what's on your agenda for me. I would like a review, I'm not sure, I don't know what you're expecting of me, I see myself as kind of normal, I don't want to go to therapy forever, I have anxiety, you'll make me feel I can't live on my own. When I know I can. . . ." She asked for me to give her my approval to stop treatment, which I told her I could not do.

She was filled with feeling, and pressed on. "I don't want to go to therapy. You make me regress, I feel you want me to have structure, you make me want to come. I can't just stop, I'd feel bad if I was impulsive. . . . You've made me have so many feelings." Despite all my efforts to keep her from leaving, she rationalized that she couldn't continue and stopped abruptly.

Three months later, just one week after my return from vacation, Elizabeth called, desperate to return to therapy. Initially, she felt relieved to be back in treatment, reluctantly acknowledging that she never should have left, expressing her anger that her transference feelings were so strong. During her hiatus, Elizabeth's suicidal ideation increased. She presented familiar conflicts that she had attempted to solve through action. Almost casually, she revealed she had seen a male behavioral therapist for biofeedback, and wondered whether she should continue to see us both. We explored her efforts to dilute the transference. In tears, she revealed that she was upset at the depth of her feeling for me, and in fact wanted to continue to see this other therapist in order to hold back her feelings from me.

She had come to the conclusion that her illusion of self-sufficiency was no longer helpful, and that she realized she could not heal herself in isolation.

I made the interpretation to her that she had left therapy in order to avoid feeling abandoned when I took my vacation, to which she snapped angrily, "That's right, I'm the one who does the leaving. No one is going to leave me again." Her anger became more prominent. "I don't want my life to be one crisis after another. I'm angry, angry, angry. Life wasn't fair to me and I'm gonna show it."

Elizabeth revealed more self-destructive behavior during her hiatus from treatment that demonstrated her lack of self-care. She had been responsible for a car wreck that left her with a concussion and severe whiplash, yet she did not seek medical treatment for weeks afterward. She revealed a self-destructive pattern of getting stoned and going for a ride in her car late at night, observing, "It's the most relaxing thing—like a cocoon." Countertransferentially, I felt traumatized by these revelations, fearful that she would manage to kill herself. Less catastrophic indications of her failure at self-care revolved around her inability to set limits at her new workplace, so that she was perpetually tense and overworked, since she allowed no time for lunch, exercise, or socialization. Still, she sporadically initiated more acceptable soothing rituals, using herb teas and hot showers to help her to relax. She remained hopeful that she would eventually succeed in taking better care of herself.

Elizabeth's fear of attachment and abandonment was highlighted following the departure of a kindly maternal figure she had befriended at her workplace. "As soon as I get a good one," she muttered, "she leaves. I'm so sick of being hurt, it's going to happen again. I'm not that secure yet, I can cry, be angry. . . . Maybe I'll have to be in treatment for the next five years, or the rest of my life."

Resisting the positive transference, she complained, "I don't want to get close to you. You're too sweet, too nice. That's transference. Like my mother. I want you to care, but you're just a therapist, because I know it's not true. It's a bubble, it's going to burst. I don't want that to happen."

We explored her fear of attachment, fear of loss, and her lack of trust. I began to feel that she would not be able to continue, that she needed to do to me what had been done to her—abandonment. "There must me some truth, you must be nice. Am I supposed to be attached? Why should I? Eventually it would end."

"How do you think it would end?" I asked.

"You might die," she replied automatically. "It happens." She laughed reflexively as she recognized the overdetermined nature of her response, continuing, "[or] then you'd go on vacation, I'd have to worry, that you wouldn't come back. I do need you, but I don't want to."

I was hopeful that perhaps she would remain in treatment. I continued to interpret the fear of becoming attached and losing me, and to help her express the negative transference feelings that were generally projected onto her "evil" stepmother while she continued to idealize her dead mother. This strategy wasn't effective; I couldn't find a way to maintain a holding environment that would contain her. She managed to sabotage her treatment by moving a sufficient distance away to rationalize that coming to my office was inconvenient. "I liked three times a week. I liked it. I was attached," she told me at a point where she was certain she would leave treatment soon. I asked her if she would prefer for me to have an office in her new neighborhood. "Oh yes, you'd be right there. Close by. It would be free of wear and tear. I wouldn't have to do the work. I deserve it."

In our final session, it was clear that she was resistant to any and all interpretations; she had to act the drama out and leave me, preserving her sense of autonomy. Coyly turning toward me from her position on the couch, she asked, with a challenging sparkle in her eye, "Am I a difficult child?" I felt that she was demonstrating to me an important part of her identity while she was in the protective structure of the holding environment. In Elizabeth's mind, she equated her resistance with autonomy and survival. I was unable to hold on to her. She left treatment, fully aware that she was putting me and everyone else close to her through "hoops" in order to be assured that they really cared for her. As she had said earlier, she would be the one to do the leaving.

With the conviction that she was strong enough to live with her symptoms, Elizabeth felt she could cope with them. As she noted, she was working, had a good relationship, and felt she was aware of her problems. Keeping the door open, she said, "Maybe I'll be back [implying the anniversary time]."

Later in the week she left me the following phone message, "I'm not coming in anymore. I can't afford it, or have time for it. Right now I'm too busy and too stressed out. I'll call, when I have money and time, in the future."

CONCLUSION

During the course of her treatment, Elizabeth's somatization decreased, but it did not disappear. She became more able to articulate her feelings, although she struggled to tolerate the intensity of her feelings. "I'm angry at the world . . . my mother died." She reached a point where she was able to express her anger toward her parents, and no longer felt she had to protect her father from the anger she feared would kill him. In the maternal transference Elizabeth struggled with positive and negative feelings toward me, which decreased the idealization of her dead mother by allowing herself to experience both loving and hating feelings. She maintained the split, however, in attributing all negative qualities to her stepmother.

Elizabeth remained susceptible to abandonment and loss of self-esteem, which she defended against by creating a facade of self-sufficiency: "If I let myself go, I'd be a mess. I'm not going to be that helpless. I will take care of myself."

In the time I was working on this chapter, I found myself unable to sustain my efforts to reconstruct Elizabeth's story and her course of treatment. The fact of the trauma, in combination with what happened in the transference as well as extratransferentially, coupled with my own counter-transference, made for a discomforting experience. I found this case, which I had originally developed as an oral presentation, hard to write and easy to avoid. I found myself full of resistances to writing and organizing the material; I would start working, write up a fragment, then need to drop it for a time. While I watched myself going through this avoidance as the affects surrounding the case pressed in on me, I was aware that this sensation must be similar to Elizabeth's daily experience. She was unable to escape the breakthrough of affects or her compulsion to repeat, except through efforts to self-medicate through marijuana or alcohol. In the process of bearing witness to her trauma and pain, trying to create a safe holding environment, I was unable to shake ongoing feelings of helplessness in the face of her losses and her pain.

Without my superimposing psychoanalytic ideas of cure on her, she has made substantial gains, and her subjective report is that today she is content and has a positive outlook on life. My hope is that this is true more often than not. Although she cannot be considered to be cured, applying the psychoanalytic notion of cure, Elizabeth did, however, meet the criteria psychologist Mary Harvey (cited in Herman 1992) lists for the resolution of trauma:

> PTSD physiological symptoms become manageable.
> The individual is able to tolerate the feelings associated with the traumatic memories.
> Memory of the event is a coherent narrative, with feeling present.
> Self-esteem is restored.
> Important relationships are reestablished.
> A coherent system of meaning and belief encompasses the story of the trauma. [pp. 212–213]

During her treatment, she increased her capacity to differentiate and to tolerate her affects, increased symbolization and verbalization, and decreased her somatization. Through her treatment, she was able to mourn her mother and sibling's death, to establish internal representations of them, and to openly memorialize them with her family. She reconnected with the lost maternal relatives. By working in the transference, she became more conscious of her guilt, fears of loss, wishes for union, fears of dependency, dangerous tendency to repeat, and need for self-care.

REFERENCES

Herman, J. L. (1992). *Trauma and Recovery*. New York: Basic Books.
Krystal, H. (1978). Trauma and affects. *Psychoanalytic Study of the Child* 33:81–116. New Haven: Yale University Press.

Silverman, P., Nickman, S., and Worden, W. (1992). Detachment revisited: the child's reconstruction of a dead parent. *American Journal of Orthopsychiatry* 62(4):494–503.

Terr, L. (1987). Childhood trauma and the creative product: a look at the early lives and later works of Poe, Wharton, Magritte, Hitchcock, and Bergman. *Psychoanalytic Study of the Child* 42:545–572. New Haven: Yale University Press.

CHAPTER SIX

Failure in the Mother–Child Dyad

ELIZABETH FLYNN CAMPBELL

PSYCHOSOMATIC ILLNESS FROM AN
OBJECT-RELATIONS PERSPECTIVE

The advent of an object-relations framework in the 1950s provided a wider window through which we could view psychosomatic expressions. While Freud and other early theorists explored the mind–body relationship, they did so under the rather constrictive constructs of drive theory, wherein psychosomatic illness was considered a pathological outcome of drive conflict. Object relations offered a broader perspective that considered the relationship between infant and caregiver as a critical determinant of the child's ability to establish internal affect regulating and elaborating functions. Specifically, the quality of the early mother–child dyad was seen to determine whether the child could create an internalized, self-soothing "other" to help differentiate and integrate the ongoing onslaught of affects.

In recent years, much has been written about the psychic repercussions of the very early mother–child relationship, particularly in regard to elaboration of affects. Winnicott (1953), Krystal (1988), McDougall (1991), Deri (1984), and others have added much to our understanding of how failures in the mother's ability to receive and elaborate on the child's communication can lead to psychosomatic expression.

The following case vignette illustrates the failure of the mother–child dyad in regard to affect regulation and elaboration. While it is virtually impossible to conclusively establish whether this failure resulted from constitutional proclivities or from problems with the mother's attunement and response to the child's affective experience, it does seem that, in this case, the mother had considerable trouble with affect tolerance and elaboration, and thus was unable to foster a self-soothing internalized presence within her child.

THE CASE OF EMMA

Emma sought my help in a last-ditch attempt to alleviate her suicidal depression. She was clearly desperate for someone to help her with her overwhelming feeling that life was just too much. For most of Emma's 52 years, life had felt like an impossible struggle, and, for the past several years starting shortly after her mother died, Emma would comfort herself with the mantra-like chant of "I just want to die." This ultimate lullaby would soothe Emma because it offered the promise of final rest from her lifelong struggle to tolerate her experience of the world as traumatic and catastrophic. In fact, Emma's early life was rife with trauma and catastrophe. However, it is not entirely accurate to interpret Emma's suicidal longings as the direct result of her early trauma. Rather, her desire to die was the result of her severe emotional depletion from trying to cope with so much early loss and trauma without the presence of an appropriately self-soothing, comforting maternal representation.

While trauma at an early stage in life always poses substantial challenges for the developing child, the presence of a soothing, affect-elaborating other can go a long way in mitigating the harmful effects of trauma on the developing psyche. Unfortunately for Emma, her mother was unable to help her integrate the considerable loss, anxiety, and terror she experienced early in life. In fact, in addition to not having an internalized maternal representation who could provide comfort and continuity while Emma struggled with severe loss and trauma, Emma also experienced her mother as needing her to "hold things together." When her analysis was dealing with particularly painful and threatening early childhood experiences, Emma would often say, "I'm falling apart" or "I'm going down the drain." I believe these utterances reflected her sense of having no internalized, affect-regulating, maternal representation to hold onto when she felt overwhelmed by affect.

In elaborating on Winnicott's (1953) concept of the "holding mother," Deri (1984) writes, "A mother who holds well gives her infant an initial feeling of unity within his or her skin. Loving and secure holding lay the foundation for basic trust; bad holding for distrust and 'unthinkable anxieties,' such as sensations of falling into a bottomless abyss" (p. 258). She then describes an infant's experience of abandonment as a "narcissistic mortification of such intensity that its effect is most probably experienced as mutilation of the incipient body-self." While Emma was not an infant at the time of her trauma, I believe that she needed the kind of "holding" mother that Deri and Winnicott describe the infant as needing. In other words, serious environmental trauma in the life of a young child may require the attuned kind of mothering most often associated with the infancy stage. Unfortunately, many traumatized children develop precocious adaptations to the external environment, making them even less likely to get the "regressed" mothering they actually need. In Emma's case, her mother's failure to provide this attuned kind of mothering in the face of severe trauma meant that Emma's soma was forced, in the absence of an internalized, affect-elaborating, maternal representation, to compensate for the absence of this psychic structure.

Trauma and the Developing Psyche

When Emma was 3½ years old her life changed in two important ways. Her little sister was born and her father left the family farm to work in a war-related job in a faraway city. Six months after her father's departure, her mother left the farm with Emma and her two sisters to join their father for a new life in the new city. A week after Emma and her family were reunited with their father, he kissed the girls good night, went to work, and was killed in a catastrophic, work-related accident. Two days after her father's death, Emma's mother drove the children away from their short-lived reunion with their father and back to the family farm. Immediately following the funeral, her mother drove the girls to a different faraway town, left Emma and her baby sister with a relative, and left Emma's older sister with another relative in another town. Then the mother drove to a relative's home several hundred miles away, came down with the flu, and spent several weeks away from her daughters while she recovered from her illness.

While she was separated from her mother during her mother's recuperation (and within a month after she had suddenly lost her father), Emma developed a hard and enlarged stomach. Following her mother's return and after several intrusive and painful procedures, Emma was diagnosed as having a rare and terminal liver disease. Her stomach grew rapidly, and she soon looked like a pregnant little girl. Over the next nine years, Emma was in and out of the hospital and doctors' offices for many painful, humiliating, and intrusive procedures. Finally, when she was 12, a biopsy revealed that the diagnosis was incorrect and that a life-threatening operation might remove the six-pound tumor that was found to surround her liver. The surgery was successful, but upon awakening after the operation Emma bitterly regretted that she had not died and ended her long and lonely travail.

Most readers would agree that Emma's sudden loss of her father at such an important oedipal age, her mother's temporary "abandonment" of her within weeks of his death, and the onset of a freakish and humiliating physical deformation would all have a tremendous impact on a child's developing psychic structure. However, my point in describing this case is not to expound on the psychic consequences of early trauma, but rather to demonstrate the critical importance of the mother's role in affect elaboration and integration, especially under traumatic circumstances.

Symbolization and Psychosomatic Illness

Emma's case is particularly interesting because she manifests strong psychosomatic tendencies at the same time that she possesses an exceptionally rich ability to symbolize her emotional experience. The capacity for symbolization is contingent on the infant taking over (through internalization) the affect-soothing and affect-integrating function of the mother. This internalization then allows the infant some independence from the mother, as it learns to symbolize or "think about" its experience. In writing about the failure of symbolization and resulting psychosomatic expressions, Krystal (1988) states, "Symbolization of a conflict makes possible dealing with the cognitive aspect of an affect such as anxiety. In the absence of such capabilities, patients have to contend with the 'expressive,' that is, the physiological aspects of their affective responses, and thus are prone to psychosomatic illnesses" (p. 249). Without this capacity to symbolize, the child would continue to experience strong affect as potentially annihilating (since without an internalized representation, there is no "psychological distance" from the child's affective experience). Lacking an internalized, self-soothing mental representation that enables children to "think about" and thus acquire some mastery over their affective experience, they may use the soma as a means of expressing "unsymbolized" affect. Given the trauma of Emma's early life and her mother's inability to help her process affects related to the trauma, we might expect Emma to exhibit a marked inability to symbolize affective experience, thus resulting in psychosomatic illness.

Maternal Influence on the Psychic Elaboration of Affects

In describing her understanding of the genesis of some types of affective disturbances, McDougall (1991) writes:

> In several personal histories of [patients with affective disorders], one parent, usually the father, had died or left the family in the patient's early infancy. The mothers were frequently presented as overpossessive and overattentive while at the same time heedless of the child's affective states. It seemed to me that, for whatever reasons, a truly caretaking mother-image had never been introjected into the child's inner psychic structure, there to remain as an object of identification, allowing the child to become a good parent to itself. [p. 157]

This description bears some resemblance to Emma's early life situation. Emma describes her mother as a woman who had no tolerance for emotions and, in ways large and small, gave her the message that emotions were "silly" and indulgent. Emma recalls that at her father's funeral, her mother admonished her not to cry because she didn't want people to feel sorry for them. She also recalls that following her father's death she often said to her mother, "I don't like anything." I understand this vague, generalized expression of negative affect to be the result of her mother's intolerance and rejection of a more articulated and precise expression of Emma's intense pain, anger, and guilt about her father's death. As a 4-year-old who had just lost her father at the height of her oedipal infatuation, Emma was in desperate need of a mother who could help her to elaborate her overwhelming and confusing affective experience.

Unfortunately for Emma, her mother was particularly unable to process her own affects, and consequently communicated to Emma that she was on her own as far as her emotional experience was concerned. In fact, due to her inability to tolerate or "know" her own feelings about suddenly being a widow with three little girls, her mother's debilitating flu following the death of her husband could be understood as a psychosomatic breakdown in the face of overwhelming affect and inadequate psychic structure to elaborate and consequently integrate that affect.

As mentioned earlier, within one month of her father's sudden death and her mother's temporary abandonment while she recovered from the flu, Emma developed a hard and enlarged stomach, which ultimately turned out to be a tumor growing around her liver. While it is impossible to know for certain, one must wonder if this physical growth was in any way a psychosomatic expression of Emma's terrible loss, confusion, and aloneness at this time. In light of Freud's understanding of identification as the primary means through which we integrate the loss of important people in our lives, we can only speculate that Emma's tumor might have represented to her young psyche the internalized presence of her father or possibly a baby from her father.

Two realities marked Emma's ensuing childhood. The first was that she learned early on that her pragmatic mother rejected the reality and validity of affective experience and thus failed to help her manage and psychically process her considerable emotional experience. This maternal response is summed up by Emma's remembrance of her mother's oft-repeated query, "Don't you ever do anything you don't *feel* like doing?" with a derisive emphasis on the word *feel*. The second was that Emma was in and out of hospitals for months at a time from the ages of 4 through 13, undergoing scores of procedures as the doctors tried to understand her rare, puzzling, and life-threatening illness. Thus, while her emotional reality was consistently rejected and dismissed by her mother, her soma was the subject of intense scrutiny.

Following her father's death and the onset of her enlarged stomach, Emma began a lifelong history of somatic manifestations. She was a chronic bed-wetter until the age of 11 and has had a serious and disruptive sleep inhibition for the past fifty years wherein she either cannot fall asleep or wakes up suddenly with a tremendous sense of impending catastrophe. She has had urinary incontinence since her mid-forties and rheumatoid arthritis since her late forties. Her skin feels painfully dry and the soles of her feet itch so badly that she often has bleeding sores from prolonged scratching. During the winter months she complains of intense coldness in her hands and feet. Early in her analysis she would experience diarrhea in anticipation of my vacation. Since starting her analysis she has developed a new symptom wherein she must vigorously rub her eyes because of intense itching. While many of these ailments can be explained in terms of physiology (i.e., a failed surgery from her childhood disrupted her circulatory system, thus causing coldness in hands and feet and itching), the onset and timing of these various ailments are indicative of Emma's failed psychic communication system.

When the Soma "Communicates" in Place of the Psyche

Many patients who lack adequate psychic structure or adequate internalized self and other representations are forced to "express" psychic conflict and pain through psychosomatic illness. McDougall (1991) has written extensively about alexithymics, who have no words for their emotions and thus often use the body to express their "ejected" affects, leading to various psychosomatic expressions. She writes, "Affect that receives no psychic elaboration or compensation for its suppression, leaving in its wake nothing but a mental blank, runs the risk of continuing as a purely somatic event, thus paving the way for psychosomatic disorganization" (p. 153).

Krystal (1988) has described how psychosomatic expression can become prevalent when the child experiences the mother as prohibiting the internalization of maternal self-caring functions. In light of this prohibition, the psychic elaboration of affects is derailed, thus leaving the soma to bear the burden of psychic expression. He writes, "In the experience of 'good enough' mothering there develops the crucial feeling that it is permissible for the child to exercise a certain measure of self-regulation of his affective and hedonic states, as well as exercising for himself the subjective part of self-comforting so that he can relax and sleep" (p. 194).

Deri (1984) has also written extensively about how the mother's inability to help the child differentiate and elaborate her affective experiences leads to a failure of symbolization. This means that affective experience cannot be worked through by the normal psychic elaboration processes of dreams, metaphor, and sublimation. Consequently, affects are too dangerous and overwhelming to be "known" in a traditional psychical fashion and must be experienced (or more accurately, not experienced) through psychosomatic symptoms.

Unlike many patients who have experienced early trauma without adequate psychic elaboration and integration of the experience, Emma is not alexithymic. In fact, she has a very rich symbolic life and uses dreams extensively to express psychic conflict. One early dream Emma had a few months into her analysis illustrates, among other things, her mother's failure in helping her to psychically elaborate and hence integrate her traumatic affects. In this dream, Emma is up in a loft with other people and wants to get down to somewhere she has been before. She knows that there used to be a way down from the loft but that was long ago and she's not sure if it still exists. There is a gauzy drape that hangs from the loft to the floor but she's not sure if it can support her.

We came to understand this as an important early transference dream that explores whether I can support her as she "descends" into her past to integrate the split-off feelings resulting from the sudden loss of her father and the trauma of her illness. I believe the loft represents her internalization of a mother who valued "lofty" rational and intellectual qualities and dismissed emotional experience. It also symbolizes her own intellectual defense against her traumatic childhood experiences. Emma's psyche was asking the critical question of whether I could "hold" her emotionally (unlike her mother) as she descends into her heretofore mostly split-off experience of the world as a brutal, unsafe, and generally traumatic place.

Symbolization as Compensation for the Failed Dyad

In addition to a very rich and elaborative dream life, Emma is also a poet. I have understood much of her tendency toward psychosomatic expression as a result of her mother's inability to receive and elaborate her emotional experience. Emma's early traumatic experiences of the world were then relegated to somatic expression. If we view this as a failure of psychic elaboration and symbolization, how is it that this same woman can exhibit such a highly developed capacity for symbolization, as expressed in her dreams and in her poetry?

I believe that her facility with words and symbols is somewhat compensatory. That is, while Emma clearly exhibits a critical failure in her symbolization processes (resulting in serious psychosomatic expression), she also has tried to compensate for her mother's rejection of the symbolic (emotional) world through a strong identification with the power of words. In fact, early in her analysis Emma brought me copies of several poems she had written over the years, one of which in particular expresses her desire that words (symbols) will provide the psychic elaboration she needs to integrate her past trauma.

This poem, which dramatically expresses her love affair with words and symbols, illustrates Emma's lifelong struggle. While it expresses her hope that her mastery of language will provide the integration of early trauma that her mother could not, this hope is couched in the imagery of the soma (e.g., "I eat it and drink it, shit, pee and sweat words. . . .") This is her dilemma; she needs to have access to her split-off, traumatized early experience in order to feel whole, and yet so much of this experience is imprisoned in her soma, and thus not accessed psychically. In her attempt to compensate for her mother's failure, Emma has mastered several foreign languages and written her doctoral dissertation on the use of ambiguity as a poetical device. She has tried to master words and language in order to release those aspects of her experience held hostage in the somatic prison, but, as analysts well know, words alone are not enough. If they are to heal, the words must be expressed within a relationship that embodies the original failed dyad.

Use of the Body to Express the "Unthought Known"

Another way of looking at Emma's dilemma in integrating her traumatic loss of her father and her ensuing illness is through Bollas's concept of the unthought known. In describing a child's limited capabilities to resolve traumatic situations successfully, Bollas (1987) writes,

The concept of working through or of time's contribution to the resolution of life issues is unknown to the child, as traumas are not experienced as events in life but as life defining. It is my view that if the parents are unable, through perception and appropriate empathic understanding, to transform the particular fix that a child is in by virtue of some life problem, then such a fix becomes an identity sense that is conserved by the child as partly definitive of life itself. . . . All persons will, in my view, therefore, conserve rather than represent some states of self. The unthought known is a substantial part of each of us. [p. 111]

It is the continual task of each parent, as a transformational object, to perceive and identify the nature of a child's ongoing needs and dilemmas, then to find some appropriate way of speaking up about the specific issue, and then to find some means of facilitating a negotiated solution which enables the child to develop. [p. 114]

In these terms, her mother was unable to provide such perception and transformation of Emma's experience, thus leaving Emma to "conserve" her experience of the world as terrifying and catastrophic. I believe her conservation of early traumatic experience is expressed in her soma, particularly in her sleep patterns. In a very real sense, Emma's lack of psychic elaboration and integration of early trauma is evident in her ongoing vigilance and need to wake abruptly from sleep. She regularly wakes feeling she is on the verge of falling into a bottomless abyss, thus expressing her sense of impending annihilation.

Psychoanalysis and the Subway

In describing the critical role symbolization plays in the efficacy of psycho-analysis, Deri (1984) writes,

If a person has not had the experience of a "good-enough" mother, psychoanalytic treatment later in life can offer a second chance to remedy the deficiencies caused by the unsatisfactory manner in which the unempathic mother handed over the world to her child. Thanks to the multiple function of symbolization, the psychoanalyst, within the framework of the psychoanalytic situation, can *symbolically* re-create and rectify the original mother–child situation, in which the mother failed her child. [p. 327]

Emma entered treatment with an exceptional capacity for symbolization. Early in treatment she used the following metaphor to describe her dilemma in trusting the "holding capacity" of the analytic space. She likened her early experience in therapy to holding onto a strap handle as the subway train is moving, describing how difficult and scary it is to let go of the strap to switch to another, even when one knows that it is necessary to switch in order to approach the exit door.

Much of our work together has been about the terrifying and vulnerable transition between removing one's grasp on the old strap and finding the new strap. In the intermediary space and time between the two "straps" (the psychoanalytic space), Emma has had to risk reexperiencing the traumatic feelings from her early childhood. As far as her soma is concerned, this intermediary space is terrifying, for as long as her split-off childhood experience is expressed somatically, there can be no elaboration, mastery, and integration of past trauma. In some sense, the terror of her fourth year of life is timeless, as long as it is "locked" in her soma.

Despite the terror of this "soma to psyche" translation process, Emma has, for the most part, been an eager analysand. Much of her poetry (written prior to entering analysis) contains language about making connections. I believe that she has brought this yearning for connection into her analysis. She strives for a mother who will help her to psychically elaborate her traumatic experience and thus escape the closed system of somatization. Emma's tenacity for healing and her eloquent use of metaphor, dreams, and poetry have contributed not only to her own renewed interest in life but also to this therapist's respect for the human capacity to creatively survive trauma.

REFERENCES

Bollas, C. (1987). *The Shadow of the Object.* New York: Columbia University Press.

Deri, S. K. (1984). *Symbolization and Creativity.* New York: International Universities Press.

Krystal, H. (1988). *Integration and Self Healing.* Hillsdale, NJ: Analytic Press.

McDougall, J. (1991). *Theaters of the Mind.* New York: Brunner/Mazel.

Winnicott, D. W. (1953). *Playing and Reality.* New York: Basic Books.

CHAPTER SEVEN

Trauma, Fantasy, and Psychosomatosis: A Case of Long-Term Treatment

FREDERICK FEIRSTEIN

This chapter presents the case of a thirteen-year analysis occurring when society is challenging us to drastically shorten treatment, when there is pressure "to accelerate the tempo of analytic therapy to suit the rush of American life." This quotation does not refer to pressure from the HMOs or the psychiatric establishment or support groups offering shortcuts. Rather, it was written in 1937 by Freud in "Analysis Terminable and Interminable." The pressures earlier analysts encountered have been obscured by history, partly because one of the ways they have had of dealing with such objections was to explore them as analytic issues, which in turn had a way of reaffirming their values and conviction about doing analytic work. It is in this spirit that I present a case of long-term treatment, trauma, and unconscious fantasy.

A background of trauma often leads to a long-term treatment, not only because it intensifies the repetition compulsion but also because of what it does to our symbolization processes, one of our strongest allies in doing analytic work. Trauma teaches us to constrict or bypass our symbolization processes altogether for fear our fantasy life might bring on catastrophe again. In place of relatively flexible symbolization processes leading to more pliable neuroses, trauma leads affect to be bound in severe obsessionalism, buried in addictiveness, or minimally symbolized in clichés and discharged in rigidly repetitive acting out and somatization.

These were the various ways that John came to handle his affect, each of which I am going to highlight in this chapter. In the 1970s John was referred by our clinic for twice-a-week treatment. He was 23, tall, and good-looking. He came from the kind of unsophisticated background that these days might have led him to a trauma support group or an HMO for a quick fix instead of to a clinic attached to an analytic institute. He was the son of a blue-collar family from a Pennsylvania factory town where he played high school soccer and was a highly talented young cellist. But he didn't carry himself in a way that suggested he could have mixed it up on a soccer field or lose himself emotionally in playing a stringed instrument. He moved stiffly and tentatively, as if my office was a minefield. He talked in a flat, affectless way as he described his girlfriend's list of complaints that brought him into treatment. She said he was passive and procrastinating, without any ambition, and was always in control of his emotions. When I asked him what was troubling *him*, he said she was right, that he wasn't feeling much, that he was all bound up and uptight. He said that he was stuck in his relationship with her, that they were constantly fighting over who took in the laundry or did the bills, and that he was tired of it, tired of her complaints about his lack of ambition because it frustrated him.

He then said, with practically the only bit of feeling in the session, that he felt like a car in neutral. John taught me to pay careful attention to such a felt cliché in the first session because ultimately it would lead us both to aspects of trauma and to the unconscious fantasies that helped make his traumas psychically enduring ones and keep him stuck in neurosis and somatization. The car would become a key symbol that would repeat itself in transferential communications and dreams throughout the case, and signal shifts in his psychic equilibrium and, therefore, where the course of treatment would go.

When I asked him in what ways was he feeling like a car in neutral, he said that he should either commit himself to going ahead in business (he had a low-level job in a market research firm) or go back to the cello. But he hadn't picked up the cello in years and now it seemed too late. He then described how he came to give it up. He said that he had played from age 9 until he was in college, where he won a competition to study in Vienna. But then after winning it he doubted that that was what he really wanted, and he quit school and went home to his blue-collar family. For two years he hung around, working like his father in the factory or in a grocery—a locale connected, as I'd learn, to childhood trauma. He drank, took drugs, ate "crap," as he put it, although his mother tried to push him to go back to school. He couldn't explain the depressed state he was in to his parents or himself, except to say he wanted them, particularly his father, to tell him they loved him.

He described his father as a silent and abusive Scandinavian who would come home from the factory, down two quarts of beer, and take a nap. When John would wake him, his father would hit him, sometimes chasing him around the house first. He'd hit John practically every day, and on top of that, John said, "He would give me no real guidance." On the other hand he described a warm Italian mother with intellectual interests, and a cross to bear—this violent husband who was beneath her.

One of the things that fascinated me about the case was the way the picture of his parents would change dramatically, as I worked with his resistances and the repression of affect lifted.

His initial resistance was to come in with prepared material and little affect, and bury me in content about his work and problems with his girlfriend. He'd sometimes seem clinging, inviting me in to comment, looking for answers in my expressions. But practically every time I did say something, he'd say, "Oh, I thought of that" and go right on talking. I'd feel frustrated and confused by this. On the one hand I was seeing a "good patient," trying to please me with his content. On the other hand he was shutting me out with his style.

If I were beginning to work with a patient like him today, I'd probably first say to myself that, given the history of his father's abusing him, this resistance is reflecting an alexithymic defense, that is, a cognitive failure to recognize or acknowledge affect. Transferentially, John is inviting contact with me as he tried to wake his father, and at the same time he's keeping his distance to protect himself from being retraumatized by his father's sadism. But that's now and from the perspective of trauma theory. Back then I got some clarity by thinking he was an obsessive, trying to control what went on between us as he controlled his emotions. In retrospect, that way of thinking about resistance was very helpful because, as it turned out, there was an overlap between his obsessiveness and his alexithymia, reflecting the interplay between his unconscious fantasies and traumas. The alexithymia protected him against trauma, and the obsessionalism against the wishes the traumas both evoked and seemed a fitting punishment for.

As we'll see, this resistance of speaking with a barrage of content and little affect, and cutting me off at the same time, would be a key one throughout the case. By addressing his constricted symbolization processes as they manifested themselves in his flat, colorless style of talking, I would find a way into both his obsessionalism and his alexithymia.

After a few sessions I called attention to how he was talking to me in an airtight, emotionless tone of voice, when the content called for it to be charged.

This intervention brought up striking memories of how he'd defend himself against feelings of fear and rage when his father hit him, how the only way he could keep himself from crumbling was to say to himself and sometimes to his father, "You can hit me but you can't touch me."

Over the next few months, as John tried to come to grips with his father's abuse, I felt very empathetic to him; his father hit him almost every day. He had real rage, which he expressed at times, and deep resentment. But most of the time his style of talking, especially when he tried to connect all his present problems to his father's abusiveness, struck me as having a manufactured quality, as if he were talking by rote. I began to feel at these times as if I were listening to an open-and-shut case against the man and started to feel bored.

In a session six months into treatment, I reflected to John how the way he was talking was making me feel, and that I was puzzled by it. He laughed and said with some relief that he felt bored, too; even more, sleepy. He associated to feeling sleepy around his mother, and for once didn't follow up on his association with affectless content. He fell silent.

In the next session he brought in a piece of a dream, his first dream. He was in a sportscar he couldn't start up, an old car, from the late 1950s, with leather seats. He first associated to a leather soccer ball and how he would play defense brilliantly but when it came to taking the offensive, he couldn't score a goal. Then he associated to one of his rare visits home a couple of years ago and seeing a strap in the attic. He said it was a short piece of leather that his *mother* had strapped him with, and then went on to tell me the history of the strap, how his mother had inherited it from her father, who strapped his son, who in turn strapped *his* son. I sat there dumbfounded. Here he was talking about his mother beating him, and he was chatting about the strap like it was a family heirloom.

When I brought him back to his association about his *mother* using the strap on him and asked him for details ("How often did she strap you?" "Oh, about once a week." "How did you feel about that?" "She strapped my brother, too"), he got irritated by my questions and kept minimizing what his mother did and said his real problems were with his father.

I now began to understand why I'd feel bored sometimes in his describing those hitting scenes: he'd been leaving out his mother and his feelings about *her*. Where was she? Why wasn't she protecting him both from his father and her own sadism? I couldn't get that short strap out of my mind.

Following that session we went through a rough period before John got to any feelings about his mother for hitting him too, and toward me for calling attention to her. He acted out on his girlfriend and at work. He picked up another woman whom he wasn't particularly attracted to, had a brief affair, and then dumped her and provoked battles with his boss, a woman, at work.

As I began to interpret his behavior as expressing feelings he must have toward me, the acting out gradually stopped and the intense affect still unconnected to his mother came into the transference. He missed sessions. He wanted to cut down on treatment because he had credit card debt. He'd forget to pay me and wondered if treatment was any good at all. When I'd ask him about this "forgetting," he'd tell me in an affectless way about "the reality," or say, "Can't a cigar just be a cigar? I just forgot."

I said to him, "I think that what you're forgetting are feelings you can't seem to tell me directly." Then all hell broke loose. He'd tell me with great emotion that he was on the verge of tearing my "fucking office" apart, of ripping every book off my shelves, of throwing his chair through the window, of getting me in a headlock and controlling me physically.

For a couple of weeks his explosiveness was intense. Although I was glad to see emotion, I'd also feel a little scared, and sometimes counterphobically tough. I struggled for a while, trying to sort out what he was inducing in me from my own countertransference.

Then a breakthrough came in a session nine months into treatment, when he was going to pay off the bill he'd run up with a bonus he was getting from work. Instead he came in with a spanking new pair of leather boots and wanted me to admire them. I asked him, "With your cash flow problems, how did you manage to pay for them?" "Oh, with the bonus I got yesterday."

I asked, "How did you expect me to feel?" He thought about it for a while, then said, "Angry. That I'm sneaky." Then he had an association to stealing money from his mother's leather purse when he was 8 or 9. I asked him how he felt when he did that. He couldn't remember but said he felt very angry at her. For the first time affect toward her, but not attached to memory yet, was coming in.

I asked him, "Why did you have to steal? Couldn't you ask for money when you needed it?"

He remembered with some puzzlement how, when he needed money and didn't want to steal, he'd go to his father, who would give it to him gladly. Then he told me, with more puzzlement over the warm feelings he was remembering, how his father would drive him for two hours to another city to take cello lessons, wait for him there, and then drive back the two hours. Over the next few sessions, as John started to recover some tender feelings toward his father, he began to express angry feelings at his mother for being tight with money, for her fears he'd get hurt if he played a rough sport, and, finally, contradicting his overprotective version of her, for hitting him with that strap.

At this point I felt the time was right to interpret his defense of displacement, of putting *all* of his rage onto his father, rage that also should be addressed to his mother, rage that we were seeing in the transference and in his acting out.

As he struggled to reconcile his memories of good moments with his father with the hitting scenes, I could finally ask, "Where was your mother when he did that?"

Slowly, angrily, with more anger than I'd yet seen, John supplied the missing details of his set story. His father would come home from work, down two quarts of beer, and try to sleep. But then John's mother would present a list of complaints about John's behavior during the day. Then his father would hit him to "discipline" him. Or his parents would get into an argument. He'd take his mother's side, and his father, feeling betrayed by John, would hit him.

Now, looking back, I can understand where some of the earlier transference was. When John first came in with a list of complaints that his girlfriend made about him, he was complying with his mother and masochistically bringing himself to his father, but also an idealized father who he hoped could stop her and give him guidance.

What I did learn then, by the end of the second year of treatment, as John got in touch with these memories and feelings about his mother, was that our working alliance was getting stronger in part because a grandmother transference was beginning to develop. This was his maternal grandmother who had suffered from a severe chronic illness, and whose home was a haven for John amidst abuse. Her house was the only place where he could relax and eat calmly, and not have to sneak sweets as he did at home. With my office becoming that kind of place for him, John felt safe enough to "let go" and talk about his mother.

With rancor he'd talk about "that bitch who'd sic her German shepherd on me if I didn't behave. She'd turn me into her 'little man' because she wasn't getting enough from the factory worker she felt she'd married beneath her." Hints of the oedipal issues that would emerge were here. But it was his narcissistic rage and mortification that were at the forefront of treatment now.

Although John got upset at the extent of the rage he was experiencing toward his mother, and toward both parents for not protecting him from each other, he also expressed relief at finally being able to get to a real emotionality. He felt a sense of adventure in experiencing it and in analysis. Looking back, this was the beginning of a long separation process from his parents—another element along with the dogged interlocking of trauma and fantasy—that made for long-term treatment.

About his newfound emotionality he'd say with optimism, characteristically using the symbol of the car, "Maybe I'm beginning to get out of neutral. I really want to move with this." We'll see that whenever John was ready to move into a new phase of treatment, whether related to separation or to a piece of trauma emerging from repression or to instinctual material connected to it, images of the car (representing his self) or leather (representing trauma to the self and his response to it) would come up, as it was coming up now, as it had come up in the first dream and his association to the leather strap, and as it had come up in his transferential communication with the leather cowboy boots and his association to the leather purse.

In response to his expression of adventurousness, in his saying he "wanted to get out of neutral and really move with this," I suggested that it would be helpful if he came three times a week and used the couch.

John was intrigued. He eyed the couch and said he'd thought of going on it several times before and wanted to take it up as a challenge. But when he got on it he expressed, along with bravado, fear—of my being out of sight, being distant, of my "withholding" myself from him. He also now felt fears that my suggesting he come more often meant I thought he was crazy. He brought up memories of being 3 and hearing how his father went "out of control" in the grocery store where he was working when his factory went out on strike, how his father threw things off the shelves before the police could get there and hospitalize him. And then when his father came home from the hospital, and for years afterward, he'd obsessively ruminate about how he had caused the fiery deaths of a flight crew during the war in Korea where he worked as an airplane mechanic.

As repression partly lifted here, John connected his fear of being on the couch with the distancing way his mother said the doctor told her she and John should treat his father when he was released from the hospital.

When I asked John if his mother would act this way with *him*, he got very upset, and angrily remembered how often she'd go in and out with him emotionally, being there one minute and suddenly not the next, and how he hated that.

He then remembered having fears she'd also physically abandon him as she'd threaten to abandon his father. Sometimes when his parents would fight, she'd pack her bags, gather the children, walk out, and once made it to the bus station. Sometimes she'd threaten John with a similar abandonment. When John didn't behave, she'd threaten to send him packing to "The Farm," a mysterious made-up place that terrified him. As he lay there, the thought of that terror put him in a rage.

Over the next few weeks the old transference resistances, partly representing the asymbolic discharge of affect connected to trauma, reappeared. He missed sessions, he got into battles with his girlfriend, and when she left him to go on a business trip to the Caribbean, he had a one-night stand and confessed it to her.

When I interpreted how his missing sessions and leaving his girlfriend when she left him was an acting out of feelings toward me for removing myself physically when he went on the couch, John brought in a dream. He was going into a department store with a woman who reminded him of his mother. They went to the children's department on the third floor to shop for clothes, but then he got lost.

His associations led him back to age 3 again, when he felt he actually had lost his mother, and his father as well. Over the next several sessions he recovered lost affect from that time. He remembered sadly the time before age 3 when things seemed golden, when both parents got him whatever he wanted. He remembered going into the hospital for a tonsillectomy. (He had suffered from earaches for his first three years and was in a lot of pain from which he'd get relief when his mother held him.) He remembered how after the operation his parents filled his bed with toys. But then immediately things became leaden. His father was hospitalized. Not long afterward John's mother went into the hospital to give birth. She came out withdrawn from him in what sounded like a postpartum depression. His grandmother helped take care of him. But then his grandmother's illness worsened, and his mother left him with a next-door neighbor for most of the day—as she'd never done before—while she tended to her own mother.

John felt totally abandoned by his mother, and with his father "crazy" and his grandmother not available, he remembered getting into rages. He'd take his toys and kitchen equipment apart as he had wanted to take my office apart. His parents nicknamed him "Destructo," and from then on his mother decided John had to be "disciplined" and, as John remembered it, *that's* when his parents started hitting him regularly.

With the emergence of these affectively charged memories, we rounded out the first phase of treatment. What seemed clear now, in the fourth year of treatment, was that the rage John had been expressing was narcissistic at the traumatic loss of his self-objects. It also seemed clear that his main resistance— his flat, distancing style—not only reflected an alexithymic defense against trauma but also an identification with his mother to help him defend against rage at her withdrawals. But it was only months later when we got to the anal defenses he also employed to contain his rage that John was finally able to emotionally connect what was going on in the transference with the rest of his life.

The anal material came up with a somatic symptom, constipation, which I would learn was not only a lifelong asymbolic way of dealing with trauma but also a mute expression of a powerful unconscious fantasy. As John came in talking with anger about his parents hitting him, and his anxieties at being abandoned by them, he also would casually mention that he was feeling constipated. I asked him if there might be some connection between the constipation and what he was talking about. He said that from the time he was 4 or 5 until he was 12 (when his grandmother died), he would withhold his bowel movements and not defecate for a week at a time. He would lie down near the stream by his grandmother's house, relax, and then run back to the dark comfort of his grandparents' bathroom and finally let go.

I interpreted that to defend himself against his rage then, which he was expressing now, he had to find a way to contain whatever was inside of him. After all, if he expressed it, not only could "Destructo" be hit, but he could lose his parents completely. He could be sent away to "The Farm" if he didn't behave. So he kept his bowel movements in, until he could let go where he felt safe—his grandmother's house—just as he was letting go in the safety of my office. With this interpretation his constipation cleared up, although it would return time and time again until it reached full symbolic expression in a dream that would lead us back to a key unconscious fantasy.

For now, I'd make transference resistance interpretations along these lines: for instance, now when he'd withhold money or time, I'd interpret his actions as ways of defending himself against anger and anxiety he'd feel when he got close to me, because he needed to defend himself against the same feelings when he got close to his abandoning parents. As we dealt with this in the transference, John would verbalize his wanting not to pay his bill or to come in late, instead of doing it.

So now, in his fifth year of treatment, as we worked through his conflicts over intimacy as we were experiencing it, John was able to clearly connect it with the rest of his life—how when he felt close to his girlfriend, he would get anxious she'd leave him and would try to control his anxiety by seeing other women, or angrily test her by procrastinating or withdrawing emotionally, or doing whatever would drive her up a wall.

As this behavior became more and more ego alien, John also began to see how very frequently she *would* withdraw from him emotionally and get depressed like his mother. He began to feel that in many ways she actually was like his mother, and he started questioning why he picked someone like her in the first place and if it was good for him to be in such a relationship.

As John began to understand how the transference and his relationship with his girlfriend repeated his early object relations, he was also able to see how his work problems repeated them. Now he partly understood how he

could be "Destructo" with his cello. Although there was an oedipal component here, which we'll get to later, the narcissistic rage and separation fears
were what he was able to understand and express now. He said the cello was
something his parents had wanted for him, and giving it up was a way of
getting back at them for abandoning him. He began to see, dimly at first,
how anxious he was now in separating from the self representation (the
"image of myself," as he put it) that connected him to his blue-collar father.

As we'll see, conflicts around making this separation would lead him
both to prolong treatment and to try to short-circuit the termination phase.
For now it would keep him working with his pencil, as he put it, as his father
pushed a factory broom. At this point John would be unable to get out of
neutral, put his words into action and leave his low-level job, or come to a
realistic assessment of his girlfriend, until the next phase of treatment having
to do with earlier trauma that resulted in fixation of affect at the anal stage.

As we were into the sixth year of treatment, John, having missed the
deadline for applying to college one semester, now was about to miss it again
and tried to draw me into "helping" him to stop procrastinating. He would
tell me he was procrastinating with what I realized was a sly pleasure in his
tone of voice, which I reflected back to him. With that, his tone of voice and
imagery changed. His speech became flavored with a great deal of anal
expressions. He'd say "Oh shit" or "Holy shit" at least ten times a session.
He'd say things like, "My basic problem is staying in neutral, not wanting to
get off the pot" (the early, stalled vehicle for him). "It's up to me now, I'm
going to get rolling, I'm going to get my ass in gear." And when he felt some
enthusiasm about following through with his plans to go back to school,
he'd say, "I'm really flowing with it now. I have to let go."

I called attention, as always, to his style of talking, in this case to his
imagery, and in one session John suddenly had an association to a pink
plastic seat his parents put on the toilet when he was 2. He'd sit backward,
despite his mother's admonitions to turn around. He couldn't or wouldn't
defecate and remembered his mother getting angry and his father hitting
him. It shocked him that the hitting began that early, in this idealized time.
He remembered his mother sitting for long periods of time on the bathtub
ledge, waiting for him to defecate, and when he couldn't, giving him enemas,
and being angry at her for that. And he remembered with anger how later on
his mother would stretch his anal opening because the doctor had told her it
was too small and that she had to stretch it.

Over the next few months John would express great rage, rage generated by an anal battle with an intrusive mother, traumatizing him with her
aggression and seductivity, as well as the narcissistic rage that had ensued
from her abandoning him—rage from two different sources but handled by
the defenses around the anal stage.

Along with John's expressions of anger, there was a great release of
material having to do with how problems at the anal stage led to a
compulsivity that lasted through adolescence up to the present. He described
compulsive rituals of studiously cleaning his anus after he defecated, and if it
weren't purely clean, plunging himself into the shower even if he was at a
friend's house. As he brought up more and more affect-laden material, he
began to make changes in his career. As he put it, he stopped walking around
with his "finger up his ass." And he began to make changes in his relationship with his girlfriend. He quit his job where he was in a masochistic
position of low pay and abuse from a woman superior, and found a
managerial job with another market research firm at a higher salary. His talk
of picking up his cello turned into action and he began to practice and joined
a chamber group.

As he engaged less and less in petty power struggles with his girlfriend
and tried to get closer, she got more and more depressed. Without him to
criticize, she fell back on her own problems with work. He began to see more
and more how she was very much like his mother. He broke up with her and
got involved with a kinder and warmer woman whom he would marry.

His manner of moving and talking also changed in this period. He no
longer walked stiffly but with a certain fluidity like the athlete he was. His
speech became more animated; it had feeling—and I no longer felt at all
bored listening to him. As we worked through his anal conflicts, he stopped
his compulsive scrubbing of his anus, and he actually took the offensive in
soccer for the first time.

And the nature of the transference changed too in this phase. For
instance, he not only verbalized about not wanting to pay or come on time
but laughed at the impulses and, identifying with my analytic stance toward
the resistances, easily analyzed them himself.

We were now in the seventh year of treatment and about to enter a
phase in which John started to come to grips with his failure to idealize and
identify with his father, leading to failures at the oedipal phase. This phase

was keyed in with a dream in which he had intercourse in the backseat of a car with his best friend's wife and then couldn't face his friend afterward.

His associations led him to recall a conversation he had with an older woman the day before in which he felt I was taken down a peg. He said he confided in her that he was in analysis. She told him she couldn't understand why he was trying to get help from someone like me, someone who wasn't a doctor. I asked him how he felt about that woman putting down my work. He said he felt angry, that I was a terrific therapist and thought of defending me but didn't. I asked him how he felt about that. He said guilty, that this little triangle reminded him of his mother and father and him. He then went on about how his mother would tell him that his father was crazy and bad and how dissatisfied she was with her lot in life.

I asked him how that made him feel. He said that he would agree with her. He hated his father for his craziness and rages and said with anger that "she got me to hate him—more than any other kid. She wanted me to protect her, to be her 'little man,' her second husband."

I wondered aloud what *his* stake was in collaborating with his mother by taking this view of his father and its consequences. John dismissed my musings by saying, "You mean that oedipal shit?" and laughed.

Shortly thereafter his father's brother died. John said he wanted to see his father cry—not be macho but to let go as he himself was learning to do now. He talked angrily of how with his mother all emotions had to be under tight control. But somehow he felt his father was capable of being more emotional if she'd just let him be. On the other hand he said he felt afraid that if his father cried, he could fall apart and go crazy. I asked him what that would mean if his father fell apart. He said that would mean he'd be stuck with his mother, he'd actually become her little man. And that made him feel terrified.

Over the next few sessions he brought in dreams of phallic women stabbing him in the back, dreams with knives and rape in them. His associations led him to remember how as a child he'd keep his father's knife hidden under his bed, for two reasons: in case his father went crazy and would try to kill them all, or in case his mother followed through with her threats to cut his penis off if he played with it. He said he half-believed she'd do it, and he would cut it off himself before she did.

As this material became conscious, John found himself able to mastur-bate without anxiety for the first time in his life. He was so delighted, he masturbated frequently and in front of his girlfriend, as if he had found his penis for the first time.

He also revealed that he hadn't been able to maintain an erection during sex in college. And he described numb feelings in his penis during and after sex. Now, he said, these numb feelings were beginning not to happen.

Over the next couple of months, more castration material emerged, this time from his adolescence. He recalled how his mother talked frequently about her periods and about her having an awful miscarriage in the toilet before John was born. She would warn him that if he made a girl pregnant, there would be no question: she'd cut his penis off.

During this period of time in treatment, John's father got laid off from work. His mother would call John at his job and playfully announce it was his girlfriend calling. Instead of responding as one might think, given the castration anxiety and anger he'd been expressing, John would joke back or would call her to tell her a dirty joke.

I said this seemed odd, in the midst of these expressions of anger at her. He said, laughingly, that he guessed he did get some pleasure out of being her "little man," that, sure, he had a stake in seeing his father as crazy and, in fact, maybe he provoked him to get him crazy. He described how when his mother would back down in readying to leave his father, he'd actually urge her to do so. As this little murderous man began to emerge, John went back to his earlier resistance of making a case against his father.

At this point I could see the interplay of John's trauma and his instinctual wishes and how they led to the form his neurosis took. As Henry Krystal (1988) put it, "The development of, say, a neurosis would be a reaction not to the traumatic experience itself, but to the fantasies to which it becomes attached in terms of an attributed meaning, e.g., as a confirmation of the threat of castration, as evidence that dangerous wishes may come true or bring punishment" (p. 142). We saw evidence of John's dangerous wishes not only in his incestuous phone calls and memories but in his dreams and associations. One dream led him to an interesting association that revealed how his food addiction (which we'll get to later) helped defend him against his murderous wishes. In the dream he went to a drugstore to buy a doll for his nephew that would replace one he had lost. The store was a Genovese drugstore, which John associated to the Mafia crime family. "The doll," he said, "was round and fat like I'm getting, and green like an elephant." He associated the elephant to peanuts and the peanuts to penis. He laughed, "If I get any fatter, I won't be able to see my own penis."

But he didn't make a change in his telephone sex with his mother until I happened upon a piece of acting out that helped bring the oedipal conflict back into the transference and led us to work toward resolution.

After one session when John had regaled me with details of his father's bad behavior, I was buying tickets to a movie, and I glanced back at the ticketholders' line. There was John with a woman who I assumed was his girlfriend. He took one anxious look at me, waved, and walked off in the opposite direction. In the next session he came in shamefaced and said he wanted to reveal something he had been keeping from me. The woman I saw him with wasn't his present girlfriend but the old one whom he had broken up with.

I asked him, "Do you think there might be some connection between your going out with her and what we've been talking about?" Yes, he said, and wondered if that's why he'd been having difficulties lately in being intimate with his present girlfriend and actually didn't like being with his old girlfriend. He added that he had the feeling that being with the old girlfriend was a way of undermining me and our work together, and that being with her was a way of going back to Mom.

Between this and the next session his mother made another call and told him sexual jokes. But this time he didn't feel the usual amusement. He felt irritated and anxious when she did it, and shame for contributing to the joking. This led him to angrily associate to memories of his mother's seductivity, how she'd "parade around the house in her bra and panties" and would have John zip up her dress. I asked him how that made him feel. He said that he felt all mixed up, that he felt much more anger than pleasure.

I interpreted how his anger at this was like his anger at his mother's castration threats. She had been arousing him and then rendering him impotent, like when she told him she'd cut it off if he made a girl pregnant. He took the interpretation and talked about how he felt this had kept him from maintaining an erection when he was an adolescent and led to feelings of numbness in his penis later on.

After this session, when his mother would call and tell "dirty" jokes again, he'd ask her to stop. He stopped seeing his ex-girlfriend completely. Once he did both, he began to express feelings of guilt for the view he held of his father and began taking the first steps toward valuing the strengths and skills, such as carpentry, his father actually had.

Now I finally could say to John that by siding with his mother in his parents' battles and by identifying with her contempt of his father, it not only affected his relationship with his father but caused problems with his own self-esteem and helped lead to feelings of depression. With this interpretation, John's depression lifted more. He found he could do some of the things that had once seemed impossible for him, from scoring his first goal in soccer, to enrolling in college, to setting up playing engagements for his chamber group.

So the analysis of his complicity in the denigrating attitude of his mother enabled him to identify with aspects of his father, which, along with the idealizing transference, helped him repair his sense of self. His idealizing of me and natural feelings of competition at the same time at first led him to set up as a goal—which turned out to be temporary—to study psychology and become "a doctor," unlike me. A normal oedipal phase now came into being in which John could feel he could safely compete with me without worrying that he would destroy me, that in fact the competition was useful for firming up a sense of self.

By the end of his eighth year in treatment, John improved his relationship with his girlfriend, considered the possibility of marrying her, and then married her. He also made a significant change in his career. He was able to accept his father-in-law's offer to train him in his successful business with the view of making him a partner. His idealization of me in the transference and his minimal identification with aspects of his father shifted now to an idealization of his father-in-law, and then through the identification with him, to more of a separation from his mother. It now seemed, given all his progress in treatment and outside in love and work, John was ready to enter a termination phase.

In one session John came in saying that his wife wanted to stop using contraception and make a baby. He smiled at me uneasily, and I asked him how *he* felt. He said, "She's right in this. She's almost 35, and I'm ready." I thought, This makes sense. He's firmed himself up enough to become a good, supportive father and this will be reparative for him as well as fun. But as he went on with an odd, unconvincing bravado, I heard him talking to his mother, who would threaten to cut off his penis if he made a girl pregnant and who had abandoned him when his brother was born. I wondered where those anxious or angry feelings were, and how they'd show up and if he was ready to leave treatment quite yet.

The next session John came in with more of that bravado, saying now that he had come this far, he wanted to end treatment, in the next session or two. He asked me what I thought, although from his manner he didn't seem to want me to reflect on it and give him an answer.

I started to tell him that I was having thoughts myself that he was ready to enter the termination phase. "Termination *phase?*" he cut me off sarcastically. "How long is that phase, a year?" He shook his head. I felt irritated as he sat there smirking, reeking of cigarettes and looking fat. Then I said to myself, *Wait a minute, you're teaching addictiveness in your symbolization course right now, and lately he's been telling you he's been smoking two packs a day and eating whole Entenmann cakes and you've been missing his communication! He's been signaling with these addictions to cigarettes and sweets that there's important affect being buried around this looming pregnancy and separation from you. With his content about his accomplishments he's telling you he's ready to leave, but with his defiant style you're seeing the adolescent John who both wanted to get out of the house and run right back there to get fat and take drugs.*

"What do you *feel* about this?" he asked me almost mockingly. I wanted to say, *I feel conflicted like you. On the one hand I don't want to be like your controlling overprotective mother and give you an enema for your feelings about pregnancy and separation. Yet on the other hand I know we need time to work out a termination, and I also know that you're keeping anxieties out of here with this show of bravado.* I finally said simply, "From the changes you've made in your life and how you now feel about yourself, you are moving toward termination. But I think we also need to take some time with this, as we have with everything else."

"Bullshit," he said contemptuously. "I'm cutting it down to once a week, as we talk about this," and he did.

A week later he came in late, shaken, saying that he'd just had a scary experience on the road. He had been tailgating another driver and loudly beeping his horn. Then he raced ahead of the guy and cut him off. He added laughingly that he'd been doing this lately on the highway, beeping and giving the other driver the finger. But this time the guy was crazy and pulled alongside him with a gun. A wild chase, reminiscent of his father's chasing him, ensued, until John managed to exit quickly and drive off.

I said to him, "You've got the car out of neutral now. What are you trying to say with it, the way you're driving?"

I half-expected him to say sarcastically that he wanted to cut me off and give me the finger and get out of here. Instead he sat silent and looked genuinely upset and said, "Maybe I'm trying to hold onto my out-of-control father with this. Look at me," he said despairingly, "I'm doing the same damn thing with my weight and smoking like him, two packs a day."

Over the next several sessions John talked at times with feeling and at times in a somewhat intellectualized way about his difficulties in separating from his blue-collar father—how he seemed to be trying, as he had in adolescence, to stay close to some of the worst aspects of him by smoking and putting on weight. As he went on to rehash more of the car chases and tried to connect all of this to ambivalent feelings about his father, I'd find myself feeling bored as I did at the beginning of treatment when he tried to connect everything to his father's abuse and left out his mother. I wondered where she was in all this acting out, especially those aspects of her the prospect of his wife's pregnancy had to be evoking. I finally said to him, "While you're talking about how these cars are nearly banging together and how you're getting fatter, what's going on with your wife's getting pregnant?" He smiled slyly and said that they were "hitting a wall." Now that she had stopped using contraception, he'd been having difficulty with maintaining an erection.

Then he told me this dream he had had the night before: "I rented a used car and went with my father and sister to a car dealership. My father was thinking of buying a car. We get ready to leave. We get back in the car I rented. I put the key in the ignition. I notice the key is broken. I look on the seat and see the other half of the key. How am I going to start this car? One of the guys at the dealership says he could get the car started without the key. I said, 'That's great thinking. I can get ahold of some Krazy Glue and put this key back together with Krazy Glue.' I was concerned would it hold, would it be strong enough once I started, would I be able to turn it off?"

I thought, there's the missing connection—the key—between his anxieties about the pregnancy and his wanting to race out of here. Fittingly, in a dream about a car, as in his actualizing an out-of-control car on the road, he's telling us what he needs and what he fears he's lacking and is contributing to his erectile problems: a broken father whose Krazy Glue he's trying to use to insert his own key into the ignition and become a father. Would such a key be strong enough to overcome his mother's castration and abandonment threats? Would he become his "out of control" father, as he was being on the road? Was I colluding with him in even thinking that he could terminate now, that he could drive off in that car with that kind of a key or, like the car dealer, with no key at all? Was his dream's concern and his thrusting a finger up in the air instead of a hardened penis into his wife's vagina communicating an anxiety that he hadn't symbolically internalized his father's penis enough to be his own man?

After these thoughts raced through me, probably true as they were, I said to myself, Look at what he's doing to you. With this racing style of thinking right now you're experiencing his anxiety and, at the same time, he's making you feel helpless, that the work you've done all these years won't be able to help him overcome his father's failures.

"My father was like a used car, never right after he got out of the hospital. My father was the other half of the key. As a kid I remember driving to my dad's hometown. The sister in the dream is my father's sister. There was something weird about her. She was mentally incompetent—maybe it runs in the family. She couldn't stick to a topic. She'd jump from one thing to another. My father talked like this, too. My mother kept cutting him off when he talked. He was labeled as crazy. I believed for so long my father was crazy. If I separate from my mother, what am I left with but my crazy father? He's the Krazy Glue in the dream I'm trying to get myself going with. I have these fears about what kind of father I'll be, and also what if my child winds up with his family's genes?"

Over the next few months as he verbalized these anxieties and retraced part of the course of treatment, John rehabilitated the fuller picture of his father he had recovered—not a crazy person who could give him nothing, but a man whom he loved who had a depressive breakdown and out of guilt and "father-hunger" he had difficulty separating from. As he recovered what he had accomplished in here, and his hard-won self-esteem took over his bravado and his terror, his erectile problems ended and he and his wife conceived.

During the pregnancy his best friend from childhood, Tommy, became critically ill of liver disease and died. Over the past few years John had tried to rescue him, making trips back to Pennsylvania to try to get him to stop drinking heavily, which Tommy had begun to do after his father had died. "He couldn't leave home," John would say. "He couldn't move out of his mother's house. He couldn't be any different from his father." As John went through a period of mourning, he fascinatingly described a whole community of self-destructive young men in this dying factory town, addicted to alcohol and drugs, unable to separate and make new lives for themselves as John was now doing. He expressed guilt, about separating not only from his father but also from a whole community of people he cared about. He expressed anxiety that the work we had done couldn't hold and that, when all was said, he might not be able to make it on his own. He not only expressed anxiety that he was irreparably damaged by his background, but continued to express vague fears that damage would come from his genes and that his wife would be damaged in childbirth. He couldn't say why he had this fear about his wife except, in an intellectual way, to recall that after his brother was born the doctors told his mother she could very well die if she became pregnant again. But the memory didn't help him dispel this anxiety. The cause we would learn came in hints he was dropping in these sessions and which I didn't register, matching his process of denial. For instance, a few times during her pregnancy, he mentioned that one of the reasons he was putting on weight was because she wasn't playing tennis with him—not because she was pregnant but because she was complaining of physical symptoms not having to do with her pregnancy. He was irritated at her for this, as if she were being hypochondriacal.

What he was communicating here didn't become clear until after his son was born. Their doctor sent his wife to a specialist who confirmed the diagnosis of symptoms, the meaning of which John well knew and had been denying. His wife had developed the dreaded illness his grandmother had, which led him to feel abandoned by his mother and ultimately by his beloved grandmother.

This time, though, by allowing himself to feel the urgency and pain in tending to the ailing one, feelings that his mother had to have experienced with his grandmother, John was able to feel sadness for all of them in his family and began to make reparation and forgive his mother for the times she had to leave him. Now a more three-dimensional mother began to appear, not the idealized one he had come in with, or the mother whose narcissistic deficits were made more monstrous by his rage. Over the next several months, as he came to terms with his loss of his grandmother, John was able to get into feelings about losing me and we set a termination date.

But now, as John was about to leave treatment, tragedy struck for a second time. His son injured himself in an accident for which John felt responsible. Over the next few months his guilt and anxiety were severe. He felt that he really was crazy like his father, who couldn't stop ruminating that he had caused the fiery deaths of those pilots during the Korean War. As we slowly worked through this identification with his father and how he was trying to hold onto him by joining him in this sense of guilt, John began to separate from it. He came to a realistic assessment of the accident and began to feel less guilty about his son. Yet he wouldn't get to the full meaning of his sense of guilt and fully free himself until we were led by another piece of reality to an unconscious anal fantasy that, like his oedipal one, had contributed to making his physical traumas an enduring psychic one.

The piece of reality was his wife's pressing him to have another child, one who, as John bitterly put it, wouldn't be damaged. But as his wife continued to press him, John went into another physical stall. This time, instead of developing erectile problems, he buried his affect in constipation. This symptom, which we had dealt with only in part before, led us to reconstruct an unconscious fantasy that had made the physical abuse he had suffered in childhood seem a just punishment, and now fed his sense of guilt over his son's injury. In a session in which he came in complaining of days-long constipation, he told me this dream:

"I'm in a car in Pennsylvania with my son. I drive downhill and the lights go out. I'd had a couple of beers and was light-headed and thought maybe I shouldn't be driving at all. I pull over and try to get the lights back on. I'm seven or eight blocks from home" (the age he was when his mother was pregnant with his sister). "Something in the car broke. I had Elmer's glue and leave the top off. I go down an embankment. The glue gets all over my son's face. I try to ask my mother to help get the glue off. She's not helping."

His associations led him to "glue when it dries becomes crusty. Having wax taken out of my ears. Severe pain in my ears before I went into the hospital for the tonsillectomy. Another association to glue is sperm when it dries. It becomes crusty, too. My wife and I are having sex again without birth control. Thoughts of a second child coming stir up feelings about my brother coming, that something will be taken away from me. My mother's attention. With another child and her physical condition, my wife will have less time for me and my son. He needs a lot of attention with the emotional part of his recovery. And he's at an age when he's very accident prone. He's opening doors, safety latches, everything. He has to be watched."

I said, "In the dream you leave the top off the glue, and it gets all over your son."

"Everything I do has to be out of reach. The top's got to be on."

"You want to cap your penis so the come doesn't get all over your son."

"I'm upset about another baby coming! And for him, too! He's still having trouble with his body because of the accident. Also a child will be coming around the time he's going to be toilet training. I don't want to screw up. I'm not going to push him, force him to sit on the seat like my mother did. He'll be close to the same age I was when my mother was pregnant. It will be upsetting for him when we get pregnant."

I called attention to his using "we," which he had used several times to describe pregnancy.

"That's how I think of it. Maybe," he laughs, "that's why I'm putting on weight."

"And keeping your shit in."

"Maybe the glue is also shit."

"Glue keeps things stuck," I said, "like that car in neutral. I wonder if you're not keeping your shit in, and your penis capped in the dream, to keep the new baby back."

"Holy shit," he said. "No wonder I have this whole thing about toilet training. How's my son going to handle *his* shit?"

Over the next several sessions and more dreams about cars and keys and images equivalent to glue, we were finally able to reconstruct a fantasy of anal birth and how through the sympathetic magic of holding in his feces he had tried to keep his brother from being born.

With the reconstruction of the fantasy, his constipation stopped. John was able to see how guilt over the fantasy had attached itself to the present trauma with his son, and this insight finally helped free him of his guilt. He was now able to see how guilt over these early murderous wishes not only attached itself to the current trauma but also plagued him all his life when traumas occurred or change and separation loomed—how, for instance, it had contributed to his running back from college and wanting his damaged parents to tell him they loved him.

The complex and delicate relationship between traumas, unconscious fantasy, and separation seemed clear to me now, and indicated why a multi-model approach, addressing each element in that relationship—and leading to long-term treatment—seemed necessary.

With a profound sense of what guilt had cost him, and determined to lead a life different from the depressed and sadomasochistic style of his original family, John, secure in his individuality, left treatment.

For a couple of years after John left, I'd think back with pleasure about how much he had accomplished, how much he had grown emotionally and had developed the symbolization processes of a mature, self-reflective man. His feelings and thoughtfulness had guided him to make a good marriage, become successful at work, and, perhaps most reparatively of all, become a caring parent. I thought how he taught me that in adult trauma, when it comes under the charge of a strong ego like that of a protective parent, we not only can soothe ourselves, but can also rework our unconscious and repair some of the damage done by childhood trauma.

I heard from John once in this time. He called to tell me that his wife had given birth to a daughter, that she was beautiful, and that things were really going well.

Then, less than a year later, he called again, this time very depressed, and asked to come in. There was something seriously wrong with his daughter. The doctors said she was mentally retarded. He came in despairing, guilt-ridden, angry, and frightened. He was guilt-ridden that his genes had caused the damage. He was angry that maybe the medication the doctors had given his wife for her illness caused it. He was angry at his wife for pushing him to have another child.

We would spend months with his depression, with helping him feel and grasp the enormity of how his life had suddenly and permanently changed. The medical news about both his daughter's and wife's conditions got worse and worse. After a while the affect he was experiencing became overwhelming and he went numb, addictively eating so much kids' food, Twinkies, and potato chips that he became eighty pounds overweight.

What we worked on was his recapturing his now well-developed capacity for self-care after trauma. Once again it was the reconstruction of his murderous birth fantasy—in this case a later version of it—that enabled us to dissolve his addictive symptom that kept him insulted against grief and mourning in the present.

In the dream about Elmer's glue getting all over his son's face, he was seven or eight blocks from home when something in the car broke. What we now got to, as we worked through his resistances and his alexithymic defenses loosened, were affective memories from that period between 7 and 8 when his mother, against her doctor's advice, became pregnant again because she wanted a little girl. There was constant talk in the house about how his mother could die because John's brother had been a breech baby.

As he remembered this, John brought in dreams to which he had a recurrent association about crawling into an igloo some kids had built on his street. His mother warned him not to go into igloos because he could get killed. One such igloo had collapsed, suffocating a neighbor's little boy. But John crawled into this symbolic womb nonetheless.

From such associations and others he'd already told us in other contexts (like stealing from his mother's purse at this age) we could reconstruct a later fantasy of once again wanting to destroy the second unborn sibling, played out in his entering the dangerous womb so that there would be no place for the new baby. As we reconstructed it, he began to own up to wishes that his daughter had never been born, and wishes for her to die now so his son could get all his wife's attention as he had wanted it from his mother. He remembered how much he had wanted it, and the immense sense of loss he felt in this period when he didn't get it. Not only did his mother give her attention to his baby sister and her own ailing mother, but when his father's union went out on strike again his mother had to go out and take a part-time job to help support them. It was then that John started stuffing himself with anything he could find to eat so he would get some relief from profound feelings of abandonment and isolation. He gained proportionally so much weight then (as he had now) that he had to wear fat boys' clothing.

As repression lifted he began to allow in the grief he felt then and now, for the limitations of his parents and his daughter, and he began to regain his self-caring capacities and started a diet. It was a diet very specific to the grief he felt over the loss not only of his mother, but also of his failing grandmother. He cut out sweets and fat and made up a diet of pasta with varied condiments as his main meal. Pasta was the food he had loved eating the most at his grandmother's house. After six months he lost the eighty pounds, all the while mourning the end of our relationship as he hadn't mourned until now his grandmother's death. With a solid sense of his own regained autonomy and an awareness of his abilities to cope—so long as he allowed himself to feel—he left for good.

In this final year of treatment what he had accomplished was the possession of a flexible affective life in the face of tragedy. As John went through mourning and his depression lifted, he began to take great pleasure in his son and wife, his business successes, his winning tennis matches, and his cello playing. One of his last dreams perhaps sums up this development: "I am driving a white BMW. I won it in a contest. I'm driving down a street with the windows open. It's a beautiful day. I never thought a car would make me feel so good. It's a statement of being well-off, things going well, Fred. I'm just cruising along. A BMW. This is nicer than I thought."

REFERENCES

Freud, S. (1937). Analysis terminable and interminable. *Standard Edition* 23:209–254.

Krystal, H. (1988). *Integration and Self-Healing*. Hillsdale, NJ: Analytic Press.

PART III

Treatment Issues—
Transference
and Countertransference

CHAPTER EIGHT

The "Tell-Tale Heart":
Responding to a Patient's Somatic Language

LAURA ARENS FUERSTEIN

Now, I say, there came to my ears a low, dull, quick sound, such as a watch makes when enveloped in cotton. I knew *that* sound well, too. It was the beating of the old man's heart. . . . The old man was dead. . . . Yet the sound increased—and what could I do? They heard!—They suspected!—they knew!—they were making a mockery of my horror! . . . Louder! louder! louder! louder! "Villains!" I shrieked, ". . . I admit the deed!—tear up the planks! here, here!—it is the beating of his hideous heart!"

Edgar Allan Poe, "The Tell-Tale Heart"

In Poe's tale of murder, the killer is driven to declare his guilt; he has the illusion that the "beating" of the victim's heart (really the ticking of his watch) after death is pointing the way to the perpetrator. The murderer is tormented by the increasingly louder "heartbeat," which speaks out, giving life to both the crime and the superego, while keeping the dead man alive to haunt him. The concept of a body organ that communicates is associated with the patient to be discussed in this chapter, Beryl, who uses her somatic symptoms to express her emotions and belie her inner deadness.

In recent years, the literature has increasingly addressed the issue of the mind–body connection. Areas of focus related to the psychosomatic patient that apply to Beryl include a deadening of feeling with poorly defined affect (alexithymia); an inability to experience pleasure (anhedonia); and a deficit in early object relations, which leads to short-circuiting of feeling paths to consciousness and a resultant substitution of emotion with somatization (disorder of regulation).

While this chapter discusses how these elements are reflected in the case of Beryl, the primary focus is on the interpretive process and how it is infused with the intersubjective experience. Through this means, an attempt is made to break through the patient's outer wall of deadness to reach the affect within her psychosomatic armor.

The creation of the interpretation in the vignette to follow is delineated in two major phases: the *approach stage* is defined through capturing the heightened transference moment; proceeding from this, the *wording of the interpretation stage* is viewed as a two-part process, that is, the therapist's internal and external communication experience. This involves first internally "reading" the patient's nonverbal language, and ultimately transforming it into externalized words to be shared with the patient.

The heightened transference moment delineated within the approach to interpretation reveals Beryl's core issue: the use of the psychosomatic symptom to prevent damage to the fragile maternal object. I attempt to demonstrate how Beryl's lifelong struggle to preserve the wholeness of a mother perceived as teetering on the edge of fragmentation from the time of her daughter's infancy is a fundamental cause of her psychosomatization.

Within the second phase of interpretation, that is, the therapist's formulation of words, the powerful use of my own body's responsiveness to Beryl's somatic cues is pictorialized; the visceral reverberation and heightened visual sensitization triggered in me by her physical communications are transformed into a verbal language, which in turn melds with her own metaphorical expression to form the affect-evoking interpretation.

The aforementioned basic elements of interpretation are depicted in this chapter as they appeared in the intimate analytic space of one woman's treatment; however, an underscored thesis is that they might be applied in a more universal way to psychosomatic patients in psychotherapy. It should be noted that the interpretive process described is not meant to be taken as a schematized entity. In practice, there are obvious overlaps of and interactions between the phases described.

This interpretive approach is offered as a uniquely personal (for both patient and therapist) piece of the intersubjective experience, which always involves creation; in this case, the therapist's "listening" to the patient's nonverbally defined affect through the language of the body leads to some transformation of both participants in the therapeutic space.

Illuminating this idea, Ogden (1994) writes: "The analyst must be prepared to destroy and be destroyed by the otherness of the subjectivity of the analysand and to listen for a sound emerging from that collision of subjectivities that is familiar, but different from anything that he has previously heard" (p. 3). This chapter represents an effort to make this "collision" come alive.

THE PATIENT'S PRESENTATION AND HISTORY

Beryl came to treatment in her early twenties with a symptom of experiencing a sensation of a punching at her heart and, concomitantly, an expansion of her chest. This somatic event would be accompanied by an amorphous sense of anxiety, and would almost always occur after she had had a pleasurable experience (which could be barely identified as such).

My first impression was of a lovely young woman whose large, sad, blue eyes took up much of her face; the glimmer of light in them was obscured by heavy dark-framed glasses and short, blonde, curly hair. Through my connection with her gaze I could sense a deep well of mourning and pain but she seemed to carry it alone, in some remote place.

Upon entering the room, she immediately conveyed the outer layer of herself, the false self which, as Winnicott (1956) states, conceals and shelters the authentic one. The latter is denied a rich emotional life experience because the false self "develops a fixed maternal attitude towards the true self, and is permanently in a state of holding the true self as a mother holds a baby" (p. 456).

Beryl's false self, made known to me from the start, was one of utmost self-sufficiency: *she* would be the one to hold *me* up, her eyes told me at first glance. I instinctively felt that she had learned well, through some as yet unknown contradiction of nature in her developmental process, how to achieve this goal of supporting me, the would-be caregiver. As her ego structure was gradually developed, and layers of defense were peeled away after several years of treatment, her inner fragility came to light; there was a helpless, neglected little girl hidden beneath the facade of independence and strength.

Her self-reliance was buoyed by a hyperactive way of life; frequent, purposeful activity without much attached pleasure during the day and sleeplessness at night kept Beryl from staying with herself long enough to feel the inner hurt of emptiness or defectiveness.

Her words, although often used to describe seemingly painful events, would lie flat in the treatment room; they seemed weighed down, powerless as evocative tools, with little capacity to pictorialize the feelings they were meant to express; moreover, they were useless as creators of transitional space between us for play, in Winnicott's sense. Her free association was not free—it was brittle, and would seem to break off whenever she would get close to expressing a need or an angry feeling.

Further, it appeared that the link between Beryl's two worlds of fantasy and reality had been severed at some very early developmental point. In Loewald's (1975) terms, in the healthy adult the play arena and the rational realm coexist and often mingle, as they do for the 2-year-old, and in the analytic setting this collaboration reaches an apex through the intensification of the transference.

It was evident to me from the start that for Beryl this melding of the abstract and the concrete was not permitted, and that, paradoxically, in order for her tenuous sense of self to remain in some whole form, these two worlds had to be kept divided at all costs. As I came to know her better, a point was being driven home: from very early on in life, Beryl had learned that playfulness was dangerous; it would mean diversion from the serious mission placed in her hands from infancy onward—that is, to ward off her mother's fragmentation.

Beryl is the older of two children (a brother is 18 months younger). Her mother told her with pride that she was given the bottle propped up in an infant seat from the age of 3 months (and seemed to "like it better that way") and was toilet trained ("with no problems") by 15 months. In her mother's words, she showed an "inborn self-reliance."

For the first few years of treatment, Beryl conveyed a sense of very little available memory and affect in relating her history. Her past was often described as if she were giving a narrative of someone else's life; the connection to feelings seemed tenuous.

She did have a vivid memory of her mother lying in bed in a half-stupor in the early evening, often while having Beryl serve dinner to the rest of the family. Next to the bed would be a glass of water and a bottle of tranquilizers. Another clear memory appeared of herself at age 10, being asked by her mother to take over the housekeeping and mothering tasks related to her father and brother.

Around puberty, Beryl heard her mother say to a neighbor that she was "going to fall apart," and did not know if she could go on. Soon after, her mother suffered hemorrhaging from fibroid uterine tumors; her memory vividly depicted the "bloody sheets carried to the laundry room by my aunt."

Beryl's reaction to these circumstances was ascertained only after years of attempts at reconstructions; her image of her mother was a body literally falling to pieces, but the striking aspect of this scenario was Beryl's feeling totally removed emotionally, and fascinated, as an outside observer would be, by the blood on the sheets. The dissociation, which would be applied so effectively in the future through psychosomatization, had worked for the moment to block out the fear. When she began menstruating soon after, she feared that fragments of her body would fall into the toilet with the blood.

Beryl's father was an archetypal macho man, with a chest that she described as "pumped up fireplace bellows." She felt her husky voice resembled his, and that had always made her feel that inside she was really more boy than girl.

She was conscious of both her attraction to and fear of him, and her wish to identify with him as the more vigorous parent. He was the one who would not "fall apart"; she saw his aggression in the context of strength and vitality, in contrast with her victim-mother who seemed sick and emotionally dead throughout most of Beryl's developmental years. At the same time, she was terrified of his sudden physical attacks, alternating with sexual seductions that conveyed a message that she was the oedipal winner.

The onset of Beryl's symptoms occurred when she went to sleep-away camp for the first time, during puberty. One night, she had been petting with a boy she had had a crush on, and could not fall asleep later as "it felt like a large thing was jabbing away at my heart, and my chest blew up." The phallic connotations are most obvious.

In describing this event, she stated, "I think Mother gave me a message that if I was free, she'd be threatened. Maybe I thought she would literally break apart or go crazy if I left her. It's as if I had to abuse my own body in order to be loved by her, and not be abandoned by her. My heart becomes like an enemy, beating me up, when it gets like that, and I get afraid that I will ruin it; it too, will go to pieces, like Mother, and I'll have a heart attack and die. But somehow, we're still together—even in death."

TREATMENT ISSUES

By the third year of treatment, when the transference had intensified (she could now at times express a feeling of seeing me as a nurturing figure, whom she would miss during weekends or vacations), the symptoms increased in frequency and quality, but they were not yet made visible in sessions. As she began to get more in touch with the emptiness and sadness beneath her outer layer of self-reliance, her dependency wishes in the transference began to emerge, as did her relational need for me as a real object.

One day she described a dream she had had the night before: "I'm undressing my baby niece, and there's a gaping wound on her chest, with all the cartilage and muscle showing." She went on, "That must be me. It feels like if I take away these symptoms, like the battering of my heart and the pressure pushing my chest outward, that something will just pop out of me; there won't be anything left inside me. It's funny, too, I had that dream after a day in which I had tried on a nightgown, and had admired my breasts— thought they were full and sexually exciting to Ray [her boyfriend]. The dream must be some punishment for thinking of myself as a sexual woman who can have more pleasure than Mother." We were then able to look more carefully at her fear that I, as the bad mother, would desert her for her sexual expression.

It should be noted that for the first two years of treatment, Beryl had been unable to directly express any anger at me. The only available conduit for it was through indirect cues, saying that she was being made to suffer through the rigors of the treatment. For example, right before sessions were over, she would "shut down," saying, "Why should I allow myself to be vulnerable at the end of a session, when I know you will break off the connection?"

At a later point in the treatment, she was able to metaphorically describe her experience, which triggered her closed-off behavior at the ends of sessions (particularly those marked by a gradual increase in her capacity to link words with emotion): "It's as if I have been a tightly wrapped mummy throughout the session—my fear is that one of the bandages will come undone at the last moment, something will start to leak out of me, and I won't be able to put it back." We were able to define her fantasy that anger toward me for leaving her after she had begun to open up would spill out of her uncontrollably, as it would have after each of her mother's abandonments of her—if she had not kept it "under wraps" inside her psychosomatization.

There were reflections of her identity with her martyred mother, such as slightly pained facial expressions upon entering the office. At these moments I could so clearly see in her the long-suffering woman on the bed; moreover, I became aware of a countertransference reaction of responsibility for her pain—I experienced what I thought she must have felt as the little girl whose mission is to take away the mother's suffering, particularly because *she has caused it.*

It should be noted that there was always a certain hidden grandiosity in Beryl's sense of victimization—that going through this purgatory (which included her experiencing somatic symptoms) ennobled her, made her superior to me and to others. But the grandiosity was deeply buried and could only be confronted at a much later date. The martyr self-image was ego-syntonic and essential, to buttress her defense of the self-sufficient child image. To identify the secret wish for exaltation would highlight the idea that she had a *need* of any kind—and at this stage in the treatment, this would have been intolerable.

OVERVIEW

In providing a view of Beryl based on the aforementioned discussion, several related elements come into bold relief. First, she has experienced a number of traumas and deprivations early in life, before and during the period of language development, and continuing through adolescence. These circumstances revolve around the core issue of the mother's narcissistic fragility and emotional unavailability, linked directly to the powerful unconscious maternal message that her daughter must become the parentified child, existing to maintain the maternal equilibrium, and act as the buffer to ward off her fragmentation.

Second, the father is too seductive and abusive to function as a healthy source of rescue from the bad maternal object, but his vitality, in contrast with the mother's deadness, makes him the more desirable source of identification (it should be noted there is some healthy ego reflected in this choice). Third, Beryl uses powerful defenses to isolate affects from words, and conveys these painful emotions through her bodily symptom.

Fourth, Beryl evinces a marked inability to play and have a humorous side, both in the treatment room and the outside world. Fifth, a harsh, archaic superego leads both to pervasive projection of the superego onto me (the preoedipal object), and a need for utmost control over impulses, which leads to great restriction in expressing dependency needs and hostile wishes in particular.

To sum up Beryl's plight, one might say that, in order for her to preserve the mother, she cannot move too far from her side, feel too much, play, or be creative; moreover, the effect of her merger with the bad maternal object is that she maintains the reflected self-image as the sick, defective female. In other words, the great paradox of her life, is that *she must remain dead like the mother in order to feel she has the right to live.* Further, to be like the father is to be alive and vital, but also destructive and frightening, and in some ways to lose herself as a female.

The following vignette reflects many of the aforementioned dynamics and reveals aspects of my processing of Beryl's body language. It provides a description of my experience in capturing the transference dynamic—that is, the moment of linking the symptoms expressed in session with the specific object relations pattern being played out with me. The vignette also helps to pictorialize the internal and external aspects of an intervention. Following this vignette from the treatment setting, I shall present a conceptualization of what occurred.

It should be noted that I have homed in on a single vignette, purposefully, to provide an intimate view of the intersubjective process. There were, however, other transference–countertransference enactments at other moments in Beryl's treatment, and in that of other psychosomatic patients of mine, that resembled the one described in the vignette.

It must also be pointed out that Beryl's symptoms are not reflective of a disease; hence, an approach to her treatment may or may not parallel one applied to patients whose psychosomatization is interwoven with an organic illness. With these ideas in mind, the following therapeutic process is discussed with the hope that it might stimulate further exploration and clinical validation for a wider application.

VIGNETTE

In the beginning of the third year of treatment, after a day in which she had been told by her employer that she was to receive a considerable salary increase, Beryl entered the treatment room conveying a bodily stiffness and a pained expression on her face. As she began to speak about her success that day, her musculature became visibly contracted, her legs stiffened, and her hands were folded rigidly; she reported that it felt as if her heart was being "jabbed," while her chest was "blowing up."

When we explored what had set off these symptoms, Beryl could begin to recognize that her fear of some unknown devastation was reminiscent of an amorphous terror during her teen years, when her mother would seem to pounce on her for a pleasurable growth experience, statement of her own opinion, or sexual enactment. She remembered a day when her mother became silent, and went to "the bed and the pills" after seeing Beryl on the front lawn laughing with and hugging a boy she had developed a crush on.

My countertransference reaction to her body language and symptom was to want to reach her and comfort her in some way, and yet I felt a distance, as if her putting a wall between us would protect her from some unknown harm. I also felt some vague sense of responsibility for causing her pain. I asked myself, What unconscious message might I have passed on to Beryl to contribute to this set of circumstances? Was I the one who had created the space between us?

I realized, through internal processing, that a projective identification process had occurred. She had had to project onto me her identity as the toxic one, the child with the capacity to hurt that defective, fragile mother through growth or separation. In this way, she could be rid of the painful sense of herself as the destructive one, the one to cause fragmentation of the maternal object. In turn, I had taken on the persona of the destroyer.

Through this empathic connection, I could further understand why her body had become such a useful sidetrack for impulses that she experienced as aggressive missiles of maternal destruction. For a short time in the intersubjective experience of the treatment room, I was Beryl as a small child, and she was her mother, suffering, and *letting me know it in a big way* through her body language. I felt my own visceral response—a tightness in my chest and a constriction of my musculature. In a fleeting moment, I saw the lifeless woman on the bed who could *break into pieces at any time*; I saw the frightened little girl who might save her mother from disintegration if she could just take enough of the pain into her own body.

It struck me that my image of the child and mother was very detailed and specific: they each respectively reflected the physical qualities of one of my childhood friends and her mother. When I looked further at this vivid picture, I remembered that this friend had always exuded some quality of sadness. She had acted as a caregiver of her five younger siblings, as her mother had been chronically ill and her father was an alcoholic. I realized that my visceral and visual senses had been heightened in my effort to reach an empathic level with Beryl, and that perhaps her psychosomatization had triggered this reactive sensory response in me.

CAPTURING THE OBJECT RELATIONS/
TRANSFERENCE MOMENT

Hogan (1995) elucidates an important aspect of the intersubjective process described above. When he considers the transference of psychosomatic patients, he reports a phenomenon commonly observed by him and his colleagues: the patients *"very seldom demonstrate their somatic symptoms during treatment sessions. When they do, it is an acute, important unverbalized presentation of a negative transference* that must be explored, understood, and verbalized by the patient and physician" (p. 195, my emphasis).

I find it useful to broaden the negative transference concept by translating it into object relations theory. In considering the dynamics of the vignette, I believe it is particularly effective to focus on the specific moment when Beryl's terror of destroying me, the maternal object, through separation or growth is evident through her body's response, as revealed in the session. This brings out what I view as her core issue, embodied in her role as the parentified child.

A Core Issue: The Breakable Maternal Object

In regard to this concept, Miller (1981) provides an elucidating discussion of the feeling-attuned child who is used, from infancy on, to maintain the emotionally deprived mother's narcissistic balance. This type of mother conceals her deep sense of fragility behind a veneer of authoritarianism. The child chosen by her to play this role is given unconscious cues to behave in a carefully defined manner that will prevent the mother's disintegration.

One tragic repercussion of this situation is that this child develops "the art of not experiencing feelings, for a child can only experience his feelings when there is somebody there who accepts him fully, understands and supports him. If that is missing . . . then he cannot experience these feelings secretly 'just for himself' [and] fails to experience them at all. But nevertheless . . . something remains" (Miller 1981, p. 10). The "something" that remains is often the psychosomatic symptom.

It is a corollary that this same child would never feel free to move far enough from the concrete mother to explore the realm of fantasy, transitional objects, play, symbolization, and humor. This impediment is accentuated, as in Beryl's case, when the father cannot function as a true rescuer from the maternal engulfment. These issues are well reflected in Beryl's statement regarding the sense of herself as a "mummy on the couch" or similar statements: "If only I could fly and soar high and away." "If only I could break out of this wall around me, then my life would be so free." "Sometimes it feels like my body is a barrier, not attached to my feelings, and not letting them out."

A related concept is found in McDougall's (1985) case of the "chasmic mother and the cork child." In this situation, the child is given the unconscious message that the only way for the mother to survive is through her daughter or son's acting as a plug to fill up the infinite void within her. In applying these formulations to Beryl, I began to think of her as a "glue-child"—that is, a child who not only is called upon to *fill* the infinite maternal cavity, but also acts as the mortar that *holds together* the shards of the shattered maternal object.

When Beryl would describe a wall around her that she could not go beyond, we began to see it as representing the entry to the outside world, the world that would take her away from the "Humpty Dumpty"[1] mother—the

---

1. I must share a moment of astonishment with the reader. Several months after I had completed this chapter, and *without hearing it from me* at any time in the treatment, Beryl used the Humpty Dumpty metaphor to describe her symptoms as they appeared in session! While experiencing the sense of her chest inflating, she stated that she felt like Humpty Dumpty, who had a thin outer shell. Further, she said with a sad tone, "It's as if this fragile layer is lifted up, creating a space between my real, feeling self down below and this external shield, presented to the world. I have to constantly work at keeping

one who sat on the wall and would certainly fall into little bits as soon as her "glue-child" would part from their merged realm of defectiveness. The maternal object in this case is kept whole by her child's providing a webbing for her tenuously attached fragments. The meaning of the expression "coming unglued" was driven home to me!

This element is related to another concept embodied in Beryl's dynamics: the mother who cannot consciously tolerate the dependency of her child (but unconsciously promotes it), and is crushed by it when it is formed into a real demand. This is a leitmotif in O'Neill's most autobiographical play, *Long Day's Journey into Night*. Mary, the mother who represents O'Neill's mother Ella, is addicted to morphine. Edmund (who represents O'Neill) says to Mary, "Mama! . . . All this talk about loving me—and you won't even listen when I try to tell you how sick [I am]." . . . Mary responds, "Now, now. That's enough! . . . You love to make a scene out of nothing so you can be dramatic and tragic. If I gave you the slightest encouragement, you'd tell me next you were going to die. . . . I hate you when you become gloomy and morbid!" (O'Neill 1956, p. 788).

It is interesting to note that Edmund has consumption. In real life, O'Neill was often ill; he smoked and drank excessively, and toward the end of his life suffered from an untreatable hand tremor and displayed subtly suicidal behavior, mostly through self-neglect and the resultant physical deterioration. His last wife said of him, "When he was hurt, he never said a word. He just sat there and died" (Gelb and Gelb 1962, p. 896). There are clear parallels between Beryl's mother's and Ella's relatedness to their offspring, and equally visible similarities in their children's lifelong efforts to rescue their mothers from destruction through turning against their own bodies.

The above discussion underscores the concept that in many psychoso-

---

it up, because if I let up for a moment the whole thing will crash down, and my free self will be let loose. I guess that thought still frightens me."

While I had used Humpty Dumpty in writing to evoke the image of the breakable maternal object, Beryl had, in free association, applied it to her false self—the scaffolding used to prevent the mother's fragmentation. Our separate use of this term as closely wedded entities might be viewed as a graphic example of Beryl's symbiotic fusion. Moreover, in recognizing this evidence of the meeting of our unconscious minds, I experienced a sense of the uncanny: while our bodies had resonated in the intersubjective experience of the treatment room, our words, in parallel fashion, now reflected the congruity of our psyches, and depicted in microcosm the metaphorical leap from the somatic to the verbal realm.

matic patients such as Beryl, *preoccupation with the survival of the maternal object* is the primary focus from infancy. The self-abuse directed at the body is viewed, paradoxically, as a necessary lifesaving act, since it begins before self-object differentiation occurs. This self-attack serves several functions: first, it is a biochemical track for discharging unacceptable feelings, ultimately leading to "disregulation of affect" (Taylor 1992); second, on a preoedipal level it rescues the mother from possible destruction by taking back into itself the primitive aggressive impulses initially aimed at the depriving or attacking object; third, it provides superego punishment for any guilt connected with separation, which can take form in hurting the mother through feeling too much (perhaps feeling too alive), experiencing one's sexuality in a free-flowing way, or just differentiating (becoming too different from the mother); fourth, it provides a momentary sense of aliveness— since symptoms provide evidence of bodily sensations, the fear of falling into the mother's state of deadness or fragmentation is diminished.

THE TREATMENT APPROACH

Attunement to the Heightened Transference Meaning of the Somatic Symptom

To summarize, how do we apply these ideas to the therapist's response, in connection with the vignette presented? The first element in the approach to interpretation of the patient's somatic shorthand is found in exquisite attunement to the heightened transference expression. I believe that the most palpable fear for Beryl, expressed through the transference by way of somatization, is of harm to the mother caused by her growth (described as her core issue).

Specifically in the vignette, separation, evoked by a pleasurable feeling of professional achievement, is equated with destruction of the mother. It should be noted that other events with a common thread of individuation occurred throughout treatment that seemed to set off the somatic response in the session following the particular experience felt as growth: a night of heightened sexual pleasure along with greater orgasmic intensity; a relaxing weekend in which Beryl was engaged almost solely in pleasure-seeking activity; a newly experienced sense of excitement felt during a surprise party arranged for her by a friend. Theoretically speaking, Beryl experienced herself as saving me, the maternal object, from destruction triggered by signs of separation, by hurting her own body.

Interpretation—Internal and External Phases

The next stage in the interpretative creation is defined by a two-part process, similar in form to one that might be used with a more verbal patient. Poland (1986) delineates this experience by identifying an intrapsychic and a dyadic phase. The therapist must move from a level of self-analytic work in which speech (within himself) is silent to one of verbal sharing of parts of himself to the patient.

In the case of the psychosomatic patient, we are one more step removed, since we must create words that will signify the meaning of someone else's language without access to his or her own verbalization. We lack the key to more precise meanings that might otherwise be supplied by the patient with spoken associations to the unconscious. Poland writes that, as it is, verbal derivatives "even at their most free, are already translations. Interpretations, thus, are translations of translations, having passed through the filter of the analyst" (p. 257).

Recognizing this added obstacle can facilitate the interpretive process with the psychosomatic patient. Hogan (1995) reports that these patients *can* be reached through intensive treatment, contrary to a popular belief that the content of the fantasy life has been too deeply buried to be analyzed. He finds that, as opposed to their sole use of immovable repression, a good deal of *suppression of content* and *denial of feeling* is employed by these patients (both defenses can be affected by analysis and, at times, in-depth therapy). While I might take issue with this view when applied to some of the more disturbed, severely ill patients with ingrained disease, I find it useful when related to Beryl and other patients with like dynamics, manifesting fleeting clusters of physical symptoms.

In applying this finding to the intrapsychic part of the interpretive process, it is a corollary that the therapist will be required to augment his listening skills and attunement to transfer from a process of deriving meaning from the patient's words to one of decoding the message buried within the patient's body language.

Interpretation—Internal Process:
Reading the Patient's Somatic Message—Heightening the Therapist's
Visceral and Visual Sense

What elements enhance the therapist's inner process of creating the words to describe the meanings of the cryptic psychosomatic code? One is the concept of integration of cognition and creativity—science and art are joined in formulating any interpretation. There are many suggested facets of this melding process, for example, Greenson's "working model" for developing empathy and Tansey and Burke's "internal processing." What I would like to focus on here, however, is the use of the therapist's senses, particularly the visceral and visual ones, in internally translating the patient's physical symptom that substitutes for a verbal expression.

Fuerstein (1984, 1992), Jacobs (1973), and McDougall (1989) address how well suited the therapist's body response is in achieving an empathic connection with the verbally blocked patient, because it so powerfully evokes the preverbal primary experience with the mother. In discussing this element, Jacobs considers that the treatment setting might be particularly adapted to the use of "body empathy," when partial regressions are experienced by the analysand (the psychotherapy patient can go through some regressions, albeit fewer and less intense). The author writes, "This temporary reinvestment of the body, which revives the latent sensitivity to kinesic cues that played so large a role in infancy and early childhood, then allows the analyst to react with bodily responses that reverberate with the unconscious communications of the patient" (p. 87).

In the vignette, my own use of body empathy is demonstrated in interpreting my somatic responses to Beryl's physical stirrings in the session; not only did I have a sympathetic visceral response to her symptoms, but I felt the countertransference and relational-based desire to *reach* her. When I examined this feeling, it involved wanting to move beyond the emotional touching to hugging and providing physical comfort. Moreover, in applying this concept in a broader sense of treatment of the psychosomatic patient, it may act as a particularly effective transition vehicle from observing the symptoms to translating the patient's code. As one body reaction "speaks" to the other, it creates a common language ground from which a verbal communication can evolve.

The use of the therapist's visceral response, felt while the patient is describing the physical symptom as it occurs, is part of the intersubjective experience; the speaking and listening that normally take place in the therapy setting through a verbal process is substituted with a language of the body. Further enhancement of this communication, however, might be found through the *visual* sense of the therapist.

It is theorized here that if the therapist can heighten her seeing response to the somatic expression of the patient, a picture will be available as a springboard to the hidden meaning(s) beneath the symptom. Freud's (1900) theory of dreams is most explicit in providing a description of the regressive process involved in pictorializing thoughts. He states that the visual sense leads to a regressive experience in which ideas are transmuted into images. However, he emphasizes that the key thoughts that go through this conversion are those that are closely tied to suppressed or unconscious memories.

Hence, the therapist's need to experience partial regressions in order to empathize with the more verbal patient is intensified in responding to somatic symptoms. "A picture is worth a thousand words" underscores the effectiveness of the therapist's returning to a preverbal era of her own, when sense images such as vision defined her experience of the outside world, when words were not available as signifiers of affect.

Interpretation—External Process: Use of Metaphor in Communication with the Patient

The final phase of interpretation of the psychosomatic symptom begins with the therapist's awakening of the patient's slumbering affect buried within the body's symptom. Once it is brought out into the light, it can be moved toward a reconnection with the primary, intolerable fantasies into which it was once melded. To achieve this end, the therapist must take the product of her internal work, that is, understanding the meaning of the transference expression of the somatic symptom and the magnified use of her kinesic and visual senses, which interweave with other aspects of theory and technique applied to forming an interpretation, such as her associations, awareness of the patient's ego strength, deficit versus conflict elements, transference–countertransference, and relational issues.

The literature addresses the concept of the metaphor as the most basic form of language, powerfully evocative of the preverbal period of life. Sharpe (1940) writes that metaphor, as the earliest form of figurative speech, is developed in tandem with the period of learned control of the bowel and bladder; hence, the feelings that were connected with the related body functions find substitute paths during verbal development through metaphors.

Searles (1962) presents the notion that perhaps the metaphor's power to evoke strong emotion is due to its capacity to rekindle a preoedipal memory "when we lost the outer world—when we first realized that the outer world *is* outside, and we are unbridgeably apart from it, and alone" (p. 583). He views this part of speech as both a sign and facilitator of transition from concrete to symbolic thinking.

Arlow (1979) highlights the idea that metaphor evolves at that developmental period when the complexity of thought cannot be expressed by the limited number of words available to the child. In relating this to the treatment process, he states that the analyst's use of metaphor in interpretation at a moment of heightened anxiety is particularly effective, because, due to its cryptic quality, it provides the patient with a reasonably safe space from content that might prove too anxiety-producing if more direct language were used.

Hammer (1993) underscores the potential role of the metaphor to evoke emotion in the clinical setting. He describes it as enhancing a participatory, shared experience of therapist and patient—a sense of trying on the image." The patient can "think-feel" the interpretation; a metaphor, as a word-picture, gives the patient the power to reach into unconscious, preverbal experience.

INTEGRATION OF THE INTERPRETIVE PROCESS

In applying these ideas to Beryl's case, we might ask what metaphor is being expressed through her "punch-in-the-heart/inflated-chest" symptom. In other words, what is she saying with her "body speak" when her heart feels like it is pounded, and her chest seems to blow up like a balloon, empty inside, but showy and defined on the outside?

One imagined, all-encompassing response from her might be, "My battered heart makes me feel alive, like my father, and unlike my deadened mother—and touched, in contrast with me as a child, in the void of mother's neglect. At the same time, it beats and abuses me, as both my mother and father did, to punish me for separation and sexual wishes, or for being a woman. My blown-up chest gives me the sense of power of Father's phallus, with its combined penetrating and distancing capacity. There is also a sense of a fusion of abuse and stimulation, just as in Father's way of relating to my body when I was a child."

Hence, there are preoedipal and oedipal meanings, elements of the drives, object relations, and gender identity issues reflected in her symptoms. The task at hand, in leading to the ultimate communication to the patient, is, as with any interpretation, to select the words that will have the greatest degree of resonance, based on what is relationally sensitive, closest to consciousness, and respectful of defenses, and based on the intensity of the transference, object relations, and ego strength.

In returning to the vignette and the approaches to interpretation previously discussed, the most pressing transference issue is viewed as fear of destruction of the mother, due to an individuation experience (in this case, professional growth). This leads me to think in terms of object relations issues of separation—particularly during the rapprochement, when the child might look back at the mother while stepping out into the world. The mother's accepting glance, energetic body language, or tone of approval through words are seen as crucial reinforcers of growth at this stage. The related element of frightening aggression aimed at the maternal object is woven into the concept of Beryl's career advancement. Oedipal guilt over beating out the pitiable mother also colors the picture.

The internal work in forming the interpretation involves selecting the issues that can best be taken in by the patient, to lead to insight based on the patient's relational needs and transference state. For Beryl, one issue is the surfacing of her preoedipal fear of losing me through separation; in contrast, her anger seems too amorphous and defended against at this point in the treatment, and her oedipal fear of competitiveness with me too threatening to be usable; further, gender issues are certainly not yet definable. Hence, I believe that the fear of loss of the object is closest to consciousness.

Tone, manner, and timing are important in presenting the interpretation. As Greenson (1976) notes, it is these nonverbal nuances conveyed in the therapist's speech to the patient that evoke the earliest object relations experiences, which become a heightened issue with a psychosomatic patient such as Beryl. More specifically, in this case the importance of a warm, nonconfrontational tone is stressed, because the fear of causing destruction to the maternal object can only be allayed by a lack of retaliation—a reversal of the pathological object relation.

The final phase of the interpretive process then evolves, using a melding of the above thoughts with a metaphor that incorporates the patient's own metaphorical description (e.g., a punching heart) of her symptoms. An example of this unifying verbal process is found in my words to Beryl: "Maybe you're afraid that I would be angry and hurt if you grew, so you put your heart and chest in the boxing ring instead of me—that way, I won't leave you—I'm still here." Her immediate reaction to this was silence, then shared thoughtfulness. Over time, a shift in the treatment evolved, which will be described.

CONCLUSION

There had been a number of moments throughout Beryl's treatment when her symptoms had been expressed, and I had used the aforementioned means of communication, without conceptualizing it. It was not until I began to write this chapter and I reviewed the treatment that I identified the patterns of the relational-interpretive process described. Throughout the course of the work, there were many times when my words seemed to fall on deaf ears, when the resurfaced early fear of loss of the object would trigger her need to hold on to the pyschosomatization. This grasping for a safety zone would become overriding, as it provided an escape from the possible dangers of taking in the bad maternal object, who would fragment. At these moments, I often experienced the sense Beryl must have had as a child with her martyred mother, repeatedly feeling shut out, deadened, and, often, harmful to her, the helpless victim.

All in all, however, there was a gradual expansion (with many difficult setbacks) of Beryl's capacity to positively internalize my maternal function, which allowed her to make more connections between feelings and thoughts; this, in turn, led to a dramatic lessening of the psychosomatization, to a point at which it no longer interfered with her outside functioning. It should be noted that during the middle phase of treatment, along with this internalization of the good maternal object who would not break as a response to affect-laden words, came an increase in Beryl's presentation of her symptoms in session.

I vividly recall the beginning of the period when I recognized a shift; it was several sessions after the one involving the vignette. Beryl described her sense of utter desolation when she had left my office on a gloomy, windy winter afternoon. A description of the deep void within her was *articulated* for the first time, as she linked the experience of leaving the office with a feeling of being forsaken by her mother. Further, I remember that this was the first time I was *moved* by her words and felt the poignancy of her deep sadness. It also was the first time she allowed tears to flow, as if the "mummy" could allow some of the bandages to fall off without danger of complete leakage of her inner self.

During this phase I also sensed for the first time Beryl's incipient capacity to empathize with the neglected little girl within. She saw a child at the park who clutched onto her babysitter and could not mix well with the other children, and was reminded of herself as a 3-year-old, needing to cling to her aunt's leg when she attended her cousin's birthday party. In relating this event, she remarked with some awe in her tone, "I can't believe I always thought of myself as so self-sufficient before this, but when I saw that little girl at the park I saw me, needy and scared at that age."

Other shifts that occurred over time involved Beryl's increased capacity to express anger directly, at me and others in the outside world. Her ability to relax, be playful, and find more humor in things was enhanced, but there remained a difficulty with free association and spontaneity. The self-ennoblement through silent suffering lingered, too, although in some milder form. Her sex life became freer; on a preoedipal level, she could move from the mother to the father, because her separation was no longer felt as quite the threat it had been to the maternal object's survival; concomitantly, she seemed less constricted by superego guilt.

This chapter has depicted the use of the therapist's interweaving of relational and interpretive communication to facilitate the psychosomatic patient's linking of affect with thought. Further, it shows how this process in turn leads to an enhancement of verbalization, and a lessening of somatization for the patient.

Sugarman's (1995) ideas about the need for integration of the relational and structural models are illuminating, particularly when considering the need to form an affect-evoking interpretation for a patient like Beryl, whose emotions are strangulated and buried in psychosomatic symptoms.

He writes that the relational model highlights deficit and the real interchange between therapist and patient; the structural model, in contrast, underscores transference and interpretation of conflict leading to insight. It is felt that the interpretive process presented incorporates some synthesis of the two models at work.

These ideas are considered within the context of current theory. As Ogden (1994) states, "acting in" (such as that expressed through Beryl's physical symptom in session) is defined by the author as a "communication-in-action," which might not be seen as growth-producing simply because it is immediately substituted with words; rather, if first given its own place in the treatment sphere, it might then be viewed as a significant element of the intersubjective experience, which interpretation can subsequently bring into bold relief. Ogden emphasizes that with less reachable patients this process is made more effective when the interpretation is a melding of words and responsiveness, synonomous with the holding environment.

Related to this idea is McDougall's (1985) description of the therapist's translating function for the psychosomatic patient. She writes that bodily representations become feelings that can be "named, symbolized, verbalized, and elaborated" (p. 196). Through this process, the therapist provides a validation of the true self; as real feelings are freely named, they no longer need to be disguised behind physical symptoms.

Another way to view this evolution is to link it with Shengold's (1989) concept of *soul murder*. He applies this term to the deadened psyches of abused children, who have been repeatedly given the message that their authentic feelings are in question, or worse yet, obliterated. The author writes,

[Soul murder] is . . . the deliberate attempt to eradicate or compromise the separate identity of another person. The victims . . . remain in large part possessed by another, their souls in bondage to someone else [the early caregivers]. . . . Therefore murdering someone's soul means depriving the victim of the ability to feel joy and love as a separate person. [p. 2]

In applying this concept to the theme of this chapter, one might say that in helping the psychosomatic patient move from body sickness to verbal expression of long-buried true affect, the therapist is "raising a soul up from the dead."

REFERENCES

Arlow, J. A. (1979). Metaphor and the psychoanalytic situation. *Psychoanalytic Quarterly* 48:363–385.

Freud, S. (1900). The interpretation of dreams. *Standard Edition* 4/5:1–627.

Fuerstein, L. A. (1984). A case of exhibitionism: self-hatred beneath a mask. *Current Issues in Psychoanalytic Practice* 1(3):69–81.

——— (1992). The male patient's erotic transference: female countertransference issues. *Psychoanalytic Review* 79(1):55–71.

Gelb, A., and Gelb, B. (1962). *O'Neill.* New York: Harper.

Greenson, R. (1976). *The Technique and Practice of Psychoanalysis,* vol. 1. New York: International Universities Press.

Hammer, E. (1993). The use of imagery in interpretive communication. In *Use of Interpretation in Treatment,* pp. 148–155. Northvale, NJ: Jason Aronson.

Hogan, C. C. (1995). *Psychosomatics, Psychoanalysis, and Inflammatory Disease of the Colon.* Madison, CT: International Universities Press.

Jacobs, T. J. (1973). Posture, gesture, and movement in the analyst: cues to interpretation and countertransference. *Journal of the American Psychoanalytic Association* 21:77–92.

Loewald, H. W. (1975). Psychoanalysis as an art and the fantasy character of the psychoanalytic situation. In *The Work of Hans Loewald,* ed. G. I. Fogel, pp. 128–152. Northvale, NJ: Jason Aronson.

McDougall, J. (1985). *Theaters of the Mind.* New York: Basic Books.

——— (1989). *Theaters of the Body.* New York: Norton.

Miller, A. (1981). *Prisoners of Childhood.* New York: Basic Books.

Ogden, T. (1994). *Subjects of Analysis.* Northvale, NJ: Jason Aronson.

O'Neill, E. (1956). *Long Day's Journey into Night.* In *O'Neill Complete Plays,* ed. T. Bogard, pp. 717–851. New York: Library of America.

Poe, E. A. (1843). The Tell-Tale Heart. In *Edgar Allan Poe Greenwich Unabridged Library Classics,* pp. 354–357. New York: Chatham River Press, 1983.

Poland, W. S. (1986). The analyst's words. *Psychoanalytic Quarterly* 55:244–272.

Searles, H. F. (1962). The differentiation between concrete and metaphorical thinking in the recovering schizophrenic patient. In *Collected Papers on Schizophrenia and Related Subjects*, pp. 560–583. London: Maresfield.

Sharpe, E. F. (1940). An examination of metaphor. In *The Psychoanalytic Reader*, ed. R. Fliess, pp. 273–286. New York: International Universities Press.

Shengold, L. (1989). *Soul Murder*. New Haven, CT: Yale University Press.

Sugarman, A. (1995). Psychoanalysis: Treatment of conflict or deficit? *Psychoanalytic Psychology* 12(1):55–70.

Taylor, G. J. (1992). Psychosomatics and self-regulation. In *Interface of Psychoanalysis and Psychology*, ed. J. W. Barron, M. N. Eagle, and D. S. Wolitsky, pp. 464–488. Washington, DC: American Psychological Association.

Winnicott, D. W. (1956). On transference. In *Classics in Psychoanalytic Technique*, ed. R. Langs, pp. 456–458. New York: Jason Aronson.

CHAPTER NINE

A Case of Severe Anxiety and Panic Manifested as Psychosomatic Illness

B. SUE EPSTEIN

Thus the print is our opportunity to interpret and express the negative's information in reference to the original visualization as well as our current concept of the desired final image. We start with the negative as the point of departure in creating the print, and then proceed through a series of "work" prints to our ultimate objective, the "fine print." . . . A fine print has been generally assumed to have a full range of values, clear delineation of form and texture, and a satisfying print "color." . . . There are different schools of thought in photography that emphasize different palettes of print values.

Ansel Adams, *The Print*, p. 3

As in the art of photography, the art of psychoanalysis is intrinsically bound with the concept of development—development of a theoretical orientation; development of a diagnosis; development of resistance, transference, and countertransference; development of the patient as a human being, replete with drives, defenses, ego functioning, capacity for relatedness, and sense of self and identity; and development of the therapist as a clinician. Original visualizations undergo an intense process before a patient's own "fine print" can emerge from the solution baths of the darkroom of the mind. Form, texture, color, and shadows all express, in some measure, the essence of the evolutionary process. In presenting this case, I have sought to focus, expose, and enlarge upon the patient, Cara, a woman who experienced severe anxiety and panic attacks that became manifest as life-threatening psychosomatic illness. Through a series of "work prints," I have attempted to rework the analytic camera's negative with an eye toward the emergence of self, her own "fine print." A major feature has been Cara's movement from a self state to a more clearly delineated, emerging object relatedness. Just as there are different schools of thought that emphasize different palettes in photography, so there are different theoretical underpinnings in psychoanalysis. As Pine (1990) and Chessick (1989) would have one listen, I have tried to be in tune with this patient from the perspectives of drive defense, ego, object relations, self, and relational theories.

THE PATIENT/SUBJECT

At the time of our first contact, Cara was in her early thirties, married and the mother of a 2-year-old daughter. She had been referred for treatment by a former patient, a counselor in the school in which Cara taught. When I returned her initial telephone call, she briefly spoke in an urgent, pressured manner about feeling depressed and extremely anxious about her health, and asked for an appointment as soon as possible.

Cara presented as a petite, elfin, Caucasian woman with close-cropped dark hair and an acne-scarred complexion. She appeared younger than her age, wearing loose-fitting jumpers and blouses and large, chunky jewelry that gave the impression that she was a child in adult clothing. During the initial sessions, she had a wide-eyed look as she sat perched on the edge of the couch with a riveting stare. As in her telephone conversation, she spoke in a pressured, nonstop manner about feeling depressed and anxious. She was especially ruminative about fears of dying from cancer or a brain tumor and of losing her daughter, Candy, to accident or illness. These fears became manifest in frequent visits to physicians. Her calling me had followed several months of debilitating depression coupled with panic attacks when she was apart from her daughter. She spoke of having been depressed following the birth of her child and of continuing depression and panic attacks upon returning to work when the child was 11 months old. During these first sessions, several themes began to emerge, namely, family chaos and trauma, chronic and acute anxiety that became somatized, and profound emotional pain and sadness.

Cara recalled many painful experiences in a vivid, descriptive manner, as if they were still happening. At 18 months, Candy was suspected of having cystic fibrosis, which proved to be negative after extensive medical testing. Almost in the same breath, Cara said, "I know I'm afraid to die and leave Candy." She associated these feelings to the death of her mother from breast cancer when Cara was 20. In addition, Cara had lost her maternal grandmother to breast cancer the Christmas before entering treatment. As Cara related incident after incident, she seemed to soak me in with her eyes. As she spoke in this intense manner, biographical material evoked associations to her low self-esteem, distorted body image, and feared illness and death. I felt like I was being asked to provide a lifejacket as her ship was sinking. Later, with the transition to the couch, I was to learn of a near-fatal drowning incident at age 5. Despite her intense anxiety and depressed mood, Cara was fully oriented and did not appear to be suicidal or disordered in her thinking. She was very motivated to begin therapy. She was seen twice weekly in face-to-face psychoanalytic psychotherapy for ten months during which time a neutral stance was maintained so as not to compromise the potential for psychoanalysis proper. After Cara began to develop sufficient trust in me and to form significant selfobject transferences, she become eager to explore further the origins of her feelings of despair and anxiety. Increasingly, she seemed better able to take in and assimilate certain aspects of her self. She was in a better position to explore her defenses in an intensified way through the use of the couch and increased sessions. However, it was first necessary to analyze her anxiety about not seeing me and the increased somatization that preceded her use of the couch. As of this writing, I continue to see Cara, who is in her fifth year of treatment.

RELEVANT HISTORY/FOCUS

Cara was the third of four children born within a five-year period to a middle-class family in a suburban town in the Northeast. She has two older brothers and a younger sister. The family atmosphere was one in which Cara "never felt secure, always worried." While there were many medical and psychological problems within the family, such problems were seldom given importance. This was a family that had great difficulty allowing members to express their feelings, to become differentiated.

With disdain, Cara described her father, a retired fireman, as self-centered, moody, and given to verbally abusing her, her mother, and her sister. He was physically abusive to her brothers. The father would not talk to the family for a week at a time for no apparent reason. Discussing his stinginess, Cara related an incident whereby the family had run out of toilet paper because her mother had used up the allotted weekly household allowance. Her father hoarded a roll for himself while the family was left without. Cara spoke of her father as being a distant, self-absorbed man with almost no interest or compassion for his children, except during their illnesses. Apparently, he was rather hypochondriachal himself. Six years ago, he moved to a remote area in another state with a female friend. Cara had never seen his new house nor had she had much contact with him. Despite Cara's claim to want nothing to do with him, I had the sense that she was very conflicted about her father.

Cara remembered her mother as a depressed, overwhelmed woman who was very unhappy in her marriage and chose to focus on her job and children. Her mother, an only child of "refined" Scottish parents, married "beneath her" when she married Cara's first-generation Italian father over protests from her parents. Money seemed to be a constant source of tension between Cara's parents despite her mother's working as a teacher and part-time in a department store at night and on weekends. The children were cared for by an older, "grandmotherly" neighbor about whom Cara has fond memories. Cara was intensely attached to her mother, enhanced even more by the father's distance and abusiveness. In the early months of therapy, she appeared to be in a reverie as she described her mother protecting her from her father's unpredictable behavior. Often, she would lament, "When we [she and her siblings] lost her we lost our buffer." She spoke poignantly of her mother's poor health throughout Cara's childhood (kidney disease, cancer) and of a family history of depression (mother, maternal grandfather, brother). Cara's mother had a history of "breakdowns" beginning when the mother was 7. Cara's second eldest brother has a history of hospitalization, medication for depression, and acting-out behavior. I began to consider Cara's physiological predisposition to depression, given this family history.

Prior to Cara's entering treatment, she had been medicated by her family physician who placed her on a benzodiazepine used to treat anxiety but not recommended for use with depression. The physician requested a consultation with me during which I made him aware of her depressive symptoms. He then changed the medication to Tofranil and Xanax, placing her on and taking her off medication several times. After a year of inconsistent medication, Cara sought psychiatric consultation. She currently takes a lowered dosage of Norpramin and Xanax in consult with a psychiatrist. Two previous psychiatric consultations ruled out major depressive illness, emphasizing instead her psychosomatic nature. Most recently, she has begun "weaning" herself off the medication, in part due to her desire to have a second child.

When her mother was diagnosed with breast cancer, Cara was a junior in high school. According to Cara, her mother had known about a breast lump for several months before seeking medical help. Following a mastectomy and chemotherapy, her mother lived for three more years, always assuring Cara that she would not die. Cara would return from college each weekend to see her mother, keep house for her father, and tend to her widowed maternal grandmother. As her mother's health declined, Cara subsequently began to reexperience panic attacks while at school during the week. Her mother died on Christmas Eve of Cara's sophomore year in college, while Cara was en route home. Her recollection is of feeling profound relief at first, because she no longer had to worry about the inevitable. She and her siblings attended the wake and funeral, adhering to their father's prohibition against any public show of emotion.

Following her mother's death, Cara continued to be the only family member who cared for her grandmother, including placing her in a nursing home and arranging for her funeral when she died the Christmas before Cara entered treatment. She recalled feeling it was her obligation to care for her appreciative grandmother. It seems that caring for her grandmother served as an extension of being with her mother, thus providing an alter ego dimension.

Cara's elder brother, three years her senior, was the child most favored by both parents. Cara grew up idealizing him and he was very protective of her. She and this brother attended the same college that her mother attended, where he would oversee her social life and introduce her to his friends. What little extra attention her mother had to give was lavished on this firstborn child, leaving Cara to feel that if she had been a boy, she might have been more prized by her mother. Since entering treatment, Cara had begun to see her brother in a less idealized way and actually felt sorry for him because he was in what she described as a "loveless marriage" with a very domineering wife and two children. She saw him as constantly repressing anger toward their abusive father in order to retain the favored-son status.

The other brother, two years her senior, was remembered as a narcissistic, provocative, and impulsive youngster who always had problems. He constantly acted out as a child and, indeed, continued to do so as an adult.

Cara recalled this brother's symbiotic ties with her mother, who would "bail him out" behind her father's back. It seemed that her brother stood up to their father and, subsequently, was more physically abused. Both brothers were excellent athletes in a family that placed great value on aggression, competition, and physicality. Cara recalled playing the flute in the band at football games with hopes of being valued by the family. Throughout the first two years of treatment, Cara continues to be overprotective of her brother, feeling it was her duty to bail him out, as her mother had done in the past. This included allowing him to live with her for several months when he separated from his second wife. He proved to be a selfish, manipulative, dishonest house guest. Following months of analysis in which she lamented about performing many of the family functions her mother had done, Cara got tired of being his doormat and asked him to leave. Bailing out her brother also caused considerable stress within her marriage. Cara's husband, John, was intolerant of her siblings and Cara's tendency to place their needs above those of her immediate family.

The sister, younger by one year, was alternately both dependent on and resentful of Cara. She has had a history of emotional problems, promiscuity, and marital discord. When Cara first entered therapy, she would send money to her sister, who often was in crisis. Later in the treatment, Cara's refusal to rescue her sister proved both wrenching and rewarding.

Cara's obesity throughout her childhood was ignored by family members. She recalled an incident at age 13 as the family was enjoying pizza when her father said that she had eaten enough. She ran to her room and cried for hours, after which she ate sparingly for the next six months, losing sixty pounds. This anorexic bodily response to a narcissistic wound was totally ignored by both parents despite her dramatic weight loss, hair loss, and amenorrhea. Cara explained that, in her family, you did not go to a doctor unless it was life threatening. I began to deepen my understanding of what the frequent trips to doctors' offices served for her, of how profound the annihilation anxiety was, and how intimately linked her existence was to ungratifying objects. Further, I felt her deepening sense of the need for splitting between doctors and keeping constancy in the transference (a doctor always being there). As I pondered the relationship between her father's rejection and Cara's extreme response, I speculated about the injury of unmet oedipal yearnings, about rivalry with her brothers (losing her femininity), and about identity development. While still idealizing her mother, Cara credited her with helping with the anorexia by teaching her to count calories once Cara shared how difficult it was for her to maintain her weight.

Cara continued to struggle with fluctuations in her weight, which she sees as an eating disorder, although clearly this problem needed to be seen in the context of her overall difficulties with her sense of self. I say this because the body-image problems became manifest in so many of her ways of being, particularly with regard to the acute anxiety about the wellness of her body. It is interesting to note that she rewarded herself with sweets (candy), and when she binged it was usually with sweets despite a hypoglycemic condition. Also relevant to body image was her past difficulty with acne. While thus far in the treatment she has related the acne to self-esteem problems, she has yet to be able to fully chance looking at the depth of the emotional scarring.

As Cara related story after story of her parents being unattuned to her, I found myself experiencing her projected despair. Anger at her parents for their remoteness and lack of protection struck a chord in my own experience of growing up in a large extended family wherein individual needs were often unmet. While I recognized the importance of being able to perceive her life experience with accuracy and objectivity, I sought to use these communicative transference/countertransference interactions to deepen insight for each of us into her terror and despair.

Anxiety about illness and her body pervaded much of Cara's life. The fear of her being at high risk for breast cancer produced anxiety, panic, regression, somatization, and a cascade of obsessive-compulsive symptoms. When I began seeing Cara, she was so ashamed about her propensity to do what she called "check myself out medically" that she had taken to going to walk-in emergency medical centers where she could maintain some anonymity while seeking assurance that whatever somatic symptoms she was experiencing were not life threatening. She compulsively checked her breasts for lumps. Her helplessness became so palpable that all else was negated. She became overwhelmed and disorganized by anxiety, so much so that she considered prophylactic mastectomy. These practices have largely abated with her emerging capacity to self-soothe. I've come to understand such panic and regression within the context of selfhood, namely, annihilation of self, fear of fragmentation, and self representation and identity. Freud's (1914) discussion of the relationship between hypochondriasis and narcissism is brought to mind as both interest and libido were drawn back into herself. My thinking also took me back to the extent of her narcissistic injury at age 13 as well as to the precursors of such an injury. I could not help but wonder about the relationship between this "breastless" body image that was thought to be life preserving and her sibling wish to be like her brothers, to identify with the aggressive father, perhaps to preserve her existence by denying her femininity and her oedipal wishes for her father. Later in her development, breastlessness became translated as to be a woman and have breasts is to be dead, and to be a woman and have breasts means you take your mother's place with your father. This primitive material at first induced in me a parallel response, wherein I found myself questioning the effectiveness of the treatment, my skills as a clinician, and her ability to change. I came to understand that as I remained calm and available to her, Cara was able to sort out the complexities of her repetitive pattern with a subsequent abating of symptoms.

Another salient feature of this case that related to self-soothing and to her obsessive-compulsive style was Cara's reliance on transitional objects and phenomena (Winnicott 1953). While this will be discussed below, it is significant to note that Cara still has a teddy bear that was hers as a child. She recalled her father's sharp verbal rebuke when he "caught" her masturbating with "Teddy" at age 3. Today, Teddy maintains a prominent place in Cara's china closet, next to her maternal grandmother's china, and among her numerous collections of antique dolls, doll furniture, doll tea sets, and cherubs. In addition, Cara has kept every item of her daughter's clothing and toys. She regretted her parents saving nothing, not even her communion dress, something that apparently her grandmother had done for her mother. She has been adamant about "building a history for Candy, unlike what was done with me." Indeed, it was only after her husband pleaded with her that she agreed to discard the piece of umbilical cord that separated from Candy's navel as an infant. In addition to these tangible transitional objects, Cara's obsession with her health and doom served in some ways as transitional phenomena wherein she seemed to seek to preserve her well-being through omnipotent fantasies about controlling her fate. Three years into treatment, at the height of such grandiose fantasies, she began to substitute religious symbolism of the Catholic Church, which became transitional in nature. Winnicott (1953, 1971) addressed this tendency, particularly with regard to Roman Catholic doctrine. While Cara's family had not been very religious, she has moved toward theology, particularly "signs," to soothe herself when she feels vulnerable.

Cara's relationship with her husband, John, seemed based in love as well as strife. On the one hand, she was overly dependent and attached while, on the other, she had an impaired capacity to maintain a consistent, meaningful relationship. This pattern was reflected in other personal relationships as well, in that Cara tended to chronically either ignore or envy friends and family members. Her frequent fantasies about ideal love ranged from having an affair with a man who would be unconditionally adoring of her to having a family, particularly a mother, who would be ever available to her.

John was portrayed as a rigid, compulsive man. He is three years her senior and works as a technical mechanic. Cara was insightful to point out that she married a man who did not go to college, just as her mother had. John came from a strife-ridden, intrusive family in which his father was physically abusive to John, his mother, and brother, but not to his two sisters (Cara's family pattern as well). John was very adoring of Cara; however, he became easily frustrated by her depressive, anxious, and hypochondriacal tendencies. The parallels of John's family to her own were glaring as she spoke of John being one of four children, also two girls and two boys. I wondered, too, about Cara's adoration of her elder brother as John is the eldest in his family and that brother's age. As I pondered these family constellations, thoughts took me to my own family in which I am in the same birth order as Cara. I realized the importance of remaining keenly aware of my own origins so as not to form an unconscious twinship with her.

Despite several other dating relationships throughout college, John is the only man with whom Cara has had sexual relations. When she met John at age 25, she was teaching school and keeping house for her father. They dated for a year and a half, during which time Cara said John was very patient with her inexperience. They became sexually active just prior to marriage, which apparently engendered considerable guilt on Cara's part. When I tried to explore her sexual life, Cara was unable to discuss sex without feeling shame and guilt, which became manifest in embarrassment and self-deprecatory statements. More recently, she has been more open and accepting of herself when sexual material is presented.

Candy was the result of a planned pregnancy when Cara was 29 years old. Candy had been difficult to soothe as an infant. That, together with the postpartum depression Cara was suffering, left her feeling very alone and anxious during her year-long maternity leave. Cara named the child Candy because she herself had always wished to be named Candy. Naming her child Candy, her most desired oral indulgence, appeared to be both identificatory and reflective of instinctual drives and ego functioning. The closeness of the name Candy to cancer also aroused my interest as what began to emerge was a very ambivalent tie to the child, through whom Cara had previously acted out psychosomatic renderings. Candy was considered to be a failure-to-thrive baby, with her weight and overall health monitored closely by pediatricians. My countertransference led me to explore my concern for the welfare of this child, seemingly in response to Cara's seeing me as the transferential mother/grandmother/caregiver. Not surprisingly, Cara began the practice of bringing Candy in with her for a session whenever there was to be a break in the treatment (her vacation or mine). The excuse would always be attributed to difficulties with child-care arrangements. I felt as if I was being cast in the role of approving mother and that the imminent separation was stirring up a great deal of anxiety and hostility. Following interpretation of the significance of her need to have me be with Candy prior to a break in our work together, much work ensued regarding separation fears concerning the child and the degree to which she and Candy are merged. Cara could not tie this practice to transference feelings when I again introduced the idea of its relevance to our relationship, further supporting the selfobject nature of the transference. While Candy continued to serve as a narcissistic extension, Cara has been able to understand and internalize, to some degree, that she needed to allow Candy to be a separate person. I was reminded of McDougall's (1989) concept of "one body for two" and how intricate the representation of one's own body is for a vulnerable patient like Cara.

DYNAMIC ASSESSMENT/THE NEGATIVE

My early impression of Cara was that she seemed to be a woman with a characterologically narcissistic personality formation. In addition, she had an obsessive-compulsive style with a heavy reliance on somatic and depressive expression. Her anxiety was so profound as to have a life/death quality to it that was represented through the soma. For Cara, the body took on symbolic meanings, and had its own language that initially I could only imagine. The origins of her extreme vulnerability, self-contempt, identity diffusion, and impoverished sense of self appeared to be embedded in the early mother–child relationship replete with primitive defenses, oral strivings, and arrested development. As the work unfolded, these initial impressions became more illuminated with the emergence of material about her mother being overly cathected to her own body. In the beginning phase of treatment, the nature of historically presented early object relations coupled with the use of me in a mirror-hungry manner in the transference further supported the premise that Cara had experienced very early narcissistic damage. For Kohut (1971), diagnosis was based less on history or symptomatology and more on the nature of the unfolding transference.

Despite this obvious lifelong pattern, my early impressions were tempered by some engaging shows of ego strength, most notably her desire to gain relief from her obsessive ruminations, her motivation to change, and her developing trust in me. While these tendencies were most evident, it became too easy to slip into a comfort level about her approach to analysis. Countertransferentially, I had to guard against just experiencing Cara as a compliant, motivated patient who took in whatever I said as if it were the absolute truth. I saw this tendency not only as a resistance to doing her own work, but moreover as reflective of an undifferentiated sense of self. It felt as if she were the infant and I was the "feeding" mother. Indeed, Cara showed a capacity to find caregivers, particularly women, whom she then tended to idealize.

In thinking diagnostically, it is necessary to distinguish Cara's dynamics from other, higher-level character organizations. Many writers (Akhtar 1992, Akhtar and Thomson 1982, Kernberg 1975, Volkan 1976) have reported that narcissistic patients seem most like hysterics, with both exhibiting similar symptoms. The differentiation is seen with regard to the patients with a hysterical structure and those who are more characterologically obsessional. It seems that Cara had difficulty tolerating separation, unlike hysterical and obsessional patients, who have more success in the separation-individuation process, greater ability to internalize conflict, better identity formation, more integrated superego functioning, a deeper capacity for object relatedness, and the usage of repression rather than splitting as the main defensive mode (Akhtar 1992). Rather, she struggled with self/object differentiation, handled intense feelings of shame and powerlessness by becoming rageful, and had identity issues with regard to gender and overall selfhood. Furthermore, she had an unduly harsh superego and distorted object relations fraught with the terror of annihilation. Her profound ambivalence, manifested in a manner that led to the development of a "false self" (Winnicott 1960), had been a major defensive posture. Other ego defense mechanisms that were an intrinsic part of Cara's character structure may be organized along a developmental continuum.

Cara's reliance on psychosomatic defensive functions, particularly with regard to body distortion, further suggested primary narcissism. Her defensive functions generally associated with the oral stage included denial—her childlike use of fantasy to disavow both pleasurable and painful material; introjection—she psychically took in and transformed object representational material into self material with indistinct boundaries between the two, thus losing her sense of separateness; and projection—her paranoid fantasies about how other people could harm her, use her, abandon her. With her obsessive-compulsive style, Cara manifested many anal-stage defenses, namely, turning against the self—by redirecting aggressive and sexual impulses from outside to inside; undoing—contradicting what might have developed in a previous session; committing transgressions and then reversing by self-destructive and/or religious expiation; and displacement—diverting the cathexis of various ideas onto the soma. Generally associated with the beginnings of identity formation in the phallic stage, isolation of affect, as evidenced in her tendency to dissociate and to have fleeting thoughts of an aggressive or sexual nature without associated feelings, was seen as an emerging higher-level defense (Blanck and Blanck 1979).

Other clinical features that distinguished Cara's dynamics from other disorders were bound in her history of having been treated in an unempathic, neglectful, yet somewhat "special" way (first-born girl, ties to her mother). In contrast with the more traumatic backgrounds of borderline patients, her origins speak more to a shame-laden, hungry self-representation as delineated by Kernberg (1970, 1975) and Volkan (1976). Although there certainly are borderline features to Cara's way of being in the world, she appeared to have greater cohesiveness, which became manifest in her tolerance, even preference, for aloneness, her excellent work record, and better ability to control impulses. While she tended to become very regressed, it did not feel like there was the potential for her to dissolve into a psychotic-like state as she showed the capacity to reconstitute. Rather, her dynamics may be thought of within Balint's (1968) concept of the basic fault characterized by a marked discrepancy between needs and the material, attention, care, and affection available to meet such needs.

The role of envy was very pronounced in Cara's dynamics. She would tell you that she mostly envied young women who had mothers who were alive and available. She also would say that she was desirous of a "charmed life," one in which she had a husband who would be attuned to her every need, in which she was surrounded by adoring family members, and one in which she was prized and appreciated for her hard work as a teacher. The early oral and oedipal struggles were represented in her rich fantasy life in which she was actively engaged, both in waking and dream states, with union with her mother and with mythical sexual liaisons with idealized men. She became extremely envious of people who seemed to have mature relationships. In the idealizing transference, this envy extended to me as well; yet Cara was not able to express her anger directly. She saw me as having a "put together life," quite unlike her own. She fantasized that I have an adoring husband, loving family, successful children, and work satisfaction. When asked how that left her feeling about me, Cara denied the envy and projected onto other, less threatening objects. While this material signaled a budding object transference, it was too soon to expect that she would risk being directly rageful (or loving) toward me. Rather, she began to do things such as coming late or canceling sessions. When I tried to explore or interpret the underlying meaning of such actions, she became concrete and childlike, denying her anger. I realized that she needed to resist in this rapprochement manner in order to begin to potentiate ego functioning. Beginning with the third year of treatment, she acted out less in this manner and had become more willing to express intense feelings in the room.

As Ansel Adams reminds us, the final expression of the photographer's visualization is the print, the final image, revealing what one saw and felt. As in the creative process of photography, wherein once the picture is taken the negative is viewed, studied, analyzed, felt, sometimes printed, and sometimes discarded in quest of a more real print, so the process of psychoanalysis unfolds as the analysand is exposed to the lens of the analytic camera revealing in the darkroom of the mind the potential for a fine print of her own. The revising, discarding, interpreting, and feeling that happen along the way speak to the belief that dynamic assessment is an ongoing process, the clarifying of which is based on an integration of theoretical leanings.

Over the years, as my work has evolved with this case and others with severely regressed adults and children, I have moved toward integrating a classic drive model with its emphasis on drives, urges, wishes, conflicts, and early psychosexual development with analytic underpinnings related to ways of understanding object relations, ego, self, and, more recently, relational experience. Drive theory has been most useful in conceptualizing Cara's dynamics with regard to the vicissitudes of her struggle with sexual and aggressive urges. Particularly salient is the conceptualization of primitive drives as being biologically based yet being forged by early bodily and familial experience. Early on, Freud (1900) addressed the development of a wish as a way in which the individual links a current tension state to the memory image of a previous satisfaction of such a state. He thereby spoke to the way in which bodily urges achieve cognitive representation, thus becoming part of the wish/fantasy network of the mind. These concepts resonated for me with regard to Cara as I thought about the very primitive, preoedipal manner in which her drives were organized. Seemingly, her lack of adequate discharge heightened the tension that became manifest in bodily symptoms. Fenichel (1945), in discussing hypochondriasis, referred to a transfer of libido from object representations to organ representations (narcissistic withdrawal) as a way of reacting to a state in which the person is "dammed up." The depth of Cara's narcissism was such that she omnipotently fantasized having an ability to control disease and illness, replete with a heavy reliance on obsessive-compulsive defenses. One is reminded of Freud's (1931) description of the narcissistic character type, in which he emphasized the patient's main interest as being directed toward self-preservation.

Identity issues, a prominent theme in Cara's dynamics, seemed to underlie her disturbed object relations, impaired ego functioning, impoverished sense of self, and character pathology. As I considered Cara's development within the domain of object relations, attachment and loss immediately came to mind. Failures in basic trust at the very core of primary object attachment seem to explain the development of many of Cara's symptoms and character traits. Most salient among such symptoms were extreme anxiety in the form of annihilation anxiety and panic attacks based in unmet need gratification; untamed (unneutralized) aggression; primitive defense structure; and the failure to establish positive self-esteem. Within object relations theory, an individual has a representational world, one in which the experiences of early internal object relations are coded. As I sought to understand Cara, Winnicott's (1953, 1960) concepts of the holding environment of movement of the self from an archaic false self to an emerging true self and his work on transitional space echoed in my mind. Emphasis on the nature of the object as intrinsically related to early maternal provisions as reflected by the individual's need for a holding environment, for mirroring, for actualization of omnipotence, for usage of the object, and for toleration of transitional phenomena were underscored as I saw Cara struggle to rework early maternal and paternal deprivation, with her reliance on both concrete and fantasized transitional objects and phenomena, potential space, and her difficulties with authenticity and self-esteem.

The concept of selfhood as developmentally linked to identity formation is delineated further within the domains of psyche and soma. Embedded in object relations theory yet extending to ego, self, and relational psychology, this concept speaks to a "psychosomatic being" with the true self coming from the "aliveness of body tissues and working of body functions" (Winnicott 1960). In contrast, Cara seemed to have a primitive false self, in which the mind and body split, with mind being the locus of identity while body became a disavowed vestige. Indeed, mental functioning and her whole experience of being took on somatic meanings with very little capacity to self-soothe. As the analysis progressed, Cara began to emerge as a somewhat more differentiated self. Her response to the therapeutic holding environment provided the solution bath in which her work prints could continue to be reworked and to take form.

COURSE OF TREATMENT/WORK PRINTS

In discussing the course of treatment, I shall be focusing on several aspects of the work that illustrate movement within the analytic experience and within Cara's internal and external worlds. Work in the transference and countertransference provided the template for analysis and synthesis of therapeutic experience. Within this context, Cara's development as an emerging self was considered. Particular attention was paid to the lessening of resistances and drives, the emergence of new ego adaptations, the tempering of somatic symptomatology, the movement toward a more cohesive identity, and the budding expression of more fulfilling interpersonal relationships. The dream record was particularly vivid in tracing the development of transference from self-state to emerging object relatedness.

In the initial phase of treatment, once the historical material was elaborated upon, Cara was able to enter into a therapeutic relationship, albeit deferential in manner. Yet, her tendency to talk nonstop in a ruminative manner suggested fears about getting too close. My overriding impression was that Cara was too fragile to tolerate direct confrontation of her ego-syntonic resistances. Fluctuations between her being overly compliant or controlling provided a window into her ego development and the ways in which defensive operations were forged by her early life. She was most responsive to the mirroring provided, which stimulated memories of a fantasized closeness with her mother. This closeness seemed to be experienced by her as ideal attunement.

In the selfobject transferences that developed, it seemed that, as Kohut (1984) suggested, mirror, idealizing, and alter-ego transferences occurred in tandem. Cara's initial hunger for mirroring coupled with the intensity of idealization in the very beginning phases of treatment seemed to lead to her propensity to use me as an alter ego selfobject. The quality of the alter ego and mirroring transferences seemed to preclude any place for me as a separate object in Cara's life. Her intense fears of illness or injury occurring to herself, and, by extension, to her daughter, echoed her tenuous self experience. In this beginning phase, it often was difficult to listen to the repetitive, highly charged ruminations. I had the sense of not being in the room, which is characteristic of the narcissistic transferences. At times, I found myself feeling helpless and incapable of providing an environment that could ensure containment. I also felt frustrated that, when flooded with extreme anxiety, Cara did not seem able to care for her daughter adequately.

As the treatment progressed, I settled into the idea that this would be a long process and that the very nature of her archaic intrapsychic world necessitated handling her resistance within the context of the self experience. This was reflected in her first reported dream, several weeks after beginning treatment. The dream came during the first week of her summer vacation from teaching on the night following her having to make day-care decisions for Candy for the following year: "I was in the park with Candy and a woman approached me and was going to steal Candy." Her spontaneous associations to the woman in the dream seemed to speak poignantly to fears about treatment, merger, and loss of self, as Cara mused, "I could sense when she talked to me she would take Candy. [Silence] Since having Candy, I worry about her waking up." Was she afraid of Candy or herself dying? Indeed, entering treatment incurred imagery about awakening. Cara then went on to recall an incident a year earlier when Candy had fallen down the basement steps. Lamenting that the child could have died, Cara spoke about feeling protective but not protective enough, about wanting to be on top of things at all times, and about being upset that she had let her guard down. This may be seen as fear of loss of self in the therapeutic process with Candy representing the infantile fears and wishes. The transference seemed to relate to whether I would "steal" the child in her, thus the relinquishing of infantile longings. She seemed to have been defending against a fear and wish to be merged with me. I also thought of this theft as her being stolen from her mother or, more aptly, her mother from her. I wondered if Cara felt I would protect her, even if she let her guard down. Her rich fantasy life underscored the need to allow potential space within the treatment to flourish, thereby enabling internal representations to coalesce into a cohesive, strong whole, integrating good self/bad self. The resistance became evident in that shame was defended against by somatic preoccupations and a punitive superego as when Cara would constantly endeavor to punish herself or feel guilty.

Ten months into treatment, shortly after making the change to the couch, Cara reported yet another self-state dream: "Yesterday I took a nap and had this dream. I dreamt about water. It was so strange. I had to walk up this big hill to save this little fish. Up a steep hill to get to it and I don't even like fish." Her associations spoke to frustration and anxiety about trying to get up the hill and not falling back. Upon inquiry, Cara reflected, "Maybe that was me trying to save myself. Maybe I'm the fish." When I explored her not liking fish, Cara's immediate response was that they are "slimy; I don't even like goldfish." Her thoughts then moved to a lifelong fear of water, of not being able to touch bottom. Yet, there was one fish she "had to save."

I saw this dream as a reaction to intensification of the treatment through increased sessions and use of the couch. She had begun to be more self-reflective and somewhat cognizant of her part in "saving herself." The dream may be thought of as affirmation of the treatment, whereby to save the treatment is to save the self. Transferentially, Cara seemed to be struggling with the breast image (big hill) and the hard work of therapy, especially in light of feeling abandoned on the couch, which we had been analyzing for the weeks preceding this dream. The dream seemed to re-create her difficulty with feeling safe in a relationship, in connecting with me, yet another merger issue. The symbol of the fish may be thought of in several contexts—the "slimy" penis, fetus, or umbilical cord or as a condensation of her fears and wishes; thus, the word *fish* serves as a concatenation of *fear* and *wish*. Or she might be saying that she does not like either the good or bad introjects, neither the "slimy" fish nor the golden one.

With the shift to the couch, several powerful memories emerged that seemed to echo in this dream. Cara recalled an incident at age 2½ when she was sick with the croup. Her throat closed up, cutting off her breathing. A neighbor ran outside with her and placed her in the snow to "shock me into breathing" while her mother waited for an ambulance. She and her elder brother, who also had croup, were hospitalized for several days. Once recovered, they remained in the hospital for tonsillectomies. Throughout her childhood, Cara heard the story of how "we almost lost you and your brother." Being on the couch also evoked the memory of the near-fatal drowning experience at age 5. This occurred when Cara slipped into the water at the child-care worker's backyard pool. She recalled going underneath the water and looking up toward the surface. Unclear as to how she was rescued, Cara still retains a fear of water. I pondered the relationship between her feet being "off the ground" in both these traumatic situations and her being "off the ground" on the couch as well as the presence of water, frozen being life preserving and warmed being life threatening. Cara went on to relate that at age 7 she had experienced periodic yet severe separation anxiety. She recalled a panic attack when left in a parked car while her mother went into a convenience store for groceries. It seemed this dream spoke to the panic states associated with life-threatening traumas as well as being an organizing dream for her sense of vulnerability.

In some profound ways, the dream related to the previous one in that again there was the fear of therapeutic intrusiveness as well as a sleep-like state and eventual awakening. In this second dream, however, she took a more active role. If we think of these two dreams in terms of a contemporary view of self-state dreams as discussed by Aron (1989), the dreams may be considered in light of their adaptive, self-regulatory, and organizing functions. Thus Cara's dream state may be thought of as not only mediating conflict, but as a means by which she attempted to integrate and synthesize her world, to create order out of internal chaos, while asleep and awake. These dreams also served as messages about her precarious capacity to organize, preserve, and grow. As Winnicott (1971) reminded us, dreams are transitional phenomena that, however seemingly trivial, provide the space in which profound issues can be addressed.

With entry into the second year of treatment, we began to analyze the remembered closeness with her mother, indeed a profound issue. What emerged was that this closeness was a fantasized relationship Cara had longed for yet never had. She was willing to examine her longing for closeness and ambivalence about attachment. The following clinical vignette, which took place at the start of the second year of treatment, helps to elucidate the flavor of the emerging insight that Cara had begun to gather. It also serves to illustrate the shift in interaction in that Cara moved from not allowing me to speak to tolerating my reflections and her own silence.

C: When I started this last year, I didn't think there was a problem with my mother. When I got older and was in the band, she'd go to see [brother] play football. I hated being in the marching band, only liked the concert band.

SE: So your mother came to games to see your brother and not you.

C: Oh, she would come when I played in concerts. I hated playing in the marching band but you had to in order to play in concert band. But I wasn't mad. She always compared our band to H.'s [district where mother taught] band. (This was said in a contemptuous tone.)

SE: You sound scornful.

C: I was hurt more than angry. She made friends there. I would clean for her. She'd go to work and complain that nobody helped. I had no acknowledgment from my mother or father for helping around the house. Nobody did anything but me. She always complained.

SE: So you did your mother's work.

C: Yes, but not to get credit. When she became very sick, she complained about no one washing dishes. My grandparents got her a dishwasher. I felt bad because she complained. (Prolonged silence. I wondered about the theme of separateness of self, the guilt about her anger toward her mother. Cara felt freed up to be able to be silent, seemingly as her ego struggled to organize her feelings. My thoughts ran to the transference that seemed to be unfolding in a different way. Was Cara expecting to be the parentified child in our relationship? Would I be at the game for her and no one else or would my work take me away from her? Or would I need her to clean my house?)

C: This is freeing me up to understand. It really helps. She wasn't able to make me feel special. I always had to pursue her. (Climbing the big hill.)

SE: Always waiting for the pat on the head.

C: It's interesting you say that. When I would do dishes, she would pat me on the behind. I loved the attention. (I wondered about her mother's sexuality and the degree to which this pat became an arousing gesture.)

C: (Prolonged silence) There were a few times when I would rebel and not do things. (Like now, with me. Yet there was never total abdication to her mother.) Because she expected it. She'd give a look of disappointment. (Cara went on to describe incidents in which she was expected to keep house for her parents and later, after her mother's death, for her father and grandmother. Her tone was full of resentment followed by retraction). My mom was a very weak person. I feel bad saying that.

SE: You seem to feel regret about your anger toward her.

C: It's true. She did the best she could, but it wasn't enough for me. My sister would get real mad at her.

SE: But you remained there for her.

C: A lot of good that did me. (Close of session.)

Reflecting on this vignette, it seemed to illustrate the extent of Cara's increasing ability to express inner rage and not turn it against herself. It served as further confirmation of her fears of connection and exploitation. With this gradual internalization of vital selfobject functions, a shift became evident—a shift from her experiencing the person of the selfobject to her experiencing her own self. The path toward more separate relatedness was in the process of being cleared as was the emergence of competing oedipal feelings. One can readily see the reversion to obsessive features as Cara engaged in doing and undoing. At this point in the treatment, Cara began to develop greater object constancy between sessions, as she would recall things that I had said in a previous session. She continued to hold onto interpretations much in the same way she had always utilized transitional phenomena. In this manner, she demonstrated an improved capacity to maintain a more permanent mental representation of me between sessions.

With the emergence of increased object constancy toward the end of the second year, Cara also showed a greater tendency to share her "secrets," things about herself that caused her great shame. She confided that she was very ignorant about her body and had not explored her genitalia or masturbated since the incident at age 3 when her father found herself masturbating with her teddy bear. Another "secret" had to do with the occasional eating binges in which she engaged. These secrets seemed to be oedipally tinged as she struggled with instinctual drives. Following the sharing of a dream in which she had an affair with an ex-boyfriend, Cara was able to talk about her sexual naïveté and desire to be loved. When I questioned how that desire related to our relationship, she blithely said that she knew I cared about her. My sense was that she was uncertain about her worthiness of my love. When I pursued this further, Cara broke down and cried, lamenting that she did not deserve my attention, verbally reminding me of how sick and disturbed she was. These types of interchanges were very characteristic of the flavor of our working, as Cara tended to revert to her heavily defended self whenever she dared to try to relate in a dyadic or triadic way. While this pattern of steps forward and steps backward continued, she had begun to show an ability to reconstitute more readily following these primitive regressions. There was a shift in the defensive structure away from archaic mechanisms such as ambivalence, denial, omnipotence, projective identification, somatization, obsessive-compulsive traits, and primitive idealization. Instead, Cara showed a capacity to listen quietly rather than talk nonstop, to distinguish both positive and negative aspects of interactions and relationships, to lessen her need to control, particularly with regard to health-related matters, and to not be as hard on herself. As the selfobject functions become more internalized, there was an easing of the defenses with resultant magnification of obsessive-compulsive features and increased oedipal longing. Her ability to explore shame-based material suggested a necessary level of self cohesion. Morrison (1983) reminds the reader that shame presents one of the central, excruciatingly painful experiences of narcissistic patients. The movement of treatment to allow for the analysis of shame-laden material underscores the importance of this theme in Cara's dynamics as she sought to become more self and other accepting.

A curious shift occurred toward the end of the second year. Cara began to talk about her father more frequently, at first denying any feeling for him, followed by lengthy bouts of anger or compassion for him. This was especially prominent when he had surgery for a hernia and Cara was conflicted about whether to contact him. The vicissitudes of the love and hate she harbored were played out as she agonized over whether to call him, send flowers, or do nothing. At times, Cara was able to take in my interpretation of her conflict around being the responsive daughter. Other times, she responded in anger that he had failed her miserably her entire life, adamantly stating, "He had something to do with my creation, that's it!" As I further pursued her anger toward him, I wondered silently about the castration implications of hernia surgery and the oedipal significance that bore. She went into a tirade about how everyone thought her father was such a great guy when they met him, adding, "You would if you met him." I stated that I thought she seemed quite rageful and frightened. After a long silence, she shook her head affirmatively. I reflected her fear that I might abandon her for her father (as her mother had done). She responded, "The man has never given me anything materially." So it seemed, even the hope for daddy's penis has been dashed with the threat of castration and the competition that his having a woman friend presented. The drive-defense aspect of the transference became more salient as Cara saw me as an oedipal rival, the transferential mother.

This session was followed by one in which Cara reported a dream she had had following a call she made to her recuperating father. "I had a dream. Dad was in it. I had lost weight, was in a bathing suit. I have spider veins in my legs and he said, 'Too bad you have those veins.'" Her associations were that it was so like him to focus on the "bad stuff," but that she had had a surprisingly nice conversation with him. She immediately switched to talking about anxiety about her upcoming semiannual appointment with the high-risk breast cancer clinic, thus repressing the latent content by focusing, instead, on somatic ruminations. While there are self-state qualities to this dream, it and the concomitant material were illustrative of the shift in the treatment from a dyadic to a more triadic constellation, from an archaic structure to one that allowed for a more cohesive self and object relatedness. In the dream, she was looking for her father to admire her figure. It was as if she was asking, "Am I desirable to my father?" If so, the anxiety was such that the "bad breast" takes over (in the form of spider veins, high-risk cancer clinic). With the gradual movement from primitive defenses to a more complex, higher-level defensive structure, Cara had begun to move away from conceptualizing her mother as all good and her father as all bad. Even though, in the dream, her father represented the critical, bad introject, she saw her body in an integrated manner, as having both good and bad characteristics (weight loss and spider veins). This dream came at a time when the transference has begun to reflect a gradual change toward relating to me more as an object and less as a selfobject.

Taken in a series, the dreams speak to the different palettes of psychoanalysis, namely, Cara's drive-defense conflicts, improved object relations, emergence of self, ego defense organization, and relational yearnings.

Four months after her father's surgery, Cara had a car accident. Her father called her, apparently concerned about her welfare. Several weeks after the accident, Cara approached him to lend her money for a down payment on a used car she was buying to replace the one destroyed in the accident. Cara was unable to connect the crisis created by the accident with her desire to reunite with her father. Rather, she was elated as she discussed how generous and unconditional he had been in lending her the money, even driving a long distance to take her and Candy out to dinner when giving her the money, which she promptly paid back. According to Cara, he had become much more expressive of his feelings since living with his female friend. I wondered if his living with a woman made him a safer object. She tried to imagine what it would have been like if her mother had been different with her father. There was more observing ego about the parents' marriage and her own relationship with him. Cara seemed to bask in this newfound relationship with her father. She even went with her husband and daughter to visit him in the house she had never seen.

As the relationship with her father has evolved, a subtle shift in the transference has been noted. It felt more oedipal as she began to express anger about other patients of mine whom she fantasized as being much healthier and, therefore, did not need as long-term a treatment. There was a sibling feel to the interaction, a vying for my attention. Cara also confided that even though she felt better now that she was working out things with her father, she was afraid that I would say that she did not need to come anymore. Now, well into the second half of the third year of treatment, this rapprochement continued with her being able to take in and make her own interpretations of conflicting material and affects. She had yet to chance full expression of her anger toward me for fear of abandonment and/or annihilation. In her archaic state, she still tended to use me as a selfobject, someone to be idealized, and as an alter ego. When this happened either in the therapy or outside with others, nobody else but Cara seemed to exist. It was anticipated that as she continued to move toward object relatedness, Cara would realize that I would not be destroyed by her rage or by her love; rather, she would experience me as a human being replete with both positive and negative propensities.

With the beginnings of such movement, as treatment intensified, several changes occurred. Namely, Cara seemed to have less shame about her body image and feel less vulnerable about her personal safety. There had been an intensification of obsessive-compulsive defenses before being open to triadic development. It should be noted that the increased attention to oedipal yearnings may also have been stimulated by Candy being in the oedipal stage herself. Lastly, grandiose, depressive, and envious feelings had become more integrated as the true self emerged in a cohesive manner, thereby allowing unacceptable feelings open, rather than shame-laden, expression.

With the budding emergence of a more integrated sense of self, Cara had been better able to achieve increased autonomous functioning. This was evidenced, for example, by her improved ability to anticipate my absence during a recent vacation without bringing her daughter to sessions, her maturity in settling the copayment part of her therapy fees, and, most recently, her finesse in convincing her husband to enter treatment. She seemed to be less psychosomatic. An example of this was underscored by her observations that she used to get upset by concerns that no longer send her into panic states in which she assumed she would die. She also began to consider having a second child, a decision that she had previously assumed would put her at higher risk for cancer. She was able to enroll Candy in a preschool program, thus letting go of her in yet another way. I found myself feeling like I was more in the room as a real person, despite her occasional lapses into deeply regressive states. She seemed to be less fragile and diffuse, less inclined toward projective identification, and more accessible, vibrant, and willing to tolerate the analytic situation in a classical sense. As her health narcissism began to bloom, the true, adult self was coming into clearer focus. With a more cohesive sense of self, she appeared as more the center of her own world rather than relying on magical thinking, religious expiation, grandiosity, or fate. Superego development had progressed sufficiently to allow Cara to be less harsh on herself. With the gradual acquisition of improved reality testing, Cara could take in more data rather than depend on others to situate herself in the world. Less of her psychic energy got drained off to defend against fragmentation; rather, the reconstructive focus was on helping her to maintain her own inner world. While there was still the tendency to long for fusion in an oceanic way, Cara seemed to be in more of a working alliance as she continued to move toward self differentiation and object relatedness. She would probably say it in much simpler terms as when in a recent session, she hesitantly stated, "I used to be such a mess, but now I can see that it's possible to have some happiness."

As Ansel Adams so poignantly wrote, a fine print requires interpretation and expression of the negative's information through a series of work prints. Cara's work prints continue to develop, as form and texture become more delineated, essence become apparent, and black and white moves to shadings of gray as well as a full range of color. Through the process of psychoanalysis, Cara's work prints speak to a change in both her intrapsychic and external life, shifts in object relations, and to a wider range of affect. As the work continues with full recognition that there is more structure building to do, the form that her true self takes is unique to Cara, enabling her to find and ensure her place in the world.

REFERENCES

Adams, A. (1983). *The Print*. Boston: Little, Brown.

Akhtar, S. (1992). *Broken Structures: Severe Personality Disorders and Their Treatment*. Northvale, NJ: Jason Aronson.

Akhtar, S., and Thomson, A. (1982). Overview: narcissistic personality disorder. *American Journal of Psychiatry* 139:12–20.

Aron, L. (1989). Dreams, narrative and the psychoanalytic method. *Contemporary Psychoanalysis* 25(1):108–127.

Balint, M. (1968). *The Basic Fault: Therapeutic Aspects of Regression*. New York: Brunner/Mazel.

Blanck, G., and Blanck, R. (1979). *Ego Psychology: Theory and Practice*. New York: Columbia University Press.

Chessick, R. (1989). *The Technique and Practice of Listening in Intensive Psychotherapy*. Northvale, NJ: Jason Aronson.

Fenichel, O. (1945). *The Psychoanalytic Theory of Neurosis*. New York: Norton.

Freud, S. (1900). The interpretation of dreams. *Standard Edition* 4, 5.

———— (1914). On narcissism: an introduction. *Standard Edition* 14:67–204.

———— (1931). Libidinal types. *Standard Edition* 21:215–258.

Kernberg, O. (1970). A psychoanalytic classification of character pathology. *Journal of the American Psychoanalytic Association* 18:800–822.

———— (1975). *Borderline Conditions and Pathological Narcissism.* New York: Jason Aronson.

Kohut, H. (1971). *The Analysis of the Self.* New York: International Universities Press.

———— (1984). *How Does Analysis Cure?* Chicago: University of Chicago Press.

McDougall, J. (1989). *Theaters of the Body: A Psychoanalytic Approach to Psychosomatic Illness.* New York: Norton.

Morrison, A. (1983). Shame, the ideal self, and narcissism. *Contemporary Psychoanalysis* 19:295–318.

Pine, F. (1990). *Drive, Ego, Object, and Self.* New York: Basic Books.

Volkan, V. (1976). *Primitive Internalized Object Relations.* New York: International Universities Press.

Winnicott, D. (1953). Transistional objects and transitional phenomena study of the first not-me possession. *International Journal of Psycho-Analysis* 34:89–97.

———— (1960). Ego distortion in terms of true and false self. In *The Maturational Processes and the Facilitating Environment.* New York: International Universities Press, 1965.

———— (1971). *Playing and Reality.* New York: Basic Books.

CHAPTER TEN

Treatment Resistance in a Psychosomatic Patient

CHARLOTTE SCHWARTZ

This case report demonstrates the interrelationship between a specific psychosomatic symptom and the role of hypochondriasis in the progressive deterioration of a borderline patient. I shall also discuss the relationship between the patient's incestuous behavior, her prostitution, and the mutual prostitution enactments by the patient and her mother and their impact on her progressive ego deterioration. The interconnection between psychic conflict and object loss is pivotal to an understanding of the patient's somatization and pathological development.

On the continuum between health and psychopathology, the psychosomatic symptom appears to point to a higher level of ego defense and ego integration than the hypochondriacal symptoms. Furthermore, the psychosomatic symptom indicates an ego organization that is more commensurate with relatedness to the external world and the stabilization of internalized object representations. I believe that the development of the psychosomatic symptom represents an attempt by the patient's ego to bind her libidinal longings, while the hypochondriasis represents her attempts to manage her conflicts over aggression, which in its uncontrolled and unmodified form would result in the destruction of the self and the object. Of course, these are issues of degree, for both libidinal and aggressive drives are copresent in all psychic functions. At the level of psychosomatization there was greater stability in ego function, while the onset of the hypochondriacal symptoms coincided with an increased loss of ego structure and function. Yet in tandem, both processes—psychosomatization and hypochondriasis—indicate a regressive process (Freud 1914, Reiten 1992). Simultaneously, these processes also represent an attempt at restitution of the body ego at the state when narcissistic ego structure (Hartmann 1950) was firmly established.

CASE PRESENTATION

Barbara G., a Caucasian woman of 40 of middle-class Jewish origins, exhibited her first psychosomatic symptom at age 35. She complained of numbness, tingling, and coldness in the extremities of her fingers. This was diagnosed as Raynaud's disease, a vascular disorder. Fenichel (1945) refers to this disease as a severe "vegetative neurosis" about which little is known psychoanalytically regarding its possible psychogenic components. The hypochondriacal symptoms had a somewhat later onset and were evidenced by her complaints of abdominal pains, headaches, dizziness, and shortness of breath. No organic etiology could be found for these symptoms. The respiratory distress suggested a conversion symptom in which the unconscious fantasy had both pregenital and genital elements. Thus, it is possible to suggest in this case a borderline state between conversion symptoms, psychosomatic symptomatology, and hypochondriasis. In general, the expression of psychological conflicts in the various gradations of a somatic mode suggest an underlying ego withdrawal from the external object world to a narcissistic state of hypercathexis of the body ego. There is an additional feature in the manner by which the patient used the symptomatology that further suggested that the somatization was erotized. Laforgue (1930) discussed a patient who had been able to cause great anxiety for her friends and herself by arousing in herself "a real death anxiety." In Laforgue's case the somatization was related to the erotization of anxiety, which had been placed at the service of her neurosis. For my patient the psychosomatic symptoms also indicated an erotization of anxiety. She became very involved with her physicians, mainly males toward whom she behaved in a sexually seductive manner. Seemingly, in these relationships she was enacting a genital sexual scenario, but fundamentally, the anxiety, a product of dammed-up libido (Fenichel 1945), stemmed from the frustration of infantile oral wishes. Since the infantile wishes had been inconsistently gratified, her ability to trust in any object was impaired. Thus, all object relationships were fixated at the level of narcissistic development and omnipotent wishes. This inability to elaborate psychically libidinal wishes within the context of a safe object relationship resulted in enormous anxiety. Somatization proved to be the only viable means by which her ego could assimilate this anxiety. Further, the sexualization of anxiety discharged through somatic symptoms also provided the patient with a defense against massive separation fears from her mother, an ambivalently loved object. Yet, equally significant in her development of Raynaud's disease was a hysterical identification with her grandmother's death, which this disease simulated. The symptoms of numbness and frigidity in her extremities duplicate a dead body. Further, the symptoms suggest a powerful death wish, an identification and rejoining of the grandmother whose body she found when she was 10.

The patient presented a diagnostic picture of a borderline personality disorder with psychopathic features. In her adolescence a somewhat better prognostic picture had been indicated, that of an adjustment reaction with reactive delinquent features. I am using the nosology of *borderline* more in keeping with Knight's (1953) use of the term, a continuum from neurosis to psychosis, rather than Kernberg's (1975) conceptualization. As the case progressed, this patient evidenced many more features of an affective psychosis. In spite of her three years of psychotherapy beginning at the age of 15, there was no improvement. In fact, a steady deterioration was evidenced by the nature of her acting out and her labile affective state. A second traumatic event had occurred in her sixteenth year—that of a sexual relationship with her mother's boyfriend. The question as to whether this trauma of an incestuous nature was the pivotal point in her psychic deterioration or whether the already pathological structures from infancy on were largely responsible for the regression and pathological ego organization is a central issue.

When I first saw Barbara, she was initially referred for treatment by a high school guidance counselor. There was concern that this bright adolescent was beginning to exhibit signs of antisocial behavior. She was truanting from school, not doing assignments, and was involved with a semi-delinquent group of adolescents.

In the first session, I observed a very pretty, intelligent young girl who behaved impulsively and was easily angered. It was clear that there was an underlying depression. The relationship with her boyfriend was volatile, and her behavior was very provocative; she was physically abusive and provoked constant emotional crises. Barbara was sexually active with her boyfriend, and intermittently, when they broke up, she would become sexually involved with other boys.

Her parents had separated when she was 1 year old and were subsequently divorced. Barbara, an only child, resided with her mother and maternal grandparents. The grandfather died when she was 3 years old and her grandmother died when she was 10. The grandmother was the primary caregiver, and her death was a profound loss. The trauma of her death was further exacerbated by the experience of Barbara discovering her dead body. For Barbara to talk about her grandmother, to recognize her loss and sorrow, and especially her fear of separation, was extremely difficult. While she admitted to loving her, there was very little expression of affect. To mourn this loss was too painful since the objects in her life were not very reliable. She had already developed a rigid defense structure that denied the need of any object. Any expression of loving emotions exposed her to an intolerable longing that she was incapable of assimilating.

I saw the patient for three years in once-a-week psychotherapy. During this time, I had some contact with her parents and her boyfriend. Her mother, an attractive, infantile woman, showed little awareness of her daughter's problems. She was adolescentlike in manner, and had little awareness of generation boundaries, sharing the most intimate details of her life with her daughter. Certainly, leaving Barbara in the care of her boyfriend while she was hospitalized for a hysterectomy indicated some unconscious incestual wish that was then acted out by the daughter. In later years they would both sleep with the same man, prostituting themselves for money.

Her father, a rather ineffectual man, was unsuccessful in every business he attempted and could barely support himself. He tried to help his daughter but was unable to sustain any real constancy. Essentially, he lived in a world of fantasy. Eventually, he was hospitalized and diagnosed as a manic depressive. He later died of a stroke. In the early years Barbara had idolized him, but in adolescence she could no longer sustain this idealized image. This disillusion was a contributing factor to her promiscuous sexual behavior, her continual search for the idealized, oedipal father.

While the treatment provided her with a supportive object relationship, it could not prevail against the destructive force of her inner rage. Her behavior was both self-punitive and destructive to the object. She continued in high school until several months prior to graduation, and then precipitously left without graduating. What I had not known at the time was that she had had an affair with her mother's boyfriend. Barbara's guilt, and her rage at the boyfriend, her mother, and me for not preventing this incestual enactment, played a significant role in her leaving high school. Further, her guilt and anger made it impossible for her to continue the treatment. In her relationship with her boyfriend and husband-to-be, these conflicts were reenacted so that she eventually destroyed the relationship.

Barbara's behavior with men became increasingly promiscuous. Psychically, to sleep with men, to control them sexually, was tantamount to destroying them. She taunted them and tried to make them feel inadequate; this also provided her with sadistic pleasure. Yet a good deal of her behavior was defensive against her guilt for her betrayal of her mother by the incestuous act. Although I attempted to interpret the multilayered meanings, and tried to make the connection between her rage at men and her deep disappointment in her father, she was unable to make use of this understanding. Underlying the oedipal conflicts and rivalries was the powerful pre-oedipal fixation to a narcissistic mother. Barbara's relationship to females was tumultuous, marked by extraordinarily close ties, conflicts that became physically abusive, breakups, and reconciliations. She was unable to tolerate any cognitive or affective awareness of her longings for a protective and loving mother. Thus, almost all her relationships evidenced the mechanism of "doing and undoing." Rage at the object and self-directed rage made it difficult to sustain the object relationship. When her abusiveness drove the object away, this seemed to be proof that no one could be trusted to love or to take care of her. Qualitatively, her guilt and self-rage reflected a harsh infantile superego. The superego as a structure was too weak to modify her aggression; quite the contrary, it became the vehicle for the discharge of the aggressive drive. There was little capacity for self-regulation, an ego deficit due to the impaired dyadic relationship with her mother (Taylor 1994).

After Barbara's precipitously leaving therapy, I heard from her intermittently. Some three years later she again resumed treatment, and remained in therapy for about eight months. Barbara had married and divorced Bob who had now matured and attained some stability and financial success. She continued to pursue him and then reject him, so that he finally refused to have any contact with her. Subsequently he remarried and had a child. Barbara was visibly distressed over the loss of Bob and made repeated attempts to seduce him. It was clear that her character structure had developed an omnipotent defense, and she believed that she could control and possess whomever she wanted. The reality of her loss so enraged her that for some time her behavior became dangerous. In intoxicated states, she would pick up strangers and have sexual intercourse with them; she barely knew their names. At times, she experienced a fugue-like state, not quite sure of the sexual act, where or how it occurred, and even if it was a real event. In part, this was also a result of heavy drinking. Although she did not tell me directly, there were implications that at times she took money for sex. Underlying her prostitution enactments were oral incorporative fantasies; the penis was a symbol for the breast. The alcoholic state and the blanking out resembled the sleep pattern of the infant after a feeding.

In the treatment, she could be verbally abusive, cursing at and demeaning me. On one occasion, as she left my office she turned at the door and asked if I were not frightened "to be here alone, as someone could kill you." I answered that I was not scared and that I could get the person before they got me. She gave me a strange smile and left. When I went into the waiting room, I saw that she had knocked over a flower arrangement and scattered the magazines. In truth, I did feel an eerie sense of trepidation, for this was the first time that I really sensed the quality of her aggression. There was no thought that she would harm me, but what she was capable of was arousing my own masochistic fantasies (Balint 1959). This was another clue to the perceptiveness of her unconscious and her excellent ability to seduce the object into an enactment or affect state.

The patient continually interrupted the treatment with me, sometimes for months, sometimes for years, although she always maintained telephone contact. In the interim, she saw a psychiatrist, Dr. X., who put her on medication. This relationship, although ambivalent, was highly erotized and in part, this erotization kept her bound to him by a repetitive need to seduce him. She had become addicted to Valium, which she had secured from various physicians. Subsequently, she also became addicted to Xanax. Barbara was extremely skillful in securing prescriptions from various physicians and psychiatrists while she continued to be in treatment with Dr. X. Her resistance both to psychotropic drugs and psychotherapy was difficult to counteract. She had allergic reactions to some of the medications, which resulted in Dr. X.'s experimental usage of a wide variety of others. A number of attempts were made to detoxify her on an inpatient basis, but this only led to repeated failures. The efforts were unsuccessful due to her powerful destructive resistance to getting well, and in fact her treatment with Dr. X. suffered the same fate. Her need for control of the object and her erotization of the object relationship interfered with the possibility of establishing new identifications. Her defenses against feelings of helplessness were too powerful to overcome; thus, she reversed the passive wishes by an active seductive behavior in which she was partially successful. She learned intimate details regarding Dr. X.'s private life, including information about his divorce and his girlfriends. Much of this information came from his secretary, but she was also able to seduce him into revealing these intimacies. At times, he would try to withdraw from treating her or she would initiate the separation and seek another psychiatrist, but in the end she would return to him. She continues to take multiple medications, abusing the dosage and drinking alcohol.

When Barbara returned to treatment with me in her mid-thirties, she had already remarried. I believe that this return was precipitated by an abortion that caused her much distress. Barbara blamed her husband for the abortion and projected onto him her self-hatred. True, Don was not very supportive regarding the pregnancy, but I believe he unconsciously understood her rage and rivalry toward this unborn child. He had been married previously and had custody of his son. Because of Barbara's resentment and rage the boy lived with Don's parents. She refused to permit the child to visit their home, and was relentless in her animosity to him. She was extremely jealous of any attention paid by her husband to his son. At moments, she would express guilt over her behavior but was unable to modify her negativism and unkindness. This hateful rage at objects was also self-directed. Not only did her ambivalence deprive her of a child, but by aborting the pregnancy, she exacerbated her self-loathing. Since the mechanism of projection was so much a part of her character structure, it was inevitable that her attitude toward her husband would become increasingly scornful and abusive.

Until this marriage, Barbara had worked as a highly paid administrative secretary. The marriage precipitated a marked regression; she developed a subway phobia, and it became increasingly difficult for her to leave her apartment unless accompanied by another person. She feared the crowds in the train, and expressed anxiety over suffocation and fears of dying. In the subway, she was overwhelmed by panic, nausea, and dizziness. The phobic symptom proved inadequate to bind the anxiety and gradually more and more areas were invaded by the underlying fears of danger and anxiety. Soon she could no longer tolerate her office atmosphere, where she also experienced feelings of suffocation. The phobia was symptomatic of her intensely ambivalent feelings toward her mother. It symbolized a powerful wish to be loved passively and cared for, and in this regressive state, oral longings to merge with her mother were also aroused. Despite these oral wishes, the feelings of suffocation secondarily represented an unconscious fear of a mother who wanted to destroy her. In part, this fear indicated a projection of her own death wishes toward her mother. A further complication to the phobia defense was a very powerful wish to die. Thus, to leave the house represented a separation from an ambivalently loved and hated object, and exposed her to vague, unknown dangers and the dread of death. In this infantile state, she could only leave the house in the presence of another person, and thereby undo the feared separation and danger of death.

Oedipal issues, that is, the infantile rivalry with her mother for the father, converged with the preoedipal anxieties. Due to the impoverished preoedipal relationship with her mother, the oedipal conflicts could only increase her fears of separation and contribute to an already weakened ego structure. These unresolved oedipal conflicts interfered with the development of genital-level identificatory mechanisms. Although her fixation to her mother was very powerful, she could only internalize a very diminished ego ideal, which resulted in a weak but punitive superego structure.

Despite the ambivalent and destructive relationship between mother and daughter, her mother moved into the same apartment building where Barbara and her husband lived. The male became the intruder between these two women, who were bound by a powerful narcissistic identification, oral sadism (Klein 1932), and oedipal rivalry. They both scorned Don and finally succeeded in driving him away. Barbara was enraged when Don left, but she had no awareness of her role. She could only experience this as another desertion, which contributed to her infantile projections regarding the bad object. The relationship between mother and daughter can best be described as an oedipal perversion; they slept with the same man for economic favors and money and shared in the mutual pleasure of destroying the male. We can only speculate as to the meaning of the unconscious fantasy in which they both had access to the oedipal father. This behavior also represented correlative prostitution fantasies. Simultaneously, a sadomasochistic rivalry would ensue in which each was physically and emotionally abusive to the other. While a strong homosexual tie between mother and daughter existed, I am inclined to regard the relationship as more indicative of an infantile narcissistic relationship, interchanging mother and daughter roles.

As long as the patient could maintain a superficial oedipal position her functioning was moderately adequate. Despite self-destructive behavior, there were still sufficient ego gratifications from her sense of mastery in relationship to men. The aggressive drive was used defensively against powerful oral needs, and thus her ego could maintain a level of defensive functioning that enabled her to work and maintain relationships with men and women. Once Barbara married, her defenses against the infantile pre-oedipal wishes were weakened. Her ego, under enormous pressure from the force of these wishes, which the marriage was bound to exacerbate, could no longer sustain the fragile defenses. Also, with diminished sexual enactments, her ego lost another line of defense against the emergence of preoedipal needs and wishes; the pretense of oedipal behavior could no longer be sustained. The development of phobias, somatization, and hypochondriasis were attempts to halt ego decompensation.

With the onset of Raynaud's disease, a psychosomatic symptom, we observe an attempt by the patient to bind the unfulfilled libidinal longings and her aggressive drive. By means of this somatic discharge mechanism the ego could still maintain a modicum of adequate functioning. The emergent hypochondriacal symptoms pointed to a severe ego regression indicating a body ego organization for which the body functions as a conduit for diffuse narcissistic drives. The ego is then organized around a narcissistic body ego. At this point, she was unable to leave her home; she spent days in bed, and she complained of multiple somatic symptoms.

That the patient made use of various organ responses as a means of dealing with internal conflict and structural deficits enables us to observe an interesting relationship between hypochondriasis and psychosomatic symptomatology, and somatization with fantasy. In this specific situation, the somatization—Raynaud's disease—represented a reenactment of a traumatic situation, that of her grandmother's death. Barbara's cold and numb fingers replicate the grandmother's cold and rigid body. We may conjecture that the somatic symptom embodied a fantasy by which the object was retained by means of identification (Fenichel 1945). Her death wish symbolized linkage with the grandmother and also contributed to the development of Raynaud's disease. Thus, she could sustain an immortal inner representation of the protective object by means of this imitative identification. With the onset of hypochondriacal symptoms, there was a commensurate increase of narcissism and withdrawal from the object world. It would appear that hypochondriasis points to a more regressive mechanism than psychosomatization (Schilder 1964). The psychosomatic symptom had indeed responded to medication and after a year improved, while the hypochondriasis remained intractable and appeared exponential to her deterioration.

TRANSFERENCE

The patient's inability to remain in treatment without continuous interruptions was multidetermined (Waelder 1930). She repeated in an active form what she had experienced passively, the abandonment first by father, then by mother, and finally by grandmother. Thus, she repeatedly abandoned me. Oedipal conflicts further interfered with her ability to remain in the treatment with me. Barbara created a triangular constellation in which her psychiatrist, Dr. X., was experienced by her as my rival. Therefore, I became dangerous to her as the mother who would prohibit her from having a man. Further, to trust, to permit the emergence of her infantile needs, created overwhelming annihilation anxiety, and thus she could only deal with these fears by leaving me. In reality, no object could meet the immensity of her infantile wishes, and only disappointment could ensue. Also, to experience the impact of these wishes in relation to an object challenged her omnipotent defenses. Her transference struggle with me entwined two very powerful wishes: one, the wish to have me as the preodipal mother who would nourish and care for her, and two, the wish to experience me as the oedipal object of identification. As an oedipal object of identification, I aroused for her the danger of oedipal jealousy and, thus, due to the precarious preoedipal attachments and ambivalence, endangered her primitive object relations. It was due to these two powerful forces that the transference resistance could be maintained with such resolution. To accept me as a fantasy mother, to experience the force and pain of the early deprivations, and to begin the process of reidentification (Strachey 1934) and emotional relearning was too great a challenge to her omnipotent defenses. To permit new ego identifications would impose the realization of a more potent oedipal rival. Thus, from the position of the regressive oral phase and the reinforcement from the genital phase, the transference was regarded as too threatening. Further, I believe the more basic constituent of the resistance was her fear of destroying me as an internal and external object. Barbara had established a relationship with me that she had always tried to convert from a transference object to a real object. Validly, her fear of my becoming a real object could only intensify her object hatred, and thus she would destroy me as an internal object representation and the external object. In essence, she tried to make me into an external need-gratifying object. Yet, since I understood that to attempt to gratify her in any real way was doomed to failure because of the intensity of her oral rage, I tried to remain strictly within the transference frame. Support and empathy were focused on her affective state, and I tried to avoid suggestion, personal revelations, and any activity that she would interpret as a "real" relationship. Her frustration with me was enormous, not, I believe, because of object hunger, but rather because she could not seduce me into this love—hate web. It was at these times that she had to break the treatment for fear that her aggression would either push me away or destroy the internal representation. If at times the transference affects became too powerful, especially if rivalry was evoked by any interpretation or more likely by clarification, this too was experienced as threatening. Barbara resisted the translation of affects into language. Joyce McDougall (1982) has described patients for whom the continuity between affect and words had never been established or had become discontinuous as in alexithymia. I consider that this patient had to maintain the isolation (Eissler 1959, Freud 1926) between affect and word, and between affect and meaning due to the enormity of her guilt and the fragility of her ego structure.

CONCLUSION

To present a case of failure has its historical referent in Freud's 1905 treatment of Dora. Similarly to Dora, the negative transference here was exceptionally powerful. Although my patient refused to relinquish contact with me, it was essentially the force of her aggressive drive infusing her oral wishes to possess me that was the force behind the continuity of contact. In this sense, the destructive drive had gained a victory over her libidinal wishes for the object.

The development of Raynaud's disease, a psychosomatic symptom, was the first line of defense against the more regressive narcissistic defense of hypochondriasis. The psychosomatic symptom enabled her ego to maintain a wider arena of psychic functions by the binding of libidinal and aggressive wishes. Just as in psychological symptoms, psychosomatization as a compromise formation can function as a defense mechanism. Psychosomatic symptomatology attempts to maintain a compromise formation between wish and defense through the vehicle of specific organ discharge. Unfortunately for the patient, the development of hypochondriacal symptoms indicated that the ego's relationship to the external environment was increasingly compromised. Regression to a body ego that utilized diffuse discharge mechanisms, and where affects are isolated from ideational meaning, indicates a more serious pathological state. Treatment was unable to spare this patient profound psychic and body disorganization.

REFERENCES

Balint, M. (1959). *Thrills and Regression.* New York: International Universities Press.

Eissler, K. (1959). On isolation. *Psychoanalytic Study of the Child* 14:29–60. New York: International Universities Press.

Fenichel, O. (1945). *The Psychoanalytic Theory of Neurosis.* New York: Norton.

Freud, S. (1905 [1901]). Fragment of an analysis of a case of hysteria. *Standard Edition* 7:3–112.

———— (1914). On narcissism: an introduction. *Standard Edition* 14:67–102.

———— (1926 [1925]). Inhibitions, symptoms and anxiety. *Standard Edition* 20:87–156.

Hartmann, H. (1950). *Essays on Ego Psychology.* New York: International Universities Press, 1964.

Kernberg, O. (1975). *Borderline Conditions and Pathological Narcissism.* New York: Jason Aronson.

Klein, M. (1932). *The Psychoanalysis of Children.* London: Hogarth, 1975.

Knight, R. P. (1953). Borderline states. In *Psychoanalytic Psychiatry,* ed. R. P. Knight and C. R. Friedman, pp. 97–109. New York: International Universities Press, 1954.

Laforgue, R. (1930). On the eroticization of anxiety. *International Journal of Psycho-Analysis* 11:312–321.

McDougall, J. (1982). Alexithymia: a psychoanalytic viewpoint. *Psychotherapy and Psychosomatics* 38:81–90.

Reiten, R. (1992). Pax de deux: on origins and ends of Freud's "narcissism." In *Psychoanalysis and Contemporary Thought,* ed. L. Goldberger, pp. 411–482. Madison, CT: International Universities Press.

Schilder, P. (1964). Personality development. In *Contributions to Developmental Neuropsychiatry,* ed. L. Bender, pp. 61–101. New York: International Universities Press.

Strachey, J. (1934). The nature of the therapeutic action of psychoanalysis. *International Journal of Psycho-Analysis* 15:127–159.

Taylor, G. J. (1994). Psychosomatics and self regulation. In *Interface of Psychoanalysis and Psychiatry,* ed. J. W. Barron, M. M. Eagle, and D. L. Wolitzky, pp. 464–488. Washington, DC: American Psychological Association.

Waelder, R. (1930). The principle of multiple function. *Psychoanalytic Quarterly* 5:45–62, 1936.

PART IV

Specific Mind—Body Problems

CHAPTER ELEVEN

The Stress Connection: Arthritis and Related Diseases

BERTRAND AGUS

It is well established that psychological factors play an important role in the painful and sometimes deforming rheumatic diseases (Moldofsky and Rothman 1971). They certainly can occur as a reaction to illnesses that are often chronic, and in some instances may be important contributing factors in the causation of these diseases. While it is controversial whether there is a specific kind of personality type that is prone to develop arthritis (Crown and Crown 1973), it is clear that the way one reacts psychologically to rheumatic disease helps to determine the eventual outcome of the disease (Rosillo and Vogel 1971). In my experience, there is great variability in the way people react to the symptoms or diagnosis of rheumatic disease. Surprisingly, there are some people who seem to accept the diagnosis well with all of its negative implications; some patients may have anticipated the onset of disease because of a family history. More commonly experienced is the sense of anger, frustration, guilt, and fear because of the disruption of a previously normal, healthful life and the prospect of being permanently disabled. Although mild depression is common, suicidal behavior is extremely rare, and most patients learn to cope with their situation.

It is not surprising that psychological stress, like physical stress, can have profound effects on body chemistry. It is known that stress increases the levels of corticotrophin-releasing hormone (CRH) in the hypothalamus of the brain, which in turn regulates the release of adrenocorticotropic hormone (ACTH) from the anterior pituitary gland, located at the base of the brain (Taylor and Fishman 1988). ACTH then stimulates the adrenal glands to release corticosteroid hormones. These hormones raise blood pressure and blood sugar, speed up the heart rate, and increase the kidney function. On the negative side, steroid hormones can impair immune defenses, and lay the body open to infections, both from without (exogenous) or within (endogenous). This potential breakdown in immunity can also lead to autoimmune disease, whereby the body cannot distinguish self from foreign, causing a misguided attack upon itself. This is the paradigm for the autoimmune dysfunction seen in systemic lupus erythematosus and rheumatoid arthritis.

Changes in physical appearance can occur as a result of rheumatic disease. For example, in rheumatoid arthritis the joints can become gnarled and disfigured. In systemic lupus erythematosus, hair loss and rashes can be very embarrassing, and treatment with corticosteroids can lead to massive weight gain. The tight, sclerotic skin of scleroderma can make one appear wizened and prematurely aged. This change in body image can reflect on one's own sense of self-esteem. It frequently manifests itself by loss of sexual interest and difficulty with normal sexual function. Sexual counseling can be very helpful to these patients. One such protocol that is widely used was devised by Ferguson and Figley (1979).

Pain per se exerts a powerful effect on personality and emotions. It can severely interfere with intellectual and emotional coping responses (Earle et al. 1979). Similarly, powerful pain medicines, including both narcotic and nonnarcotic agents, can cause cognitive difficulties. Nevertheless, serious drug abuse and addiction is not common in patients with rheumatic disease. As in the general healthy population, thresholds for pain perception vary widely among rheumatic disease patients.

Age of onset of disease profoundly influences the psychological response. Consider the interesting example of juvenile rheumatoid arthritis.

McAnarney and her colleagues (1974) did a detailed investigation of forty-two children from a pediatric rheumatology clinic. Whereas children with arthritis had more psychological problems than normal controls, the ones with the least disability had more problems than those more severely impaired. This surprising result stems mostly from the fact that the most disabled were perceived by others to be ill and were catered to. The minimally disabled were commonly thought not to be ill at all.

The loss of functional ability often makes rheumatic disease patients dependent on other people. The simplest of tasks can become very demanding, and it can be devastating to patients when they can no longer carry out routine bathing and personal grooming. A factor that has important psychological impact is the financial cost of chronic illness. Having arthritis means frequent doctor visits, laboratory examinations, medications, and occasional lengthy hospitalizations.

TYPES OF RHEUMATIC DISEASE

To better understand the way stress impacts on rheumatic disease, one must have basic knowledge of the types of rheumatic disease.

Degenerative Disease

Degenerative disease of the bone and joints results from disintegration of the normally articulating structures, such as the cartilage, as a result of a lifetime of wear and tear. The best example of degenerative rheumatic disease is osteoarthritis, where joint cartilage, the main "shock absorber" of the joints, disintegrates, a phenomenon that will occur in almost every person to some extent, should they live long enough. The main contributing factors to degenerative arthritis are advanced age, genetic predisposition, occupational factors (such as typists who get osteoarthritis of the hands, or football players who get arthritis of the knees), and traumas (such as old fractures). Although not a main cause of degenerative arthritis, psychic tension can aggravate symptoms of arthritis by causing muscular tension in those areas that are mechanically altered. The pain of the common "pinched nerve" occurring in the cervical spine or low back ("sciatica") is often exacerbated by psychic muscle tension. Thus, psychological factors in these instances are most often a consequence of the disease, rather than causative. Patients sometimes manifest depression over the prospects of aging or not being able to carry out ordinary lifestyle activities such as a favored sport, or being forced into early retirement.

Metabolic Disease

Metabolic disease causing pain in the muscles, bones, and joints results from an upset in body chemistry. The most notable condition in this category is disease of the thyroid gland, either overactive (hyperthyroidism) or underactive (hypothyroidism or myxedema.) Importantly, thyroid disorders frequently cause neuropsychiatric symptoms as well. Prompt recognition is critical to rendering the proper treatment for these patients. Hyperthyroidism (Graves' disease) typically causes symptoms of anxiety, insomnia, weight loss despite excessive appetite, tremors, weakness, palpitations, and muscle and joint pains. Often patients can be recognized by the prominence of the eyes with enlargement of the eyeballs in the sockets. A battery of tests must be performed to diagnose the condition, including thyroid function tests and radioactive uptake scanning of the thyroid gland. Hypothyroidism can be more subtle in its presentation. It may develop slowly over twenty or more years, sometimes in patients previously treated for hyperthyroidism. Classically, patients are slowed mentally, are overweight, and have coarsened hair, constipation, and slow pulse rates. Patients can also manifest a wide array of neuropsychiatric symptoms, up to and including the so-called myxedema madness. Obviously, psychological treatment for such patients has limited value except as an adjunct to appropriate medical therapy. Should one suspect any kind of thyroid disorder, prompt referral for medical workup is indicated.

Of importance are the multiple pain syndromes caused by diabetes mellitus. Diabetes is mostly thought of as a disease of abnormal sugar metabolism, but in reality it is a complex illness affecting the nervous system, blood vessels, muscles, bones, and joints. Many patients suffer from reactive hypoglycemia, in which excessive amounts of insulin are produced in response to a sugar challenge. Hypoglycemia can cause headaches, anxiety, and cognitive problems Many of these patients will develop frank diabetes in later life due to the development of insulin resistance. They must be counseled not to eat diets high in simple sugars, such as the typical American junk-food diet, but rather diets high in protein, which is more slowly metabolized to sugar, thereby avoiding excessive insulin secretion response.

Diabetes can also affect the nerves, a condition labeled *diabetic neuropathy*. This can cause lightning pains in the extremities, and a severe degenerative arthritis called Charcot's arthropathy, because patients may lose their sense of joint position and appreciation of pain, thereby traumatizing their joints with the simple activities of daily living, such as walking.

Inflammatory Diseases

Inflammatory diseases are a heterogeneous spectrum of diseases of unknown cause in which there is a systemic inflammation that can lead to damage of many organ systems. These diseases can be referred to as connective tissue diseases, because they can affect any part of the body at one time or other. At one end of the spectrum is rheumatoid arthritis, the commonest form of disease in this category, where the brunt of the inflammation is sustained by the joints, often leading to destructive arthritis over months and years. At the other end of the spectrum is systemic lupus erythematosus, where the disease is not confined to one organ system but can affect the connective tissue of any organ, including the skin, heart, kidney, blood-forming elements, and the nervous system. Muscle and joint involvement in lupus is therefore much less severe than in rheumatoid arthritis.

There is considerable scientific evidence that diseases of connective tissue have a genetic basis. It is also well known that disorders of the immune system play a role in these conditions, and that stress can alter the delicate and modulated functions of the immune system (Ader and Cohen 1985, Solomon et al. 1974). There is also a female proclivity for connective tissue disease. For example, the female/male incidence is 2–3:1 in rheumatoid arthritis and 10–13:1 for systemic lupus erythematosus. Several genes have been linked to rheumatoid arthritis, notably human leukocyte antigen (HLA), DW2, and HLA B27 in the rheumatoid variant of spondylitis. Twins separated at birth have an extraordinary concordance for systemic lupus erythematosus.

It is also known, however, that simply having a gene for a particular trait or disease does not guarantee that one will get a particular disease. Even if one inherits a genetic disease, for example, the gene does not necessarily determine the severity of the disease. For example, in psoriasis, a common skin disease with a high tendency to cause a rheumatoid-like arthritis, called psoriatic arthritis, it is known that psoriatics have a gene deletion on the short arm of the sixth chromosome, in a zone near the one that controls the proteins of the immune system. If one has a parent with psoriasis, then there is a one in four chance that the gene will be passed. In the overwhelming majority of cases, the psoriasis may be only barely manifest, such as simple "pitting" of one or a few nails, or a hidden psoriatic plaque in the cleft of the buttocks. There will be others where the psoriasis will cover over 80 percent of the body surface. About 10 percent will develop a chronic rheumatoid arthritis, and some will have the presence of the arthritogenic gene HLA B27 as well. The association of stress and flares of psoriasis is well known, emphasizing again how diseases that are genetically determined can be influenced by environmental factors.

Clearly, other factors, probably environmental, must be important in unlocking certain gene functions, allowing for partial or complete gene expressivity. In the case of systemic lupus erythematosus, the damaging ultraviolet A and B rays are one such environmental factor that brings on the lupus diathesis. Thus, a patient's lupus may become evident after exposure to the sun during a day at the beach. Psoriatic patients will relate that their skin disease and even their joint disease flare if they are under psychological stress. The role that stress plays in flaring rheumatoid arthritis can be seen in the two following examples that I have documented in my medical practice in the past twenty-five years.

CASE PRESENTATIONS

J.B. was a normal 26-year-old man who, on his honeymoon, while driving at high speed in Nevada, lost control of the car and skidded into a ditch. His bride was killed instantly and J.B. survived with only minor scratches. Profoundly saddened and depressed, he returned home. Two weeks later, he developed pains and swelling in many joints, including the hands, feet, and knees. Blood tests showed an elevated sedimentation rate, a measure of inflammatory activity, typical in rheumatoid arthritis. There was no family history of rheumatic disease. He was diagnosed with rheumatoid arthritis, which remained very active despite drug therapy for one year, after which the joints improved, and he has not had any recurrence ten years later.

W.S., a 104-year-old man, was hospitalized for an acute myocardial infarction. He did very well with subsidence of chest pains in a couple of days, and return of his electrocardiogram and blood tests to normal. Ten days later, while awaiting discharge home, he developed symmetrical swelling of hands, wrists, knees, and ankles. He never had any history of any kind of arthritis or gout. He was diagnosed as having rheumatoid arthritis by examination and blood tests. He was placed on antirheumatic medication and improved in a few months.

Discussion

These two cases show the importance of stress as a trigger for rheumatoid arthritis. Neither case had any kind of genetic predisposition as far as is known, but both suffered from severe stress, one emotional and one illness-driven. Cases of rheumatoid disease have been noted in surgical postoperative periods as well. Moreover, many patients can date their onset of disease to a particular stressful time of life. It is reasonable, therefore, to suggest that psychological counseling for such affected patients is an important adjunct in their treatment and ultimate rehabilitation.

FIBROMYALGIA

In the past two decades, a relatively common recognized pain syndrome called *fibromyalgia* was recognized. The possible psychological basis for this syndrome is still being hotly debated among rheumatologists (Bradley et al. 1985). Typically affecting young women in their thirties and forties, but not exclusively restricted to this age or sex, the condition can be so severe that the individual cannot carry out the activities of daily living. In some cases, fatigue is the major presenting symptom, and these cases have been labeled *chronic fatigue syndrome*. In others, muscular pain and stiffness are predominant, and the term *fibromyalgia* has been applied. Objective findings are few in these conditions, except for the presence of selected tender points, sometimes called "trigger points," in the muscles about the neck, shoulders, low back, and epicondyles of the elbows. Almost all laboratory tests are negative, although some claim that there are inordinately high serological titers against certain viruses, like the herpes virus HHV6 and Epstein-Barr virus. These patients commonly have a sleep disturbance with frequent nocturnal awakenings, and in about 40 percent of cases have irritable bowel syndrome. Many of the patients have been found to be clinically depressed. Indeed, treatment for this disorder includes the use of low-dose antidepressants, which are believed to work by favorably altering the sleep cycle. In fact, most of the patients are not clinically depressed, and many are unwilling to entertain the possibility that their condition could have an emotional basis. They tend to agree with the contention that stress exacerbates the condition, but tenaciously deny any hypothesis that would make stress the etiology of the problem. Treatment for fibromyalgia is extremely disappointing. No drug, or combination of drugs, works uniformly to alleviate the symptoms. Physical therapy is of transient benefit, as are chiropractic treatment and acupuncture. Even less valuable is therapy with "alternative" approaches. Most patients resent psychological or psychiatric interventions, and even when they participate, results of long-term psychotherapy are mixed.

CONCLUSION

Stress plays an important role in the rheumatic diseases, mainly as a catalyst or promoter of disease. Stress, whether physical or psychological, is important to the biology of all living beings. It serves a useful purpose by stimulating the nervous system and keeping it in a state of high alert. It serves to stimulate the immune system to fight off infection and to provide surveillance against the emergence of cancer. Prolonged and unremitting stress, in contrast, has negative consequences for the body, by causing depression of the immune system, raising the blood sugar and cholesterol, and facilitating life-threatening infections. To the extent that chronic stress can do this, it facilitates the onset of degenerative and inflammatory musculoskeletal disease. It is important, therefore, to employ a multidisciplinary approach in the treatment of rheumatic diseases. Such treatment should not only attempt to suppress inflammation where necessary, or improve biomechanical situations to allay abnormal forces on bodily structures, but should also address the stress itself. Modalities that may be useful in stress reduction include biofeedback, anxiolytic and antidepressant medications, and psychotherapy.

REFERENCES

Ader, R., and Cohen, N. (1985). CNS-immune system interactions: conditioning phenomena. *Behavioral Brain Sciences* 8:379–395.

Bradley, L. A., Anderson, H. O., Young, I. D., and McDaniel, L. K. (1985). Is psychological disturbance highly associated with primary fibrositis? Evidence that primary fibrositis is not a form of "psychogenic rheumatism." *Behavioral Medicine Abstracts* 6:145.

Crown, S., and Crown, J. M. (1973). Personality in early rheumatoid arthritis. *Journal of Psychosomatic Research* 17(3):189–196.

Earle, J. R., et al. (1979). Psychosocial adjustment of rheumatoid arthritis patients from two alternative treatment settings. *Journal of Rheumatology* 6(1):80–87.

Ferguson, K., and Figley, B. (1979). Sexual counseling in the arthritic disease. *Sexual Disability* 2:130.

McAnarney, E. R., Pless, I. B., Satterwhite, B., and Friedman, S. D. (1974). Psychological problems in children with chronic juvenile arthritis. *Pediatrics* 53(4):523–528.

Moldofsky, H., and Rothman, A. I. (1971). Personality, disease parameters and medications in rheumatoid arthritis. *Journal of Chronic Diseases* 6:363–372.

Rosillo, R. H., and Vogel, M. L. (1971). Correlation of psychological variables and progress in physical rehabilitation. IV. The relation of body images to success in physical rehabilitation. *Archives of Physical Medicine* 52(4):182–186.

Solomon, G. F., Amkraut, A. A., and Kasper, P. (1974). Immunity, emotions and stress. *Annals of Clinical Research* 6(6):313–322.

Taylor, A. L., and Fishman, L. M. (1988). Corticotrophin-releasing hormone. *New England Journal of Medicine* 319(4):213–221.

CHAPTER TWELVE

Psychosomatic Telemachus:
The Body as Oracle, Armor, and Battlefield

JOSEPH SIMO

The complexity of the multiple aspects of this bewildering case have forced me to pack into its title as much signification as possible, in order to alert us that the raging inner battles of this man-child take place simultaneously on many fronts. I will concentrate my narrative on three of the dis-ordered and dis-ordering ways in which the patient, whom I will call Telemachus, "misuses" his body. These misuses, I hope, will help us understand his *misconceptions*—in Money-Kyrle's (1968) sense—of the body's natural functions. Thus, I will refer to Telemachus's use of the body as:

1. an *armor* against contact and relationship;
2. an *oracle* that reveals somatically—with his perennial colds, flus, and skin rashes, all the way to his pneumonia and his unconscious suicide attempt—that which he cannot "say" verbally; and
3. a *battlefield* where he enacts the savage fights of his "combined" parents, strifes that he cannot metabolize psychically and has to expel and banish from his mind.

I will use the separation-individuation paradigm to retrace the twisted road that led me to the door of Telemachus's enigmatic soul. In that paradigm the child, on his way to becoming an individual, has to move away from the symbiosis that keeps him/her fused psychosomatically with mother and enter the world of differentiated bodies, of distinct minds, and of one-to-one relationships. He/she has to travel the psychic distance from the absolute symbiotic mother

to *m*-other (the dawning of the awareness of an-other object not me/mother) to *me*-other (mother as the other separated from me by psychic space).

This is the essential split that tears the symbiotic proto-space where experience is only felt and not perceived by the infant and marks the outset of the interpersonal world in psychic life. These early sensations, when they are not properly signified by the mind, may lead to severe misconceptions of body functions. The main factor in this split that marks the onset of psychic structuring, the something that is not me/mother, is the entry of the father into the field of experience of the child and his active presence in its psychic life. To ensure a successful entrance of the father in the psychic life of the child, it is essential that the parental figures(s) who look after the child be *good enough*, as Winnicott said, so they can provide a safe holding environment where the child's development can proceed in an orderly fashion. Unfortunately, often the child's environment, far from being safe, is a traumatizing one in the sense that Ferenczi (1932) used this concept. The trauma creates an extreme rise in tension in the relationship of the child with the adults in his environment that endangers the emergence of trust in the significant other as a separate and benign entity. Instead, the other is "felt" as a part of the self that can be omnipotently manipulated and controlled. If (s)he does not get help from the environment to solve this rise in tension, a split in the personality will ensue, one part suffering the effects of this intolerable situation and another part observing detachedly, and hardening in an unbridgeable paranoid/schizoid position. This original trauma can be made a permanent part of the personality by means of the introjection of the traumatizing agent that Garcia Badaracco (personal communication) calls the "maddening object." I will add that a precondition to the success of this process of separation-individuation that leads to triangulation and to the necessary creation of psychic space where objects can exist and take on stable identities is the relatively successful differentiation of what Klein (1952) described as the "combined parent" figure. This is an unconscious fantasy formation characteristic of the earliest stages of psychosexual development.

Klein wrote of the combined parent mostly as the main source of envy. When the mother—a mother experienced symbiotically as part of the infant's own body, meaning that originally she is experienced somatically—is not there to fulfill the needs and symbiotic desires of the infant, he fantasizes (obviously an archaic proto-fantasy) a deformed being, *mother-plus-not-me*, who is taking mother away from him. This monstrous combined being is not only engaged in an endless cycle of self-gratification of oral, urethral, and anal nature, which is experienced as catastrophic in the infant's proto-fantasies, but can be experienced as tearing apart, taking away, or physically injuring a part of the child's own body. Given the infant's lack of set boundaries, its ignorance of physical laws, and its not having a secure location in time and space, I consider the inability to metabolize psychologically this most archaic of objects into its "adult" form (one body for each, one sex for each, and one mind for each) to be a source and a main theater-of-the-deformed kind of object relations that we observe in psychotic and borderline patients and in the curious lack of feeling and rigidity in the expression of the somatizing patient. This dual separation-individuation process—baby-from-mother and mother-from-father—contributes as well to the preconscious delineation of the body's natural boundaries and of its distinctive features: me–not me, inside–outside, body–mind, physical–emotional, and boy–girl. These differentiations are essential in order for the child to succeed in the task of establishing a clear sense of gender identity and fairly healthy relationships, both within the self and with significant external objects.

Given the importance of the preoedipal father as a critical factor in a successful separation-individuation process, in the marking of body boundaries, and in the differentiation of the sexes, I will call this patient Telemachus because in classical mythology Telemachus was a boy who grew up without a father. However, in my own deconstruction of the Homeric myth, varying notably from traditional interpretations that stress the undying faithfulness of the good wife Penelope, Telemachus is the boy who grew up next to a psychotic mother who didn't want him to have a father. Despite not knowing for sure if this fateful deprivation perpetrated by Penelope stemmed from her hatred of men or from a Lacanian desire to turn Telemachus into the phallus that she lacked, what is clear is that she succeeded in separating young Telemachus from his father and tried hard, later on, to separate him from his analyst-father.

The implicit thesis that we are contemplating is that a serious paternal failure in this crucial stage of development, due to either critical deficiencies or to absence, can have catastrophic effects on the child's tender psyche. Among these, it can contribute to the solidification of a terrifying symbiotic con-fusion of genders, of psyche and soma, of child and mother-as-part-of-me, and it can thus become a main factor in the creation of a somatizing patient. The case of Telemachus sadly illustrates this kind of failure and its costly consequences to the child. Deprived of a basic identification with the father, as both male and different from mother, Telemachus became a strange hybrid to himself, a shallow false front to the Other, and developed a deformed and bizarrely working psychic apparatus. This psychic apparatus foreclosed the products of intolerable needs, impulses, and desires for other human beings that it could not metabolize, and tossed them away to get lost in some forgotten corner of the body, a body that Telemachus experienced as a terrifying curse ever since he became conscious of it. That is why he has always tried to forget that he had a body and preferred to live in a permanent dream state where the body is not *felt*. (This "disappearance" of the body from the field of direct experience, in my opinion, hasn't received enough attention in the literature on dream interpretation or in the evaluation of the role of conscious fantasy in psychic life.) Grotstein (1994) suggested that Klein's

> concept of the infant corresponds to that of Tausk—that it is born as a psyche who first discovers its body—and its body's needs—through *projective identification* and then claims them through *introjective identification*. In addition, however, since the infant is identified with its psyche, then all needs and feelings, at least at first, are believed—in phantasy—to be (a) originating from outside its self-as-psyche, and (b) to be inextricably associated with the arrival and departure of mother-as-breast. [p. 729]

Thus, needs are originally experienced as alien and persecutory and the desire emerges to rid the psyche of them. The idea that the physical body may be constructed in the psyche by means of archaic projective identifications suggests an intriguing hypothesis—that those unyielding symbiotic fantasy structures that we encounter in so many of our "difficult" patients have as one of their main functions not only the maintenance in the preconscious of the combined parent proto-phantasy, but the maintenance of the unity of the physical body as well. We will see in the case of Telemachus that disturbances in his fantasy structure produced by the analytic work caused a direct somatic response.

In 1894 Freud introduced the concept of "forclusion" (*Verwerfung*) when writing about psychosis: "Here, the ego *rejects* (*verwirft*) *the incompatible idea together with its affect* and behaves as if the idea had never occurred to the ego at all" (p. 58, my italics). Lacan elaborated this rich but neglected concept, adding to our understanding that foreclosure consists in not symbolizing that which ought to be symbolized (castration). M. Safouan applied this concept to the psychoanalysis of transsexuals. The ability shown by some people to annihilate the psychoemotional significance of their real experiences has pushed many psychoanalytic authors to pursue the urgent understanding of this most strange and elusive human behavior. Concepts like Laing's (1959) *death in life*, McDougall's (1974) *psychological foreclosure*, Meltzer's (1975) *absence*, Green's (1975) *blank psychosis*, Grotstein's (1979) *psychotic not-being*, Ogden's (1980) *state of nonexperience*, and my *psychic vampirism* (Simo 1993) are some of the many attempts to throw some light onto the dark clinical maze where these most puzzling patients lead us. This is a most difficult category that includes the somatizing patient.

McDougall (1989) wrote about patient Christopher:

> A radical split between body and mind had occurred. Messages sent by the psyche were not transmitted through the symbolic chains of verbal thought and word-presentations; rather short-circuiting the links of language, they were registered only as *thing-presentations*, provoking a direct somatic response, such as we observe in small infants. The persistence of this kind of mental functioning reveals frequently in the course of analysis, its roots in the early mother–child relationship. [p. 64]

I will add to my agreement with McDougall's portrait "a disturbed mother–child relationship" due to the absence of the structuring function of the father. This is a function that establishes the triangulation necessary to the development of the psychic space where relationships can appear and grow. To relate, we know, is to connect that which is apart. And its opposite, leading to serious psychotic disturbances, is, as Bion (1957) taught us, "attacks on linking." Thus, I will conceptualize my approach to the somatizations and distortions of body image and gender identity presented by Telemachus as follows: a psychologically absent father, hated and devalued by a bitter, *hateful* psychotic mother (I emphasize her hate as the pathological aspect of her personality), prevented the boy from achieving both a modicum of separation from his destructive mother and the creation of a psychic space large enough to contain in the psyche the vicissitudes of that which belongs to the domain of the affects that regulate intrapsychic and interpersonal relationships, that is, the immaterial but essential space where we feel the intimate affective connections that we establish between *I* and the significant people in our experience, our inner objects. Instead, he felt pulled by destiny into an inescapable and asphyxiating spaceless folie à deux with his mother, which carried with it an endless string of catastrophic effects, real and imaginary. Of these, I refer briefly only to the most relevant:

1. the failure to differentiate the "combined parent" imago in his unconscious, with the inevitable misconception of people as fused in cruel, sadistic, and indivisible units, from the ensuing confusion about gender and male-female characteristics, and
2. the failure to symbolize his overwhelming castration fears, to nurture a healthy male identification, and to acquire the basic psychoemotional benefits of such an identification.

Such developmental failure had the effect of keeping this young man functioning psychically at the level of an infant. When this kind of archaic mental functioning is maintained in an adult it appears to us as either psychotic or borderline. Instead of using verbal thought and symbolic language Telemachus "said" many important thoughts with his body. At the same time he expressed verbally, and in the images he wove into his cherished fantasies, his bizarre misconceptions of the body, of feelings, and of human relationships. Then he tried to force his body to actualize and to perform these aberrations. The only window that afforded him a few breaths of fresh air uncontaminated by the permanent panic of mother-as-body and body-as-mother was his fantasizing himself and the world around him into oblivion, literally, and not only to forget his devalued self and his badly battered identity but, most of all, his body, perceived as an unbearable cross.

Let me introduce you to Telemachus. In the early 1980s I conducted workshops on "Masculinity, Myths, and Realities" as my contribution to the profeminist men's movement. Telemachus was sent to me by his female therapist in order to inject some life into his severely stifled sense of masculinity by "being and working with other men." At the end of this workshop he "thought," and his therapist agreed, that he would be "better off with a male therapist." I became Telemachus's fourth therapist and, with me, he started his first analysis, which he initially regarded as something "adult" and as something "masculine" a few years after. Telemachus had been in therapy since he was about 10 years old, which, by then, amounted to twenty years. When we started the analysis the most dramatic feature of his life was being trapped in self-castrating female identifications (I prefer *fusions* because, despite their fantasy nature, he experienced them concretely and believed that "they" performed from outside of his self many of the psychic functions that he refused to perform as himself and as a boy). These were fusions with his psychotic mother—experienced as his bad but powerful self—and with female characters of TV comedies of the 1950s (the period of his babyhood and early childhood). The most notable were Lucy of "I Love Lucy" and Alice Kramden of "The Honeymooners"—women idealized as the good parts of his self, even if they were silly or apparently powerless (in his psychic reality all women are powerful). He was so concretely attached to these characters, not only as his "family" but as an external part of his true self, that he watched reruns of these shows every single day in order to feel himself "at home." He had memorized all the dialogue of each episode, in order to block the intrusion of reality in his endless daydreams and to reach a state of unreachability and nonunderstanding that would protect his fusions. Betty Joseph (1975) describes a similar process as a specific kind of splitting and projective identification that enables the "difficult" patient to get absorbed into his own thought processes and fantasies, "leaving me in contact with only a pseudo-understanding part of the self and therefore unable to give him understanding" (p. 57). To this, I will add the severe degree of isolation from reality that this kind of absorbing daydreaming is supposed to achieve, isolation that is qualitatively different from the psychotic distortion of reality. Reality, to Telemachus, is a bad dream, a terrifying black hole that threatens him with sucking into itself every tiny bit of pleasure that he manages to scrape, with the greatest difficulties, from the bottom of life's barrel.

According to Telemachus, he was a "basket case" ever since he could remember. That's the reason he started therapy so early. For he was terrified of nearly everything: older boys, girls, dogs, heights, sports, school work. These were his conscious fears, the ones he denied or foreclosed related to the terror that his perpetually angry and castrating mother inspired in him. She was a "mother" not fully differentiated in his mind: not truly female, nor male either, but, as all combined parents are, was neither and both. It took him ten years of analysis to verbally acknowledge this terror of his mother. As a terrified child, the only thing that calmed him down was his fantasizing and his playacting at being a woman. Telemachus loved to wear towels as shirts or as turbans around his head. If this had been the extent of his female identifications, they would fall within a normal range of childhood exploration of gender characteristics, similarities, and differences. But in Telemachus's case they were still solidly entrenched when he was in his thirties, well beyond the usual range of exploration, and he not only had managed to bury these identifications in his unconscious, but had fused them with his flesh as well as with his mind. In a psychotic delusion that Telemachus enacted in his strange masturbatory rituals, it seemed not only that he was trying to change his sex but that he easily succeeded in this strange task.

Telemachus is past 40 and has never had sex with anyone, male or female. His internal fusion that keeps him welded to his "mothers"—the good soothing ones and the bad killer ones—prevents him from getting close to another human being. He uses his body as an armor, made of ailments of all kinds—especially skin disorders—against the battlefield of physical and emotional contact. He reacts still to the idea of touching or being touched by another human being with an anticipated painful feeling. No wonder that during the first years of the analysis, whenever he allowed us to get "closer" in the transference, he experienced real and dramatic physical pain, in the form of his self-induced skin rashes. Telemachus started building his body as an armor against contact when he was an infant and, he believes with horror, his mother was disgusted by the contents of his body: feces, vomit, or urine. Telemachus was a colicky baby and he is convinced that whatever his body expels is truly bad, foul smelling (it contains as well the rotten smell of dead babies), and deeply humiliating. This is why when, already as an adult, he felt a need to defecate (which he did several times a day because he "stuffed his face with food"), he behaved in another bizarre way. If he was at work (he works in lower Manhattan where municipal government offices are located) he left his office, "armed" with matches and odor-erasing sprays, searching for solitary bathrooms in little-occupied buildings in order to have his bowel movements in as close to total secrecy as possible. The idea that men using his own office's bathroom could detect the smell of his fecal matter—equated with his entire body and its shameful secrets—filled him with an intolerable sense of humiliation and shame. The notion that the fecal matter of other men using the bathroom had the same odor as his, despite his having experienced it, was dismissed before it could be integrated into his psyche. Any hint of an identification with male peers or senior men in his office was violently attacked and destroyed by him-as-mother. On the other hand, he always felt at home chatting and gossiping with "the girls," something he believed was tolerated by mother even if she didn't fully approve.

It took a few years of analysis for him to be able to use the same bathroom as his male co-workers and a few more to stop using matches and other erasers of natural odors. His accepting a bit more of the body that had been an endless source of shame and of panic attacks was felt by him to be a major therapeutic victory. Previously, he had to disguise the humiliating pain of whatever some evil force had turned him into behind an unbroken chain of colds, hives, flus, and bugs (intestinal and otherwise), and in the clumsiness that had alienated him from any athletic pursuits and signified a further denial of his maleness. This denial was embodied in an ill-defined heel "injury." He was convinced that his "limp limb" would always prevent him from walking away from the chains that tied him to his destructive mother. This limp limb was a symbolic expression of his missing father, and of the accepted castration that in his fantasy kept the rest of his "old-womanish" body "safe," a belief that proved to be an insurmountable resistance to "get it up." Not only did he angrily refuse the idea of having sex with another human being, but even to masturbate as the other boys, the normal ones, do was unthinkable to him.

Deeply humiliated by the growing awareness of how bizarre his fantasies and practices were, after a few years of struggling with his terror of "it," he decided to take a sex course in order to end once and for all his "frustration with it." He consulted a sex therapist who referred him to a surrogate for a twelve-session program. He was supposed to start working in the nude on his "body image," and end the program having sexual intercourse with the surrogate. The entire program was supposed to last three months. After two years of weekly sessions, his surrogate—a woman much older than himself and an obvious preoedipal mother figure—decided to retire to Florida. Telemachus never completed his program because he couldn't manage to have successful sexual intercourse. The female "cavity" hid a dragon in disguise (a devouring-aborting mother), waiting there to "get" him in order to castrate and destroy him. He very much liked his weekly visits to the surrogate, as they had become friends, according to him, and he enjoyed "dancing and talking in the nude." It appeared to me that their interaction had little sexual content, other than his waking up to skin eroticism, which coincided with a notable decrease in his skin disorders and a promising replacement of the painful skin sensations with pleasurable ones. Without a doubt Telemachus's most pleasurable experience was his being held, as if he were a baby, by the good, loving, and libidinally gratifying mother he had turned his surrogate into. Notwithstanding his failure at becoming sexual, he became far more accepting of his body and, for the first time in his life, allowed himself to be touched by another human being. Adding some further confusion to his already confused gender identity, he enjoyed dancing in the nude with his sex surrogate, and having joined a gym and beginning to feel like one of the boys, had an erection when he felt the touch of his male masseur.

Despite this momentous breakthrough in his social isolation, masturbation—his peculiar version of it—remained his only form of acknowledged sexual activity. His favorite sexual scenario always opens his quite frequent masturbation. In it, he imagines a man—abnormally large in muscles and sexual organs—who displays them to a captive "sex kitten." She touches them in awe and disbelief and anticipates a "big" sexual experience, which is never clear in his narrative if it is pleasurable, painful, or—given the way in which he experienced his body—both. Pain and pleasure are indissolubly fused in his mind, like the sexual excitement and the terror of brutal castration, and his version of the combined parent. His is the praying mantis model of the combined parent, the one where the female part kills and devours her male counterpart. In this fantasy of the beefy man, a silent copulation follows the exhibitionistic display of muscle, a copulation broken only by faint pleasure (pain?) moans, uttered by the sex kitten. The beefy man is "totally steely." This means that he does not show any emotion of any kind and, most importantly, he does not sweat at all. Losing anything that reveals the inside of the body—sweat, odor, excrement, semen, vomit, even thoughts and words—has caused him intense shame and intense panic for a long time. I suspect that revealing the natural contents of the body is, in his deformed mind, the signal that triggers off the praying mantis's insatiable cannibalistic appetite for her mate.

Telemachus forces his body to perform a strangely unnatural exploit when he masturbates. I had never heard before a similar misconception of male masturbation. Lying in bed face down, holding a pillow as a love object, he rubs his penis against the mattress and fantasizes about the cartoonish muscle man receiving the sex kitten's look of disbelief and admiration. Although he bends his erection in a most unnatural way—he holds down his hard penis between his legs while rubbing it (his apparent anatomy changes from male to female)—he manages to achieve an orgasm. But this is not the most remarkable feature of his odd masturbatory practices. When he reaches the orgasm, he ejaculates without much pleasure (perhaps he expels from his body his maleness with his semen). Then he cleans himself methodically, walks to the bathroom, and, holding on to the towel rack and the door handle, he experiences what he describes as an "internal" and "satisfying full orgasm," without any further ejaculation. His whole body convulses, as if he's having a pleasurable spasm or, even more intriguing, as if he's having a female orgasm.

We know about the permanence of the hardened combined parent imago in his psyche, and his chaotic fusion with good and bad mothers. We know as well that in his most terrifying fantasy one of the babies aborted by his mother was a female (he always says "abortion" when he intends to say miscarriage). This clarifies another possible source of his "female" orgasms as part of his deep female identifications. "She"—he as his dead sister—could not be reached by the psychotic rages of his mother because, by not being endowed with a penis, a girl cannot lose the penis that she does not have. We know that his own real penis "disappears" when he masturbates. Telemachus has always believed that he has a better chance to survive as a girl than as a boy, or maybe he is as dead to sexuality as his dead sister is, or, even more dramatic, in the depths of his unconscious he tries to revive his dead sister with his complex, hermaphroditic sexuality.

Fears of annihilation have always tortured Telemachus mercilessly, especially since he was 11 years old when his father died, according to his mother, of a heart attack. I write "according to his mother" because Telemachus has spent his entire life chained to his mother's voice like a slave to his master's dungeon. He never had an opinion of his own that he expressed verbally because he didn't allow himself to know them. The only way he "spoke" his own version of events that dissented in any way from his mother's version was with his body. With his mind, he never questioned anything that his mother said, no matter how absurdly contrary to the laws of logic or reality it might have been, because his mother *was* his mind. And yet, unconsciously, he managed to project into me small fragments of knowledge that had been deeply repressed but not somatized. From the beginning of our analytic work, I had a strange conviction that his father, of whom Telemachus knew practically nothing, had killed himself.

Mother's version of his father's death never made any sense to me. According to her, he had his heart attack while he was walking on the FDR Drive in Manhattan. This proved to be a lie that, nevertheless, contained her buried confession that his "heart"—his strength, his feelings—had been "attacked" repeatedly by her, and these attacks, in some way, had contributed to the depression that led to his suicide. After almost six years of bloody transferential battles between the analyst-as-father and the folie à deux team Telemachus—mother, battles that resulted in the defeat of the all-powerful but evil mother, he allowed himself to look with his own eyes at his father's death certificate. This was a symbol of his allowing himself to finally feel the loss of his father, a new and notably different object from his mother's hated and devalued husband. Although he worked in the city government, and presumably would know how to obtain a copy of a death certificate, he had never dared to find out how his father had died. Telemachus was devastated by the conscious knowledge that his father had killed himself by jumping into the East River from a bridge. This was the reason he had been walking along the FDR Drive, and the reason his casket had been closed at his funeral.

The discovery of an important truth about his father, the separation of his own perceptions from mother's eyes and the capacity to feel autonomously his own feelings, succeeded in freeing the masculine strength he had acquired after many years of savage transferential wars, and marked a turning point not only in the analysis but in his life. Needless to say that the conscious memories he had of father and mother together were memories of brutal, endless verbal fights. These were fights that, according to him, were always started by mother who won them, easily, after sadistically humiliating the weak father in front of him. Telemachus could think, for the first time, that his mother had "pushed" his father off the bridge with her hatred. And he could hate her for "pushing" him as well, symbolically at least, off the bridge that would allow him to walk away from her and toward father, toward men, and a needed and secretly yearned for masculine identification.

When he got his father's death certificate Telemachus called my office, for the first time ever, asking me to call him back at home no matter how late into the night I might get his message. When I returned his call, he cried his overwhelming distress, burying his tearful face in my telephonic lap. It was the first time that he cried in front of me, even if it was at a safe distance. This was the first time that he had allowed himself to transform his unbearable emotion into an appropriate reaction, tears, by crying his distress and his need for a good-enough and soothing mother rather than attacking himself by attacking the body that he had always blamed as the cause of his overwhelming anxiety and sadness. He recognized me for the first time as a good-enough mother containing a real father in herself, a good combined parent who could metabolize his distress and return to him soothing words that he could reintroject into his psyche. This fateful event flung open the door to his much-needed male identification, even if it progressed very slowly.

This was a momentous transformation if we take into consideration that when we started the analysis, a few years earlier, he lived alone in his mother's apartment (she had retired to another state). Telemachus was isolated, literally, in this imaginary "maternal" space that he had created. He was unemployed—he had been fired again for daydreaming while on the job—and slept in his mother's bed, wrapped up in his mother's bedsheets. I have to emphasize the psychotic content of this dramatic depressive regression. I compare it to the horror movie *The Silence of the Lambs* in which a psychotic killer murders young women in order to cut slices of their skin and stitch together, literally, a new "female" skin for himself, even if the comparison sounds exaggerated. And yet if we consider that (1) he cut himself off from the outside world in order to create this new "skin" that glued him to a soft "mother" (Harlow's experiments with monkeys—the wire-and-cloth mother—come to mind), and (2) he attacked his own skin by developing extensive and painful hives, which he scratched compulsively, whenever he felt me trying to separate him from mother with my probing questions about their relationship, we can see how close he was to literally tearing off his own skin in order to replace it with the concrete skin of a soft and warm mother. Finally there was an imaginary but desired mother who, being all good and all loving, allowed him to fantasize grand destinies for himself, something that he felt that his real mother had always forbidden him.

His daydreams—accepting his third or fourth Academy Award for Best Director, or waving triumphantly to the enthusiastic crowds that elected him to the U.S. Senate as the new John F. Kennedy—were the sole narcissistic nurturance that his starving anorexic self had received until then. Telemachus was trying to deny the suffering inflicted by his life-long feelings of being a powerless pushover who had always been easily controlled by everybody: his mother, his teachers, the children at school, his boss, or his neighbors. The "best" director is the man who controls *all* aspects of the movie and *everyone* who works in it. It also speaks of an invisible strongman behind the frightened and sick weakling that in his fantasy everyone sees and despises. Telemachus began to decrease the length and the frequency of his phone calls to his mother, which for years had been a daily routine. In the analysis, the transference became far more peaceful than it had ever been, and he started to substitute his "girlish" activities—talking on the phone about movies and movie stars—for manly ones. He joined a gym, which for the longest time had been an unthinkable feat, where he built the real muscles of his own body, instead of the fantasy body of his muscle man. Finally, after escalating the Himalayan mountain of shame that separated him from everybody else, he could show his nude body to the other men, be a boy among boys, instead of "bitching on the phone with my two girlish friends," as he put it.

Telemachus felt humiliated by his mother and was angry at her instead of becoming "colicky," breaking into skin rashes or catching the flu (which had been his usual responses to feeling something not sanctioned by her), when he realized that he was the only one who did not know about his father's suicide. We can see how Telemachus had used his body throughout his life as an armor and battlefield. Somatizing prevented any external input from disturbing his much needed and hated fusion with mother, and it prevented as well any autonomous feeling from doing the same from inside. He had always dreaded the possibility of getting to know his real hate for her, because that knowledge included the possibility of viciously and impulsively attacking her with this hate.

The discovery in his mind of the mutilated body of his father, a body that he could finally lay to rest, consolidated a plurality of analytic transformations and was felt by him as an awakening. He was getting to know parts of his mind that he had never felt before. Upon this rude awakening, he could feel how bitter the unreal world in which he had spent his years dreaming impossible dreams had always tasted to him. He could then feel his own anger at his mother's hatred of him, when he asked her why she had never told him about his father's suicide, and all he got as an answer was an indifferent shrug and a cold "Because." It is interesting to think that I am talking about a dyad, he and his mother, who fought and argued angrily and endlessly, especially since his father's death. And yet that brand of anger had never disturbed Telemachus, because he never considered it to be his own. Being as fused with mother as he was, it was her anger in him that they jointly directed at the father in him and in the outside world, as they for years had directed her hatred at me in the transference. Now it was quite a different picture, for it was his anger at her, as a feeling belonging only and exclusively to him, even if helped by the fantasy that I-father also hated her.

Telemachus, in the process of acquiring a self more separated from mother and closer to father, made a considerable breakthrough in his capacity to feel, to remember, and to verbalize. And, being quite an intelligent and insightful man, he began to understand the place and the role that somatization played in his psychic life. As a result of the dramatic improvement in his capacity to remember, he recalled two significant incidents that had followed his father's death. The first was that, at the beginning of the school year that followed his father's suicide, he had to stay in bed for a few weeks with his lungs full of liquid, because of a serious bout with pneumonia. The second was that, after he had recovered from the pneumonia and was back to school, one day when he was distracted he walked into the incoming traffic, and was hit by a car, but fortunately was not seriously injured.

Telemachus understood that he had "told" with his body that he knew about his father's suicide by drowning. This was knowledge that, at the time, he could not think with his thinking apparatus, or verbalize to himself or to another. He understood his signifying with his "body talk" his identification with his father's escape from the hateful mother, via suicide, and recognized his own attempted suicide as the ultimate destructive attack on the body as the container of his own and his parents' rages and hatreds. Telemachus began to integrate his understanding of the complex paths he utilized when he expressed somatically forbidden and foreclosed thoughts and affects. When he could acknowledge his longing for the analyst father—as a nurturing breast-penis that was replacing the bad breast that fed him anger, fear, and hatred—he developed a remarkable ability to interpret to himself his less frequent somatic reactions to psychic distress. He marveled at the fact that for the first time in his life he was free of the endless string of colds, flus, stomach viruses, and dermatitis that previously lasted from September, when we started the analytic year, to July, when we ended it.

After ten years of analysis he revealed his most terrifying fantasy, that his mother had tried to abort him—as she had done to both his unborn brother and sister—and in some magical way she still could do it. (I have already noted that he always said "abortions" when referring to the two miscarriages that preceded his own birth.) Fornari (1982) studied the dreams of women at all stages of pregnancy, parturition and postpartum, and concluded that their unconscious fantasies in these stages are related to the actual survival of the mother, fetus, and baby. The mothers-to-be studied dreamed of killing and being killed by the fetus or the baby and their anxious fantasies intensified at parturition. Fornari argued that, unconsciously, contractions actualized a maternal fear of killing the baby, and relaxation manifested the anxiety of being killed by the baby in the process of parturition. He also emphasized the capital importance of the father in containing and metabolizing the psychotic anxieties and primary paranoia revealed by the dreams of the expectant mothers.

Fornari's work makes me think about the possibility that, in the case of psychotic pregnant women who do not have effective partners helping them to metabolize these psychotic anxieties—as most likely was the case with Telemachus's mother—these frightening anxieties are neither metabolized nor successfully repressed. Instead, they are projected into the actual relationship of the mother with her baby, which is then flooded with an ever-present but nameless dread. Telemachus often describes his experience of feeling a sense of danger in relating to his mother, ever since he can remember. We know about his mother's sometimes psychotic behavior and the miscarriages—experienced by Telemachus as murdered babies—that preceded his birth. We know about the lack of support that his mother got from his father ("he was never there"), Telemachus's fears of being torn apart physically, and his mother's open expression of disgust for his body when he was a baby. The sum total of these parts seems to indicate that the psychic space that contained the relationship of Telemachus to his mother during most of his life was fenced in by preconscious psychotic fantasies, similar to those described by Fornari.

The meaning of his favorite angry fantasy—a sadistic, psychotic "torture of ex–S.S. Nazi officers"—became a bit clearer. The assorted torments he delighted in inventing included "cutting them open and eviscerating them," and "cutting off their limbs and sexual organs, and feeding them to the dogs" (I sometimes have one of my dogs in the office). If we can get past the obvious countertransferential repugnance produced by these sadistic fantasies, we realize that underlying them is an unconscious but anguished belief in a fragmented body whose parts are not well glued together, like those of aborted babies and perhaps his own body and mind. A conscious manifestation of this belief can be seen in Telemachus's rationalization of his old masturbatory habits: he cannot masturbate like other boys (men) do because he's not convinced that his penis is solidly attached to his body, and he is afraid that he will pull it off if he does.

We can see here a concrete manifestation of Bion's concept of *attacks on linking*, not unrelated to the permanent attacks of the psychotic patient on all the links with the analyst that could lead to analytic progress and that, in the case of Telemachus, lasted for several years. Grinberg and colleagues (1975) describe these attacks:

> The origin of this aggression can be traced back to the phantasized and primitive attacks on the breast and the penis, as described by M. Klein, in the paranoid-schizoid position. But the psychotic tends to attack repeatedly links with the object and between different aspects of his self, the links between internal and external reality and the apparatus that perceives these realities. As a consequence of these "attacks on linking," the psychotic part is left pre-eminently with apparently logical almost mathematical relationships, that are never emotionally reasonable. These surviving links are of a perverse, cruel and sterile character and are associated with arrogance, stupidity and curiosity. [p. 29]

The evisceration of the bad Nazi "butchers" was a projection onto a deserving bad other of the fate that, in his unconscious, he still believed awaited him: being aborted violently after being cut open, the mark of the female genital. His endless fantasizing had a subsidiary function—to reassure him that his mind was "together," capable of weaving complete stories, and of a continuous existence, by recalling these stories and thinking them over again and again.

It is obvious that Telemachus's relationship with his mother had been highly traumatic. As he became able to use his own psychic apparatus, rather than cloning his mother's feelings mindlessly, he began to remember aspects of his complex relationship with his father. It had been a gentle relationship that most likely kept Telemachus from becoming a hospitalized mental patient. He verbalized the portrait of a gentle man (this characteristic was stressed over and over again as opposed to the aggressiveness of his mother), who was a hard-working, gifted, and devoted high school teacher by day and who held a second job in the evenings. It is not clear if father's second job was a response to a real necessity or if, as mother managed to force Telemachus to accept as a fact, it supported father's alleged gambling debts and provided an excuse to be out with women. In any case, it contributed substantially to Telemachus's feelings of abandonment, to his adopting as his own his mother's perception of father as a no-good gambler and womanizer and to his distorted view of sexuality as an attack on mother. This meant that Telemachus was left alone with mother (a schoolteacher as well) when she was at home. This real event of childhood, once it became ossified in his mind, cemented the fantasy that relating to another human being means remaining a student for life, that is, a student who is not only told what to do by the other-teacher, but who is punished as well by this formidable other who is always in control of the situation. We can understand better the deep roots of Telemachus's fantasies of being a winner, the most charismatic young senator or the best movie director, emerging from his overwhelming sense of being totally powerless. I have already alluded to this aspect of his fantasy life when pointing out that the only person with whom he had physical contact, the surrogate, was considered by him to be a teacher of sex and himself a student. Mother had always accused father of being out "with women" or gambling, accusations that are the likely onset of Telemachus's isolation and of his avowed preference for being at home with TV's female characters. It is interesting to note that she accused his father of being out "with women," not "with other women." Given Telemachus's bizarre ideas of what women are, I wonder what she thought herself to be, for he was always ashamed of mother (shame that was known to her and that she resented), and never thought of her as being like the other mothers. In any case, why did a gentle man choose to marry this chain-smoking, angry, and clinically paranoid woman?

Father's mother, the grandmother that Telemachus knew only as an abandoning internal object of his father, died when his father was only 2 years old of a tuberculosis that had kept her in bed since before his birth. This fact warns us against an easy division of Telemachus's parents into a "bad" mother and an innocent "good" father. The hate of Telemachus's mother was manifest. Yet Telemachus proved to be a master of passive-aggressive needling, a mastery that cannot have its origins in the crude hysterical outbursts of his mother. I suspect that he inherited his mastery in the art of gently provoking people and driving them crazy from the unmetabolized rage of his father at his own abandoning mother. Telemachus continued this cycle of abandonment that he inherited from the father who repeatedly abandoned him—first by barely being home and ultimately by his suicide—by passively-aggressively forcing people to abandon him, a cycle that he also attempted to enact in the transference.

As a child, Telemachus loved to get into father's bed on Sunday mornings and feel tightly held in his arms, after his angry mother got out. This was a ritual, he admitted, that excited him sexually. Despite the complications that this excitement added to his confused gender identity, the fact that he had desired his father, that he had invested libidinally a loving and erotic space next to his father, and that he had felt that his father's genitals were attached to his father's body were hopeful signs for the outcome of this analysis that had always appeared as interminable. Finally we had found hopeful traces of a living eros in action, despite the extra twists and turns that it added to an already complicated picture. Did his father transmit to Telemachus, while holding him in his arms, his own desire that the boy should be like the female companion that his mother wasn't? Was he asked to bring him the love and comfort (and perhaps the warm body) that neither mother nor wife had brought him? In the recent homosexual fantasies that Telemachus allows himself to be conscious of, he is "fatherly" to the young men he's with. These men-boys sound in the narrative of these fantasies a great deal like he sounds when he's in session with me.

A close relationship to father, besides being a needed good omen and adding to his gender confusion, also contained a well of guilt. Father had told him that the only reason he didn't go ahead with the divorce that the endless fights were always forecasting was that he did not want to be separated from him. His father's words had translated in his mind as "If father had left he would not have killed himself, and he only stayed because of me." In Telemachus's tortured mind love kills and hate keeps alive. This deeply buried guilt played a major role, I believe, in his somatization of father's drowning, his own pneumonia, and in his own suicide attempt.

Early in the analysis Telemachus felt claustrophobically trapped in a treacherous no-man's-land. Being terrified of what he believed to be the magical powers of the mother who possessed him, he did not dare to leave her by establishing a working alliance with the analyst-father. Humprey (1992), in his reformulation of Descartes' dictum "I think, therefore I am" as "I feel, therefore I am," proposes that sensory consciousness arises out of bodily responses of pain and pleasure, which are validated by the human environment. I would add to Humprey's proposal that the mother is the most important source of this validation. Validation by the mother acts as the thread that joins together these responses into a unified body, while nonvalidation—either real or imaginary—of these responses results in a body fragmented (and the possibility of somatizations) and to the experience of the body and the self as dangerous aliens. Telemachus believed that his mother could literally break his body at will (castrate him) and/or his mind (drive him insane with anxiety and fear). He was afraid as well of the powerful analyst-father (conceived initially as a super-mother, the secret half of the combined parent), who could punish him harshly for his guilty alliance with mother in his father's murder-suicide. Driven to a frenzy of hate and panic by the maddening maternal object and by his own fear, he insisted in attacking the analyst-father (the weak-as-daddy one) with foolish viciousness. Here was an analyst-father who in exchange for his transferential attacks showed him that, in reality, he was stronger than his terrifying mother had ever been and reversed the rapport of forces between male and female parts of his combined object. This brings us to a brief consideration of the transference.

I have pointed out that the bloody wars enacted in the transference pitted the team Telemachus-mother against a pitiful and weak father who wanted to leave mother but could not muster the courage to divorce her (to

Telemachus it meant that father was also symbiotically tied to mother, and that only death could part them). Despite often verbalizing how horrible he felt about the endless fights that opposed father and mother, when he/mother attacked me in session (outside they attacked "me" all the time), I could witness a kind of psychotic fusion way beyond identification that I had never before seen in treatment. I felt that I was watching another old TV program, "The Twilight Zone," for my astonished eyes witnessed how the face of Telemachus mutated into that of an angry, vengeful, and sadistic old woman. If this wasn't strange enough, his gestures, tone of voice, and body language completed this bizarre and quite frightening transformation. This became a kind of somatization I had never found in psychoanalytic books and only seen in horror movies like *The Exorcist*. Once this bizarre "possession" was completed I had to listen, over and over again, to his contempt and furious hatred of me. "They" sadistically ridiculed my accent and my background, my taste in clothing, furniture, art, or music, and dismissed me for not understanding American people and culture, for not getting how American people think (he always said "we"), "better than Europeans," according to him. Totally absorbed in his grandiose fantasies, he sounded wholly patronizing as if he was talking to a stupid servant. Probably he was acting the role of a southern belle during the Civil War in some favorite movie of his, but his bizarre performances made me think rather of the behavior of the servant sisters in Genet's play *The Maids*. The servant sisters Solange and Claire suffer from their envious admiration of the lady who employs them. When Madam is away Solange and Claire take turns at "being" Madam, a game that frees their cruelest and most murderous impulses. Given the fact that Madam is the product of an idealizing and alienating process and consequently unreachable, it is the envious self that has to be murdered in order to silence the torturing envy, a process that Telemachus knows quite well.

This astonishing possession of Telemachus by an evil mother, a malignant goddess in a variety of female vicissitudes, a possession that he enacted day after day, year after year, made me often feel that I didn't want to continue with his treatment. I felt truly sorry for his sad lot in life, but at that particular point in my life I didn't want to have that kind of daily irritant in my practice. There was no gratification of any kind in this treatment, not the scientific kind brought about by seeing a difficult case progress toward the resolution of complex conflicts, nor the narcissistic kind of being at the receiving end of someone's gratitude. Most of the time I felt like a kindergarten teacher, having to put up with an unteachable and extremely obnoxious child. I wanted out. Whenever I reached this crucial point, almost with clockwork precision, Telemachus would become suddenly "depossessed," look and sound overwhelmed by sadness, and I did not go ahead with my "divorcing" him and the mad mother who had clawed her way into the deepest corners of his soul. Like his father had done before in the real situation, I stayed in this insanely destructive transferential "marriage" that he experienced psy-chotically out of pity for this pathetic boy, whom I thought and felt that I could not abandon. My staying seemed at times to increase the amount of his anxiety and somatizations, because he transferentially "felt" with his body more than with his mind that it would inevitably lead to my second murder-suicide. In this important transference enactment he was pushing me toward a divorce, by forcing me to end a treatment that he had managed to make very unpleasant. I wish to convey Telemachus's desperate transferen-tial efforts to save his father's life (by pushing me to throw him out of treatment, so his mother could not kill me again), as well as trying to infuse new life in the father in him (by witnessing my withstanding the vicious attacks that in his fantasy were supposed to drive me to suicide, the father in him was slowly becoming stronger than his mother).

CURRENT EVALUATION

It is easy to describe the psychosomatic symptoms that got worked through. Yet to assess with some accuracy how it was done, especially in a case as complex as this one, is a difficult task that keeps me guessing far more than affirming. A truly humbling task. To describe Telemachus's inner world would require a full-length book, in order to be able to look in some detail at a few corners of this irritating and tricky psychosomatic labyrinth. I trust that I managed to convey at least a sense of its cognitive and emotional intricacies.

Telemachus is in his twelfth year of analysis, at the same frequency of four sessions a week. I can say that Telemachus now "works," not only in his profession—he has been at his current job for almost eight years and has been promoted to a managerial position—but in his analysis as well. During the first five or six years of the analysis we didn't have a proper working alliance that could solidly anchor the therapeutic process. He came to his sessions with a negative attitude—to "see the doctor," a doctor that he despised *with* his mother, despite his own fear of him—and to take his "unpleasant medicine," a dose of hatred reality. His secret mission was far worse: to act as a hit man for his destructive mother and try to maim his pathetic and already castrated father a bit more, if possible. Yet, despite all the endless roadblocks, we managed to work through to a satisfying extent both his hypochondria (his chronically feeling weak, tired, and needing to rest) originating in the introjection of his "old" mother, as well as his somatic delusions (fear of pulling off his penis or of losing his internal organs if he vomits). Heimann (1964) indicated that the difference between hypochondria and somatic delusions resides in the strong sense of shame that accompanies somatic delusions, shame that is rooted in a deeply wounded narcissism and fears of helplessness. Telemachus's somatic delusions did contain deeply buried somatic memories of painful sensations that were reactions to early experiences of being touched and handled by harsh and angry hands. That's why his physical experiences with the sex surrogate and the masseur, his using the bathroom in his office, and his walking nude in the men's changing room of his health club were promising indicators of the possibility of his working through his somatizations to an extent that he had never allowed himself to dream of.

Today, Telemachus is looking well and doing reasonably well. Anyone seeing him in person would never guess that this kind, albeit narcissistic, gentle yet reasonably strong man is the same boy that went in and out of the jungle of somatizations and psychotic ideation for so long. He is the same boy who had his mind so devastated early in life that, in order to survive, he had to eject his unbearable psychic pain from his mind and, lacking any other available container, had to use his own body—experienced as an alien burden that he had to carry—to dispose of that unwanted pain. He is tolerably depressed because he is no longer denying the high cost of the psychotic symbiosis with his mother and the endless years of bloody wars with real and transferential paternal figures. At 40 he is single and has never felt a sexual or intimate relationship with either a woman or a man, although the dawn of adult intimacy is arising in the analysis where the early tenderness he experienced with his father is slowly awakening the possibility of becoming dependent on a true holding environment for the first time.

I have emphasized earlier the importance of the attacks on linking in psychotic ideation and psychosomatic conversion and how Telemachus attacked relentlessly all possibilities of being constructively connected to me. It is interesting to note that today he has developed a solid working alliance and he feels solidly attached to his analysis and, transferentially, to me. This attachment has given way to an important transformation in his fantasy life; today he also feels that his penis is solidly attached to his body and he is no longer afraid that he will pull it off if he masturbates as boys do. It is interesting to see that his attachment to the symbolic father has freed him from his painfully submissive position of being his mother's Lacanian phallus.

He doesn't know for sure if he wants to be gay (his fantasies are overwhelmingly homoerotic, but he's paranoically concerned about looking bad as a gay man to "them," his internal public) or if he wants to be heterosexual and a father (perhaps a mother). He's never given any indication of wanting a woman. Women, other than dim-witted but glamorous couture models, are still a deeply humiliating curse that one has to suffer if one cannot avoid relating to them. To him all this "relationship stuff," as he puts it, is still a matter of theoretical choices intended to boost his starved narcissism. Yet, his growing submission to the respected analyst-father and the beginning of an identification with him is the axis of his emerging new "I." He feels much better about himself than he ever dreamed of feeling, is reasonably at peace with himself, and is far more successful at work. Even if he's not sure if he is gay or straight, there's no longer any doubt in his mind that he was a boy—a very sick one, but nevertheless a boy—and that now he is a man—a frightened one, but a man. To him, this means a great deal. For the first time in his life he's able to feel gratitude where before he only experienced corrosive envy. And, as a clinician, as the contemporary version of the old Mentor in the Iliad, and as one of the warriors in this contemporary version of the Trojan war, it also means a great deal to me. At this point I can say that I'm grateful for the benefits that his analysis has brought to me.

Listening to the psychotic tortures and eviscerations that he repeatedly described for years brought back from the depths of repression to my conscious memory the religious paintings of hellish tortures, the art of the Middle Ages, that as a child had frightened me so much. The world they depicted was so terrifying to me that I even forgot to remember it in my training analysis. Listening to Telemachus I remembered how happy I felt when I left the Middle Ages room in the museum and could move to the Renaissance. I've always loved Giotto and Fra Angelico with a tender fondness and more than gratitude for their light-filled, gentle, and loving paintings. Working with this disturbed man-child helped me to reach a degree of metabolization of my own childhood fears, and an understanding of the "psychotic" Middle Ages that I had somehow internalized but had never approached during my analysis. In exchange for his considerable help, and despite my often strong desire to divorce him and his mother, it was only fair for me to help Telemachus to leave his dark Middle Ages, lead him to the Renaissance room, and introduce him to the light and the loving tenderness in the paintings of Giotto and Fra Angelico. And slowly, very slowly, we are finally getting to see that there's a gentle light at the end of this dark tunnel.

REFERENCES

Bion, W. R. (1957). Differentiation of the psychotic from the non-psychotic personalities. *International Journal of Psycho-Analysis* 38(3–4):266.

Ferenczi, S. (1932). The clinical diary of Sándor Ferenczi, ed. J. Dupont, trans. M. Balint and N. Z. Jackson. Cambridge, MA: Harvard University Press, 1988.

Fornari, F. (1982). *Il Codice Vivente*. Turin: Boringhieri.

Freud, S. (1894). The neuro-psychoses of defence. *Standard Edition* 3:58.

Green, A. (1975). *On Private Madness*. Madison, CT: International Universities Press.

Grinberg, L., Granel, J., Grimaldi, P., et al. (1975). *Introduction to the Work of Bion*. London: Maresfield.

Grotstein, J. (1979). Who is the dreamer who dreams the dream and who is the dreamer who understands it? *Contemporary Psychoanalysis* 15:110–169.

——— (1994). Projective identification reappraised. *Contemporary Psychoanalysis* 30:708–746.

Heimann, P. (1964). *About Children and Children-no-longer*. London: Tavistock.

Humprey, N. (1992). *A History of the Mind*. New York: Simon & Schuster.

Joseph, B. (1975). The patient who is difficult to reach. In *Melanie Klein Today*, ed. E. B. Spillius. London: Tavistock/Routledge, 1988.

Klein, M. (1952). The origins of transference. In *Melanie Klein*, vol. 3, ed. R. Money-Kyrle. New York: Free Press.

Laing, R. D. (1959). *The Divided Self*. Baltimore: Pelican.

McDougall, J. (1974). The psychosoma and the psycho-analytic process. *International Review of Psycho-Analysis* 1:437–459.

———— (1989). *Theaters of the Body.* New York: Norton.

Meltzer, D. (1975). *Explorations in Autism.* London: Clunie.

Money-Kyrle, R. (1968). Cognitive development. In *Collected Papers,* ed. D. Meltzer. London: Clunie.

Ogden, T. (1980). On the nature of schizophrenic conflict. *International Journal of Psycho-Analysis* 61:513–533.

Simo, J. (1993). E. narcisismo primitivo como vampirismo. *Gradiva* 5(3):225–240.

CHAPTER THIRTEEN

Psychoanalytic Psychotherapy of Borderline Patients with Anorexia*

HARRIETTE PODHORETZ

Diagnosis, developmental determinants, and treatment modalities of anorexia nervosa have been traditionally linked to medical pathology. The genesis of anorexia, according to Fenichel (1945) is "a denial of sexual longings" as well as evidence of hostility, noting that children who refuse to eat are expressing negative feelings. The resultant oral conflict is directed not only against frustrating objects, but also against oral drives, resulting in a sadistic character. Fenichel divides anorexia into two stages of drive theory: pregenitally as an oral conflict—"I will not let myself be controlled; I eat what and when I like"—and as an anal component that is revealed as wishes for revenge; and genitally as the unconscious significance of a pregnancy wish, which incorporates both oral and anal fantasies. Masserman (1941) feels that oral aggression and guilt over the wish for father's phallus play a crucial role in self-starvation, while Moulton (1942) cites severe family

---

* This chapter is a revision of a paper presented at the American Psychological Association, Los Angeles, 1980.

conflicts and overprotective mothering as causal factors. Lorand (1943), in a detailed analysis, observed that early envy and frustration over competitive strivings were expressed as a reaction formation to intense feelings regarding destructive wishes and fears about oral incorporation.

Etiology and insight into anexoria took a new turn after Mahler's (Mahler et al. 1975) seminal work on separation-individuation. Theorists and researchers viewed it more exclusively as an intense, bitter struggle around control between parent and child. Steiner-Adair (1991) discusses relatedness among female anorectics, finding that they "confuse engagement with enmeshment" (p. 230) while fearing connection because it represents the loss of a separate sense of self. Anorectics believe that their "need of others is dangerous" (p. 231). Consequently there is both a hunger for attachment and a defense against yearnings.

Bruch (1980), in addition to citing oedipal determinants, emphasized the failure of preoedipal development, as well as the fear of sexual involvement that occurs at puberty. She catalogues the failure to separate due to early developmental deficits. The developmental history of anorectics includes a "fight against enslavement" with the illness resulting from the failed struggle for independence. The anorectic, resisting the new demands of adolescence, keeps the concerned parent involved in and focused on her body. Bruch finds that the mothers of anorectics tend to ignore separation-individuation clues.

Crisp (1980) agrees with Bruch and cites maternal overinvolvement while other researchers note conflicts around body image and identifications. For instance, Wooley (1991) sees eating disorders as the inability to integrate "feminine and masculine poles of personality organization—[as] undeniably gendered disorders" (p. 246), concluding that the anorectic rejects "female nurturance" (p. 246). On the other hand, Johnson (1991) discusses the anorectic's body-image distortions resulting from the attempt to defend against "intrusiveness that is experienced as malevolence" (p. 176). His research indicates ambivalent themes around attachment that is both longed for and feared. Additionally, his findings show that the mothers of anorectics are restrictive; consequently, when the second major phase of separation occurs at puberty, it threatens symbiosis. Anorectics fail to successfully negotiate the developmental thrust of sexual awakening.

Horner's (1989) findings show that the anorectic regards food as a displacement for toxic wishes. Furthermore, Rampling (1980) addresses abnormal mothering and excessive symbiosis that include an emotionally weak and passive father. His findings include ambivalent maternal attitudes, preoccupation with feeding, and a reaction formation to infanticidal desires that include starvation.

Not surprisingly, Winokur (1980) found primary affective disorders to be more frequent in relatives of anorectic patients, which is consistent with his findings of the relationship of depression to anorexia.

Treatment approaches are varied, and in some cases contradictory. Bruch (1980) directs the therapy toward the interruption of intense enmeshment with the family via the therapist's affirmation of the anorectic's self-initiated behaviors. Davis (1991) sees treatment as having a unique form and resistance and suggests a here-and-now treatment experience, even going as far as to disclose personal revelations to the patient.

Wooley's (1991) conjection is that successful treatment is twofold. In the earlier phase the therapist must relinquish as much control and absorb as much hostility as possible until the latter phase, when the therapist exercises confrontation and assertion of feelings that are vital to the completion of therapy. Fischer (1989) found that utilization of Mahler's (Mahler et al. 1975) developmental perspective enabled the analyst and patient to make sense out of a relationship that initially seemed "chaotic and . . . stagnating" (p. 53).

Intensive psychoanalytic psychotherapy with two anorectics pinpoints the diagnosis of anorexia nervosa as a borderline syndrome with paranoidal, obsessive, and depressive undertones, but basically presenting as a hysterical type (Kernberg 1974). Outlined are the condensed genetic determinants reflecting massive developmental conflicts and/or arrests at the oral, anal, and phallic levels that gave rise to distorted internalized objects that contributed to the orally tinged, primitive behavior patterns, a description and illustration of the treatment of choice—expressive psychotherapy (Kernberg 1974) with modifications proposed by Podhoretz (1980) that link the present with the past via the transference. Kernberg's criteria include the phenomenon of unstable boundaries between the self and others as the hallmark of the borderline, which aptly describes the anorectic who falls into the classification of hysterical personality, low-level borderline. Although the flamboyant symptoms of anorexia suggest a hysterical borderline syndrome, the diagnostic picture quickly shifts to an obsessive/paranoidal frame when the anorexia lifts. Viewed from the perspective of object relations, the self is nondifferentiated and nondiscrete due to a prolonged symbiosis with mother that is fraught with separation-individuation conflicts, implying fears and longings around separation and closeness. Reconstructing the symptomology and character style of the anorectic would imply that the pathology of an eating disorder indicated conflicts at the oral level, pointing to a very early mother–child interaction.

The anorectic's style of denying self-gratification (oral pleasure) as well as life sustenance points out the conflicted emotions regarding "taking it in" versus withholding or "letting it go," and suggests that fantasies around food, ingestion of food, and the mechanics of eating and digestion contain nonneutralized, unintegrated libidinal and aggressive components.

Starving controls the love–hate relationship to the representations of the self, that is, it maintains the split and regulates self-esteem and remains the primary fulcrum of controlling intrapsychic and interpersonal relationships. In short, the anorectic experiences herself as about to lose control of sexual and aggressive impulses; controlling and manipulating these impulses through control of food intake primitively effectuates nonthreatening, "safer" internal and external relationships.

Anorexia's symptoms—extreme weight loss and amenorrhea—are mainly manifested as an eating disorder. The rejection of food implies the early onset of suspiciousness and mistrust of the goodness of supplies as well as the inherent goodness of the self. If the breast or the self is regarded so mistrustfully at this earliest stage of development, then the note of ambivalence is rung upon all present and future feelings, perceptions, and objects, and the acceptance or rejection of all subsequent supplies, objects, and desires. This heightened ambivalence will manifest itself at all further stages of psychosexual development and alter internalized objects and their harmonious interrelationships, resulting in distortions of the superego that impair subsequent ego development.

This ambivalence results in very early splitting of feelings and perceptions and brings about distortions around the body image, the self, and others. Emphasis here is on feelings and perceptions, since both are needed for critical discriminations of the good and bad images of the self and others. Whether or not in Jacobson's (1964) terms this early splitting is due to inappropriately timed frustrations or too much gratification, pregenital hatred accrues and mistrust of the mother-breast then raises suspicion and ambivalence in regard to the poisoned breast or the poisonous self.

The longing for the "good" breast, in turn, will arouse suspiciousness and terror toward impulses to take in and enjoy when impulses to destroy and mutilate become interpenetrated with gratification, that is, the sadistic character wins out.

At the anal stage, this earlier ambivalence about the self is further reinforced when demands on the child to give must be met. Here again, spitefulness and withholding keep mother involved with body functions, preventing separation-individuation and the furtherance of stable ego boundaries.

The ambivalence in regard to the goodness of the self reechoes at this new stage of development, reflecting in the "goodness" versus the "badness" of the body's products, forcing us to hypothesize that the already critical and rejecting self is now reinforced by a new round of rejection of mother and the self. Consequently, the tasks at the phallic stage, staggering under the earlier traumas, cannot be successfully negotiated while natural, competitive strivings suffer from nonneutralized instinctualized aggression or the splitting of love and hate, making appropriate feminine identification impossible.

If the breast-mother is so envied and consequently so good, these feelings and perceptions must be denied and rejected; on the other hand, if the breast-mother is so bad, why should one want it or wish to make an identification with the hatefully regarded mother? The child is then forced to reject the perceptions and feelings, that is, her needs and strivings, because of the massive infusions of hatred and envy unmitigated by the love for the mother and the representation of her body. Therefore, instead of the emotions of pride and pleasure in anticipation of the mutating feminine self, feelings of shame and envy predominate. Resultant distortions and representations of the self as well as of others, due to earlier ambivalence over mother's breast, serve to further distort structural differentiation and discriminations between self and others. This seriously affects all ego functions. Therefore, oedipal resolution becomes impossible, since genital strivings toward father revolve around earlier oral fixations and take on oral reflections, whereby fantasies of oral impregnation and confusion between the phallus/breast predominate.

The primitive defenses invoked throughout this developmental process occur at the juncture when synthesis and integration failed, producing projective identification (this defense involves splitting off at the negatively cathected emotions and projecting them onto others), projection, and denial.

The anorectic's most obvious employ of the defenses of denial and projective identification is her insistence that she is grossly overweight just at the time when she has gained weight and looks both more humanly and sexually attractive. This distortion of her reality testing (body image) is a result of the splitting and projecting of the negative critical disapproving self (superego) around developing curves and voluptuousness onto others by calling herself "disgusting," that is, "shameful." Therefore, the most longed for and desirable sexual characteristics are also those that she must assiduously defend against.

CLINICAL CASE MATERIAL: BETH

Beth's mother had been my patient from the time Beth was about 14 years old, after she had undergone ten years of prior psychiatric treatment. Understandably, my views of the family dynamics were primarily fixed upon her mother's conflicts. The mother presented as a severely depressed woman who periodically caved in under a load of psychosomatically related illnesses, at which times she removed herself from her family. Prior to treatment with me (when Beth was 7) she was hospitalized for acute depression. Subsequently, she divorced her very wealthy husband and reared Beth and her younger son in their family home. There ensued years of bitter, ongoing litigation around finances. My impressions of Beth over the years were that she was a loner, a good student, and socially inhibited, and she tended to exhibit very controlled behavior. I also intuited an intense symbiosis and overidentification on the part of my patient with her daughter. Mother had mentioned, but was not unduly alarmed about, Beth's developmental problems, both physiological and emotional, such as one brief menstrual period at 13, little contact with or interest in boys, and disappointing relationships with friends. At age 14, Beth "heard voices." She underwent brief psychotherapy and the "voices" disappeared.

At the conclusion of the mother's treatment, Beth was finishing her freshman year at a nearby boarding college. At this point, her mother became openly alarmed because Beth was eating only jarred baby food. Worried, she took Beth to Babies' Hospital where the diagnosis was anorexia nervosa and the mandatory three-month treatment design was incarceration with forced feeding. Her mother rejected this plan for an alternative at Montefiore's Anorexia Clinic, but Beth failed to relate to her psychiatrist. Would I see her daughter? My resistances battled with intrigue at the challenge of treating a case of anorexia. The consideration of Beth's success in school made outpatient treatment desirable since school was her only major source of ego strength. Yet her failure to make contact with her prior therapist warned me of the pitfalls and types of transference resistance I could anticipate— primarily hostility and resistance on the patient's part. However, I was still ill-prepared for the shock of our first meeting. Beth, a competitive runner, confessed that she had been controlling her food intake for years, which finally escalated into virtual starvation during her freshman year. This regimen, coupled with running, equaled both starvation and enervation and produced the likeness of an Auschwitz victim or a human skeleton. Her other acknowledged presenting symptoms were gastritis and constipation.

About this time, I received a concerned phone call from her internist, who related a diagnosis of anorexia nervosa and amenorrhea, and that there were no patella reflexes and dangerously low blood pressure with the incipience of structural damage to the heart muscles. He pronounced her "schizophrenic" and was predictably gloomy about analytically oriented therapy without benefit of hospitalization and/or psychopharmacological aid.

Our initial sessions exposed Beth's extreme negative hostile transference to treatment per se and to me in particular. Her scornful, mocking comments induced my own complementary negative emotions that I contacted and used as a springboard for our first confrontation. My therapeutic interventions with her included transference observations and interpretations directed toward her withholding type of behavior, intransigence, remoteness, rage, and hurt. These reflections produced heavy weeping interspersed with revelations of important memories from childhood, such as separation at the age of 7 from her mother when her mother was hospitalized for depression. These experiences left her feeling frightened, isolated, and abandoned; all of these emotions were painfully reinforced by an indifferent maid and an absentee father. Feelings of loss, helplessness, fury, and longing emerged again when her parents divorced. Beth linked these affects to those she experienced whenever her mother's depressive episodes broke into their closeness.

Memories about her father revealed him to be nonchalant about their meetings, frequently coming late, and often forgetting to pick her up at school as promised, or leaving her alone, while at the same time making explicit and harsh demands upon her performance both as a student and "good" Jewish daughter. Here, the interpretations were aimed at her lack of control and loss of security over the frightening events in her life, primarily separation, which reinforced her sense of isolation and mandated a need to control the terrifying feelings that accompanied these experiences.

As Beth's affects (libidinal and aggressive) surfaced and were clarified and explored, her shame conflicts around hunger and longings for both parents as well as rage against them became more apparent and tolerable, and the unconscious demand to control these emotions was supplanted by her understanding of them. As she worked through them, she began to eat.

Initially, Beth ate nonstop, starting with milky foods, such as ice cream and cookies, and progressing to fish, chicken, and finally very well done meat. As the conflicts around eating were reduced, the onset of a somewhat better alliance for further conflict resolution occurred. This new arena surfaced when the anorexia lifted and the patient waxed nubile and voluptuous and was no longer hysterical, obsessional, or phobic in regard to eating, chewing, and swallowing. She now obsessed about her bowels, stomach pains, and constipation. She shifted from an oral to an anal character style, but kept her mechanisms of defense intact and unchanged. This heightened cathexis and preoccupation with her body parts reflected her mistrust of relationships and functioned as a replacement and substitution for controlling good and bad internal and external objects. Beth's lack of object-relatedness manifested itself through her rejection of close friends, heterosexual contacts, and an inhibited, nonspontaneous style of relating to me.

Her feelings of mistrust were frequently acted out by responding to me in a suspicious, remote, contemptuous, and sadistic manner. Interpretations centered on her intense conflicts around strivings, which always brought up the specter of possible rejections. Beth's longings for intimacy and sexual attractiveness conflicted with her denial of these needs. Further transference interpretations at this juncture were addressed to her denial of and shame over her longings for love (positive feelings) and her denial and repudiation of her caring feelings for me; controlling these loving feelings compelled her to deny and project only her cold and critical emotions onto me. My interventions spoke to her paranoidal and obsessional defensive structure—denial, projection, and projective identification—as well as her intellectualization of her basic emotions. The interpretations of the negative transference focused on her control over her negative feelings of hate toward herself, her mother, and me.

Working through invoked changes around her self and her object relationships; eventually she took close and loving girl friends for apartment mates during the remaining three years of college.

During the five years that spanned her treatment, she left twice. She interrupted her treatment by neglecting to show up for an appointment, then phoned an "I'll be in touch with you." My response twinned her indifference and I did not pursue her rejecting behavior, nor, of course, whatever transferential emotions (due to my failure to understand my countertransference) lay behind her act of abruptly dropping her treatment and disappearing. There is a clear identification with the aggressors (both parents) who dropped her or disappeared whenever she began to experience closeness and security in her relationships to them. An additional interpretation of this abrupt departure from treatment may be explained as separation-individuation versus rapprochement needs, since the consequences of her treatment were developmental gains in the physiological sphere that conflicted with pregenital longings.

In the middle of her senior year of college, she reentered treatment. Her anorexia was now cured, and during this interim she had been menstruating regularly, regained her patellar reflexes, and looked very healthy. Her general physical demeanor was excellent, but she still rejected heterosexual gatherings, because of extreme sexual anxiety, and she reported crushes on men whom she tended to idolize from afar. Surmising that graduation was reviving her unresolved separation-individuation conflicts, her return bespoke a rapprochement and return to the touchstone of a constant relationship.

Initially, much of the treatment focused on here-and-now conflicts, such as getting a job in her chosen and highly competitive field, breaking up the harmonious and close relationships with her friends, and a generalized anxiety in regard to her future.

After a summer vacation and some more sessions, she called to ask my advice and opinion about two jobs offers, and said goodbye over the telephone. Essentially, Beth acted out, with some help from me, her primary conflict—an "abandonment syndrome"; that is, she repeated her earliest experiences of "dropping out," assuming the role of the aggressor or the powerful parent who controls the separation.

Subsequently, upon getting in touch with my rage at her, I then understood the inconstancy of Beth's object relationships, her dropouts, and her disappearances; I could also appreciate the impact on her of her parents' abrupt departures. I understood and resonated with her primary abandonments, her rage when her mother dropped out due to depressions and illnesses, and her deep disappointments when her father dropped and picked her up whenever it suited him, unattuned to his daughter's feelings.

The third time she reentered treatment was stimulated by the reactivation of this as yet unworked-through theme.

In the intervening year or so, she replaced running with an equally demanding sport, competitive bicycle racing, lost a job, and experienced some severe interpersonal rejections from her new circle of friends; these cumulative rejections produced a moderately severe depression. Her father agreed to support a limited five-month time frame for treatment. Direct observations of the transference, that is, her quick departures from our relationship, opened her up to more memories and feelings around abandonment from both parents. We focused on her inability to express anger or hurt toward anyone who rejected her, which then turned to self-blame, depression, and finally isolation. Her withdrawal and depression were not only a repetition of her mother's behavior, but also kept her close to her mother through this negative identification. Using myself as the transference or screen figure further helped to clarify and explore Beth's emotions of rage and hurt over her experience of rejection.

Her increased freedom to talk about feelings or rejection, both to me and important people in her life, led to a more integrated self and object relatedness and closer, more authentic interpersonal relationships. She began to express her anger, hurt, and disappointment instead of attempting to control her emotions.

The analysis of her conflicts over rejection, hurt, and anger promoted her interest in her appearance and enjoyment at perceiving herself as a sexually attractive 24-year-old woman. She had had some dating experience during this time with very rejecting men who induced emotions and memories of prior abandonments and betrayals. Finally, she felt ready for sexual involvement and began to date a young man who valued her.

The sight of this now stunning young woman invoked memories of our first encounter and compelled me to contemplate the ego's capacity to heal by reintegrating and renewing good internalized relationships through the use of constant dyadic therapeutic relatedness.

Initially, Beth controlled her emotions in a primitive fashion by controlling her food intake, distancing herself from relationships, and putting her body through rigorous and painful ordeals. Eventually, this control gave way to her compassionate understanding of her history. Our allotted time was up and it was necessary to talk about separation. Beth now permitted herself to get closer to her feelings about me, our relationship, and our impending good-bye; she was able to experience the manifold and ambivalent emotions of sadness, tenderness, and mourning that accompanied termination.

CLINICAL CASE MATERIAL: WENDY

A 19-year-old female anorectic presented the following symptoms: amenorrhea, no breast development, and failure to complete her out-of-town college studies. She threw tantrums, threatened suicide, and had refused to eat solid food since age 12. In appearance she was emaciated, childish, clumsy, and unfeminine; she had few female friends and no apparent interest in men.

From the outset she showed her resentment and suspiciousness of me; indeed, she was remanded into treatment by her endocrinologist and her mother. By refusing to acknowledge her conflicts or her need to resolve them, she clearly made me "the enemy."

An appraisal of her symptomatology coupled with her refusal to speak during our first session dictated the diagnosis—borderline personality, hysterical type—and the tactical line that treatment would assume: expressive psychotherapy with *active interpretation* of her oral and anal rage. Linking up her refusal to speak in the transference with her refusal to eat and give herself or anyone else, namely her parents, satisfaction precipitated copious weeping. In subsequent sessions, her ambivalence around separation reflected by her need to keep her parents involved with her bodily functions as a defense against her sexuality was persistently interpreted through the transference.

For example, she was obsessed with her lack of breasts and was consumed with envy over her mother's and sister's endowments. Since she couldn't personally afford reconstructive surgery, she begged, whined, and demanded that I compel and instruct her mother to "buy her breasts." My interpretations of these critical demands were based on the underlying wish behind this plea as well as the induced emotions of resentment and frustration in my not being able to gratify her longing.

These demands were made in an imperious and commanding manner: "You have all these books on your shelves; get off your ass, go look at them, and find out why I have no breasts." My instinctual response was to follow her directive and gratify her terrible need; my own response produced anger and confusion in me. By confronting my own emotions in the countertransference I could truly grasp what she had struggled with all her life, and so I asked her why she needed my approval to become a sexually mature woman. Also, I wondered aloud whether or not she felt furious, ashamed, and helpless whenever she could not fulfill her mother's demands.

This transference interpretation afforded her an opportunity to explore and clarify her perceptions and feelings around the unconscious demands for fulfillment and gratification of needs that both she and her mother were continually placing upon each other. For instance, she was not allowed to lock her bedroom door; if closed, her mother and father would barge in without knocking, and scold her for keeping them out. When she installed locks, her father removed them at her mother's directive; therefore, all boundaries were carefully and methodically erased. Consequently, all identifications with her sexually developing separate self were denied and ignored by her parents. Her experience of the failure to meet these critical demands set up rounds of oscillating shame, hatred, frustration, and disapproval around all subsequent attempts at achievement and identity formation, with the exception of academic achievement. She rolled up an impressive high school record that helped her to win an out-of-town scholarship; however, since she was forbidden to separate, this, coupled with her excessive inhibitions, reinforced both her isolation and fear of closeness. She returned home after the first semester.

Wendy's extremely awkward gestures, bumbling mannerisms, and gawky appearance clashed strikingly with her quick, ironic wit and sharpness of intellect, all of which was apparent from our first consultation. References to a "retarded boy" in the neighborhood became a screen figure for her father, whom she described as an oafish, "retarded," and childish man. She spoke about him with scorn and contempt, revealing feelings of rage and helplessness; yet these angry emotions were a cover for the deeper feelings of mortification that he aroused in her. He earned little money (they lived in a dangerous slum), dressed in rags, spoke baby talk, and "innocently" exposed himself by wearing torn underwear. He related to her orally by buying her cookies and candy, which, of course, she rejected. Engagement with father took place mainly at the oral and anal level—he bought food for her and she rejected it, continuing the cycle of rejections via the discharging of hostile emotions that alternately repulsed and bound him to her. His sexual acting out served to provoke, confuse, frighten, and shame her, which subsequently heightened her identification with the aggressor—her unattractive, awkward father.

Her rage and envy of her mother, a teacher, forestalled any positive identifications such as a voluptuous figure or a college degree. An additional note of confusion was added to Wendy's identity conflicts, caused by her mother's open contempt and rejection of the same husband she sided with whenever Wendy attempted separation. Additionally, Wendy was critical of her sister for openly expressing love and feelings of closeness for their father, thereby denying her own envy, and identifying with her mother's rejection of father, yet competing for his attention through infantile behavior. This behavior permitted her to keep her father involved with her body at an oral and anal level, through the cycle of starvation, rejection, and withholding from him her admiration and love, yet removed her as a sexual (oedipal) threat to her mother.

Subsequent sessions were spent exploring her sense of frustration in the family, revealing and making conscious to her her feelings of isolation, rage, and shame. She confessed to feelings of guilt and shame in the way she used refusal to eat as a means of controlling her parents.

Soon it became apparent to her that in order to avoid the painfully frustrated emotions aroused by attempts to separate, all of her authentic needs and strivings were sacrificed. Confronting and contacting these painful affects permitted Wendy, after our sixth session, to begin eating solid foods, including meat, for the first time in six years; she gained twenty-five pounds in the next three months.

Once, when I was expecting the patient at her appointed hour, her mother presented herself instead. I was surprised, but nevertheless forced to respect the full strength of the symbiosis I had intuited; here was proof that mother and daughter regarded themselves as interchangeable parts. Clearly, the mother needed to become a part of her daughter's treatment and resented any separation between them.

Nevertheless, the mother said very feelingly, "What did you do? The other day Wendy came into the bedroom and offered me a box of chocolates and then said, 'Never mind, I want them all for myself,' and proceeded to eat the entire box. She hasn't touched sweets since she was 12 years old." Her mother expressed amazement at Wendy's revived interest in and appetite for food; nevertheless, she still monitored Wendy's food intake, hovered over her, and refused to understand why Wendy needed locks on her door. Wendy's eating pattern was intriguing; from an initial food repertoire that was exclusively confined to Diet Tab, she progressed to milky foods, then solids (mainly sweets), then to fish, chicken, and finally hamburgers—very well done! Her entire oral area underwent libidinal and aggressive decathection as she worked through her oral conflicts. Essentially, she allowed herself, for the first time since puberty, to acknowledge her desires for gratification without shame. Former conflicts that had unconsciously reminded the patient of destructive and envious wishes toward her mother, sister, and father no longer interfered with the ego functions of eating, chewing, and swallowing.

At the same time, she embarked on a series of endocrinological lab tests that required much taking of blood samples and provoked intense, hysterical reactions to needles. Fears and fantasies around penetration with many associations to her father's seductive behavior became the major theme in our subsequent sessions.

Wendy became close to a young married woman who functioned as her role model and mentor, teaching her the feminine arts of makeup and dressing. She was highly invested in these pursuits and now spent the major part of her salary on clothing and makeup. These rapid changes in my patient's physical appearance provoked many emotions in me; quite frankly, I was amazed and delighted by this butterfly, who in a few short weeks emerged from her cocoon; my respect for her struggles around individuation was coupled with fear and an empathic identification with her sense of loss around her breasts. She heaped many recriminations upon herself for her prior starvation; she mercilessly attacked herself for having "fucked up" her hormone and breast development, yet she seemed notably uninterested in her absent menses. Her punitive superego, unmitigated by empathy, devalued her new gains; predictably, this weight gain revived old conflicts around her body, since with each newly gained pound she would stand up, stick out her belly, and say mockingly, "You see? Don't I look fat and disgusting?" simultaneously simulating and rejecting her wish for a pregnancy while acting out through her rejection and denial the mocking of feminine strivings, too shameful to be acknowledged.

These yearnings for feminine curves clashed with the rejection of these strivings and manifested themselves by getting her mother to participate again in her idealized body image by compelling her to sew "falsies" into bathing suits. The arena had shifted from oral to oedipal confrontations and conflicts.

As treatment progressed, she metamorphosed into a very attractive young woman, who dated, had relationships with men, and resumed her college career away from home.

TWO CASES OF ANOREXIA NERVOSA: SIMILARITIES AND DIFFERENCES

The treatment of Beth and Wendy distinguishes between developmental arrests and developmental conflicts. Comparing and contrasting the history and treatment of two female anorectics reveals the following similarities and differences:

Both entered treatment at 19 years of age, both were white, Jewish, late adolescents, who manifested physical and emotional developmental arrests and conflicts. Both had amenorrhea, but because Beth had breast development and late-onset anorexia her physiological conflicts were corrected and worked through in psychoanalytic psychotherapy. Wendy, who had stopped eating at age 12, did not menstruate, nor did she develop breasts at the conclusion of her treatment. Both related to the therapist in a cold, remote, suspicious manner, defending against pregenital longings for object hunger, closeness (love), and fear of their own hateful destructive impulses. Both restricted their eating in order to primitively control desires for and fear of incorporation of mother's breast/father's penis. Both were excellent students, utilizing their obsessive need for perfection to drive themselves mercilessly; Beth's sadistic and rigid superego forced her into punitive physical competitions without enough body fuel to sustain herself.

Both tended to internalize their rejections in an obsessive/depressive pattern, unconsciously criticizing themselves. This defensive maneuver illustrates the splitting of the love—hate identification as opposed to integrating their libido and aggression toward these objects. This failure to integrate libidinal and aggressive components boomeranged when sadistic aggression, unmodified by compassion and love, turned into severe criticism against all libidinal and aggressive desires such as eating and heterosexual competitive strivings. Both made unconscious, negative identifications with their opposite-sex parent, the father, as a defense against their ambivalently regarded mothers.

Upon the initiation of eating, both feared the loss of impulse control in regard to their love and hate fantasies, a fear invoked by the aggressive acts (mutilation and incorporation) set into motion by chewing and swallowing. Both started out with bland, milky foods, progressing from fish to fowl to meat. By the time I treated Wendy's anorexia, I no longer thought of this recapitulation of an eating pattern as pure coincidence, since it was too reminiscent of an infant's ontogenetical gustatory development. Both related obsessively to their body parts prior to relating (through the transference) to their internal and external objects.

Upon the resolution of anorexia, both shifted their paranoid and obsessive behavior onto me and others. Wendy's fear of puberty resulted in an arrest manifested by secondary sexual retardation and arrested physiological development, while Beth, who had evidenced breast development in puberty and menses in one brief period at 13, was able, with the help of analytically oriented psychotherapy, to work through these developmental conflicts.

Both, however, in their own separate ways, came to appreciate the exacting penalties demanded by their critical and punitive superegos for their longings and desires around libidinal and aggressive strivings.

Expressive psychotherapy with two female anorectics utilized interpretations that focused on the underlying pregenital hurt, shame, rage, and longings that stemmed from their conflicts and arrests at the oral and anal stages.

The failure and mistrust incurred at the breast resulted in very early splitting, which in turn affected and impaired differentiation and discrimination, creating blurring of ego boundaries and distorted body image, poor structural formations in the psyche, and contamination of all future authentic strivings and needs. The primary relationship with mother, based on rejection and suspicion, affected the harmony of all future intrapsychic and interpersonal relationships. Psychoanalytic psychotherapy, through the rigorous observations and interpretations of the transference, permitted the integration of warded-off libidinal and aggressive strivings and helped to negotiate subsequent genital aims.

REFERENCES

Bruch, H. (1980). Preconditions for anorexia nervosa. *American Journal of Psychoanalysis* 40(2):169–172.

Crisp, A. H. (1980). *Anorexia Nervosa: Let Me Be*. London: Academic Press.

Davis, W. N. (1991). Reflections on boundaries in the psychotherapeutic relationship. In *Psychodynamic Treatment of Anorexia Nervosa and Bulimia*, ed. C. Johnson, pp. 68–85. New York: Guilford.

Fenichel, O. (1945). *The Psychoanalytic Theory of Neurosis*. New York: Norton.

Fischer, N. (1989). Anorexia nervosa. *International Journal of Psycho-Analysis*. 70:41–54.

Horner, A. J. (1989). *The Wish for Power and the Fear of Having It*. Northvale, NJ: Jason Aronson.

Jacobson, E. (1964). *The Self and the Object World*. New York: International Universities Press.

Johnson, C. (1991). Treatment of eating disordered patients with borderline and false self/narcissistic disorders. In *Psychodynamic Treatment of Anorexia Nervosa and Bulimia*, pp. 165–193. New York: Guilford.

Kernberg, O. (1974). *Borderline Conditions and Pathological Narcissism*. New York: Jason Aronson.

Lorand, S. (1943). Anorexia nervosa. Report of a case. In *Evolution of Psychosomatic Concepts*, ed. M. R. Kaufman and M. Heinman, pp. 298–319. New York: International Universities Press, 1964.

Mahler, M., Pine, F., and Bergman, A. (1975). *The Psychological Birth of the Human Infant*. New York: Basic Books.

Masserman, J. H. (1941). Psychodynamics in anorexia nervosa and neurotic vomiting. In *Evolution of Psychosomatic Concepts*, ed. M. R. Kaufman and

M. Heinman, pp. 320–351. New York: International Universities Press, 1964.

Moulton, R. (1942). A psychosomatic study of anorexia nervosa including the use of vaginal smear. In *Evolution of Psychosomatic Concepts*, ed. M. R. Kaufman and M. Heinman, pp. 274–297. New York: International Universities Press, 1964.

Podhoretz, H. (1980). *Modifications of Kernberg's expressive psychotherapy with a borderline psychotic woman*. Paper presented at the American Psychological Association, Montreal.

Rampling, D. (1980). Single case study: abnormal mothering in the genesis of anorexia nervosa. *Journal of Nervous and Mental Disease* 168(8):501–504.

Steiner-Adair, C. (1991). New maps of developments, new methods of therapy: the psychology of women and the treatment of eating disorders. In *Psychodynamic Treatment of Anorexia Nervosa and Bulimia*, ed. C. Johnson, pp. 225–244. New York: Guilford.

Winokur, A. (1980). Primary affective disorder in relatives of patients with anorexia nervosa. *American Journal of Psychiatry* 137(6):695–698.

Wooley, S. C. (1991). Uses of countertransference in the treatment of eating disorders: a gender perspective. In *Psychodynamic Treatment of Anorexia Nervosa and Bulimia*, ed. C. Johnson, pp. 245–294. New York: Guilford.

CHAPTER FOURTEEN

The Significance of the Anal and Rapprochement Stages in Anorexia

ANDREA S. CORN AND ROBERT C. LANE

This chapter presents an in-depth discussion of Nicole, a 16-year-old anorexic female with rich clinical material. A discussion of the theory and treatment of anorexic issues concentrates on the patient's anality and separation-individuation conflicts. This chapter also addresses the development and outcome of this challenging and life-threatening psychosomatic condition.

To fully understand the patient's dynamics and clinical developments, theory on anorexia is reviewed from both a conflict-based and an object-relational perspective. These two aspects of development are discussed in some detail prior to the clinical case presentation.

THEORY OF ANOREXIA

Literature has appeared on anorexia nervosa from a psychoanalytic perspective since the 1930s. Early psychoanalytic investigators saw the aversion to food and the refusal to eat in terms of disguised unconscious oral impregnation fantasies. Oedipal wishes were said to be defended against by the regression to preoedipal drive components. Symptom formations were seen as converging around oral conflicts, and food refusal was attributed to a way of gaining autonomy. In the anorectic adolescent's psychopathology, the preoedipal stages had to be resurrected since the existing psychic structures were inadequately prepared to cope with the increasing demands of adulthood. This regression was claimed to bring about renewed attempts at mastery.

The Anal Stage

The anal stage of psychosexual development signifies the time when the child must learn to comply with external pressures in order to control instinctual impulses. Anal training is a pivotal experience around which intrapsychic processes and interpersonal relationships coalesce.

Freud (1908) was the first to address the existence of pregenital zones. He claimed that in the second psychosexual stage, the child was able to derive enjoyable sensations in being able to both retain and eliminate faeces. Heimann (1962) further elaborated: "The infant knows no disgust or shame and with narcissistic grandiosity highly values her faeces as a part of her own body. She keeps them back for her own pleasure and, in yielding them to her mother, confers on her the first presents that she can produce from her own resources" (p. 407). This closely follows Freud's thinking that the feces is the first "gift" the child bestows on its caregivers.

With the advent of toilet training, the child gradually comprehends that defecation must adhere to socially prescribed standards. Fischer and Juni (1981) discussed the dual nature of the libidinal process of the anal phase. They characterized the early retentive-expulsive continuum as erotogenic, due to the focus on autoerotic gratification, and the sadistic-erotic continuum as interpersonal, due to the interactions between parent and child.

The significance of the anal phase was referred to by Heimann (1962) as being a time when "the infant experiences the major clash between her narcissism and object-relatedness" (p. 408). There is the struggle between the instinctual impulses and compliance with the demands of an autonomy-robbing environment. Heimann also pointed out that in contrast to the symbiotic oneness of the oral stage, autonomous strivings mark the underpinning of the anal stage. If the mother demands rigid compliance or total conformity, on the threat of withdrawal of love, the chances are great that inhibitions in autonomous behavior will result. The final outcome will bear its mark on subsequent character development.

With respect to the anorectic patient, stubborn refusal to both produce and part with bowel contents suggests a negative assertion of autonomy through the ability to exercise such control. The anorectic withholds the discharge of aggressive affects through the defenses of repression and denial.

The anorectic's constellation of negative anal characteristics is exhibited via disturbances in ego development, body imagery, need for control, and magical thinking. Defensive anal character traits are observed in flashes of pseudoautonomy that coexist with personal ineffectiveness. An emaciated physical appearance is denied, yet a passive, stubborn defiance is apparent in the refusal to comply with parental or medical requests. Rigid eating patterns are coupled with frugal consumption. This leads to a sense of mastery that is derived from denying basic oral pleasures. These patients find a renewed sense of power in their capacity for abstinence and self-control. A significant amount of energy is channeled into the elimination process as anorectics often ruminate and obsess over matters that pertain to toileting and laxative usage. Anal behavior patterns have been mentioned in various studies, although their particular influence in the anorectic population has been generally overlooked. Anorectic patients are experienced as highly frustrating and difficult in treatment due to their strong passive-aggressive tendencies, obsessional ideations, and masochistic acting out. These patients can take sadistic delight in rubbing one's nose in not being able to eradicate their disorder (or clean up their mess), which is their way of devaluing those persons in authority.

Other tendencies associated with anal-sadism are revealed in negativism, emotional constriction, and closing off one's mind, mouth, or body. Reaction formations are expressed in demeanors of overcompensatory kindness and an incapacity for aggression. Within the anal spectrum, contradictory personalities can be expressed by anorectic patients, as they appear both kind and cruel, orderly and messy, and flexible and stubborn. Struggles regarding whether or not to eat are part of the eternal conflict between the anorectic's self-preservation and self-destruction. Conflicts around sexuality and aggression are also played out in this life-threatening symptom. Freud (1908) identified a triad of anal character traits, "orderliness, parsimony (or frugality), and obstinacy (stubbornness)." These three terms will be briefly explored in the adolescent anorectic's psychopathology.

Orderliness

For children in the second year of life, orderliness is imposed by parental demands for conformity. This is seen not only in toilet training but in all aspects of behavioral compliance. The parents' sense of themselves as orderly is mirrored by their offsprings' ability to comply with societal expectations. Harsh parental punishments shape the superego and induce a sense of unworthiness and shame. If the child experiences continual "failures," autonomy needs are not gratified and maternal symbiosis prevails. Female children may especially experience more demands during this period because their mothers may view them as narcissistic extensions of themselves. There are strong unmet dependency needs along with an identification with their same-sex role models. Children who are at risk to develop anorexia learn to repress rage while outwardly complying with maternal demands. This is further compounded if the fathers in these families are physically or emotionally absent.

Parsimony

The character trait of parsimony relates to the anorectic's constricted affect and behavior. Anorectic patients who exhibit this trait become rigidly defensive and brittle from the stress of holding back their reservoir of emotionality.

These attitudes originate in the second year of life, when the toddler views the world as alternating between threatening and unpredictable but needed for survival. Emotional compliance and an overwhelming need to be physically close to the caregiver safeguards the child from the fantasy that the parental figure has been annihilated by his/her aggression or will counterattack and annihilate the child (projected aggression).

Obstinacy

Obstinacy is perhaps the hallmark trait of the anal-stage child. The word *no* not only becomes the rallying cry for these toddlers, but also instills a sense of pseudo-power in a world that has become increasingly ordered and controlled by parental dictates. This attribute occurs for the first time as the child learns to tighten the sphincter muscles and spite parental efforts.

Mahler in 1968 regarded "the negativistic period of the anal phase" (p. 20) as a necessity for intrapsychic separation and boundary formation. For the "at risk" child, continual usage of the "no" precipitates the fear of psychological annihilation. The accompanying fears of losing mother's love, approval, and affection are potentially devastating to the child. As a result, the child no longer feels like a person who is empowered to act on her own "no." Therefore, compliance, obedience, and adherence assure a child of mother's love, while age-appropriate spontaneity, independent action, and individualism elicit overwhelming fear in relation to possible parental loss and emotional abandonment.

The discussion regarding intrapsychic development is extended into the interpersonal realm by the development of both at the same time. The interactions between mother and child simultaneously affect both the use of libidinal energy and the formation of internalized objects that shape the basis of interpersonal interactions. This brings us to a discussion of object relations.

Object Relations

Object relations theory further extends psychoanalytic principles, as the interpersonal sphere is reflected in the relationship with the primary figure of attachment. Object relations theorists stress the centrality and quality of the mother–infant attachment, and its importance in establishing all subsequent relationships.

The rapprochement crisis in Mahler's separation-individuation construct highlights this precarious juncture. The child attempts to make autonomous strivings, while simultaneously being conflicted with strong needs for contact, affection, and safety. The toddler's natural assertion may be thwarted by a controlling mother who fosters dependency and stifles individuation. A conflict arises between the need for separation and the fear of loss of the mother's emotional support and physical proximity. This crisis of the separation-individuation phase leads to a movement to "stay safe." This need for safety is manifested in the form of compliant, dependent behavior.

Inadequate early object relations and their impact in understanding the dilemma of the anorectic patient have been extensively described. Winnicott (1965) observed that if there are "good enough" caregiving functions, the child develops feelings of selfhood and security. On the other hand, when the emphasis shifts to a preoccupation with external cues and an accommodation of others, while sacrificing one's own needs, a false self is created. This results in a regression as feelings of helplessness and unprotectedness are too unbearable to manage.

Anorectic patients use food refusal and their quest for thinness as methods of obtaining a sense of mastery, perfection, separateness, and control over bodily functioning. These voluntary restrictions hold off unconscious fears of merging or identifying with an all-pervasive, powerful, and controlling mother. Food becomes the object of conflict by its identification and assimilation with the nurturing role. While the eating-disordered patient longs for oral mothering, there is a corresponding compulsion to rid the self of the introjected bad mother. This fantasy is the result of excessive frustration and rage at the mother. Food becomes the enemy through displacement, and must either be eliminated or not taken in because it does not provide gratification.

Individuals diagnosed with anorexia have been unable to internalize a good-enough mother, and consequently they feel unconsciously starved for a nurturing object. These individuals are immobilized out of fear of losing their primary attachment, although the attachment is fragile, frustrating, and conflictual. They fluctuate from retaining a desire for closeness and merger to fearing the accompanying separation and loss. As a result, splitting, introjection fantasies, and omnipotent magical thinking become prominent defenses against aggressive and sexual impulses. As portrayed in the case study, the anorectic re-creates the ambivalent struggle between the actual and internalized mother image through food denial and distorted body perceptions.

Adolescence revives the transition from dependency to autonomy as earlier infantile struggles and conflicts reemerge. The anorectic patient's need for independence manifests itself in not eating. The self-destructive act of self-starvation enables the adolescent girl to regress developmentally, control pubertal demands, and foster an internal sense of control. This pressing need for identity and independence is not verbalized but enacted in anorectic posturing: "I am me, you are you. If I do everything you want me to do, I'll become you or like you, and lose my identity." Thus, refusal becomes a means of control and defiance in reaction to the original loss of independence re-creating the earlier anal problem. Anorectic patients can display a perverse repetition compulsion by finding comfort in depriving themselves of food, while maintaining an external reliance on an object for self-regulation.

Anorectic patients have great difficulty in acknowledging conflicts regarding expressing rage, asserting oneself, and needing support. Consequently, in order to avoid feeling "consumed" by their mothers' expectations, anorectic daughters outwardly distance themselves from their mothers while simultaneously secretly longing for their nurturance and unconditional love. These individuals internalize and repress their anger in order to conceal their destructive impulses, all the while attempting to maintain an intrapsychic balance. This usually proves to be unsuccessful and is witnessed in failed suicide attempts, chronic hunger, excessive exercising, and masochistic and self-injurious behaviors that can produce irreversible bodily harm.

Regardless of the anorectic's gender, studies have portrayed maternal figures as domineering, controlling, overprotective, and perfectionistic. The anorectic is unwilling or unable to risk maternal rejection and/or separation due to the internalized mental representation of mother as one who rewards compliance while being overprotective. Humphrey (1991) has described how the holding environment becomes inadequate and deficient in its ability to "(1) nurture, (2) soothe, and (3) be empathic" (p. 324). Clinical presentations of anorectic patients often point to a pervasive and passive ego that is receptive, compliant, and ever-hungry.

According to Humphrey (1991), there is a long-standing, transgenerational pattern of developmental deficits. These did not begin with the primary parental figure nor can these conflicts end with their anorectic offspring without intensive psychotherapy. Treatment considerations must include the mother's unconscious need to deny her own early childhood pathology, and the displacement of her feelings onto her anorectic offspring in order to relieve her own feeling of inadequacy, as demonstrated in the following case.

CASE ILLUSTRATION

Nicole Valdez is a 16-year-old Hispanic girl with two prior hospitalizations. She secretly disposed of food, falsified weight gains, and was highly manipulative.

She is the second and oldest female child of her natural parents. Her older brother is two years her senior and she has twin sisters four years her junior. Nicole lived in Panama until she was 12, and then moved to Miami, Florida. Shortly thereafter, her father returned to Panama, leaving the mother as the sole provider. The father, a strict disciplinarian, contacted the children infrequently.

At mealtime, Nicole was forbidden to leave the table until all of her food had been eaten. She recalled staring at her plate as a child, silently refusing to obey her father's demands. Her mother described that scene as a painful time for all. She would helplessly watch her daughter suffer without any attempt to rescue her. Too intimidated to intercede on her daughter's behalf, she found other ways to express her rage passively. She would refuse sexual advances, eventually creating many unpleasant scenes.

In general, Mrs. Valdez was subservient to her husband, masochistic, and sacrificing her integrity while enduring scathing criticism and denigration. Nicole was described by her as a "clingy" and fearful child who required her mother's soothing. Her lack of feelings of trust, safety, and security interfered with her psychological growth. She identified with her mother's deficiencies in ego functioning as well as her sexual difficulties. Mrs. Valdez, herself emotionally starved, was jealous of any attention Nicole received.

The foundation for Nicole's later refusal to eat, reluctance to grow up, or "to give in" (implying a sexual surrender as well) were fixed early in her life. Her need for control and strong resistance, and defiance against being controlled were already apparent in the very early feeding situations. Nicole became the recipient of her mother's projected negative feelings, self-doubts, and insecurities. This enabled Nicole to remain close to her mother, dependent and loyal, which was the essence of their dysfunctional bond (similar to the mother's dependence on the maternal grandmother).

At 13 years of age, her parents divorced, and her father returned to Panama to live with and later marry his mistress. Mother found some outlet for her rage in totally destroying the children's image of their father. This created an even stronger bond between mother and daughter, causing Nicole to be more fearful of sex and of growing up. Mrs. Valdez stimulated guilt feelings in Nicole by making her an audience to intimate details. These revelations, such as confessions that mother rejected father's advances, also sexually awakened and excited Nicole, stimulating thoughts of becoming an oedipal victor. Whether mother had pushed Nicole onto father in order to get him off her back is not clear. We do know that he was pushed into acquiring a mistress. Whether he was running away from incestuous feelings for his daughter we also don't know. Although Nicole spoke about not wanting to hear about mother's intimate secrets, we also know that she was flattered by the attention (this may have been one of the primary sources of attention from mother). In one sense this ushered in a negative oedipal victory, as it fulfilled the fantasy of being rid of her father, while also compounding preoedipal drives concerned with having mother all to herself. Inwardly she resented her mother for allowing father to leave, although her outward grief (how superficial is unknown) probably served as a reaction formation against her inner guilt. She secretly desired an exclusive relationship with her mother, and now that this was a reality she despised herself for wanting to replace her father as the significant libidinal object in her mother's life. Negative feelings such as shame, guilt, and inadequacy were the result of this conflict. Instead of expressing her rage at both parents for their damaging actions, she masochistically enacted these impulses against herself.

Nicole felt alone and isolated when the family then moved to Washington, living with relatives while the mother had to go to work. She tended to escape into a fantasy world in which she was loved and adored. During this period, Mrs. Valdez began corresponding with Mr. Garcia, a man she had met in Miami. Viewing his marriage proposal as a means of attaining American citizenship and a rescue fantasy, she accepted, and the family returned to Miami.

Mr. Garcia was a superficially charming man who made many unkept promises to the children. Instead of his being the attentive, generous husband, father, and stepfather, Mrs. Valdez soon discovered that he, like her husband and father, behaved irrationally and was extremely manipulative and abusive. A disturbed Vietnam veteran, he suffered periodic flashbacks that left him hypervigilant and paranoid. Unable to work, he remained at home caring for the children while his wife became the breadwinner. Nicole's older brother could not tolerate his stepfather's unpredictability and left home shortly after their return to Miami.

Nicole supervised the younger children, prepared the family meals, and became the responsible substitute mother. She worked hard to please her mother and remain the beloved daughter. Her neatness compulsion and cleaning fetish signified the beginnings of ego regression and the covering up of immense negativity and hostility. These feelings found some release in Nicole's imposing her position of substitute mother on her twin siblings, thus compensating for general feelings of powerlessness and insignificance. She was upset to find that the twins complained of being forced to comply with her rigid expectations. Nicole apparently behaved toward her twin sisters as her parents had behaved toward her. Instead of rewarding Nicole for duties performed, as well as excellent grades, her mother, in exhaustion, withdrew her emotional availability. Mrs. Valdez was envious of Nicole's role as well as her husband's passive position. She was too needy herself to accommodate her daughter's needs and instead confided in Nicole her personal problems and financial concerns. This left Nicole feeling helpless for not being able to alleviate her mother's long-standing despondency, and guilty for having hostile thoughts toward her.

Mrs. Valdez's remarriage and subsequent emotional abandonment dramatically changed the dynamics of her harmonious dyadic relationship with Nicole. Nicole was jealous of Mr. Garcia's time with her mother and her mother's time with him, and she felt unable to please either party. Her fantasy of having her mother for herself was shattered. Even more so, Nicole feared Mr. Garcia might act on his repeated threats to restrict her contacts with her mother if she did not listen to him. She was frightened of the power this man held over her. In light of the maternal functions Nicole performed and the time spent alone with her stepfather, one might suspect *some* sexual stimulation or acting out, but none was reported. Nicole did become the symbiotic partner onto whom her mother projected her own depressive sadomasochistic rage and with whom she shared secrets. These projections and externalizations were mother's defenses against her own long-standing traumatic losses.

Nicole's fears of intimacy were reenacted at the age of 15, when she was rebuffed in her first and only experience with the opposite sex. This romantic experience culminated in light petting. Shortly thereafter, Nicole was horrified to discover that her "lover" had boasted to his friends and spread rumors about her easy availability. Nicole was ashamed she had enjoyed her sexual contact and now felt cheap and promiscuous, akin to feelings attributed by her mother to her father's mistress. What it meant to her is not clear. It may have been a combination of maturity, a need to prove her womanhood, a wish to displace feelings from her stepfather who was stimulating her heterosexually (as well as from her mother who was stimulating her homosexually), a bid for attention, and a wish to break away. There was reason to believe that each of the above prevailed at one time or another. The event apparently triggered painful oedipal memories that had to be repressed. Nicole needed to preserve her closeness to her mother, and in order to do so she had to disavow mature sexual strivings and regress to a more vulnerable and helpless position.

The onset of adolescence brought about a resurgence of incestuous oedipal longings. These apparently resurfaced through her relationship with Mr. Garcia. He was the older man who represented her absent father, and his behavior was similar in that he could be attentive and caring one moment and rejecting and hostile the next. Essentially, she played the role of the wife and mother who cooked, cleaned, and took care of the children. So on some level did she not wish to receive his love as well as to become his sexual partner? This fantasy would resurrect tremendous guilt resulting in an escalation of hostile feelings toward herself and guilt toward her mother. Despite Nicole's denial of these thoughts and feelings, she could only prevent this realization by becoming an undesirable, unattractive, ascetic female. Her conflict soon gave way to repression and to regression to a time when temptations didn't play such an important role in her life. This partial regression from the genital phase prompted an increase in all anal-phase activities.

Nicole also seemed to have an unbearable sense of guilt over the fantasy of harming her ambivalently loved object. Her shunning of age-appropriate activities enabled her to receive special privileges from mother. In this way, mother impeded Nicole's autonomous strivings while simultaneously appearing to gratify unmet dependency needs, serving both a repressive and adaptive function. This shielded the patient against experiencing age-appropriate strivings. As a result, successive developmental tasks could not be mastered due to prior unresolved primitive fears and defenses including splitting, projective identification, and apparent magical thinking. Subsequently, this reenacted a regression to phase dominance, a point where separation from her mother was feared and her mother's physical presence was sought to assure safety.

As mentioned, Nicole thwarted her own growth since she could not relinquish the preoedipal attachment to her mother and establish a normal oedipal attachment to her father. Even if Nicole had been able to turn to her father in the hope of possessing his love, her identification with and need for her mother was too strong. Intense anxiety developed in retaliation for harboring forbidden impulses. These wishes were repressed, and her love for and identification with her mother remained the dominant force during her early sexual development.

Puberty resurrected incestuous preoedipal feelings. Previously, Nicole's mind had been poisoned by mother's unhappiness as she confided in her that men were untrustworthy and only interested in using women. Developmentally, Nicole's positive oedipal strivings actually served as a defense against preoedipal longings, as she desperately needed a nurturing relationship. Nicole regressed to pregenitality with an emphasis on both the oral and anal phases of psychosexual development.

She began exhibiting a compliant and cooperative facade that masked strong passive-aggressive actions, hostilities, and rebelliousness. Nicole forced a rigid daily schedule on herself. She consumed only soft and low-calorie foods, took several showers daily, and after her mother returned from work she would walk five miles. She ignored her mother's pleading not to exercise so strenuously. Following upsetting arguments, Nicole would arise an hour early to work out as if to cleanse herself. This passive-aggressive behavior frustrated her mother, leaving her feeling helpless. Nicole further exerted herself by trying to control and dominate her surroundings, especially everything she took in emotionally, behaviorally, and nutritionally.

Nicole's symptoms were ego-syntonic in that she was unaware of her possessiveness, contrariness, and stubbornness. It seemed that her behavior consisted of reaction formations against fears of losing her bodily and emotional boundaries, as she denied her own aggressive tendencies. Furthermore, the traits she revealed were her way of keeping her distance while maintaining a sense of control, ruminating over obsessional ideation pertaining to thinness, holding in her rage, denying sexual aims, and at the same time rejecting symbiosis with mother. Negative anal character traits subsequently became the dominant expression of Nicole's psychopathology.

The emergence of Nicole's anorexia symbolized the emotional starvation she experienced as her mother became increasingly more unavailable, as well as her guilt over her hostile feelings toward her mother. Anorectics have great difficulty tolerating painful affects, their drives, or even hunger for food, because of their mortal dread of succumbing to and acting out their hostile feelings (Goitein 1942). Nicole's ability to restrict food intake was a desperate attempt to abandon her experimentation with autonomy and became a way to extinguish sexual desires and maturational fears.

Ambivalent anal behavior became the hallmark of Nicole's relationship with her mother, and punishment became the binding tie accompanied by fears of maternal engulfment. Mother perceived her daughter to be the exposer of her defective parenting and the source of her feelings of inadequacy. Nicole's frail and skeleton-like appearance (suggesting to others that mother starved her) brought both shame and embarrassment to Mrs. Valdez, who was furious with her daughter. In turn, Nicole's continuous self-starvation was her way to seek retribution, hurt her mother, and still maintain their enmeshed attachment.

In the hospital, Nicole's passive-aggressive behavior was so pronounced it became a hindrance to treatment. On the surface, she was willing to please and was soft-spoken. She clung stubbornly to her resistances, was unwilling to hear therapeutic interventions, and vehemently resisted parental intervention and medical treatment. Being obstinate enabled Nicole to hold on to her internalized aggression, while at the same time strongly controlling the external environment. Her superficial conformity and veneer of kindness (reaction formation) masked repressed and denied rage, while permitting her to appear the "perfect young lady." Nicole was consumed by narcissistic rage related to her uprooting, the various moves, her father's abandonment, and her mother's subsequent desertion and replacement with Mr. Garcia. She also resented her mother's need to infantilize her while forcing her to grow up prematurely and assume the role of her confidante. Unconsciously, Nicole was confused by her mother's need to envelop her with her own unresolved dependencies and unmet affectional needs. This latent homosexual preoedipal attachment both frightened and stimulated her to the point where she had to take flight. A negative oedipal attachment was evidenced in her mother working and becoming the breadwinner while Nicole stayed home with the children, cooking, shopping, and performing the household duties. Her behaving in a passive-aggressive, self-defeating, punitive, and masochistic manner can be viewed as attempts to avoid closeness and intimacy with mother. It can also be seen as a revenge motive to her mother and getting even with authority figures in general, and it demonstrates her general confusion concerning relationships. Nicole's efforts at resisting therapeutic endeavors were unconsciously an attempt to defeat the transference mother as well as the real mother.

Anorectic patients often appear to be notoriously evasive and secretive, misleading parents, doctors, and psychologists by omitting pertinent information. The need to withhold thoughts, negate and constrict feelings, and stubbornly hold on to internalized condemnation are thought to stem from overwhelming fears of annihilation and self-negation. Nicole exhibited these traits as she tried to preserve her sense of self as separate from the bodily and psychic intrusion she experienced. Whereas she acted "as if" she was cooperating with the medical team, in reality this was far from the truth. The medical team was worried she might die due to her lack of compliance. Her compulsion to withhold was so pronounced that she would not talk about her medical condition even when she experienced symptoms of numbness and fainting, and she had to be fed through a feeding tube. Nicole was fearful of spontaneity and imprisoned by her own self-doubts and insecurities. For over three months, her therapy progressed minimally.

Anorectic individuals like Nicole are faced with an abiding sense of incompetence and unworthiness, and a tremendous fear that they won't please mother. These negative devaluations are at the root of the pathology and serve to reinforce self-hatred. Nicole's anality was pervasive in the extent of her emotional constriction, retentiveness, and obstinacy. The devaluation and deindividuation of anal defensiveness may act as a defense against underlying rage (Shengold 1985).

During therapy, the interplay between unresolved anal conflicts and the wish to separate from an omnipotently perceived maternal figure were gradually revived in the transference. Nicole was fearful of being verbally attacked and had great difficulty sharing herself in the transference. She reacted to the transference mother as she did to her real mother—with ambivalence and suspicion, fluctuating between longing for "good-enough" mothering and hating the invasive aspect of therapy. She became disappointed easily whenever she felt the therapist failed to sense her needs and did not nourish her unconscious wish for fusion. Beattie (1988) observed this fluctuation in her description of anorectic patients. She found they oscillate between "excessive dependency, slavish conformity, and lack of self assertion, to exaggerated pseudoautonomy and defensive rejection of help and intimacy" (p. 459).

Besides Nicole's individual therapist, there was a team of doctors tending to her needs, including two male psychiatrists. She intensely resented their taking control over her life, and was especially piqued by their decision to insert a nasogastric tube and force-feed her (symbolic rape). They also came between her, her mother, and her therapist by preventing her mother from visiting her until she had gained weight, and controlling her life and medication, thus making her therapist appear secondary. Nicole related to these doctors as if they were her stepfather (and father)—the men in her life who ordered her about, did cruel things to her, and kept her apart from her mother. For months she withheld the rage she felt toward them, and via intellectualization was able to control the mounting affective volcano within her. When she finally released her rage, it erupted in a burst of explosive tears. Following this outburst, and working on it in the transference, her mistrust of them lessened. Gradually, she began to accept the necessity of their medically intrusive procedures into her bodily openings and her role in bringing it about.

The structure and safety provided by the hospital eventually fostered the establishment of a facilitative environment that strengthened the therapeutic alliance. This enabled Nicole to work toward resolving some of her predominant anally driven behavior and separation-individuation conflicts. This also helped to promote her perception that the therapist could be a constant object able to withstand hearing rageful feelings, without the gratification of unmet dependency needs.

During Nicole's first few weeks at home postdischarge, her mother hovered over her with a kind of smother-love. Her overprotectiveness and overpermissiveness dominated Nicole's eating, exercising, and peer relationships. However, her mother's aggressive impulses toward both her own mother and her daughter, not having been sufficiently worked through, were still a potential threat to Nicole's attempts at independence and recovery in general. Her mother still treated Nicole as if she were the embodiment of her mother by ambivalently giving and withholding her affection. As Nicole regressed and demanded more and more attention, treatment gains quickly diminished. Power struggles and conflicts over control between her mother and Nicole carried over into every facet of their relationship, and crystallized in their arguments over food.

Several months after termination of therapy, Nicole stabilized at a low but acceptable weight, enabling her to produce four consecutive menstrual cycles. She graduated from high school and had plans to attend a local college. However, Mrs. Valdez and Nicole could not maintain consistency in adhering to their outpatient treatment and termination was prematurely forced. It was the wish of the therapist that Nicole could have continued in treatment. However, losing therapeutic control now meant that Nicole had to differentiate her maternal identification independently while establishing her self-identity. Only by mastering this stage could she blossom into an independent, separate being who could feel love and not feel harmed when mother's approval was not forthcoming. Unfortunately, in this case it is highly unlikely that Nicole's fiercely intense anal conflicts and separation-individuation struggles will subside without continued therapy. Chances are they will continue to manifest themselves both symptomatically and defensively in Nicole's character structure and personality.

DISCUSSION

One can see the patient's lifelong struggle for power and control, first with one and then the other parent, and later with the stepfather. Forceful handling and rigid training practices with her younger twin sisters are suggestive of her own forced training by her mother. Her refusal to obey her father's demands at the kitchen table further reinforced the mother's training practices. Repeated expectations by the parents and wishes to control and dominate permeate the case history. Power struggles with parents, hospital staff, doctors, and the therapist are all evident. She wishes to control both the situation and the environment. She experiences an excessive sense of duty, and is harassed by and with responsibilities.

The patient felt unable to please her mother. Whatever she produced was neither "enough" nor "good." No matter what her accomplishments, she did not feel her efforts were appreciated. She cared for the house and the children, did the food shopping and preparation, and assumed the mother's usual functions. Yet the mother still expected Nicole to care for her. Full of rage, Nicole was unable to express her feelings, and covering up, hiding, and masking secret desires and forbidden impulses were common in her history.

Given the centrality of the mother—infant relationship, which is stressed in object relations theory, this case illustrates the conflict that can emerge during the rapprochement crisis of the separation-individuation phase of development. The patient's natural desires for assertion and separation may have been thwarted by her controlling mother, preventing normal individuation. Her need for safety was reflected in her overly compliant behavior. The difficulty in acknowledging her conflicts around the expression of her rage, self-assertion, and need for support led the patient to internalize and repress her anger.

She regressed to negativity in her attempts to establish a sense of identity, with passive-aggressive activity rampant in her behavior. Whenever upset, there was a marked increase in her anal phase activity and character traits. She showed evidence of marked ambivalence and bisexuality, with suggested phallic tendencies and wishes to be a boy. The active sadistic component reinforced and exaggerated the masculine attitude in the patient. She exhibited both positive oedipal desire for father and negative oedipal desire for mother. She wished to replace mother and possess father, and replace father and stepfather and possess mother. The patient had to be aware of the sexual difficulties between her parents—mother's reluctance and her father's looking elsewhere. The birth of her twin sisters, born when she was 4 and in the oedipal phase, suggests that there may have been an oral or anal impregnation fantasy with father. It was he who force-fed her, insisting she take it (food) forcefully into her mouth. Although her one reported unsuccessful sexual encounter (petting) is described as pleasurable, it resulted in abandonment, hostility, and rage. Sadomasochism, secrets, and exposure were all associated with sex, leading to fear and avoidance (isolating, making herself undesirable, perhaps viewing sex as impure and dirty). Unfortunately, there is no further information concerning her toilet training history, birth fantasies, autoerotic activity and fantasies, and ideas about sex.

As Winnicott (1965) discussed, the patient's feelings of helplessness and insecurity led to the formation of a false self organized primarily around external cues and accommodation to others. Through her food refusal and quest for thinness, she sought mastery over her body and fended off fears of merging with her powerful and controlling mother. Identified with nurturing, food represented her conflicts regarding nurturance and separation. At the same time, food represented her longings for oral mothering while there was an overwhelming desire to rid herself of the introjected bad mother.

The anal sadistic orientation is revealed in reaction formations demonstrating compensatory kindness, cleanliness, incapacity for aggression and punctiliousness (she did her duties and on time). The mixture of reaction formation with strong defiance and rebelliousness makes the patient appear contradictory. Polarities (antitheses) such as cruelty and kindness, aggressiveness and submissiveness, dirtiness and cleanliness, and disorder and order are all present. Defensive use of undesirability, unattractiveness, passive-aggressiveness, subservience, and self-punishment are also apparent. Anal defenses such as intellectualization, isolation (of ideation and affect), reaction formation, undoing, and regression are in evidence in her verbalization and behavior. Although these defenses are most obvious with her excessive kindness, stress on perfection, and search for the perfect body, she also gives evidence of deeper oral defenses such as splitting and idealization. Perfection, a defense against decay and death (the evils), may overcome paralysis of action because only if one is perfect is one immune to decay and death. Magical thinking and omnipotence of words and thoughts (she might cause harm) are also suggested.

Turning to Freud's anal character traits, orderliness is seen in her neatness and cleansing compulsion, her compulsion to take showers, her rigid daily schedule and school attendance, her exercise compulsion, her fastidiousness or compulsion to clean up dirt in general (her hostility, murderous rage, and sexual fantasies), and other compulsive rituals. Cleansing rituals must have been a repetition of what she heard or saw as a child and used as a defense against "dirty" thoughts. The orderliness described is used to protect against dangerous instinctual demands and impulses. Isolation of ideational and affective content serves to protect from closeness and intimacy with others. Thus, she appears cold and emotionless, unable to associate freely, and, through the use of the mechanism of isolation, prevents touching and closeness. She became more compulsive when she was with her stepfather as a defense or protection against closeness, touching, and sexual impulses in general. Parsimoniousness or frugality is apparent in her reluctance to discuss her problems, her possessiveness, her fearfulness of spontaneity, and her need to control (words, thoughts, emotional expressions, and her nutrition). She restricted her food intake and her life in general. She did not volunteer nor was she asked about avarice, saving, collecting, or hoarding. Obstinacy or stubbornness was apparent in her refusal (to eat, give in, or cooperate with the medical team and its requirements), and in her strong resistance, defiance, and struggle against any control. She held in or back everything, particularly her strong negative feelings, which she acted out in passive anal ways. Withholding became a way of life for her. She was uncooperative, and showed argumentativeness, control struggles, rebelliousness, defiance, and obstinacy in general.

Through not eating, she regressed to the earlier transition phase from autonomy to dependency with the attendant conflicts and struggles. The act of self-starvation served to allow her to regress and promote an internal sense of control; thus, refusal became a means of attaining separation from the mother and the independence originally lost.

SUMMARY

Contemporary writers have elaborated on the unresolved interpersonal conflicts in the mother–daughter dyad during the rapprochement stage of the separation-individuation phase of development. Although this phase overlaps with the anal stage of psychosexual development, anality and anal characteristics in general have received much less discussion in the literature. A principal accomplishment in both phases involves differentiating the external boundaries of the body and mind from internal ones. Anorexic patients are observed to display intense interpersonal difficulties in depicting their conflicts, such as their desire for closeness on the one hand and their fears of engulfment on the other. They have a fierce desire for independence while still craving dependence. To the anorectic patient, food becomes the object of conflict through its association with the nurturing and mothering role.

In the second year of life, ego boundaries are tenuous, and compromises occur between intrapsychic separation and self–boundary formations. Freud (1923) regarded the ego as "first and foremost a body ego," and his view envisioned how the body image becomes the entire repository of internalized images. His remarks have foreshadowed future concepts, such as fusion and introjection.

The case study was presented to demonstrate the preponderance of anal conflicts and interpersonal difficulties seen in the anorectic patient. The patient's constellation of anal character traits were presented. Hostility and dependency conflicts and ambivalencies characterized all of Nicole's interpersonal interactions. Therapeutic interventions were based on these developmental and structural deficits, which illustrated maturational and pubescent problems in general. These occurred along with inadequate autonomy strivings, a presentation of a false self, and negation of self-worth.

We hope this chapter's emphasis on the anorectic's anality and separation-individuation conflicts will help inspire innovative research into how early, unresolved psychosexual and developmental conflicts become paramount in the understanding of the anorectic's long-standing difficulties.

REFERENCES

Beattie, H. (1988). Eating disorders and the mother—daughter relationship. *International Journal of Eating Disorders* 7:453–460.

Fischer, R., and Juni, S. (1981). Anality: a theory of erotism and characterology. *American Journal of Psychoanalysis* 41:51–57.

Freud, S. (1908). Character and anal erotism. *Standard Edition* 9:167–176.

———— (1923). The ego and the id. *Standard Edition* 19:3–68.

Goitein, P. L. (1942). The potential prostitute: the role of anorexia in the defense against prostitution desires. *Journal of Criminal Psychopathology* 3:359–367.

Heimann, P. (1962). Notes on the anal stage. *International Journal of Psycho-Analysis* 43:406–416.

Humphrey, L. L. (1991). Object relations and the family system: an integrative approach to understanding and treating eating disorders. In *Psychodynamic Treatment of Anorexia Nervosa and Bulimia*, ed. C. Johnson, pp. 321–353. New York: Guilford.

Mahler, M. S. (1968). *On Human Symbiosis and the Vicissitudes of Individuation*. New York: International Universities Press.

Shengold, L. (1985). Defensive anality and anal narcissism. *International Journal of Psycho-Analysis* 66:47–73.

Winnicott, D. W. (1965). *The Maturational Processes and the Facilitating Environment: Studies in the Theory of Emotional Development*. New York: International Universities Press.

CHAPTER FIFTEEN

Irritable Bowel Syndrome

JANET SCHUMACHER FINELL

This case presentation explores the role of analytic work and interpretation in the treatment of irritable bowel syndrome (IBS). The patient was an educator who hoped that this analysis would clear up the irritable bowel syndrome that had become exacerbated when she had to make presentations. One of the key problems to be explored was the patient's negative therapeutic reaction (NTR). She battled interpretations and meaning and had a very difficult time being a patient in analysis.

Sarah was 54 years of age, of Jewish descent, and was perceived as highly attractive with blonde hair and bluish-gray eyes. She was married, with two grown daughters, and had numerous hobbies and a circle of friends with whom she was very involved. She was very intelligent and had strong coping skills. Her determination and good ego skills helped her through a traumatic childhood and difficult years when her children were young. She was courageous, strong-willed, and capable of surviving periods of great suffering.

BACKGROUND

As the elder of two children born to an observant Jewish family, Sarah, whose father owned a coffee shop, grew up in financial hard times. Her mother was an emotionally overwrought, hysterical woman who hit, screamed at, and threatened Sarah. Sarah was terrorized by her. At 5 years of age, Sarah left the playground with relatives, without informing her mother. The reaction was traumatic. Mother screamed, cried, and hit Sarah. She later said she almost called the police. Sarah pictured men in blue pouring out of cars searching for her. She was the center of attention in this anxiety-laden fantasy in a very negative way.

She was told that her mother almost died giving birth to her. Mother was highly psychosomatic and Sarah was expected to show compassion and concern for her suffering. Mother shrieked that Sarah's disobedience was killing her. Mother worried and displayed chronic feelings of doom and martyrdom. Mother did not allow any display of anger. Sarah became compliant and received love through being good and being sick. Mother enclosed her in her space, mummifying her emotionally and physically. In the winter, Sarah was so overdressed she could hardly move. She missed a lot of school for minor colds. Mother was always very worried about her health.

By elementary school age Sarah had performance anxiety and bowel problems. In college she developed palpitations. Nauseousness and anxiety accompanied the bowel problems. She felt her creativity had been killed. In adulthood she struggled with child-rearing responsibilities, and agoraphobia further complicated the symptom picture.

Sarah had an interesting phrase for her mother's attacks. She experienced them as "coming out of nowhere." This is how she experienced her bowel attacks, also. Mother's screaming, yanking her by the hair, and threatening felt terrifying and traumatic to her and were beyond her comprehension as a child. She recalled crying so hard that she was unable to stop. She felt this would also happen in treatment if she let herself go, and the session would end with her sobbing uncontrollably.

As a result of these experiences, Sarah decided at an early age not to let her mother see how much she had hurt her and not to be dependent. Her stifling these feelings resulted in their being displaced into psychosomatic and anxiety symptoms.

Sarah had an early idealization of father that was smashed when his working long hours when she was in elementary school resulted in his being absent from the home. He pulled away even further when she reached puberty. This was very painful to her. Against her mother's wishes, he supported her wish to go to college. Mother wanted her to work after high school and give her income to the family. His death from cancer when she was 19 was a loss to her. Later she blamed herself for not being alert to his ill health and possibly saving his life.

Sarah's three-years-younger sister was never experienced as an ally. Sarah first saw her as an intruder, and threw powder in her face and tried to overturn the baby carriage. Later she had to care for her sister, which she deeply resented. The sister became very compliant and never separated from the mother.

In spite of these difficulties, Sarah developed adaptive ego skills. She became a risk taker, an adventurous, fun-loving person. She loved the outdoors and had hobbies that gave her a great deal of pleasure. She was a high-achieving, bright, courageous woman. The determination she developed as a child to avoid mother's wished-for symbiotic merger made her an independent, high-functioning woman, but with many painful symptoms.

THE TREATMENT

This case discussion explores the role of the interpretive process in the treatment. Historically, in treating psychosomatic illness classical analysis attributed meaning to physical symptoms, and through the making conscious of unconscious wishes and feelings the symptoms were typically found to decrease. This patient had a great deal of difficulty with meaning as it reminded her of the meaning her mother attributed to her own psychosomatic symptoms. Mother cited drafts, weather changes, and other externalities as causes of her sufferings. Additionally, the patient saw meaning as authoritarian, and she linked me to Freud, "macho men," and medical doctors, describing us as people who thought we knew what was going on in someone else.

This presented a dilemma in treatment. Initially Sarah was compliant and fearful of expressing aggression. She had not been able to express it with previous therapists—all male. At some point Sarah read Joyce McDougall and saw herself as alexithymic—without the ability to identify and differentiate among different feelings. She realized she was avoidant of feelings, and often was operational and concrete. She spent a good deal of time discussing the specific details of either her psychosomatic illness or family issues. One of the first dreams showed her difficulty with aggression. She dreamt her hands were full of blood. She had blood on her clothes as well.

Another theme that showed up was fear of being trapped by me. She dreamt that she was immobilized in her bed in a public place. She asked passersby for help but to no avail. Control was a big issue, too. She dreamt that she was in a barrel rolling downhill, helpless to stop. She saw me as the mother who would control and imprison her as her mother had done. Analysis felt like a negative event that she had to suffer through in order to feel better.

Some dreams displayed anxiety reactions. She dreamed that someone was standing over her with a knife. She literally jumped out of bed. Her thought was that it was her mother. She had had conscious fears and nighttime dreams of locked doors. Sometimes she was unable to get in and sometimes she was unable to get out. Bears also appeared in her dreams as dangerous animals, surprising her and threatening her with attack. One association to a dream was that while she never remembered any conscious sexual wishes about her father, she recalled his "bear" hugs quite lovingly. In a follow-up meeting five months after termination, she reported a dream in which her mother was lying on top of her forcing her tongue into Sarah's mouth. The affect associated with this dream was horror and fear.

NEGATIVE THERAPEUTIC REACTION

One of the difficulties Sarah had was that following some improvement in the IBS she would have a reversal with exacerbation of her problems. When she was symptomatic, I encouraged her to trace recent events to see if something had precipitated anxiety feelings. This technique more often than not led to the discovery of some family interaction or career pressure that left her feeling inadequate, anxious, and angry. Making these linkages often brought symptomatic relief, but this would soon be followed by statements about analysis not being helpful.

The theme of deprivation and envy often came up with Sarah around material possessions. I wonder if she didn't resent my power as the analyst conducting treatment. Early in life she had decided not to allow herself to be dependent on her mother. The idea of being in treatment with a female and having to swallow interpretations she didn't like must have felt like the bad emotional food she received as a child. She felt forced and controlled and this was a painful position for her to be in.

While Sarah from time to time expressed positive feelings about the work we were doing together and reported improvement in her symptoms, at other times her transference was angry and critical. She saw analysis as inefficient, ineffectual, and unpleasant. She reported that it was hard for her to work with a female, although with previous male therapists she had been totally unable to express aggression or criticism. Paradoxically, she considered her freedom to criticize me as a milestone for her.

In the follow-up meeting she felt that after analysis her capacity to experience anger at mother was even deeper. She also realized there were times when she knew she was angry without fully feeling it. She was able also to realize that she was angry through a return of her old fear of knives. This fear had been particularly bothersome while her children were young and had appeared at times when she felt particularly overwhelmed with child-rearing responsibilities. She now had a clear perception that she projected her anger on the knives, so that she immediately recognized anger upon thinking of sharp knives.

On another level, Sarah found analysis difficult because working closer with me threatened merger and annihilation. Anger ensures separateness and shores up feelings of boundaries. In contrast, love, neediness, and appreciation threaten loss of separateness. Sarah's NTR protected her against a dreaded loss of self accompanied by annihilation anxiety. It was safer for her to feel angry, critical, and not helped by me than to feel improvement and appreciation.

Sarah could feel better in the first part of the week and rapidly deteriorate in the latter part. She saw this as the failure of analysis to make any permanent improvements rather than her difficulty in taking in anything of value from me. While she could observe this in others, she defiantly fought getting anything positive from treatment. The fear that I was the bad object who would implode her with poison and enemas in violation of her boundaries and her survival interfered with her experience of analysis as a safe haven.

COUNTERTRANSFERENCE

Two of the countertransference reactions frequently mentioned with psychosomatic patients are boredom and sleepiness. These occur as a reaction to the patient's tendency to be concrete and operational. Different analysts handle the countertransference in different ways. I have heard of analysts saying to patients, "I'm falling asleep. What is happening?" or "What are you avoiding?" My use of my countertransference when I occasionally experienced sleepiness because of distancing was to ask Sarah if she could reflect on what was happening in the process. She was able to hear the monotone sound of her voice and realized that she was holding back some hurt feelings, disappointment, anxiety, or shame around career or family. These were often accompanied by the realization that she was angry at the way someone had behaved toward her.

Another countertransference feeling I frequently had was helpless concern. I sometimes gave advice that, while it was not particularly useful to Sarah's health problems, did not evoke resentment in her. I understood my need to give her advice as part of my defense of omnipotence against helpless countertransference feelings. I believe my omnipotent rescue fantasies were triggered by her suffering and brought up my own history of trying to be a caregiver and omnipotently rescue my own psychosomatically ill and infantile mother. Sarah and I had a similar rescue wish toward our needy mothers. She recalled feeling that her mother's pain was her pain. Her wish to rescue and take away mother's pain was a core part of her personality and she became a very nurturing, caring person as a result. At times the omnipotent rescue wishes were distressing to her when she could not get the desired outcome. She fell short of her ego-ideal in this respect. I identified with her feelings and brought this into the treatment with positive results.

When I experienced deadening, a kind of mummification, which involved feeling controlled and useless, I would comment on how controlled she had felt with her mother and that this was now being relived with me. Sarah was enacting her sense of self as a narcissistic extension of her mother and the rage that this interaction evoked in her. Using projective identification she evacuated her feelings of inefficacy and hopelessness into me, rendering me "mummified" and therefore lifeless. There were times when I felt that Sarah perceived me as the mother herself, not in an "as if" manner. At these times the transference neurosis was not in evidence, but I was perceived as the bad mother to be fought and avoided. My using my countertransference helped her to work through some of this difficulty and enabled the treatment to continue. It also lessened the intensity of hostility toward me.

SHAME AND GUILT

Sarah experienced shame as a result of failing to live up to her ideal self. The IBS violated her sense of control and perfection. It was multidetermined as it seemed to be related to feeling trapped, angry, impinged on, and controlled. Her wish to strike out against the offender was symbolized in periodic bowel attacks. Guilt over her aggressive impulses contributed to the symptomatology. While she did not particularly like my connecting these feelings with the IBS, there were a significant number of occasions in which Sarah experienced some improvement in her symptom following our work together. It is possible that a constitutional predisposition existed around this problem since her mother and maternal grandfather suffered from it as well. At regular intervals, however, she denounced analysis and said that it had not helped her. My sense was that she felt helped more than she acknowledged, but that she could not bear to give the analysis the credit for helping her because of her envy and narcissistic issues.

PREMATURE TERMINATION

As we approached the four-year mark with sessions three times a week, Sarah gave me short notice of her plan to terminate. I was rather surprised and disconcerted as I saw our work together as moving along and yielding good results in spite of her often negative transference. I then made a series of interpretations that addressed Sarah's experience of analysis as enemas imposed on her from without. She responded that she found this thought disgusting. To show me that she did not believe in analytic thinking she commented that she did not have sexual wishes about her father! This referred to my effort to deepen and elaborate on incestuous sexual dreams she had had about her father early in her marriage. At the time she had these dreams she had been in couples' therapy and her therapist dismissed the dreams as not significant. In the follow-up sessions, she reiterated that she never had conscious sexual thoughts about her father, but loved his "bear hugs." I speculated that this might be related to the dream of dangerous bears about to attack. Her warm affectionate feelings to her father had a scary sexual association.

I wondered to Sarah whether she was responding with wishes to end analysis in order to avoid exploring omnipotent fantasies that had come up recently around a family cat that became ill. She blamed herself for not noticing the cat's symptoms earlier. This became linked to her self-blame for not noticing symptoms of her father's cancer sooner than she did. She wondered if she could have saved his life if she had been more attuned to his health problems. Perhaps she felt that to continue any longer in analysis would put her omnipotent feelings to a test that she could not handle.

Another motivation in Sarah's terminating that I explored with her was the wish to deprive me of the pleasure of experiencing greater success with her and of receiving the fee for the treatment. In fact, I did feel deprived and punished. She had struggled with deprivation and envy and I thought this theme might now be in play in her wish to end treatment quickly. Her mother's infantile personality and preoccupation with her own illness had made her an unempathic, nonattuned parent. Sarah's early experience undoubtedly involved much deprivation. She was now doing to me what had been done to her. She was dead set on terminating and had no interest in my feelings or ideas on the subject. She was unable to stay the month we had planned on, so eager was she to get away from treatment.

Sarah's last dream involved twins who regurgitated and then ate their own vomit, like a cow chewing its cud. This dream suggests the "mérycism" McDougall (1974, p. 447) writes of in which the baby "regurgitates and then swallows his stomach contents . . . *prematurely* (creating) an autoerotic object which enables him to dispense with his mother." Sarah associated that the twins were self-sufficient and this was how she wanted to be. Sarah had been dismissed by one of her therapists for potentially becoming too dependent on him. She was now dismissing me for permitting her to become dependent on me. My impression was that she feared any further deepening of her infantile longings and attachment to me. Her last dream reveals a narcissistic retreat in which she dispenses with the analyst-mother.

CONCLUSION

Would this patient have done better with a purely noninterpretive approach? Her dreams about the mirror and twins showed there were self problems. She experienced interpretation as a violation and could only partially internalize the analytic process. In some ways she mummified me, treating me as her mother treated her. She controlled me and rendered me helpless and ineffectual. She tried to wring the life out of the analytic process, making it a battleground in which her defenses, control, and preoccupation with her psychosomatic symptoms protected the fortress of her personality. While there seemed to be significant improvement, I felt there could have been an even deeper resolution that could have freed up her creativity as well as further ameliorate the bowel problem. Perhaps at some point she will seek out another analysis that will help her resolve these deeper core issues.

REFERENCE

McDougall, J. (1974). The psychesoma and the psychoanalytic process. *International Review of Psycho-Analysis* 1:437–459.

CHAPTER SIXTEEN

Psychosomatic Symptoms Following Postconcussional Syndrome

PAULA FREED

The etiology of symptoms following insult to the brain is intensely complex and must take into consideration the disciplines of both biology and psychology (Lishman 1988, Miller 1991, Slagle 1990). Individuals who sustain a trauma to the brain sustain a trauma to the ego functions as well. For these individuals, trauma to ego function means a disruption in their perception of themselves as successfully adapting to the external world. Cognitive deficits heighten the emotional difficulties they experience in their environment. Despite adequately adaptive coping strategies preinjury, the suddenness of loss of function following the injury presents a major challenge. The ability to function adequately in the world is now compromised by a decreased tolerance for painful affects and a loss of resources to adequately defend against anxiety. The result of increased anxiety in these patients leads to object relationships that become noticeably compromised. Often complicating this regression in object relatedness is the impairment of more adaptive autonomous functions such as memory, perception, motility, planning, anticipation, speech, and language. Cognitive deficits also affect judgment and evaluation, as well as the capacity for integration of information, flexibility of thinking, and appropriate expression of emotion.

Although patients demonstrate a vast array of brain injury–related problems, their response to adaptation depends on a multitude of factors ranging from the degree and location of the damage, prior psychic functioning, genetic history, and cognitive style. At the most severe level of brain injury, patients demonstrate measurable organic pathology that leaves them with debilitating cognitive and emotional deficits. There is no question that their injury creates a tremendous challenge as they struggle to adapt in the world with diminished capacity. However, as we move through the continuum from moderate to milder degrees of injury, we have different expectations for recovery and return of function. At the mildest level of brain injury, patients experience symptoms of postconcussional syndrome in which subtle cognitive and emotional sequelae often appear more psychoneurotic than organic. Unfortunately, at this level there is often inadequate attention given to how the organic dysfunction affects their inability to mediate the ego for adaptive psychic functioning. This chapter focuses on this change of function for the mild brain injury patients and the resultant symptom formation, and discusses the relationship between operations of the cerebral hemispheres and primary and secondary process thinking. I will illustrate how hypochondriacal and somatic symptoms in a postconcussional patient serve as a defense against preexisting unconscious conflicts that become exacerbated as a result of change in hemispheric functioning.

SOMATIZATION AND HYPOCHONDRIASIS

We have come to understand somatization and hypochondriasis as a means to communicate distress in the form of bodily complaints and medical symptoms, the latter differing from somatization by inclusion of disease conviction, disease fear, and bodily preoccupation (Barsky 1989). In Freud's (1914) view, hyprochondriasis is a withdrawal of interests and libido from objects in the external world to internal organs. Others view hypochondriasis as a symbolic displacement of an unconscious wish, an ego defense against guilt or self-esteem (Wahl 1963), a perceptual amplification of bodily sensations and symptoms, and a means for interpersonal secondary rewards (Barsky and Klerman 1983). Brown and Vaillant (1981) consider hypochondriasis as the transformation of reproach toward others emanating from aggressive and hostile wishes into physical complaints and symptoms. Ludwig (1972) distinguishes hypochondriacal patients who view somatic symptoms with exaggerated compulsiveness from hysterics who view their symptoms with dissociation and lack of concern. Barsky and Klerman (1983) distinguish hypochondriacs from neurotics in that hypochondriacs do not view their symptoms as shameful, private, irrational, or excessive. In McDougall's (1985) view, psychosomatic phenomena can exhibit the symbolic significance seen in the more neurotic structure and can be attributed to an unconscious communication to the mother. She views libidinal cathexis as bound up with narcissistic fantasies, which are then experienced somatically and perceived as hypochondriacal symptoms. Schur (1955) agrees that "narcissistic regression follows somatic symptoms" and concludes "that emergence of psychosomatic phenomena is linked to ego function" (p. 155). Of significance for this particular discussion is the predominance of psychosomatic phenomena in the postconcussional syndrome patient.

BRAIN TRAUMA AND THE
POSTCONCUSSIONAL SYNDROME

The etiology of residual deficits following concussion is often multidetermined. Psychometric testing, EEG, and computed axial tomography (CAT) scans frequently reveal little, if any, organic pathology despite the contrasting self experience of patients. Most frequently, postconcussional symptoms are expressed as headaches, dizziness, and a generalized feeling of chronic fatigue (Slagle 1990). Other typical responses are diminished concentration, memory problems, irritability, insomnia, anxiety, and depression (Lishman 1973, Slagle 1990). Significant psychodynamic sequelae are frequently "characterized by a narcissistic wound, affective regression, hypochondriac pre-occupation with the body and intellectual impoverishment" (Violon and DeMol 1987, p. 99).

A striking feature in the literature is the conflicting opinions about physiological and psychological causation, whether we are looking at cerebral pathology or conflict and anxiety (Lishman 1988). Studies indicate distinguishable differences between those patients manifesting neurological signs and those patients in whom organic manifestations are lacking (Lishman 1988, Ruesch and Bowman 1945). In the former, there is greater similarity with acute brain injuries and less resemblance to the psychoneuroses. In the latter, more covert demonstration of conflicts and life dissatisfaction is associated with prolonged recovery and physical symptom formation. Exploration reveals that prior living conditions and the mind sets of patients are often the same before and after their accident. Lishman (1988) describes patients' use of their injury as a cover-up for preexisting conflicts and difficulties as a "scapegoat motive." (p. 461) There is further indication that the longer neurotic symptoms persist, the less likely they are an expression of brain trauma (Lishman 1988, Ruesch and Bowman 1945). Lishman (1988) writes, "Ultimately . . . the organic cerebral contribution may give way almost completely, and we will be left with patients virtually all of whom are suffering from conflict, depression and anxiety" (p. 468). However, we would be remiss in attributing only persistent symptoms as having a neurotic basis just as we would be remiss in diminishing the importance of organic etiology (Binder 1986, Miller 1984, 1991, Slagle 1990). The persistence of headaches, loss of concentration, chronic fatigue, and other bodily symptoms can cause emotional distress just as emotional distress can produce the outbreak of bodily symptoms (Binder 1986).

Also of importance is that postconcussional patients with minimal cognitive dysfunction can sometimes demonstrate more disturbed ego functioning than those who are more cognitively compromised. The latter can often adjust more readily to change in cognitive functioning if preinjury psychological development has been more adaptive. We too often confuse ability to abstract with ability to function. Postconcussional patients with the most intact ability for abstraction will remain compromised functionally if deficient ego strength limits their capacity to tolerate anxiety, frustration, anger, and disappointment. For some patients, the premorbid history reflects a more developed ego structure and the ability to utilize adaptive defenses. However, for others, conflicts are readily observable in their tenuous and maladaptive behavior prior to insult. Patients who bring to their injury prior emotional disturbance also bring a level of ego functioning in which the ego capacities are already compromised and, therefore, are more likely to develop psychiatric dysfunction postinjury (Slagle 1990). The event of the trauma further reduces the state of narcissistic equilibrium, making patients more susceptible to increased anxiety and diminished capacity to utilize adaptive defenses. There may, in fact, be more resistance to admitting feelings of dependency, helplessness, and loss. We are left to struggle with how much the neurological insult is diminishing these patients' accessibility to adaptive defenses and coping strategies, and to what extent prior developmental failure is now challenging them to confront new and unwanted life situations with preexisting ego weakness.

RIGHT AND LEFT CEREBRAL SPECIALIZATION AND PRIMARY- AND SECONDARY-PROCESS THOUGHT

The integration of biology and psychology has even greater significance when looking at the connection between cerebral specialization and the concept of primary- and secondary-process thinking. We attribute certain functions and emotions of the brain to contrasting hemispheres. The left hemisphere, "specialized for linguistic processing and logical descriptive analysis, is especially good at perceptual and conceptual analysis of details" (Miller 1991, p. 223); the right hemisphere, "specialized for spatial processing and image coding, is especially good at gestaltic synthesis of forms, and is more intuitive and inferential" (p. 223). Studies in mood change following brain trauma also attribute contrasting emotional states to the two sides of the brain (Sackeim et al. 1982). More "dysphoric reactions of despair, hopelessness and anger" as well as "heightened tendencies toward self blame, self deprecation and fits of crying" (p. 210) are attributed to the left hemisphere in contrast to the right hemisphere's "indifferent euphoric reaction, characterized by minimization of symptoms, emotional placidity, joking, elation or social disinhibition" (p. 210). Alexithymic patients who have difficulty in recognizing and describing emotions or demonstrate an impaired capacity for empathy may be deficient in right hemisphere capacities (Taylor 1987). Smokler and Shevrin (1979) consider the left hemisphere more analogous to obsessive/compulsive personalities who demonstrate more "absence of affect and preponderance of ideation" (p. 950) as compared to hysterics whose "repression of ideas and emotional lability" (p. 950) is more aligned with right hemisphere operations. Right hemisphere function has been correlated with internalization of anxiety and self-report of psychosomatic symptoms (Smokler and Shevrin 1979).

An important correlation can be made between the two hemispheres of the brain and Freud's (1900) dual psychical system of primary and secondary process. Freud's two fundamental forms of psychic functioning provide us with a most fruitful means by which to understand varying degrees of organizational structure. The first system, according to Freud, is effected by unpleasure and is incapable of allowing anything negative into its thoughts; the second system cathects an idea only if it has some control over inhibiting any developing unpleasure (Freud 1900). In the system unconscious, which is characterized by primary-process thinking, instinctual impulses can coexist without contradiction; they are subject to the pleasure principle regardless of reality. In the system conscious, secondary-process thinking has evolved through the acquisition of language and the use of logic. Freud (1923) states this more clearly when he postulates thinking in pictures as more closely related to the unconscious processes and that things only become more conscious when brought into connection with corresponding word presentations.

Noy (1979) suggests that the optimal level of normal cognitive development is dependent upon the balance between primary- and secondary-process thinking: "Secondary processes are never formed to *replace* the primary ones, but are always added at another level. . . . Any disturbance in the course of development in one mode may endanger the normal balance between the two, thereby causing varying degrees of psychopathology" (pp. 180, 181). According to Noy, organizational modes of primary and secondary process form two developmental lines that reflect autoplastic and alloplastic forms of adaptation. This corresponds to the right hemisphere being less involved in modification of inner needs in response to the demands and constraints of the outside world (Miller 1991) versus the left hemisphere's ability to alter external reality to meet inner needs and wishes. It is important to look at the concept of anxiety as it relates to this organizational process. Anxiety, as an anticipatory reaction, signals danger and serves as an essential function of the ego (Freud 1926). We might then conceptualize danger as a right hemisphere/primary-process concept that is initially experienced as a gestalt, while the use of the left hemisphere/secondary process acts as a means to signal and alter the experience of the danger.

We can further state that the severity of anxiety depends on the degree to which the ego adapts to the dangerous situation. According to Hartmann (1939), "Human action adapts the environment to human function and then the human being adapts (secondarily) to the environment he has helped to create" (p. 27). He perceives the attainment of alloplastic function as an outstanding task of human development, but also believes that "alloplastic action is actually not always adaptive, nor is autoplastic action always unadaptive" (p. 27). Hartmann's emphasis on adaptation as "primarily a reciprocal relationship between the organism and its environment" (p. 24) is a further contribution to the integration of the disciplines. His proposed idea of a third form of adaptation as the "choice of a new environment, neither quite independent from nor quite identical with the alloplastic and autoplastic forms" (p. 27) has important meaning to patients who have experienced sudden change in ego functioning. Brain trauma, and its corresponding ego regression, often creates the need for environmental change. There is now a need to reorganize the environment to accommodate the shift in balance between cognitive ability and emotional response. It is the very resistance to that change that serves both as a compromise to maintain psychic organization and as a complication to present existence. Loss of normal defenses makes brain-injured patients susceptible to developing counterproductive coping strategies that contribute to depression and other acting-out behaviors, especially if they serve to compensate for the loss of ego development in other areas. For instance, highly intellectualized and articulated language may serve as a powerful defense against the inability to relate on a deeper, more intimate level. If this ability is no longer sustained due to cognitive loss, intolerable anxiety can result. This will be especially evident if content is now "ordered around libidinal and aggressive aims" (Klein 1970, p. 282) as opposed to more secondary-process thinking "around interests, values and realistic intentions" (p. 282).

Whereas the hemispheres work together in complementary ways, interruption in their normal operations can create disruption in function both cognitively and psychologically. Galin (1974) presents an interesting example of how individuals could experience conflict if the two hemispheres began to function as if they had been surgically disconnected and their exchange of information decreased: "The left will attend to the verbal cues because it cannot extract information from the facial gestalt efficiently; the right will attend to the nonverbal cues because it cannot understand the words. . . . In this situation, the two hemispheres might decide on opposite courses of action; the left to approach, and the right to flee" (p. 576). Galin's example has special significance for patients who suffer even minor changes in hemispheric functioning, and face newly ordered cognition without the defensive structure to adjust to the newly ordered emotions and anxieties created by the change. As Schur (1955) states, "Prolonged chronic illness, or any permanent loss of an important ego function increases the strain, and requires complex adaptation with a shift from object to narcissistic libido" (p. 148). Permanent alteration of hemisphere function creates interference in the integration of primary- and secondary-process thought and stirs up new anxiety for which corresponding defenses are not readily accessible. Miller (1984) addresses the unforeseen difficulty in having to transfer a more right hemisphere mode of thinking based more on primary-process emotions into more rational secondary-process language. In helping to alleviate anxiety, we need to take into consideration the negative changes in psychic functioning that result from the trauma. This may mean adaptation of the new psychic reality to the present environment as an autoplastic adjustment, alteration of the external world to eliminate the source of tension as an alloplastic adjustment, or the creation of a new environment as an integration of the two.

CASE VIGNETTE

Helen is a 41-year-old single woman who sustained a concussion as a result of a motor vehicle accident in which she was a passenger. She did not lose consciousness, but experienced disorientation, dizziness, and nausea. Following her accident Helen received an EEG, magnetic resonance imaging (MRI), and CAT scan, which were all within normal limits. After attempts to return to work intensified her symptoms, she was evaluated at a brain injury facility. The results of her evaluation revealed minimal impairment in attention, comprehension, and visual/spatial organization. Despite low-grade depression, Helen appeared to be functioning at normal levels. Although verbal fluency and comprehension did decrease when she was forced to handle greater amounts of information, there were indications that impaired performance was due to anxiety. Helen was given a prescribed treatment for six months at this facility during which time she grew very attached to her therapist. When her treatment ended she made some attempts to see this therapist privately, but Helen was unwilling to travel the distance to the therapist's office since driving out of her immediate area created undue physical and cognitive distress. The therapist, aware of my work with brain trauma, referred Helen to me. However, Helen did not utilize the referral and eighteen months later, still dissatisfied with her cognitive and physical functioning, sought treatment at another brain trauma facility. Reevaluation again indicated greater right hemisphere involvement demonstrated by a decrease in visual/perceptual skills, impaired attention and concentration, and difficulty taking in nonverbal information. Left hemisphere involvement appeared to be in the normal range, but once again there was a suggestion of decrease in overall intelligence and verbal abstraction abilities judging from her present fund of knowledge and premorbid intellectual performance. However, evaluation indicated a plateau in remediation of cognitive function and it was then suggested that Helen would benefit more from psychotherapy to address residual cognitive losses than referral to another treatment facility. Six months later, almost two years after the initial referral, Helen finally contacted me for treatment.

At our first meeting, Helen presented as depressed, bland, and desperate to have someone understand just how much the accident had changed her life. Once an avid reader, she now experienced nausea and headaches when reading more than a few pages. She had not read a book in two years. Helen was employed as a certified public accountant and returned to her previous work setting, effectively performing her job with minor adjustments. However, she frequently experienced frontal headaches that she believed were triggered by minor stress and work demands. She also experienced mild concentration impairment and short-term memory problems.

Helen grew up in a middle-class Jewish family. Both her parents were retired. Her mother was a medical social worker whom she described as overbearing and intrusive. Helen viewed her mother as "always being on the job" in that she related to her children in terms of physical illness. She described her father lovingly as a passive and benign man who provided little rescue from her mother's intrusiveness. Her sister Debra, born when Helen was 18 months old, was diagnosed as profoundly retarded. Totally deficient in self-care, Debra was attended to at home by Helen's mother. She was institutionalized out of necessity at age 8, when Helen's mother required surgery for a tumor on her thyroid. Helen described a radical change in her home life after the institutionalization of her sister. Her mother now intrusively focused all her attention on Helen. There was little rescue from her father, who apparently had his own difficulty meeting the mother's needs. While Helen managed to leave home physically and go to college, she was still controlled by her mother. A futile attempt to separate was made when she ran away with a boyfriend to another state. However, this relationship ended after two years, at which time Helen returned home to live with her parents. She eventually returned to school, developed a career, and lived on her own. Helen's social and interpersonal life remained shallow and she developed few intimate relationships with either men or women.

Helen's sessions focused predominantly on issues around the loss of control she felt over her life. Her anxiety was rigidly focused on external issues involving the outcome of a court case regarding the accident, and evaluations with psychiatrists, neurologists, and other medical practitioners. She felt unable to rely on anyone involved in her life to handle things properly. Helen was able to relate the intensity of her feelings to her childhood, in which she experienced her parents as unable to make decisions and unreliable in their support and caregiving responsibilities. Having learned early to rely on herself, she was particularly proud of her proficiency in being able to articulate her needs. She expressed her worst fear after injury as being dependent on her parents and ending up like her sister. My attempt to explore her fears about not being taken care of properly by me as well, based on her previous therapeutic experience, had little impact. Helen shared that she felt disappointed by that therapeutic experience, but viewed the therapist as being unsympathetic to her transportation difficulties, which meant she did not understand the severity of her injury. She felt confident that I was more knowledgeable about brain trauma.

When Helen's court case was finally settled and she did not receive the compensation she had expected, new anxiety occurred that was expressed somatically as a "feeling in my head." Her thoughts rapidly escalated to more severe and fatalistic outcomes such as a blood clot or tumor. Her anxiety was further increased by ongoing evaluations conducted by the insurance company to determine the merit of continued treatment. Psychosomatic complaints were expressed in the development of a breast discharge, followed by a yeast infection. Sessions became filled with rumination about both of these conditions and the rejection by a series of doctors whom she felt did not take her seriously. Some months later, her symptoms became expressed in more hypochondriacal complaints. She shared that she felt a lump in her throat that was painful when swallowing. At this time, Helen's mother became very involved in her symptoms. They mutually agreed that she had a tumor that was rapidly growing and their combined anxiety was intensified when the symptoms were not verified. The doctor's request for thyroid testing created new tension exacerbated by her mother's concern that this test would prove dangerous if the tumor was malignant. There was further talk about needing surgery if there was, indeed, a malignancy. Helen brought both parents with her for this procedure. When the doctor made a referral to an endocrinologist, Helen's mother challenged the doctor's suggestion. She felt that a surgeon would be more appropriate for Helen's condition. Helen soon began to experience her mother as "taking over," which activated her struggle between feelings of loss and feelings of intrusion. When Helen found the endocrinologist to be unsympathetic, her hypochondriacal complaints increased. She now feared that her tumor was leaning forward and affecting her speech. When her thyroid scan proved negative, she quickly found a holistic doctor who did not totally dispel her own more acceptable diagnosis. Helen continued to express a lack of energy for anything pleasurable in life since so much of her time was taken up by tests and doctors' appointments. I soon found myself becoming joined with Helen in her sense of helplessness. In response to that helplessness, I began to make more concrete suggestions for increasing her quality of life, such as outlets for socialization and different job possibilities. However, when she did take a suggestion and went out with a friend, the emphasis was on the resultant fatigue, which she felt was "the price for having a good time."

Although Helen appeared to be content in the therapeutic relationship, there was an overriding discrepancy between her implied and stated connection to me and my struggle to feel a real connection to her. There was also unquestionable countertransference stemming from my inability to break through to the anxiety that was being masked by the somatic and hypochondriacal rhetoric. I was struck by the manner in which she viewed her symptoms with dissociation and lack of concern (Ludwig 1972), and the concrete matter-of-fact reporting of physical experiences that seemed devoid of any affective response one would expect from someone who thought she had a fatal illness. My confrontation concerning her affect brought joking responses. She was unable to get in touch with what I wanted her to feel. It was not until I became aware of the intensity of my feelings concerning her hypochondriacal complaints that I realized how joined I was with how others were experiencing her. I began to acknowledge her frustrations that people didn't seem to take her seriously. I wanted to know if she thought I took her seriously. She responded that she felt I did. I talked to her about needing something concrete to be wrong with her as a way to have her suffering acknowledged. I also addressed her symptoms as a way to connect with her mother and possibly to me. She could see the connection to her childhood in that she related to her mother through physical illness; she was not certain about the connection to me. As a result, there was some transfer of focus from physical illness onto disappointment with parents and, consequently, some lessening of the symptoms.

A major conflict arose when the accident insurance company made the determination, based on a psychiatrist's report, to terminate coverage for treatment. The report indicated malingering and conversion as opposed to any sign of organic pathology. It was also filled with major discrepancies and distortions that rightfully angered Helen. She developed a stomach virus and was out of work for five days. Confrontation on her illness as being related to the reevaluation resulted in a narcissistic injury that she was able to work through. Helen then brought me all the reports to read and asked if I would respond to the doctor's evaluation. I found myself writing a very strong and impassioned response to the insurance company in her defense. However, it did not bring results and a termination date was set. Helen had other insurance that allowed her reimbursement for treatment with the company's designated providers, but she felt more secure with a therapist trained in brain injury who would understand her plight. This appeared to serve a twofold purpose. On the one hand, it provided her with continued denial of the psychic content of her symptoms. On the other hand, it served as a means for her to connect through somatic content and traumatic brain injury symptoms, rather than to me directly. The termination of her "brain injury coverage" presented a loss of this symbolized connection. Blaming the psychiatrist was an indirect way to deal with the loss of me. In some ways, my report may have been a defense against my own wish to abandon her. Although I felt the psychiatrist's report to be simplistic and unjust, I knew from past experience that my rebuttal would have little or no impact. In this way, by writing such an impassioned report, I could avoid the feeling of the wish to abandon just as Helen could avoid the feelings of the fear of loss of me.

For Helen, the intense connection with her mother around the somatic symptoms served as an unconscious communication (McDougall 1985) in which bodily symptoms served as a means through which early fantasies reemerged (Schur 1955). The somatic symptoms also served as an attempt to regressively repair the childhood experience—to be rescued by her father in order to allow separation from her mother. However, this attempt at repair was greatly hampered by extracountertransference phenomona. Whereas I never doubted Helen's self experience concerning her change in cognitive function, my treatment of her was significantly affected by the intrusion of the insurance company. Although it was clear that Helen needed long-term treatment in which I could work with her defense of somatization, the company insisted that in order to keep her coverage she needed to be making progress. In this case, progress meant focus on behavioral outcome rather than dealing with developmental issues to get to the root of the somatic symptoms. Further indication of the need to deal with developmental issues was the demonstration of narcissistic injury that was experienced whenever I deviated from an empathic alliance with Helen about her traumatic and sorrowful life. She appeared to be much more comfortable with me in the role of empathic listener rather than the role of one who would help her out of the discomfort and move ahead. I believe that what ensued was primarily a paternal transference that allowed some comfort but, in the end, reenacted her worst fear in terms of the parental constellation. The psychiatrist's report stirred up the triangle in which he became the intrusive, annihilating mother and I became the ineffective father who could not stop the mother from determining her needs.

DISCUSSION

In consideration of the interrelationship between Helen's cognitive dysfunction resulting from her injury and the psychodynamic aspects of her premorbid personality, we can better understand the prevalence of her psychosomatic symptoms. Demonstration of hemispheric specialization for different cognitive styles allows us to appreciate the left hemisphere's role in providing an analytic and logical mode where words are important (Galin 1974), and the right hemisphere as a nonverbal representation more concerned with aspects of "intrapersonal reality, somatic apperception, and body image" (Miller 1991, p. 224). Somatization based on the function of the hemispheres emphasizes the role of the right hemisphere both because of its organic relevance to arousal and its connection between right hemisphere information-processing style and primary process—like operations (Miller 1984). Overall, the literature stresses the loss of intellectual function following left hemisphere damage and the prevalence of somatic and hypochondriacal symptoms as a result of right hemisphere damage (Lishman 1968). However, despite Helen's evaluation revealing greater right hemisphere involvement, it is my contention that it was more the damage to the left hemisphere that was the main factor activating the psychosomatic symptoms. Given Helen's career choice, interests, and self-report of cognitive style, it would appear that prior to her injury Helen was more of a left hemisphere—dominant personality. The loss of left hemisphere function, as mild as it was, decreased Helen's defenses around the more primitive instincts and anxieties that were now apparent in the primary process/right hemisphere mode of operation.

Miller (1986) suggests that the patient's inability to see a rational basis for one's somatic symptoms is attributed to unconscious conflictual material generated from right hemisphere operations, which is denied secondary-process working through due to the inability to use the left hemisphere as a means of articulation. Schur (1955) perceives this regressive phenomenon as resomatization, in that psychic conflict now provokes somatic responses normally attributed to an earlier developmental stage. I believe that the prevalence of primary-process thoughts, brought about by the failure in neutralization, rendered Helen more right hemisphere—dominant and without the necessary coping skills to withstand the tension of such an abrupt change. In the primary-process state, libidinal and aggressive drives are in an unneutralized mobile state, unlike the secondary-process mode (Klein 1970). For Helen, somatic symptoms now served to ward off primary-process emotions that used to be defended against by secondary-process skills. McDougall (1989) states, "Doors open to psychosomatic functioning in response to a primitive signal from that part of the psyche that had no words to capture and contain the frightening fantasy in question" (p. 101). So in effect, Helen's anxiety was in reaction to the psychic danger she experienced at being forced to adjust to a newly ordered ego function. Her defense against this danger was the hypochondriacal and somatic complaints.

Helen's somatic symptoms provided for the expression of internalized rage in response to her loss of control in dealing with her external environment, which was in large measure a displacement from her early caregiving relationships. Helen's relationship with her mother was volatile and symbiotic. She was joined with her father against her mother in an unspoken alignment of their combined helplessness. This constellation became intensified after her injury, as her cognitive deficits reactivated early dependency needs. Somatic and hypochrondriacal complaints served initially as attachment and identification with mother. However, the wish for symbiosis through illness soon became transformed into fear when identification proved too potent and toxic. Helen's imagined tumor served symbolically as an object tie and as a representation of fusion and intrusion. As a result, it became an expression of the conflict between the wish for and fear of closeness to the mother. This was demonstrated by Helen's attempts to reach out to her mother in hopes of receiving some empathy and concern, and then having those hopes turn to disillusionment and resentment as mother's help became an intrusion and a means to feed her own narcissistic needs. Helen's expressed fear was that she would end up like her sister and have to depend on her mother.

Often children who grow up with a chronically disabled sibling observe that sibling as the recipient of parental nurturance, sympathy, and concern that they crave for themselves (Barsky and Klerman 1983). Whereas on some level Helen wished to be cared for as her sister was cared for as a child, there was also the fear that mother would ultimately cast her out—move away from her for survival—as she did with her sister when she needed the tumor surgery. This may have reactivated the toxic memory of her sister as merged with the mother. The mere fact that Helen fears becoming like her sister, a tremendous exaggeration given the reality of the injury that she has sustained, is indicative of the powerful feeling of loss of control, annihilation, and destruction that she feels could come to her. This was demonstrated by reactivation of experiences with her early objects and repeatedly shown by the expressed contempt when her self experience was not confirmed.

Brown and Vaillant (1981) describe the anger that has its origin in past rejections and losses, and gets transformed from self-reproach to reproach of others. This aspect of reproach was evidenced by Helen's verbalized despondency about her life situation and through the dynamic in which I was induced to find concrete solutions, but then seen as unsympathetic to her fatigue when my help was offered. This presented an interesting dilemma in terms of attachment. The only way to provide a connection was to keep her unhealthy because it was in her unhealthy state that she felt heard and connected. However, at the same time she induced the feeling of helplessness and incompetency that she experienced herself. It was her symptoms that provided her with a concrete basis on which to connect and enabled her to gravitate to me as an object. Her symptoms also protected her from the hostile and aggressive wishes both toward herself and toward me, in that they provided an alternate channel for her aggression. Helen's injury served both as a means of connection to her mother and as an identification with the disabled child whose mother could not care for her. This enhanced her fears about being more debilitated and having to rely on her parents, and became displaced onto caregiving professionals after her injury. Diversion from this fear came through psychosomatic complaints. It was her way to express the helplessness and hopelessness at being unable to master life in her new environment. For Helen, her somatic complaints became symbolic of being in control—a means of self-regulation.

It is interesting to note that while Helen displayed an inappropriate, almost euphoric affect in response to her somatic symptoms, she demonstrated signs of depressed and anxious mood in terms of decreased interpersonal functioning and frustration over changes in her level of cognitive skills. Given the studies that show the prevalence of intellectual disorders in the left hemisphere and the prevalence of affective, behavioral, and somatic disorders in the right hemisphere (Lishman 1968), there is indication that Helen was able in some way to compartmentalize her affect. On the one hand, she appeared to experience the feelings of loss and sadness regarding the left hemisphere/secondary-process skills, but needed to defend against the feelings she experienced on a primary-process/right hemisphere instinctual level. The more primitive instincts and anxieties that were experienced in a more right hemisphere/primary-process mode of operation needed to be transformed into the more acceptable form of psychosomatic phenomena as a flight from instinctual danger (Freud 1926). The symptoms that Helen experienced regarding her concussion were able to be observed on a secondary-process level. They were observations that allowed her to put word presentations to the feelings. McDougall (1989) puts it quite succinctly:

> Words are more effective containers for channeling energy linked to instinctual drives, as well as the fantasies to which they have given birth, with regard to the parental objects of infancy. When words do not perform this function, the psyche is obliged to give distress signals of a presymbolic kind, thereby circumventing the restraining links of language.

There is then a considerable risk of evoking somatic instead of psychological responses to the experience of wordless anguish. [p. 101]

Helen's symptoms related to psychosomatic phenomena were more in reaction to a nonverbal representation that reflected her intrapersonal reality. Lishman's (1988) study also notes that when there is a high incidence of behavioral disorder, there is a low incidence of somatic complaints and vice versa. Helen's hypochondriacal response to a tumor that, from all her medical interventions, appeared to be imagined, had a psychotic-like quality. We could then hypothesize that the somatic defense, while serving as a means to ward off the anxiety, was in some ways a compensation for even more intense unacceptable feelings to surface and become manifested as a behavioral disorder.

Helen was a bright, highly articulate, and competent woman with relatively good ego structure. In many aspects, it was her high level of cognitive function that served as a compensation for inadequacies in other areas of her life. Her self-identity was about "thinking and doing" and reflective of intellectual pursuits, accomplishment of tasks, and capacity for self-reliance. Her high level of intelligence combined with prolific language skills provided her with a means to advocate her own needs. In terms of adaptation, prior to her injury Helen was someone who was able to create an environment in a more alloplastic way, but the event of her brain trauma relegated her to an autoplastic mode of functioning. The feelings of incompetency she experienced, initially around getting medical attention for her postconcussional symptoms and then in dealing with her lawyer, court case, and insurance company, represented a loss of self through loss of left hemisphere/secondary-process skills. In one sense, the somatization served to self-regulate the impulses. However, at the same time, as Schur (1955) indicates, narcissistic regression followed the somatic symptoms and acted "as a focal point for the convergence of diverse pathological mechanisms" (p. 148). Her loss of secondary-process function represented a significant failure in her ability to reestablish neutralization and ego structure, which resulted in the exacerbation of her symptoms. She lost the ability to reorder her environment to accommodate her cognitive loss in a way that enabled adaptation and the capacity to maintain ego autonomy. Her concussion, followed by posttraumatic symptoms, set off a regressive chain of events, beginning with the failure to reestablish a sense of ego organization in her first therapeutic experience, further complicated by the flood of dependency needs that reactivated the early relationship with her mother, and culminating in a failure to repair a parental constellation by the intrusion of the insurance company.

The psychiatrist who defined Helen's symptomatology as malingering failed to take into consideration the loss of ego autonomy resulting from her loss of cognitive function and the subsequent effect on her psychic organization. There is no question that in some cases there is a histrionic component, compensation behavior, and malingering following postconcussional syndrome. However, a number of authors (Binder 1986, Lishman 1968, 1988, Slagle 1990, Violon and DeMol 1987) found significant evidence of prolonged symptomatology following postconcussional injuries when there is no litigation or compensation claim in process. Overall, the literature reveals that focus on symptoms appears far more prevalent than malingering. Although Helen displayed classic obstacles to recovery, such as financial problems and resentment pertaining to compensation over her accident, she did not appear to be malingering. She also did not appear to be looking for excuses not to function in the outside world. She seemed intent on restoring her losses, and her psychosomatic responses functioned as a defense against narcissistic rage. Through them, she enacted regressive wishes that were intensified as a result of the organic changes caused by the accident. Intellectual functioning was diminished, albeit slightly, after her accident.

When Helen was discharged from the brain injury facility, she felt neither validation of her postconcussional symptoms nor appreciation of the degree to which her life was now compromised. Although Helen felt the therapist to be unsympathetic to her symptoms in expecting her to travel a moderate distance to see her, the therapist in fact was eager to continue treatment and disappointed that arrangements were not able to be worked out. It is also significant that the therapist had little recollection of such intense somatic or hypochondriacal behavior. Helen was referred to me immediately after termination from the brain injury facility, but it was almost two years before she sought treatment. In the interim, she attempted entry into another brain injury treatment facility. The evaluator felt there was little to be gained from another treatment program and suggested psychotherapy to work through the anxiety and depression related to her residual cognitive losses. However, it took another six months for her to act on the evaluator's advise. By the time Helen appeared for our first session, the anxiety stemming from her disordered cognition had escalated to psychosomatic illness as a further attempt to get the validation she was seeking for her symptoms (Barsky and Klerman 1983). Her initial postconcussional complaints now took on a somatic preoccupation and she responded to her anxiety by redundant visits to health care practitioners as a way to receive validation of her new psychic reality and as a preservation of psychological integrity (Violon and DeMol 1987). Lishman (1988) aptly points out that "both physical and psychological traumas of the injury may thus be operating on a particularly vulnerable person" (p. 461), which raises the question if Helen's postconcussional symptoms had been responded to more seriously in her first therapeutic experience in terms of the effect on her psychic organization, would there have been less regression to earlier forms of object relating as both a connection through illness and then as a flight from fear of dependency to somatic symptoms?

We must remain cognizant that patients' anxiety as it pertains to emotional adjustment following an insult to the brain, no matter how minimal, is in response to both the disordered cognition as well as the psychological reactions to that new condition. Patients often continue to report subjective complaints of changes in cognitive function even when there is no objective verification. This is a function of preexisting psychological disorders as well as physical changes. Right hemisphere deficiencies resulting from frontal lobe damage (Lishman 1968) could be mistaken as an alexithymic quality, in that recognizing and describing emotions is impaired (Taylor 1987). Just as we need to be open to postconcussional symptoms as having organic importance where there is little or no psychometric validation, we may also need to think more seriously about the integration of biological and psychological symptomatology even without evidence of physical trauma. Subtle cognitive dysfunction can occur even in organically "normal" individuals. Our patients bring to us intensely enigmatic personality styles, complex ego organizations, and diverse modes of cognitive operations that require a plethora of multidetermined approaches in order to begin to understand their needs. Often patients' subjective needs will become expressed nonverbally as psychosomatic phenomena. Their subjective complaints must be taken seriously and respected as real feeling states even when the expected affect is hidden.

REFERENCES

Barsky, A. J. (1989). Somatoform disorders. In *Comprehensive Textbook of Psychiatry/V*, vol. 1, ed. H. I. Kaplan and B. J. Sadock, 5th ed., pp. 1009–1027. Baltimore: Williams & Wilkins.

Barsky, A. J., and Klerman, G. L. (1983). Overview: hypochondriasis, bodily complaints, and somatic styles. *American Journal of Psychiatry* 140(3):273–283.

Binder, L. M. (1986). Persisting symptoms after mild head injury: a review of the postconcussive syndrome. *Journal of Clinical and Experimental Neuropsychology* 8:323–346.

Brown, H. N., and Vaillant, G. E. (1981). Hypochondriasis. *Archives of Internal Medicine* 141:723–726.

Freud, S. (1900). The interpretation of dreams. *Standard Edition* 4/5:1–629.

———— (1914). On narcissism: an introduction. *Standard Edition* 14:67–102.

———— (1923). The ego and the id. *Standard Edition* 19:113–59.

———— (1926). Inhibitions, symptoms and anxiety. *Standard Edition* 20:7–128.

Galin, D. (1974). Implications for psychiatry of left and right cerebral specialization: a neurophysiological context for unconscious processes. *Archives of General Psychiatry* 31:572–583.

Hartmann, H. (1939). *Ego Psychology and the Problem of Adaptation*. New York: International Universities Press.

Klein, G. S. (1970). On inhibition, disinhibition and primary process in thinking. In *Perception, Motives and Personality*, pp. 281–296. New York: Knopf.

Lishman, W. A. (1968). Brain damage in relation to psychiatric disability after head injury. *British Journal of Psychiatry* 114:373–410.

———— (1973). The psychiatric sequelae of head injury: a review. *Psychological Medicine* 3:304–318.

———— (1988). Physiogenesis and psychogenesis in the postconcussional syndrome. *British Journal of Psychiatry* 153:460–469.

Ludwig, A. M. (1972). Hysteria: a neurobiological theory. *Archives of General Psychiatry* 20:771–777.

McDougall, J. (1985). Psychosomatic states, anxiety neurosis, and hysteria. In *Theaters of the Mind*, pp. 107–124. New York: Brunner/Mazel.

———— (1989). Affects, affect dispersal, and disaffection. In *Theaters of the Body*, pp. 91–105. New York: Norton.

Miller, L. (1984). Neuropsychological concepts of somatoform disorders. *International Journal of Psychiatry in Medicine* 14(1):31–46.

———— (1986). Some comments on cerebral hemispheric modes of consciousness. *Psychoanalytic Review* 73(2):129–144.

———— (1991). Brain and self: toward a neuropsychodynamic model of ego autonomy and personality. *American Academy of Psychoanalysis* 19(2):213–234.

Noy, P. (1979). The psychoanalytic theory of cognitive development. *Psychoanalytic Study of the Child* 34:169–216. New Haven, CT: Yale University Press.

Ruesch, J., and Bowman, K. M. (1945). Prolonged post-traumatic syndromes following head injury. *American Journal of Psychiatry* 102:145–163.

Sackeim, H. A., Greenberg, M. S., Weiman, A. L., et al. (1982). Hemispheric asymmetry in the expression of positive and negative emotions. *Archives of Neurology* 39:210–218.

Schur, M. (1955). Comments on the metapsychology of somatization. *Psychoanalytic Study of the Child* 10:110–164. New York: International Universities Press.

Slagle, D. A. (1990). Psychiatric disorders following closed head injury: an overview of biopsychosocial factors in their etiology and management. *International Journal of Psychiatry in Medicine* 20(1):1–35.

Smokler, I. A., and Shevrin, H. (1979). Cerebral lateralization and personality style. *Archives of General Psychiatry* 36:949–954.

Taylor, G. J. (1987). The brain, the body and the unconscious. In *Psychosomatic Medicine and Contemporary Psychoanalysis*, pp. 171–197. Madison, CT: International Universities Press.

Violon, A., and DeMol, J. (1987). Psychological sequelae after head trauma in adults. *Acta Neurochirurgica* 85:96–102.

Wahl, C. W. (1963). Unconscious factors in the psychodynamics of the hypochondriacal patient. *Psychosomatics* 4:9–14.

CHAPTER SEVENTEEN

Miscarriages

MICHAEL EIGEN

To some it may seem odd or unreasonable to treat miscarriage as a psychosomatic problem; yet it is difficult to avoid this impression in certain instances. Sometimes women with repeated miscarriages seek psychotherapy for help in bringing a pregnancy to term. Nearly thirty years of work have convinced me that psychotherapy *can* help many women have successful pregnancies. I have seen this happen with women who almost certainly would have miscarried otherwise.

I do not know why different therapies and therapists succeed or fail with particular patients, but I would like to share some impressions of work with a particular patient, Lucia. No claim is being made that miscarriages, in general, have a psychological basis, although, certainly, nearly all have psychological consequences. I simply wish to portray what can and does happen with a good number of women and discuss what therapy offers. The story of every woman is different, but exploring one case brings to light factors many share.

LUCIA AND JAN

Lucia was an engaging woman in her mid-thirties who had two miscarriages in as many years, following her marriage. She was a professional woman who scaled down her career to become a mother. Her husband's work demanded that he be away a lot, so that she was alone for weeks and sometimes months at a time.

She and her husband, Jan, loved each other, but fought a lot about how their lives were to be lived. He was picky and needed an exceptionally neat environment and well-prepared food. She seemed more involved with feelings and moods, and did not pay much attention (not as much as he would have liked) to material chores. Making a living was up to him, since she essentially stopped working to focus on motherhood. He expected more from her at home than she could deliver, since she had neither the experience nor the inclination to maintain the sort of household he envisioned.

When I met Lucia, she was despondent and fearful, anxious lest this pregnancy also fail. Friends urged her to seek help. She had been in therapy when she was single and developing a career. She left therapy when she and Jan became a solid couple, a few years before their marriage. She and Jan got along well when they were single, absorbed in their careers. At that point, neither demanded more than the other wished to give. They enjoyed each other's company when together and needed long periods away from each other for work. Neither was prepared for the strains living together and marriage with children in mind would bring.

Traits that were not intensely bothersome and even were amusing (e.g., his supercilious neatness, her inadvertent sloppiness) when they were single became incendiary in marriage. She admired and enjoyed his brilliance, the way he shone when they were with friends, the way they talked for hours and she never was bored. The cutting edge of his precocity had been aimed at objects other than herself, except in fun. She was not prepared to be criticized for being an ineffectual housewife. She expected to be accepted as she was.

What especially bothered her was that his way of criticizing was so controlled. She wished he'd get mad like she did, and she'd get furious with him for criticizing her with aloof, untouchable nastiness. Her rages appalled him. He loved her greater access to feelings before the fights began. For years he felt nourished by her emotionality and earthy perceptions. They filled him out, amplified his world. He was not ready for her stormy refusal of his mild-mannered defensiveness. She screamed at him for being withdrawn, withholding, wanting perfection. Each felt perfectly innocent, maligned by the other.

For a time I saw Lucia and Jan together as a couple, in addition to Lucia's twice weekly individual sessions, and sometimes I saw Jan alone. It took several years before their relationship reached the point where he'd see a therapist. Jan had had a lot of therapy, much more than Lucia, but quit after he met her and his life stabilized. He could not believe he needed therapy again; he felt he had enough for a lifetime. He felt on top of his problems (he was so controlled), but Lucia went wild with hers. He repeated his picture of what was wrong with Lucia every time we met. Jan was convinced everything was Lucia's fault because she was angry at her father. Her father criticized her and made her feel bad about herself. Now all men (i.e., Jan) were fathers getting the retribution due the original.

When I saw Jan and Lucia together, I could imagine them in an old-fashioned photo. He was thin, precise, straight; she was fuller, rounder, softer, fuzzier. Yet she would not let him get away with his defensive superiority, and this galled him. If he pointed at her father, she pointed at his mother. His mother was extremely self-centered, cool, and controlling, and it was easy for Lucia to see a connection between the former's emotional stinginess and Jan's fear of feelings. He found a way of living with his mother's distance by distancing himself from her. A real, live woman like Lucia was water for parched land, but also a problem. He was used to the calm of little contact, but now had to deal with upsetting emotional demands. Lucia wanted more from him than he ever got from his mother and Jan was convinced he was getting the anger due her father. They were good at finger pointing. Their relationship put more pressure on them than either could bear.

As the therapist, a lot of pressure was dumped on me. Each looked to me to take her or his side against the other. Each looked for signs of support, which meant agreement. I liked them both. They were articulate, alive, creative, caring, and doing their best. Was it their fault society provides no adequate vehicle for emotional education? It is far from clear that the human race knows what to do with itself and the states it goes through. How can two people learn how to get along, if they want to? What resources can they use?

When Lucia spoke, I felt life from her standpoint. When Jan spoke, I could feel life from his. Each spoke from wounded sensitivity and I felt the reality of both. Zigzagging between them gave me some sense of what it must be like for them to be torn apart by each other.

It is important to note that Lucia and Jan were right about what each said about the other's family. Each had truth on her/his side. Lucia felt ashamed of her family, but also proud. She had to deal with too much of the wrong kind of feelings, but at least she was used to a lot of feelings. Her parents fought all the time. She knew about people screaming at each other. Jan was all too right about her father's critical, wounded, and wounding nature. Her mother's resources went into striving and holding her own in a coarse, abusive atmosphere. The children received the spillover from these stormy, self-absorbed, childish parents, alternately fighting for their lives and succumbing to dreary accommodations to each other.

Where Lucia's father spent his spare time watching television in a daze, Jan's father was an artist. Jan's parents were better educated, refined, more reserved, and dignified, the father warmer and weaker than the mother. His parents were used to each other and put up with each other. They went their own ways, pursued their own interests, without seeming to be close. Jan was baffled as to what positive tie might hold them together. For Jan, they were a negative example of a relationship, a model of what a relationship shouldn't be; it shouldn't be nonexistent. Hostile control was quiet, indirect, but devastating.

It was inconceivable and appalling that Jan should be repeating elements of a relationship he abhorred, although he easily saw that Lucia did so. What was wrong with her family was so much more obvious, since her parents were together too much in a quasi-collapsed, explosive way. He felt his family was better off than Lucia's, steps up on the evolutionary scale. Lucia was tempted to feel coarse in light of Jan's refined background. But she was not coarse, merely expressive. Both were accomplished persons in their own right.

It would be too great an exaggeration to say that Lucia suffered from overstimulation and Jan from understimulation, since the background of each was mixed and variegated. Yet each craved a level and style of interaction that frustrated the other. When Jan wanted more intimacy in a calm, quiet way, Lucia stirred things up. When Lucia wanted more closeness, Jan was busy, preoccupied, disdainful. Each spent a good deal of time licking wounds and nursing grudges. The rhythm of their dance went awry. They could not coordinate closeness and distance and emotional (warm-cool) needs. Yet there was a deep bond between them, and now and then good moments.

I felt happy Lucia chose me as her therapist. I liked being with her. I could feel her feelings, her emotional presence, her realness. Sometimes I felt so good being with her that it was difficult to realize she was depressed. My good feelings could not delude me long. Lucia and Jan got sick often. Lucia had terrible sinus attacks that could linger for months. She had hosts of minor ills that could be debilitating for a time. Jan tended to get respiratory illnesses that responded to medication. While neither had life-threatening problems (although perhaps life threatening to a fetus, since no fetus survived their psychophysical tensions), the intensity and frequency of physical problems suggested something amiss with psychosomatic integrity. Neither had enough emotional support to promote psychosomatic cohesion, although support was not completely lacking.

They felt let down by families and each other. Neither their relationship nor their bodies could handle what they were going through. They were ripped apart by multiple cross-currents neither had the capacity to navigate without injury.

CHOICES

I held sessions with Lucia and Jan as a couple, and with each individually when hostility between them became too awful and they locked into unremitting mutual laceration. But the weight of the couple's and of Jan's problems would have sunk my work with Lucia if it were not clear to all of us that she was my primary patient. Lucia wanted a baby more than Jan, and it was she who initiated therapy. I don't know whether Jan wanted a baby or therapy less, but he was reluctant about both; he wanted neither fatherhood nor patienthood. He felt pushed or pulled into both. Lucia was the driving force where therapy and pregnancy were concerned.

I felt bad for Jan when I saw him. He felt under pressure. He worried about succeeding in his profession. He worried about the loss of Lucia's income, now that she had stopped working. It did not occur to him that he might also have lost Lucia's emotional support; he did not feel emotionally supported enough himself to emotionally support a family. He looked pinched and pained, straining at the bit. He was so tightly coiled that it was easy to see that some form of somatic semi-collapse was likely, if only to buy resting time.

Jan was sensitive and bright. I felt he would make a good father (or patient) in spite of himself, if things got started. When I saw him I could not help feeling that deep down he wanted to be a father (and patient), but needed help in taking the leap. In this regard, I suppose I was on Lucia's side. I could see why she loved him. He was a good-hearted person who felt threatened by the tumult she brought, pushing him over the edge of what he was used to. I would have loved to help him over the hurdle. But I had more than enough with Lucia and confined myself to taking the edge off the worst of it for Jan, until he realized he wanted more.

I felt a sense of loss that Jan could not be my patient in the long run, even though I was happy that Lucia was. A therapist can't have everything, and it is useful to note that tolerance of loss or not having is something Lucia and Jan needed to learn in their relationship. It is one thing to know a marriage takes work, but to actually work at it is something else. It is terribly frustrating to see that somebody needs help and not be able to help sufficiently. I suspected a sense of frustration was something Lucia and Jan also needed to become aware of.

Pain, frustration, loss, fear, anger—yet I also had a good feeling about Lucia and Jan, and about their baby. There was a lot wrong between them, but there was, also, life.

Lucia and I quickly became a therapy couple, and that both added pressure to the marriage and relieved it. If one person improves more than the other, the boat gets rocked. But the boat was rocking anyway.

THE GOOD FEELING: WAVES OF FEELINGS

The physical, familial, and marital agonies Lucia portrayed did not long dampen the good feeling working with her aroused in me. I could get into her agonies and even be stymied or paralyzed by them for a time, but the good feeling welled up. I just liked seeing her; it felt good.

At times my good feeling bothered her. She did not think I was taking her pain seriously. "You must think I don't believe you're depressed," I said.

"Yes," she nodded. "It's irritating seeing you content, smiling. Don't you know how worried I am?" She listed her worries: another miscarriage, no support from Jan, or her family, or his family.

"And now a therapist who isn't worried enough," I added.

"I'm worried you're not worried, but it's relieving," she said. "I'm used to people being nervous or angry."

"Do you fear I'm uncaring if I'm not nervous and angry?"

"I like the good feeling, too. It feels good being here, in spite of what I say."

"But it also scares you? I won't see *you* if I'm blinded by liking you?"

"How can you know what I'm going through, if you're happy?"

But I certainly was worried. Being worried and anxious is part of my nature, and I very much felt her and Jan's compression. Why, then, this good feeling?

There are plenty of bad reasons to feel good. We often substitute good for bad feelings in order to avoid, short-circuit, or postpone the latter (Eigen 1986). This can be useful, as it helps us get through things more easily. Still, fear, anger, and sadness are useful, too, since they contribute to an important part of ourselves—our capacity to experience a wide range of feelings in life-giving ways. Was I trying to wash away Lucia's apprehension and grief with my good feelings? Was I like a parent who can't bear the child's despondency and requires the child to feel good for the parent's well-being?

The above conversation suggests I did this to some extent. But there were many other moments when Lucia and I sat with her worried, despondent self and gave it its due. We went through a wide range of states together. She spoke about daily events, her life with Jan, what she gained and gave up in marriage. She spoke of ins and outs with her friends and parents and thought about going back to work. Yet whatever crises past or present we went over, we reliably reached a point where I looked at her and felt good, whether or not she felt good.

Was I feeling something her mother/father felt when she was little— pure delight in her being? Was I in touch with a nuclear goodness in her life (our lives) that came through whatever threatened to wreck it? I listened to everything Lucia had to say, including the worst. But sooner or later the smile in my heart returned, and waves of good feeling pulsated heart to heart.

Therapy involves cognitive work, going over behavioral and emotional patterns, letting thinking processes emerge, encountering eclipsed parts of self and others. A lot of rehearsal and repetition go into working on stubborn sets of problems. One sees oneself and others in new ways and tries new responses. Still, understanding is not enough and even can add further tensions to what one already is undergoing. A lot goes on outside understanding. There's a mute sensing or psychic body English in the subsoil. Whatever Lucia and I said or failed to say, we felt our beings work on each other in ways smiles, frowns, and elusive gestures express more than words.

As her pregnancy progressed, Lucia began to stain and she stayed in bed, as in past pregnancies. When she came to see me, her apprehension was palpable. Would this be another failure? I gave her plenty of room to talk herself out and encouraged her to do so. Her fears, resentments, and history of past and present injuries spilled out. Was her inability to complete a pregnancy simply biological? Was it a good she dare not give herself? Did she fear a baby would ruin her marriage? Was there too much hate in her system for a fetus to survive? Were there ways she did not survive her upbringing and marriage? Had she reached too far beyond her parents, too far beyond herself? Was failure a form of self-punishment? Did she feel she did not deserve a baby? Were the pressures of existence, together with her real and imaginary fears, too much for her psychosomatic frame to support? Was not bearing a baby linked with an incapacity to bear life? Did she dread what a baby might do to her? Wouldn't a baby reshape her life and mis-shape it?

But beneath all these apprehensions was positive desire and good vision. Lucia wanted a baby and imagined happiness deeper than misgivings. She *felt* happiness more pervasive and more basic than evil imaginings. It suddenly dawned on me that my good feeling—whatever else it might be—was akin to the happiness of a good pregnancy. When I was with Lucia, I felt a bit like a pregnant woman, without realizing it. I was resonating to and validating an affirmation at the core of Lucia's being. Her bliss/joy/ecstasy over being a mother was a yes from the center of her existence, triggering the yes at the center of mine.

It was the deep faith of motherhood at the core of life that I was called on to experience and support. In Lucia, this faith was very real, but subject to internal and external attack. Her faith in her capacity to bring life into the world was imperiled by a variety of worries, pressures, and hardships, including her past experience of failure. Could her faith in her creative capacity and life's creativeness survive failure?

So often the therapist becomes a proxy (for a time) for work the patient must do. One becomes a kind of laboratory or workshop for processes the patient must undergo in her own fashion. The work one does (or fails to do) *can* be a life and death matter. I was required to experience the antilife tendencies bombarding Lucia. I needed to struggle with destructive forces that threatened to dissolve her faith and generativity. If I could not telescope, survive, and work with forces that weighed on her, she would be alone with them, at their mercy.

In this context, my seeing Jan at his worst made further sense. The pinched, tight, naysaying Jan represented, in part, Lucia's tendency to tighten in the face of pressures. Jan's taut face mirrored Lucia's contracted muscles, nerves, and circulatory and respiratory systems. Lucia's exterior was softer and rounder than Jan's, but inside she was knotted. He looked like she felt, an external image of her internal contraction. Of course, Jan was more than this, and so was Lucia, but would the more win out?

Everything I learned about his and her parents, Lucia's and Jan's past and present lives, their hopes and frustrations, their economic, professional, and social dilemmas, became part of a high-velocity psychic particle collider. What happens to the psychosomatic self under these pressures? Add to this a baby's impact. For some people, a baby is a crashing meteor causing black winter. Not only growth in the womb stretches a mother; a child's effects on a mother's life and psyche far outweigh changes her body goes through in pregnancy.

All the pregnant women I've worked with dream of water, floods, and ocean waves, and eventually Lucia did too. I wonder if such images aren't a normal part of pregnancy. My impression is they increase in the last trimester, but can appear earlier. The reference to water and being overwhelmed is obvious, from both the mother's and embryo's/fetus's standpoints. In the dreams, it is almost always the mother who is being inundated by waves. Over the years, my patients and I have covered this territory with many permutations. The mother-to-be identifies with the growing baby within her, is concerned for its safety, fears that her own inner processes and states, physical and emotional, can upset the growing life within. In reciprocal manner, she fears for her own physical and psychical being. She, as well as her unborn baby, is at the mercy of psychosomatic processes that unfold without her governance. She, like the baby, is in over her head.

The age-old association of gestation—birth waters with catastrophe informs the dream life of pregnant women. On the one hand, fluids are life-giving. There is joy in bathing in the waters of life—cleansing, baptism, birth, and rebirth—psychospiritually as well as somatically. Waves also refer to waves of sensation-feeling, heightened intensity of emotional and mental aliveness, an increase in the capacity to generate and bear experiencing. But there is ever lurking the possibility that something will go wrong. Baby or mother may die or be ill or impaired. The peril may be psychological, as well as somatic, as in a deepening maternal depression that blights existence, or violence aimed at life one cannot bear.

The story of Oedipus involves not only patricide, matricide, and incest, but also child abuse, including infanticide barely averted (see Bloch 1984 and Young 1994 for variations on this theme). It is useful to note that our cultural heritage is informed by stories of violence in high places (including violence aimed at babies), not simply the result of crippling socioeconomic impoverishment or disenfranchisement. Violence at the top sets standards for violence at the bottom, although both make special contributions. In literature, the association between birth and murder (partly a reversal, a mastery attempt, making the passive active, controlling the uncontrollable) has a noble lineage.

Does violence partly originate in the womb? Imagine, if an embryo could feel, what upheavals it goes through in so short a time. Is it fanciful to think of these changes as violent? How much imaginary/real violence a pregnant woman must contain, ride out, and even try to process! A young child complains of growing pains. What would a fetus complain of? I believe the pregnant mother-to-be is sensitive to these complaints. She (unconsciously?) registers, experiences, and responds to violence happening to her baby and herself, of which signs are plentiful (including weight gain, change of shape, fatigue, forgetfulness, nausea, dizziness, emotional upheavals, perspectival shifts, pressure shifts, varieties of ecstasies-agonies, worries, intimations and presentiments, new desires, demands, and preoccupations).

Noah in his ark and Jonah in his whale dramatize, in part, what a mother and her baby go through: captured by a whale of a body, drawn through oceans of changes beyond individual control, floods of changes, life starting over. Mother may be less familiar to herself than her baby is to her. She may wonder who and where she is, since baby brings her to new places that are fresh, odd, challenging, redemptive/destructive. Columbus's discovery of America pales in comparison with the territory that opens with pregnancy.

Is it any wonder that psychophysical systems might short-circuit the process and recoil, in the sense of "I can't go through with it. Let's stop here!"? Excess of ecstasy wells up and floods excess agony, one offsetting the other. With Lucia and me (and, I believe, Jan) our affirmation was generally the home base and climactic movement of self, but not always.

FACTORS IN THERAPY

Why did therapy enable Lucia to have a baby? The skeptic argues she would have had it anyway; it is only an illusion that therapy made a difference. We can't know with certainty what would have happened. Yet I have little doubt that without help, Lucia would have had another miscarriage. Within weeks of her starting therapy, I could see a difference. Her face and body were visibly more open, less tight and strained. The difference was palpable. The way she carried herself was changing, and so must have been her way of carrying a baby.

Therapy is not only a talking cure, although with Lucia talking certainly helped. Throughout this chapter, I have mixed images that suggest different ingredients in the therapy stew. I have mentioned pressure, bottled-up feeling, impacts of events and affects, injury, porousness-rigidity of personality, conflicts between/within individuals, openness, flow, faith, depression, ecstasy-agony, learning, evolving, the basic good feeling that sustains therapy. I'd like to list and comment on some of the factors that played a role in helping Lucia's pregnancy come to term. The factors noted are not unique to a therapy seeking to avoid miscarriage; they likely are facets of many therapeutic undertakings.

Talking Oneself Out and Hydraulic/Eliminative Images

Therapy provided Lucia a place where she could say whatever was on her mind without retaliation. This took some pressure off her. In hydraulic and eliminative terms, she let off steam, cleaned herself out, lessened blocks and dams. Common speech associates talking oneself out with getting a load of weight off one's mind and, consequently, feeling lighter, carrying less baggage. When Lucia first sought help, she "felt like shit, clogged up." She looked low and tight. After she had some chance to talk herself out, she began to lighten. I could see tension in her upper and lower back (and, presumably, anal sphincters) ease. Her movements became more graceful and fluid. One wonders what pressure was placed on her body by holding herself in, tightening her muscles so. The tightening had become chronic, and scarcely in her awareness. As she spoke herself out, her energy-meaning flow became easier.

Psychosomatic Poisons

At various points in sessions, Lucia feared she was poisoning her baby, and, less consciously, that her baby would poison her. At times she felt poisoned-poisonous within. It is likely such feelings represented aspects of physical processes that are part of gestation, birth, and development. Normal processes often have toxic elements. However, careful exploration suggested dread of poisonous insides was, also, associated with congealed hate.

It was easy to tap Lucia's hate through grudges she bore against Jan. Marriage is a daily source of injustices. Jan was too remote, critical, ungiving, not *there* enough physically and emotionally. The rage one chokes on in daily living takes a toll. Even though Lucia got furious at Jan, the anger she expressed was a token of what she felt. One's psychophysical frame cannot possibly express the infinity of what one feels. A lot of what one feels becomes stagnant, hardens.

Also, Jan was right in linking Lucia's rage to her father. Lucia, also, tied her *injury rage* to her mother. The rage in one's life is cumulative. It sediments in the belly of one's being and corrupts muscles, nerves, veins. It not only stiffens one's body, it poisons one's thoughts. One bears grudges from early childhood on, so that one is ready to jump on others for not giving enough or, correlatively, be overly grateful for pittances. Cumulative rage helps nourish a pessimistic, depressive, semi-malevolent counterpart or undertow to one's official, happier self. In some people, bitterness/sourness is closer to the surface. In others it works more silently. One may recoil with surprise at the rage a "nice" person harbors at the secret bad taste of things. In either case, more overtly or covertly, chronic outrage over injury can eat at life like an acid and corrode psychosomatic integrity.

Hate as a poison can be linked with hydraulic and eliminative notions. Hate builds up, explodes. One tries to get rid of pressures it exerts. However, the sense of poisoning and corroding the personality does not quite fit eliminative/hydraulic concerns, or perhaps is a special case of the latter.

Insofar as hate eats away at personality, it may be said to get rid of or eliminate or kill aspects of personality functioning (Bion 1967). Explosive hate obliterates the self. Poisonous hate corrupts the self. One's efforts to rid oneself of explosive/poisonous hate backfire, so that the latter deforms the self that fights it, and the evolution of one's personality and life may miscarry.

Equipment Failure

An important source of shame is the sense that one's psychosomatic equipment cannot support real living. Whether in professional, social, aesthetic, familial, or sexual realms, there is a dreadful presentiment or conviction that, at crucial moments, one's body and mind will let one down. The most dramatic instances of this, in Lucia's case, were her two miscarriages, but it is a theme that ran through her life. By the time I saw her, her marriage was becoming a mess, and her faith in her professional self was shaky. Not only did she doubt her body's ability to support a baby, she doubted her personal ability to support a marriage and profession. She was getting ill often and felt more and more like a basket case.

Lucia felt ashamed of her inability to support life. She and Jan tore each other down. She tore herself down. Her sense of shame spiraled as her life threatened to go downhill. Her ability to process what was happening to her jammed. Her response to her situation become more constricted. She seemed to feel her inadequacy to handle what was happening was her fault, even as she blamed others. Shame and blame were like viruses taking advantage of a general weakening of her condition, and they contributed to her feeling overwhelmed and flooded.

My sense was that Lucia's capacity to process affects had, in certain ways, been compromised early. She had done extremely well working around the rage-injury-shame that were part of the background of her existence. For much of her life, she had been able to maintain a generally positive, upbeat tone and make use of her abilities. She pushed on in spite of the undertow, and even made use of the latter in her aesthetic sensitivity. Still, a shame-filled sense of injury/rage remained unmetabolized, and became more pressing as life placed her in situations she could not "solve" and no one could solve for her.

Therapy took the edge off Lucia's shame by enabling her to let down and acknowledge she was in over her head. It gave her room to realize she was spinning her wheels, flailing, collapsing in on herself. There was no place in her life she could admit she did not know what to do, that whatever she did made things worse. Jan was defensive with her and all her parents wanted was for her to be happy. Her friends supported her but had their picture of what her life should be like, and tried to bolster her will and ability to function. Therapy made fewer demands on her than anything else in her life. It gave her a chance to thaw out and experience the one true demand—to link up with herself and see what it might feel like to be alive.

One can be alive with inadequate equipment. One can never adequately keep up with all that occurs, and why would one want to? Therapy may help a person process injury and rage somewhat, and help broaden one's response repertoire to the latter. Evolution in processing ability and response capability is a real achievement. But so is evolution of the ability to live decently with the vast unprocessable, including wounds that never heal.

Therapy practices the art of making room for what another person can and can't experience, can and can't process, and so, to some extent, models possibilities of making room for oneself and others. To what extent can we become partners with the capacities that constitute us? Even a little familiarity with the packages we have been given can bring enormous relief and enrichment. As Lucia reset herself and dared to dip in (see below), she remembered/discovered how delicious being herself could be, with new appreciation for difficulties. Opening a little at a time in sessions went a long way. Just a bit of opening, with all its psychic chills, makes a difference. As faulty as our equipment is, it supplies us with more than enough for many lifetimes.

Cognitive-Behavioral Insight and Rehearsal

Lucia felt criticized, put down, and unsupported by her parents, yet she also felt loved by them. How could this be? There were many good moments. She could remember her father smiling at her, kissing her. She remembers many times her mother comforted and encouraged her. How could she love them if they were bad to her? How could she hate them if they were good to her?

The mixture of bad and good parenting can confuse a child, so that it is difficult to tell bad from good. One never knows whether one is hating or loving the good or bad parent. One often lashes out at the good one and loves the bad. Such confusions carry over into adult relationships, especially when one tries to get close to another person. To a significant extent, Jan became a target for Lucia's confusions. At one moment, he was a wonderfully sensitive, open, bright man, whom Lucia felt lucky to be with. At another moment, he was remote, self-preoccupied, critical, a source of pain. At times she beat up on him when he was good, and doubted herself when he was bad. She rarely felt she got things right.

Over the years, Lucia went through these confusions with me. She was able to say what bothered her about me and say what she liked, and experience any number of reversals of attitudes and affect. We survived myriad changes of state together. She even got to enjoy liking me when I was bad and disliking me when I was good. It was possible to have varieties of feelings without regard to "goody-goody" or "baddy-baddy" fits. This was in marked contrast with her upbringing. Often as not, she would be punished for strong feelings by parental anger or incomprehension, and she would withdraw or make a stronger display of emotions in order to feel her impact.

She was not used to being listened to easily and felt it odd to have impact on a man (me) just by speaking. She was used to having her feelings thrown back at her in some twisted way, and getting her own back by withdrawing (making the Other sweat it out) or becoming furious (provoking hurt withdrawal and further retaliation). She mimicked ways her parents reacted to her.

In our first weeks and months, it was enough to convey a sense that a journey lay ahead, that we would get to know each other over time, and that, as time went on, perceptions/emotions/words would link in ways that would make her a better partner for herself. It did not take her very long to get ready for the undertaking.

How Much Aliveness Can We Take?

The traumatic impact of "bad" aspects of parenting struck me, in Lucia's case, to be exaggerated instances of "normal" tendencies. It is not so unusual for parents to be critical of their children and each other. Parents and children strike out and withdraw from each other in countless ways. Parents also idolize their children, as well as tear them down. Various forms of destruction and love commingle. Shifting, variegated mixtures of love/anger/injury/recovery are a normal part of aliveness.

Nevertheless, some mixtures are more devastating than others. We should not minimize the damage we do to ourselves and each other. With luck, we learn to modulate these tendencies and find comfortable ways of protecting others from ourselves, and ourselves from others, and ourselves from ourselves. It is important to find forms of protective modulations that fit and extend our sense of self, so that real growth is possible. In therapy, such a desirable outcome is often possible only after an individual thoroughly satiates herself with first-hand knowledge of the feelings one needs to modulate.

There is a vast difference between acting on a hint of feeling and staying with the feeling, bathing in it. Lucia had gotten into the habit of lashing out at Jan or grinding herself into the ground in response to frustrating moments and rise of negative feeling. As difficulties in marriage mounted, her emotionality became as much a liability as virtue. Her feelings followed gradients of least resistance, compressed into ruts, congealed around fault lines of her personality, became more stereotypical. She gradually collapsed to the worst she could be, rather than best, and the former became more and more the everyday baseline.

The intensity of her depressive complaints, angry outbursts, and begrudging silences became as unbearable to her as to Jan. She was becoming the sort of person she did not like, a person she never wanted to be and had fought against being. By the time she sought help, she was ready for it, since she was reaching the point of not being able to stand herself, as well as not standing Jan.

Her pride in being the emotional one (next to Jan's remoteness) stood in her way somewhat, but she was also glad to move past this bit of marital mythology. It brought some relief, paradoxically, to realize how difficult it was for her to stay with feelings and situations, and let them build, rather than cut herself off with rage and self-hate (which were becoming her specialties). Realizing how hard it was to stay with her feeling flow (and how unflowing her feelings had become) made Lucia hopeful that there was something more to her than the reduced person she was hating, that there was more to reach for. She was too depressed, hurt, afraid, and angry to open to the larger sea within, but there was a larger sea to open to.

With help and encouragement, Lucia experienced how she short-circuited her states, her capacity to be. She was caught up in blaming self or other. With support and hard work, she could stay with feeling a little longer, increasing her capacity to *experience* who she was and what she felt. Once she located a feeling and focused on it, we could see where it would go, what it turned into, follow tributaries, guess sources. Sometimes it seemed important to investigate it, get ideas about it, map a history. But there also was a need simply to feel it, drink it in, get the most out of it. Just soaking up feeling states can be nourishing, especially if one has been deprived of space and atmosphere to let feelings be.

Experiencing a feeling takes time. One needs time to follow its waves, pulsations, as it builds, climaxes, subsides. This is as true of shame, for example, as of joy. With practice and courage, Lucia bathed fully in streams of shame, seas of shame. There seemed no end to it. Once she started, it seemed like something she needed to do, had long wanted to do. What a relief to drink deeply and undefensively of the vast reservoir of shame that consumed her! She was used to fighting or evading it. She was not supposed to give in to unending shame. She was ashamed of shame.

Arrays of feelings came and went: shame, guilt, fears, furies, doubts, accusations, pleasures, joys. She had her fill of them, got to know them. She was becoming a little more familiar with herself, learning about feelings without having to rush. Her fear of getting lost forever was followed by disappointment in not being able to get lost forever, since feelings flowed alone, one state limiting another.

How much could she take? How much would she need to take? It occurred to her that this was the best possible training she could have for being a mother. Yes, there would be practical problems of child management, daily chores, fatigue, and survival. But the simple ability to let feelings be, to tolerate buildup and flow, and how infant and mother felt together would be all that mattered.

Without quite realizing it, she had been afraid of what she might do to a baby with her fury or shame. She feared she would inundate her baby with shame, make it as ashamed of itself as she was of herself. She would make it ashamed of being a baby. Or she would be unable to break her addiction to lashing out/in. Instead of herself or Jan or her parents being objects of rage, she would rage at her baby. Suddenly, she saw herself and Jan as raging babies—screaming like mad with no parent to hear. Rage meets rage. Baby infant—baby parent. Where was the Other to break this cycle, where was the Other who could respond, not simply react?

In therapy, Lucia was learning to respond, to appreciate baby aliveness in herself and others, to give baby life its due. Life is more than baby life—but what damage results from fear of baby life and inability to respond!

Faith in Basic Goodness

A primacy of faith in the basic goodness of our time together provided a background context for everything we went through. I can't say where this faith comes from, but it is there. Without it, I don't think our work would have been as successful. It would have had a different tone.

The faith in basic goodness that made our work possible spanned many levels and dimensions. First of all, it was an immediate experience. I felt *core goodness* in Lucia and myself. It felt good to be together. We increased each other just by being. This is on a level of sheer presence. Images of tuning forks, resonance, positive reverberating circuits are among those that come to me. Perhaps the bare fact that such experience is possible is a good prognostic sign.

There were many semi-visionary experiences I kept private. There were times I imagined Lucia's insides bathed in golden light. At times, it seemed more than imaginary: I saw her embryo/fetus support system in radiant gold. I could move this golden radiance throughout her body and emotions and hoped it had some healing use. Such images seemed part of an overflow of the goodness circulating between Lucia and me, a core to core goodness.

Although we stimulated good feeling in each other, the latter belonged to neither of us, or both. While it occurred within us/between us, it was part of a good feeling flow that went beyond our relationship. It was part of the basic goodness that supports the world and makes life possible.

The concrete clinical effects of basic goodness were many. It provided a tone and atmosphere ("spirit") that could absorb psychic toxins and a wide range of impacts. All the pressures of her life, everything that went wrong between Jan and her, the pressures she put on herself—the good feeling housed them. Similarly, goodness provided a frame for poisonous and stagnant rage, and all the feeling states that had no useful place to go and miscarried. All inadequacies, incapacities, disabilities—goodness bathed them all.

The pressures, toxins, impacts, fears, and unhappiness of her life strangled basic goodness, rendering it less effectual. The spontaneous, basic good feeling that makes life worthwhile was getting suffocated. It could not do the work it needed to do. It was not getting sufficient support and education. It was too much under attack and burdened. It could not offset the unhappiness and helplessness flooding Lucia.

Psychoanalytic faith did more than bolster Lucia's core good feeling, although this was essential. Psychoanalytic therapy is more than a shot of psychic vitamins, although affective infusion is a crucial element. Psychoanalytic faith stimulates cognitive-behavioral work that enables basic goodness to circulate more freely in the psychic body. Better circulation of basic goodness supports more adequate (always partial) metabolization of emotional trauma and toxins (inevitable parts of every life). Where a sense of life's goodness is too weak to support processing of trauma/toxins, the latter spiral and life itself may be threatened.

In Lucia's case, the baby growing within her raised the question whether life was possible. Was it worth getting born? One cannot answer this question for another living soul. But sometimes one can affect conditions that form the background of a reply. Psychoanalytic faith and work provided a clearing that enabled Lucia to respond to life, rather than merely react. One wonders if the baby growing within her could sense the difference.

REFERENCES

Bion, W. R. (1967). *Second Thoughts*. London: Heinemann.

Bloch, D. (1984). *"So the Witch Won't Eat Me": Fantasy of the Child's Fear of Infanticide*. New York: Grove.

Eigen, M. (1986). *The Psychotic Core*. Northvale, NJ: Jason Aronson.

Young, R. M. (1994). New ideas about the Oedipus complex. *Melanie Klein and Object Relations* 12:1–20.

INDEX